Tony Crisp has been interested in the health of mind and body since his early teens. He began writing about these subjects in 1956. His fascination for what lay under the surface of the mind, led him to personally explore the unconscious using dreams and other mental and physical disciplines. From 1972 he worked as a psychotherapist using an eclectic, Humanistic Psychology approach. His books include *Do You Dream? The Instant Dream Book* and *Liberating The Body*.

In more recent years he worked as a dream columnist for the *Daily Mail* and *She* magazine, and is currently Dream Interpreter for LBC Radio and 'Dream On', the Teletext dream page on UK television's Channel 4.

The *New*
DREAM
DICTIONARY

*A handbook of dream meanings
and sleep experiences*

TONY CRISP

LITTLE, BROWN AND COMPANY
Boston   New York   Toronto   London

A *Little, Brown* Book

First published in Great Britain by
Optima in 1990
Reprinted 1990, 1992
This revised edition published in 1994
Reprinted 1994 (twice), 1995
Reprinted by Little, Brown and Company (UK) 1995
Reprinted 1997, 1998

ISBN 0 316 87957 6

Typeset by Solidus (Bristol) Limited
Printed in England by Clays Ltd, St Ives plc

Little, Brown and Company (UK)
Brettenham House
Lancaster Place
London WC2E 7EN

To Quentin
Who awoke in the cellar
and has had the courage
to stay awake

Contents

Acknowledgements

Without the thousands of dreams shared with me by countless people, many of the insights in this book would not have been possible. The dreams have come from several different sources. The first major influx came from readers of the *Daily Mail*. Readers of *She* magazine contributed some interesting dreams. The many people I have spoken to on the LBC radio station in London have significantly helped, because I was able to talk over the dream with them.

At the time of this revision I am receiving a fresh major influx from viewers of Teletext on Channel Four. The 'Dream On' feature has helped me particularly regarding the dreams of teenagers, especially girls, whose dreams I had hardly any experience of previously. Many of the dreams I have not been able to respond to on screen, but thank you for your letters and dreams. I have put entries into this new edition that summarise what I have learnt from them.

In this edition there are many other new entries on subjects that had been left out or new objects that have entered our life more fully such as computers, CDs and fax machines. A high percentage of the previous entries have been added to in some way. For instance the entry on **car** has 'rear view mirror', 'passengers', and other features added. So I hope this new edition will have much to offer established users of the book as well as new readers.

My work at Atsitsa, the holistic holiday community on the Greek island of Skyros, where I teach groups of people how to explore their dreams, enabled me to experiment with a format which enables a peer group to support each other in dream work. The outline on **peer dream work** describes this approach. Dina Glouberman, through her use of 'Visualisation and Life Choices' showed a way of using questions to stimulate response from the unconscious, which I incorporated in the peer dream technique.

My friendship and work with John Hodgson and all those involved in the 'seed groups' Hyone and I lead helped me define the approach described under **using symbols to change habitual life problems**, which is also a new entry.

My thanks to Marcia Karp – psychodramatist extraordinary – who pointed out to me the way basic information in some entries was lost amongst the examples. I have remedied this. Thanks to Sarah Davison for suggesting I clarify the need to look for some entries under group headings. I have listed all such headings now in the Introduction.

Loving thanks to my wife, Hyone: her ready willingness to listen to me while I explore my own dreams, her aid in our mutual work teaching seminars on dream work, and her supportive attitude while I am writing or working with individuals, has added to the quality of this book.

I want to thank my son Neal, who through sharing so much of his inner life with me while I revised *Dream Dictionary*, reminded me of some ancient truths. His courage in experiencing the emotional impact and revelation of his dreams, in being willing to share what he met, tells me again that within each of us lies a radiance that enriches us if we can meet it; that this radiance constantly tries to show us how to become whole; that becoming whole may take strength, surrender and trust.

My thanks to Hilary Foakes who encouraged me to write this revision. I am always learning more, and it is a great pleasure to be able to incorporate it into the *New Dream Dictionary*. This is more thrilling because, through the work of the publicity department, and people like Christina Macphail (who has now left the rights department of Little, Brown) and Nann du Sautoy, *Dream Dictionary* is now published in six languages.

Jayne Booth spent hours going through the manuscript editing and suggesting improvements – thank you Jayne. This book is also a joint effort with many people I do not know, compositors, printers; their effort deserves acknowlededgment.

Rhea Monro has helped me with extra suggestions for the entry on symbols and shapes, sharing some of her insights gained from working with children using art.

I have managed to keep up to date with research without an expensive news cutting service through my use of Compuserve. By linking my computer with such databases as Magazine Database Plus, which has ninety American magazines all on computer file and easily searched electronically for subject headings, the material accessible to me has been immensely enlarged.

I am thankful to all of you who have purchased the book and use it. I appreciate your support, and get great satisfaction from knowing that professionals such as Marcia Karp, already mentioned, Natalie Matyuk in Australia, and Carole D Guerrero in the United States, use what I have written in their work and life.

My love and thanks to you all for helping me to create a life so full of interest, so full of your dreams and so rich in meetings with Life itself.

Introduction

Dreams are one of nature's miracles, not the result of a wandering mind in sleep. A dream is an interface between the process of life and our conscious personality. Life existed quite capably for millions of years before the self-aware human personality came on the scene. Life's age-old processes are still the major part of our being, yet we seldom consciously meet them – except in dreams. As our physical and psychological health depend upon a reasonable co-operation between the spontaneous processes of life and our conscious decisions and actions, the encounter in dreams is vital.

A dream is a meeting between the most ancient and the most recent in evolution. It is also much more. In an overview of the study and research concerning dreams, there is evidence that a dream can be:

- An expression of what is happening in the physical body. Some doctors consider dreams to show signs of illness long before they are evident consciously.
- A way of balancing the physiological and psychological activities in us. When a person is deprived of dreaming in experiments, a breakdown in mind and body quickly occurs.
- An enormously original source of insight and information. Dreams tap our memory, our experience and scan information held in our unconscious to form new ideas.
- A means of exercise for the psyche or soul. Just as the body will become sick if not moved and stressed, so the mind and emotions need stimulus and exercise. Dreams fulfil this need.
- An expression of human supersenses. Humans have an unconscious ability to read body language – so they can assess other humans very quickly. Humans have an unimaginable ability to

absorb information, not simply from books, but from everyday events. With it they constantly arrive at new insights and realisations. Humans frequently correctly predict the future – not out of a bizarre ability, but from the information gathered about the present. All these abilities and more show in our dreams.

- A means of solving problems, both in our personal life, and also in relationships and work.
- A way of reaching beyond the known world of experience and presenting intimations from the unknown.

THE MAGICAL DREAM MACHINE

We all dream every night, so we each have what could be called a Magical Dream Machine. If we imagine ourselves locked in a dark mechanism, hardly moving, with no sounds or light from outside disturbing us, our mind relaxed – this is sleep. But now – in the darkness a light glimmers. Gradually it takes shape. The shape of a person is suggested. In the time that follows he or she evolves form, moves, and we have full sensory experience. We are totally involved, with all our emotions and sexuality responding. Changes occur and we love, fight, fear, murder or bring to life again the person, who can become an animal, a devil, God or a bodiless voice lost in a sombre countryside.

If we had been in such a machine, and on coming out of the total involvement of these moving experiences were told we had created it all ourselves – that on the black screen we had, out of our fears, habits, secret longings and passion; out of our immense store of memories; with our unbelievable range of feelings and creativity – through giving form to urges and processes in our body we had made this rich world of experience, what would we feel? Would we disclaim responsibility? Would we consider it meaningless? Would we realise what amazing creativity and potential we have?

Your dreams are such a magical place. Do you discount them? Do you see that you create your own world of experience in them? If you do, have you wondered why you may have a propensity for creating what you do? Or why, with such creative potential, you might still lack self-confidence? Just as we create our surroundings in dreams, we also create the psychological world we live in. Understanding our dreams can help us to clarify why we create what does not satisfy us and how to generate a whole new world of experience. We can take charge of our creativity and ride with it instead of being at its mercy. Such power, after all, can as easily produce misery and ill health as pleasure and ability – unless we learn to direct it.

AMAZING STOREHOUSE OF THE MIND

Although we constantly use the huge storehouse of memory and developed skill in our everyday life, we usually fail to recognise what we are doing and what a miracle it is. As an example, you now hold in store millions of bits of information. By asking you a simple question such as 'What is your present home address?' I can call to conscious awareness a minute part of the information lying in your unconscious. If I were to present you with a bicycle, or you were dropped in deep water, the skill of cycling or swimming could also emerge from latency if you had previously learnt those skills.

Apart from these aspects of our immense storage of information, there is also the possibility that by the right series of questions or experience, you could arrive at a creative synthesis of information already held. In other words something not previously held in memory could arise from putting together old ideas or experiences.

While we dream we have a very full access to the storehouse of our experience. If we learn to use the dream process we can more capably use the riches of what usually lies unconscious like treasures at the bottom of the ocean.

So how can we get into this magical world of our dreams and start to harvest the possibilities held there? The following pages of this book are designed to help, guide and inform on how to do this. The book is also a counsellor on what you may find in your dream adventure.

WHAT IS OFFERED IN THE BOOK?

The information about dreams presented in this book has been gathered during thirty-two years of working with and studying dreams and the dream process. It synthesises the experience of personally helping hundreds of individuals explore their dreams. The examples used have been taken from a collection of 3,000 dreams put onto a computer filing system. The filing system was also used to define general associations with commonly used dream images.

In the entries in the *Dictionary* are explanations of the many different types of dreams and dream images. Despite some people's attempt to explain dreams in one simple formula, dreams cover a huge range of phenomena and human experience. Amongst subjects covered in the book are thousands of entries on the researched meaning of the things, people, creatures and places we dream about. There are also many entries on special subjects such as **symbols and dreaming**; **dream interpretation**; **recurring dreams**; **nightmares**; **sex while asleep**; **teenage girls' love dreams**; **predictive dreams**; **sleep talking**; **dream as an adventure**; **science, sleep and dreams**; and many more.

Therefore, if you have dreamt of such things as your teeth falling out, being chased, or your marriage partner dying, you will find an explanation of your dream in the following pages.

The aim of the book is to help you make connections between your dreams and your everyday life; to discover more fully the powerful emotions and reactions that unconsciously direct your decisions and responses in waking. The book is not an attempt to give you merely ideas to play with, to agree or disagree with, like fortune telling. It can lead to real insights which empower you to make more of yourself and find your way through the many decisions life confronts you with.

USING THE BOOK

The *Dictionary* contains explanations on almost any type of dream subject. The entries are placed in alphabetical order for easy reference, but some, like 'dog' or 'running' are placed in certain categories such as **animals** and **posture, movement, body language**.

The major collective entries are: **animals**; **archetypes**; **birds**; **body**; **car**; **clothes**; **colours**; **dream processing**; **ESP in dreams**; **family**; **fish, sea creatures**; **food**; **furniture, furnishings**; **games, gambling**; **house, buildings**; **individuation**; **insects**; **jewels**; **man**; **numbers**; **peer dream work**; **positions**; **postures, movement, body language**; **reptiles – lizards, snakes**; **roles** (such as actor/actress, captain, dentist, etc.); **shapes, symbols**; **size**; **time of day**; **trees**; **unconscious**; **weapons**; **woman**.

So if you dreamt of a flying saucer landing in a field, and aliens getting out and taking sheep and a dog back into the saucer, you could look up each of these subjects in the text. Turn to the 'F' entries for **flying saucer**; the **animals** entry for dog and sheep, and so on.

Each entry gives the general meaning of the dream subject, just as an encyclopaedia or dictionary does for a word. Several possible meanings are given, as in the example below.

perfume, scent or smell   Bad smell: Frequently in dreams a bad smell expresses an intuition of something rotten in one's life. Rotten might mean 'bad' emotions felt in a relationship; a hunch or feelings about something, as in the example below; memories. Good smell: Good feelings; non-verbalised intimations or love; a sense of personal beauty. Idioms: on the right scent; throw someone off the scent. See: *nose* under **body**

> *Example: 'I went back in time in circles, almost as if going unconscious. I went back and back and then there came this awful smell such as I've never experienced. I always felt it was the smell of death. I would wake terrified. One night my husband, a practical and down-to-earth man, said he would read me to sleep to see if it helped me not have the dream. It made no difference I still had the nightmare. Imagine my surprise though. He said, "I knew you'd had the dream again for there was an awful smell in the room for a minute."'* Mrs E.C.

The above entry on **perfume** is typical of most entries. The example it contains is in italics and illustrates the entry, or an aspect of it. In general, the description of what the dream image means is set out as the part which reads: 'Frequently in dreams a bad smell expresses an intuition of something rotten in one's life. Rotten might mean "bad" emotions felt in a relationship; a hunch or feelings about something, as in the example below; memories.' The insertion of the semicolon – ; – means that a separate suggestion for the meaning of the dream image is being given. We could therefore read it as saying, 'Perfume or smell might mean "bad" emotions felt in a relationship. It might depict a hunch or feelings about something. It might mean memories of something – depending on the smell.'

To pack as much information as possible into the available space, the semicolons have been used to shorten statements. Therefore, in using the entries to find meanings of dream images, consider each suggestion given.

Many entries, as with the above, also give variations, as with <u>Good smell</u>. The headings for these are underlined to make them easier to find. Because many dream images depict our unconscious thought processes, as used in language, the section <u>Idioms</u>, also underlined, is frequently given. Standing in a pink room might well be our dream's way of saying we feel 'in the pink'. Coming down from a tall building to street level might be quickly understood by the idiom 'coming down to earth'.

'See' suggests reading other entries which might be useful. In this section when it says *nose* under **body**, this means look for the entry called **body** and then find the entry *nose* which is just below it. Sometimes a suggestion is made to 'See' an example. This is because the example mentions the symbol dealt with. Occasionally there is a 'See also'. This gives entries which might be interesting further reading, but are not as directly linked as the 'See' references.

A dream has in it many sources of information. Not only should you consider the basic dream images, but what is happening, how people are dressed and their posture, and what the dream environment is. A dream is often like a film. The background gives a lot of information making the foreground action meaningful. There is a great difference between a scene taking place in a farmyard and one in a bedroom. So even things such as what hand was used, left or right, should be referred to. Entries in the *Dictionary*, such as **settings** and **posture**, help to understand this aspect of dreams.

Where sex or sexuality is mentioned, I am not simply referring to the sex act. I mean sexuality in its overall aspect, which includes the urge toward parenthood, and the love and caring connected with it. Also I am not attempting to present the ideas in this book as scientific or proved. My aim has been to take what information I have gathered from dreams and present what it suggests. To save space I have not argued the points.

GETTING TO WORK ON YOUR DREAM

An example will be given to show how to arrive at a dream's meaning by using the entries. It is important first to write the dream down as fully as possible. Don't stint on your use of words. Be descriptive. Then take the very opening scene of the dream and look it up in the appropriate entry.

> *Example: 'I was standing in the back garden of a house – one of a row of terraced houses. Each garden was fenced and ran down to a large drainage ditch. It seemed to be raining and water was filling the drainage ditch. The water was backing up into the gardens because something was blocking the ditch. It started rising up my legs. It was quite hot. I realised this was because hot water was running out of the baths and sinks in the houses. I felt I must get out of the gardens. Not only because of the water, but because of how people might feel if they saw me in their garden. I managed to find a way into a farmyard where I felt relaxed.' Ted F.*

The first scene here is 'Garden'. On a piece of paper separate to the dream, write 'Garden', with space for notes to be put beside it. The entry on **garden** in the *Dictionary* says: 'The inner life of the dreamer; the area of growth or change in your life; what you are trying to cultivate in yourself; feelings of peace; being near to ones natural self; meditative attitude.'

The words **houses**, **raining**, **hot water**, **fences**, **farmyard** need to be looked up and relevant comments written down next to each word. In doing this with his dream, Ted ended up with the following:

Garden – The growth and changes occurring in my life at present.
Row of houses – Other people.
Raining – Depressed feelings or difficulties; emotions which take away enthusiasm and act as a barrier to action; tears and emotional release – an outpouring; other people's emotions 'raining' on me.
Hot water – Emotions. In the idioms is 'hot water' suggesting I have got myself into trouble.
Fences – Social boundaries.
Farmyard – Where my natural drives such as sexuality, parenthood, love of fellowship, are cared for or expressed.

When Ted added his own associations to this the dream became fully understandable to him and read like this: I am going through a lot of changes at the moment – the garden. These are to do with allowing myself to have warm but non-sexual relationships with women. I have always been too dragged along by my sexuality in the past. Just a few days before the dream I was in a 'growth' group. I had made friends with a woman there, Susan, who I was warm with, but not sexually. The group work required some close physical contact, and I and another man worked with Susan. It seemed to me to go without complications. A while afterwards a woman in the group came to me, and with evident emotion said I had made love publicly to my lover, meaning Susan. I had certainly been physically close to her and had felt at ease, but the viewpoint and feelings of the woman's accusations, coupled with her threat to expose me to the authority figure in the group, bowled me over. This is the hot water in the dream. The fences are the boundaries people erect between their personal life and what is socially acceptable. For some days, up until understanding the dream, I felt really blocked up emotionally – the blocked drainage ditch. I cut off any friendship toward Susan. When I realised that in the farmyard – the acceptance of natural feelings without neat little boundaries – I could feel at peace, I was able to allow my natural warmth again.

After writing the comments next to each dream image or setting, add any personal memories, feelings or associations, as Ted has. Put down anything which amplifies what has been dreamt. For instance a car is said to be one's drive and motivation in the entry on **car**. But it is helpful to add what personal feelings one has about one's car.

Try imagining what the absence in one's life of the car, or house, etc., would mean. A friend recently told me the absence of her car would mean loss of independence. So this was her personal association.

DEEPENING DREAM UNDERSTANDING

The method described above will throw light on most dreams, even if you do not take time to write out fuller associations. When the insights gained in this way become useful, you may wish to increase your skill still further. Therefore, below, and throughout the book, additional information is given on how to draw out the wisdom in dreams. A working attitude toward them is also outlined.

Although the dream process might not be a direct attempt to present *meaning*, a dream may nevertheless contain a great deal of *information*. This becomes clearer if we remember that not many years ago it would have appeared highly superstitious or suspect to claim to be able to tell a person details of their health and parentage from a sample of their urine or blood. Today it is common practice. We accept that a growing amount of information can be gained from these unlikely sources. Blood doesn't contain meaning, but we can gain information from it. In a similar way a sample of our dreams can also tell us an enormous amount. Sometimes this data is obvious, sometimes it needs processing to uncover, as with urine and blood.

The following dream needs no deep techniques of processing. The word 'processing' is used throughout the book instead of analysis. Analysis has the connotation of giving our own thoughts or opinions to the dream. Processing is used to suggest extraction of information which leads to insight. With this particular dream, all it needs is a few facts brought into it to make clear what information it holds. The dream is that of a young woman, Mrs C.L.

Example: 'It is a bright sunny day. I am walking across a large concrete car park. It is empty except for a huge trailer from a truck. It has "BOOTS" written on the side, and stands high off the ground. Being 4 feet 9 inches tall myself I decide to walk underneath. As I am halfway the trailer starts to be lowered on top of me. I try to shout but cannot. I get onto my hands and knees and the trailer still keeps coming down. I am now lying on my stomach, convinced it is going to crush me. Then it suddenly stops a couple of inches from my head. I wake feeling terrible.'

The dream is interesting, although the information it holds may not at first be obvious. But with a minimum of processing the dream information will become clear. The first technique of processing the dream is to recognise some of the key statements within it. These are 'I am walking' – 'I try to shout' – 'convinced it is going to crush me'. The reason these are key statements is because the dreamer is saying 'I am walking' – 'I try to shout' – 'I . . . am convinced'.

This form of processing has not added anything to the dream. It has simply drawn attention to the information already there in the dreamer's description of her experience – this is why it is useful to write the dream out fully. If we add a little more information which the dreamer herself connects with the dream, then it becomes even clearer. Mrs C.L. says, 'I work for Boots the chemist. The employees at the shop I work in were told at the beginning of the year that Boots are selling our shop. When that happens I will be made redundant. We were supposed to finish on May 26th. It is now the end of July. The deal fell through so we are now just left hanging indefinitely until a new buyer comes along. I feel very unsettled as I can't make any plans for the future.'

Having read these comments, it would be difficult not to see the dream as relating to the woman's work situation, and to her strong anxiety connected with it. She herself says – through her dream – she is 'convinced it – the situation – is going to crush' her. She also feels her strong emotions about this – expressed in her attempt to shout – are not being expressed or 'heard'. From just this one dream, we can be forgiven if we assume that dreams may express in dramatic form our feeling reaction to the circumstances of our everyday life. Taking this dream as information, Mrs C.L. could see she is feeling crushed by the situation, yet not stating her feelings loudly enough to be heard. She might therefore speak to the manager to clarify the situation for herself.

Here is an even shorter and less complex dream. It has been left just as it was written so its information is immediately apparent. The key words here might be 'trying to contact him' and 'not under-standing why he left me'. The dream is from Mrs C.J.

Example: 'Years ago I lost my first husband at twenty-nine. I had the same dream continually of being in a phone box trying to contact him, not understanding why he had left me. He died of cancer. Later I remarried and this husband died of a heart attack. Once again the same dream came back so much.'

On speculating about the dream from what is immediately apparent, we might say that although it is irrational to try to contact her husband, nevertheless, her desire to be with him continues year after year. This same part of her cannot understand why he died. We might put such feelings into words as, 'But what had he done to die so young?' and 'Why should it happen to me twice?' We can also assume that her desire to understand these questions, which is what contacting her husband represents, is expressed in the dream as the telephone. The dream process has dramatised her situation and inner feelings – given them form and made them experiential. Looking at this dream helps us see how an image, such as the telephone, performs exactly the same sort of function as a spoken word, although in a different way. Namely, it represents feelings and thoughts. That the woman's questions remain, that her problem is unsolved, is apparent from the fact she does *not* make contact on the telephone and does not find peace. Understanding her dream shows her the importance of the questions she continually asks herself, and the need to release the emotions behind them. With this she could be free of the dream. If she cannot manage this by herself, taking advantage of the professional help of a therapist might help.

It is to the possibility of finding this, and even greater degrees of information in dreams, that this book is devoted. It will do so accepting that for whatever reason, dreams do give dramatic form not only to out inner feelings, but also to our habits, our intuitions, to our physical processes and our variety of mental states and functions.

Therefore, although the entries about dream subjects or images may describe what the theme and meaning of your dream is, it must be remembered that your dream is an expression of the way you feel at the time of the dream. Dreams do not express your fate or future, only inasmuch as you might perpetuate the attitudes or feelings the dream may express. The woman who had the 'Boots' dream is not fated to be crushed by her feelings about her work. But she might very well continue to feel crushed if she carries on believing her whole future well-being depends on her part-time job at Boots, or continues without stating her feelings.

THE WORLD OF DREAMS

When we sleep and dream we enter a completely different realm of experience than when we are awake. It would be foolish to try to breathe under water in the physical world, but in dreams this is not only possible but lots of dreamers do it. In dreams we can fly. We can make love to men or women as we please, without fear of social or physical consequences. While dreaming we can die over and over. The dead can be reborn, and the world around us can be changed simply by changing our attitude. A monster pursuing us one moment can in an instant become a warm friend because we changed our fear to love.

In the world of dreams our most intimate fears and longings are given an exterior life of their own in the form of the people, objects and places of our dream. Therefore our sexual drive may be shown as a person and how we relate to them; or given shape and colour as an object; or given mood as a scene. Our feeling of ambition might thus be portrayed as a business person in our dream; our changing emotions as the sea or a river; while the present relationship we have with our ambition or emotions is expressed in the events or plot of the dream.

A dream portrays a part of us, such as our ambition, as being exterior to us, because a thought or an emotion is something we experience, not something we are. By showing our urges or fears as people or places exterior to us, our dreams are able to portray the strange fact that while, for instance, the love we have for another person is intimately our own, we may find such a feeling difficult to bear, as when one is married and falls in love with someone else. While we dream, the subtleties of such dilemmas are given dramatic form. To observe our dilemma as if we were watching it as a play, has very real advantages. The different factors of our situation, such as our feelings for our marriage partner, our love of the new person,

and social pressures such as our family's reactions, might all be shown as different people in the dream.

We can therefore not only experience these as separate from our central self, but we define in the dream's action how we relate to them. Most important, we *explore safely* the possible ways of living within, or changing the factors involved.

This exteriorisation of internal feelings is clear in the dream of the unanswered telephone and in that of the sinking Boots trailer. Dreams might do this because they frequently portray intimate parts of ourselves which have never been verbalised or made fully conscious. Put in another way, because some parts of our feelings may never have been consciously felt or recognised, they cannot be grasped by us as a thinking or perceiving being. We cannot see them with our eyes, touch them with fingers, or smell them, let alone think about them. After all, they are unknown and formless. But a dream can portray what has not yet been put into words or organised into conscious thought by portraying it in images and drama. The woman who dreams of trying to contact her dead husband may not have fully acknowledged her question of 'Why he left me?' Being able to 'think' in story form, about subtle areas of our experience, is a great additional faculty when added to our other modes of gaining information and insight. In this way, dreams are able to bring to our notice areas of our being which might otherwise never be known. The dream is thus another sense organ, looking into areas we might not have any other way of examining.

A way to understand this is to consider the now commonly used monitors one sees at the bedside of critically ill people. Such monitors depict in the form of an image – a flashing moving graph – the heartbeat of the patient. They can also portray temperature, breathing, brain pulses and blood pressure in the form of externally visible images. These internal events would otherwise be unknown or unconscious. In a similar way, dreams are a monitor, giving apparently external images to depict the subtle and otherwise unconscious processes of body and mind.

That the external person or object in the dream is actually the dreamer's own internal feelings and mental structure is difficult for many people to believe or even grasp. The following unusual dream helps us to develop a conception of this. I say it is unusual because very seldom can a dreamer admit to themselves while asleep that the world which in their dream appears as exterior is actually their own internal thoughts feelings and psycho-biological functions. The dreamer, A.B., is a man in his fifties and dreams he has found a huge thistle in his garden which is as big as a tree.

> *Example:* '*I look at the trunk of the thistle examining it. At this point it seems like a giant hardwood tree. I snap a twig and it smells very nice – a perfumed wood. Other branches are going rotten. Walking around to the back of the tree to see if the bark is rotten I notice a hole where bees or wasps have a colony. I put my left hand up to touch the bark and as I do so notice there is also a hole in the back of my hand, in and out of which wasps are flying. With great shock I look in the hole and see wasps eating my flesh away, so my hand is almost hollow. I awake with the feeling of being old and decrepit.*'

What is of particular importance in this dream is the point of transition where the dreamer moves from seeing the hole in the tree to seeing the hole in himself. But this transition continues, for the dreamer then moves to the feeling of being old and decrepit. These points of transition mark the stages of realisation that what seems exterior is not.

Some of the key statements in the dream are *examining – I notice – a hole – look in –* and *see – the feelings of being old* and *decrepit.* If we put this into a flowing sentence we have, 'In examining myself I noticed "a hole" or emptiness in myself. When I look into this I find a sense of being old and decrepit.'

In looking at his hand and realising there was a hole in his life, A.B. took note of what he felt. Just prior to the dream he had experienced a lot of anxiety about whether his marriage was breaking up. The dream made him realise that niggling thoughts and emotions were eating away at his self-confidence leading him to feelings of being near to the scrap heap, having outlived his usefulness. The dream had depicted these emotions and thoughts as wasps. This enabled him to see that if he entertained such feelings, they would certainly eat away his grasp of life. He could see that as a person he only *entertained* thoughts and emotions. They were simply what he thought and felt about reality, not reality itself. It was up to him as to what he wanted reality to be. Did he want to entertain the reality of the tired ageing man who could no longer satisfy his wife's need for love and companionship, having nothing worthwhile to contribute to others? That could certainly become reality if he allowed such feelings to dominate him. He had thought that his life was like a giant thistle, but on closer inspection he saw it was a giant hardwood. It did have branches which needed pruning, but the rest of the tree was good and perfumed – giving off good feelings to others. So he decided to put love and care into his life and marriage instead of self-doubt and a sense of defeat.

When we realise each aspect of the dream, each emotion, each landscape and environment are materialisation's of our own feeling states, we begin to see how we live in the midst of a world – the world of our thoughts, feelings, values, judgements, fears – largely of our own making. Whatever we think or feel, even in the depths of our being, becomes a material fact of experience in our dream. It is almost certainly this inner universe that religion speaks of as heaven or hell. Finding some degree of direction, mastery or harmony within this world of our own being is the great work of human life.

DREAM
DICTIONARY

abandoned A sense of how others, particularly our parents, felt about us while we were a child. This feeling of not being wanted may have become habitual. It may not be true that we are not wanted, but our feelings are saying it is.

Being abandoned in the sense of allowing sexual and emotional liberty: finding a new freedom; dropping usual social codes and unashamedly expressing ourselves. Also it can be an example of one of the functions of dreams, which is to release held-back sexuality and emotion. See: **alone**; **functions of dreams**; **hero/ine**.

Example: 'My mother asked me to go and buy some butter for her. A chain on my left leg prevented me from going very far. I look down the road and see my mum, dad and my four brothers in the back of a car. I wave and call and they drive right past me, going over the chain I am wearing on my leg.' Lorraine (LBC).

Lorraine's dream illustrates not only her feelings of being left out of family life, but also the chain on her leg shows she is not fully independent. We often feel 'abandoned' while we are trying to become more independent.

abnormal Even if parts of one's body or face are shown in a dream to be distorted or abnormal, such a dream is not usually referring to the physical body. Our own idea or image of what sort of person we are is translated in dreams into our body form. We might dream our face looks subnormal mentally, or our body has strange areas. This refers to an internal sense of ourselves not having

1

developed to our full potential, or of psychological hurts having distorted some aspect of ourselves such as our ability to reach out for help. See: **body**.

aboriginal   The part of self which still has contact with the natural life processes within and feels unified with the rest of nature and the cosmos. See: **African**; **black person**; **natives**.

abortion   Suggests one has aborted an idea, a direction or an area of one's feelings such as might surround a love affair. If dream connects with actual abortion: the emotions surrounding a woman's actual experience of abortion; sense of guilt; the fears of damage to future possibility of childbearing; the feelings about loss of the baby. All these need to be healed in some measure. Also the body was in the midst of a process if the abortion was induced. The body has powerful feeling reactions which need acknowledgement, and which are frequently presented in dreams.

above   See: **positions**.

abreaction   Abreaction is a re-experiencing of painful or traumatic events or situations. In many dreams it is obvious that the process underlying dreams is attempting to trigger an abreaction. This suggests the dream process, as Jung and Hadfield say, is a self-regulatory one in our psyche. In many cases where a person explores the feeling content of their dreams in a confident way, abreaction occurs. Although it has been given different names in recent years, such as Primal Therapy, Rolfing, Discharge, Catharsis, abreaction is still a basic psychological healing process.

Example: 'For some considerable time now I have been troubled by a nightmarish dream which is so realistic sometimes I think I am going to die. In my dream I have swallowed something which is literally choking me or is going to poison me. I wake up and rush down the stairs to the kitchen spitting and choking, holding my throat and making all sorts of disturbing noises which frighten my wife. I have had this dream as many as five or six times a night. My doctor says it could be to do with the last war. I was a child then and my dad had to constantly wake me up to take us down to the shelter, sometimes as many as four times a night, and we were bombed out twice. I cannot recall having any fears about this at the time.' Mr K.T.

Parts of our experience become repressed because there is an automatic reaction in us to avoid pain. Therefore painful experience may never be fully felt or understood at the time. Reliving such experience allows us to review and integrate vital information about ourselves. Frequently all the analysis in the world cannot relieve a neurotic pattern until the repressed emotion holding it in place is released and understood.

The strength with which we hold out against allowing our being to spontaneously abreact is seen in the above example. Mr T. is brought to the brink of reliving his very stressful childhood again and again. Yet he manages to avoid actual memory and in particular the experiencing of any childhood emotions and fears.

Example: 'For several hours I could find nothing about the dream. My mind simply wandered. But with help I persisted. Suddenly I seemed to break through, first to seeing how the shop was a place in which I had unconsciously experienced great emotional pain. My father was always criticising. Never a word of encouragement. Then I burst into powerful sobbing as I felt the pain of wanting my father to love me, instead of criticising all the time, and help me grow into somebody capable of meeting life. And then, something I just had not wanted to see, the thirty years of my life I had wasted by avoiding any contact with authority. My father was the original authority in my life. I had cut off from him because of the lack of support, and I had done the same with school and other authority situations. But what a relief to understand myself and to meet that young vulnerable boy I used to be. How I loved him and understood him/myself.' Clive.

The opposite is shown in this account by Clive, who explored with me a dream about being shot in the arm in his father's shop.

abroad   General: your feelings about that country, or the culturally held view of it. If you have lived in the country: overall experience of that place. Were you happy there, lonely, what characteristics of the people did you take in?

absorb Dreams often represent learning as an organic process. Ideas are taken in, digested, then form part of an organic whole in an integrated system. Seeing something absorbed in a dream may represent the taking in of ideas, or even poisonous feelings, depending upon what the dream images are.

abstract nightmares According to the collection of dreams used as data for this book, these usually occur to children. They often appear as a dot, small object or shape, which is, or becomes, threatening and increases in size. The examples below suggest there is some relationship between the dream and feelings connected with a parent or parents. It may be the dream portrays unspoken moods felt by a parent that the child feels anxious about. Very often we sense something going on that is not spoken about or visible externally. Such hidden things are picked up by our unconscious, which attempts to communicate them as a dream or intuition. We often feel very uneasy until we realise the situation – perhaps the person it refers to might even deny it if asked.

Example: 'When my husband was a child of about eight years he often used to have an abstract nightmare. It consisted of him (a soft wavy line) being attacked by the enemy (a pointed zigzag line). As the enemy (zigzag) overcame him (soft waves) he would wake up in terror. The nightmares ended when his father died unexpectedly from a heart attack.' Jane S. (Teletext).

Example: 'I am eighteen years old, and ever since I was eight I have been having the same dream and I cannot understand why. I dream of a small black dot which rotates in a spiral, and as it goes around it gets bigger and as it gets bigger it gets faster until in the end it laughs or glares at me and then it blows up. I used to have this dream about twice a week. I don't know why it keeps coming back.' Amanda H. (Teletext).

abyss   If feared: fear of losing control; failure; loss of identity; death. Without fear: going beyond the boundaries of one's own limitations, concepts, present experience. It represents the enormous personal potential lying beyond already formed conceptions and experience. It is the aspect of human consciousness existing beyond the opposites such as good and bad, right and wrong. Access to this gives tremendous liberation to the dreamer, freeing them from restricting, rigid concepts or habits of thinking, responding and relating. See: **falling**.

accident   Many people have strong feelings of anxiety about any dream which shows them having an accident or being injured. If we could have a record of every dream each person had, we would see everyone dreams of being injured, murdered, killed, again and again. Because these are common themes, some dreams are going to coincide with an actual accident or plane crash. Many dreamers attempt to link the dream with a later event. But such dreams are usually about psychological injury or anxiety.

General: anxiety; self-punishment or introverted aggression. Occasionally a warning to watch one's step. An accident to someone else: could be hidden aggression. Idioms: accidentally on purpose; chapter of accidents.

> *Example: 'I was standing in a hospital corridor looking through a glass partition. I could see a man having what I thought was a heart attack. Nurses and doctors came rushing to him and he was vomiting blood. I was on holiday in Canada at the time, staying in a hotel. I thought this dream was a bad omen and wouldn't leave my bedroom for ages. But this was five years ago.' Mrs F.*

The woman in the example was having her feelings, represented by her heart, massively attacked by anxiety. So much so she is laid low, unable to go out of the bedroom and lead a normal life.

acid   Something burning away at our feelings or confidence; our own vitriolic attack on someone else. Idioms: acid tongue; the acid test.

acorn   Considering that our being has emerged from the combination of tiny sperm and ovum, a huge growth has emerged from a tiny beginning. This potential is frequently represented by the acorn or a seed. Even when adult, there is still enormous potential. See: **seed**.

active/passive   When we are an inactive observer in our dream, are on the receiving end of dream action all the time, or as in the example below, make no effort to move from discomfort, we are in a passive role. If this occurs frequently in our dreams, we are probably passive in our waking life.

> *Example: 'I was in a house that I lived in many years ago, how I got there I do not know, but I saw myself sitting in an ordinary chair just behind the closed front street door. It was very quiet and I was afraid, but I did not make any effort to move.' Ms J.*

This passivity can gradually be changed by such techniques as active imagination. It is our own emotions, fears and sexuality we are meeting in our dreams, so it is wise to take charge of our being rather than be a victim. The following dream illustrates an active dreamer.

> *Example: 'As I walked toward a house a number of demons or devils came at me menacingly, trying to stop me getting near the house. Although they made all the ghostly noises I wasn't at all afraid of them. I felt they were a damned nuisance, and to show them I meant business I grabbed one and with my right hand I gripped its flesh and squeezed. It started to squeak in pain and I squeezed harder.' Clive J.*

active imagination   Carl Jung several times described a technique for using the imagination which allowed the spontaneous expression of the unconscious. Jung described active imagination as a putting aside of conscious criticism while we allow our irrational self to play or fantasize. In relation to a dream, this technique can be extraordinarily helpful and revealing. A way to learn the technique is to take a dream in which a fairly defined person appears. It can be a child or adult. One then sits in a quiet situation alone, or with a sympathetic listener, and imagines or feels oneself back in the dream. One does not need to develop clear images unless they come easily. Just holding the idea of the dream is often sufficient. Then in a playful way develop a conversation with the dream person. Ask them what they are doing; why they appear in your dream; what do they represent of yourself? With a little practice the dream characters can come to life for you if you can let yourself play or free-wheel a little.

As we learn active imagination, it can give us other ways to enter into the life of our dreams and therefore our unconscious. We can imagine ourselves *as* the dream character, or even as the objects or animals, and allow ourselves to experience and speak from their viewpoint. We can enter the dream and carry it forward from where it stopped, imaging what would satisfy us and thus becoming more active in dealing with our own inner and outer life. See: **dream processing**; **peer dream work**.

active sleep   During experiments to monitor the brain activity of animals and humans while asleep, it was noted that the brain seemed to move through a series of levels of activity. In deep sleep there are slow, rhythmic brain waves. These at times would give way to faster rhythms of a more dynamic nature. This was at first called 'desynchronised' sleep because during it the muscular system relaxed deeply even though the brain was active. It was also known as paradoxical sleep, but more recently it has become known internationally as 'active sleep'. During active sleep the rapid eye movements – REM – characteristic of dreaming occur. The brain's activity was found to be a better indicator of dreaming in animals than REM because some creatures, such as owls, do not move their eyes. In this way, all mammals were seen to exhibit active sleep or dreaming. Birds also dream, and, measured in this way, so do many types of fish, reptiles and some amphibians. See: **science**, **sleep and dreams**.

actor, actress   See: **roles**.

adder   See: **reptiles – lizards**, **snakes**

addicted   Anxiety that something or someone is getting a hold on us. Sometimes the fear of something is the power which actually dominates us – not the thing itself. Each of us have areas dominated by such fears or feelings and the dream action will point to what they are.

address   Oneself; way one lives; one's present style of life. To forget or lose your address: to lose sight of your goals or standards in life. Past address: the person you were; the traits you developed; what you faced in life at that time. Another person's address: contact with that person.

Adler, Alfred (1870–1937)   Born in Vienna, Austria. Studied medicine, later became a disciple of Freud. Diverged from Freud over the sexual impulse being all important in human behaviour. Adler saw people as goal oriented, with an urge toward personal growth and wholeness. He stated that in dreams we can clearly see our aggressive impulses and desire for fulfilment. Dreams can also help the dreamer define two often conflicting aspects of their experience – their image or sense of themselves and their sense of what is socially acceptable. Because we strive from our earliest years to have some control over ourselves and surroundings, we may develop a style of life around a sense of inferiority or lack of power. So a person who feels vulnerable may become aggressive to compensate. Adler therefore felt that in our dreams we not only see what we think of ourselves and what our environmental situation is, but we also find a definition of our techniques for satisfying our drive to deal with and succeed in the world.

adolescent   Whether the young person is your own child, someone you know, or a stranger, it is usually an expression of yourself at that age. The dream below shows Hilary taking her teenage feelings into her lovemaking. This is because Hilary had no chance during those years to mature sexually, so as an older woman she now finds herself meeting a young girl's feelings with her lover.

Example: 'My lover and I were going to try and make love, both with our own hurts and being aware of each other's difficulties. We were both very gentle with each other. A young girl came in under the bedclothes with us. I thought it would interfere, but I could see it wasn't worrying her. She was playing hide and seek. We were in bed out in the open countryside.' Hilary.

If dreamt by a child: depicts their feelings or assessment of their own future or ways of meeting future relationships. See: **boy**; **girl**; **man**; **woman**.

adoration　See: **worship**.

adultery　See: **affair**.

adventure of the dream world　Dreams give us a doorway into a strange and wonderful world. Although it appears to have many of the features of our waking world such as people, animals, objects and places, it is nevertheless full of subtle surprises and differences. To enter this world while asleep leaves us largely unaware of its possibilities. To take waking awareness into our entrance, as happens when we explore a dream through dream processing, unfolds the magic impact of what we meet.

When we open the door of dreams in this way we begin a journey. It has stages, problems to surmount and things to learn, just like any journey. Many people have already travelled before us, and there are books, such as *Alice in Wonderland, The Odyssey, Exploring Inner Space* and *Altered States of Consciousness*, which describe journeys and the terrain.

Although we might meet the heights of religious experience as well as the depths of human despair on the journey, in simple terms it is primarily a journey into a confrontation with our own potential, our own fear, our own prison bars of thought and habit, our own ability to lift perception beyond what we have known before and look at the world and our life in it from new perspectives. It is a journey toward greater maturity in which we face the humbling vision of our own littleness; the moving encounter with the vulnerable child we once were; the cleaning out of the store cupboards of resentment, hurt and anger; the DIY of conscious renewal of our identity; and the meeting with love as we experience ourselves as a living participator in the wonder of life. We look at birth, we meet death, we gaze into the vast depths of space out of which our being has arisen. Then we find ourselves seeing the faces of the other human beings we live with and recognising we are all on the journey and we only have each other. Realising we are all waves on a shoreless sea – from no port we move to no destination – we understand our self-responsibility and consider what we will to do with the momentum of our life.

advertisement   A desire to have others know something about yourself; a way of bringing something to your attention.

advice   Conscience; sense of 'ought' or 'should'; what you desire to say but haven't; what you know to be useful unconsciously, but haven't accepted. See: **talking**; **voice**.

aeroplane   General: Represents sudden or dramatic life changes. To climb aboard a plane is to embark upon a dramatic movement from one way of life to another; a leap into the unknown, into chance. Perhaps that flight into chance, into life and its mysterious possibilities may be okay. But it might fall from the sky too. The plans, the love might die, might lead to tragedy with all its rippling effects moving into the web of relationships and events connected with the flight of the plane. The crashed plane: can be anxiety bringing down our ambition or adventurousness; a loss of self-confidence or mental equilibrium. The plane journey: shows a move toward independence; leaving home or friends; success. Being grounded: sense of not getting anywhere and frustration. An attacking aircraft: feeling attacked either by our own doubts and self-criticism, or that of others.

The example below clearly shows one aspect of what a plane means, being daring in a new area, taking risks in life, braving a new work area or relationship. Sometimes the plane in the sky represents feeling threatened by something new or unknown. Thus one dreamer dreamt of bombs being dropped from a plane when she was offered a new job which would take her into the public eye.

Example: 'I saw a biplane fly overhead. Its pilot was performing daring new stunts. I ran into a house to tell a man who was in bed to run out and see the plane.' David R.

Aesculapius The Roman form of the Greek god of healing, Asclepius. See: **Asclepius**.

affair In the dream below, Andrew's fear of his wife's desire for another man is being expressed. But the dream really depicts Andrew's feelings of sexual inadequacy. Adultery dreams may also express release of sexual feelings; desire for another partner; desire for one's partner to have sex with someone else. See: last example in **dark**; **sex in dreams**.

> *Example: 'I was on board a pleasure cruiser with my wife. As I stood on a high deck I looked down and saw her sitting below with very tight knickers on and nothing else. As a man walked toward her the knickers came off or slipped down. The man was sexually aroused and started attempting to penetrate her. She only put up a token resistance, mewing a bit, but not fighting him off. I rushed toward them and kicked him off.'*
> *Andrew P.*

African This may refer to one's own feelings about coloured people or racial prejudice; Africa may have been the birthplace for the human race. In dreams we still use primitive Africans or Australian Aborigines to represent our own natural inner life. See: **aboriginal**; **black person**; **native**.

aggression See: **hostility**.

aim Suggests directing attention or desire toward what is represented by target or goal. <u>Gun being aimed</u>: directing anger, sexuality or attention.

air See: **wind**.

airport Making new departures; changes; being en route to something new in life; a checking of one's own values, identity, a sort of self-assessment in regard to independence and moving on to new opportunities. Self-doubts and uncertainties at this stage stop us from attempting the new.

air raid Feeling under attack, the severity depending on the dream damage. The attack might be emotional from people, or feelings we have about events around us. Things may be going badly at work and comments can be felt like bombshells. Very often though, the threats are purely mental. We may read of an illness such as AIDS and the anxiety we connect with the idea has a devastating effect. Idioms: I feel blitzed. See: **aeroplane**; **war**.

Example: 'I am in a house and planes are dropping bombs on it.' Mrs S.M.

alcohol An influence which changes the way we feel, moving us toward negative or positive feelings; prelude to friendliness or intimacy; an allowing of another influence into our life that we do not immediately feel is our own conscious will; dependence; in a religious sense the wine represents a life-changing influence, an influx of spiritual power – i.e. a deep self-acceptance allowing new experience both from within and from other people and events.

alien Urges or feelings we find difficult to identify with; feelings of being an outsider in a group or society; can also be something very new and previously not experienced in regard to one's own potential or mind.

alligator See: **animals**.

alone Expresses one's sense of isolation; feelings of loneliness; independence, depending on dream feelings. Idioms: go it alone.

altar Self-giving – this can be a very positive action or a sort of self-punishment out of guilt; place of death, but also of rebirth. See: **archetypes**.

ambulance See: **accident**.

America See: **abroad**.

American Indian Natural wisdom. See: **Iroquoian dream cult**.

amnesia   The example below shows only too clearly how often one may forget things that are so important and fall into old habits. The woman David was sleeping with was someone from his past he was unhappy with.

> *Example: 'I am sleeping rough in a garden with a woman I do not love. I think I should try to make the best of the situation, but my feelings against it are too strong. Then I decide I don't ever want to live like that again and tear up the mattress we slept on. As I do this I realise, as if waking from amnesia, that Pat lives just across the road. She has specially moved there because of our love. I realise with horror I had forgotten and may have lost her.' David H.*

amplification method   An approach suggested by Carl Jung. In essence it is to honour what the dream states. In the dream example above, David is sleeping on a mattress, but it could have been a bed or a hammock or even a sleeping bag. So why a mattress and why in the garden, and why not alone? Having noted the specifics of our dream, we then amplify what we know about them. We ask ourselves such questions as: what does sleeping on a mattress on the floor mean? Have I ever done it? When? Why? Where? In what circumstances? Does it represent some condition?' In other words we bring out as much information as we can about each dream specific. This includes memories, associated ideas, anything relevant. In the case of David, he was sleeping on a mattress on the floor in his present relationship. But he had slipped back into attitudes which damaged his previous relationship. P.W. Martin emphasises it is amplification not free association which is sought. Free association may lead to other ideas and feelings not directly connected to the dream specifics. See: **dream processing**; **postures**, **movement**, **body language**; **settings**; **word analysis of dreams**.

amputation   To lose or cut off by repressing whatever the limb represents; loss of adequacy, sexual or otherwise. See: **body**.

anaesthetic   Death; avoiding painful emotions; entering the unconscious; feeling overpowered.

analysis, dream   See: **dream processing**.

analyst   An analyst, psychologist, psychiatrist in our dream depicts our self-assessment. Our mind can transform itself in a number of ways. Sometimes one new piece of information or a new mental discipline can change the quality of all mental life. The analyst represents such power to transform, as well as the often avoided self-awareness.

angel   The positive side of your relationship with your mother; religious concepts; sometimes feelings about death; a need for a parent figure to guide or instruct in decision making. Idioms: guardian angel; like an angel; on the side of the angels; fools rush in where angels fear to tread. See: **religion and dreams**.

anger   See: **hostility**.

animals   Like any other animal, human beings have developed certain physical and behavioural traits. Some of these traits, such as a new-born baby attempting to suckle the breast, are rooted in millions of years of past experience and can be thought of as instinctive. In a male dog we can observe instinctive behaviour such as cocking of the leg to urinate. We can see some of our own traits in such things as the human desire to elect leaders. Many of these habits are psycho-biological or social. In our dreams we represent these drives or habits in the form of various animals. Our restrained sex drive or aggression may be shown in our dream as a dog on a lead. The power of drives such as the urge to parenthood via sex might be shown as a horse which we are trying to control. More than anything else though, our dream animal represents our powerful feeling reactions to situations – reactions developed through centuries of human experience in frequently terrible situations. This aspect of ourselves is rooted in the older portions of the brain.

Example: 'I am sitting in the hotel staff room eating lunch at a large dining table. One by one I am joined by perhaps a dozen women. The atmosphere is pleasant, easy and light-hearted. I enjoy the feeling of being the only male among a dozen attractive women. Then I notice a strange thing. One by one all the girls around me turn into cats, but carry on laughing and talking as if nothing is happening. I find this interesting and not alarming. I am aware each girl turns into the sort of cat that is right for her – a vivacious redhead becomes a purring orange tabby; an aloof, slightly superior lady becomes a Siamese; the only ex-girlfriend of mine present becomes a black witch's familiar.

I remember turning to my left and asking: "Tell me Rebecca, how did you do this?" The Rebecca cat giggles with a human voice and says: "He doesn't have a clue, does he?" As I look at the Rebecca cat I realise she still has her human eyes. This I realise is true of all the cats, they have human eyes in feline faces. As I realise this one says: "I think he's beginning to understand now" and laughs.' Paul C. (Teletext).

This graphic dream so well illustrates how we each have our human personality within our animal drives and urges. The animal in our dreams has commonly been seen only as the sex drive. A careful examination of animal dreams shows this to be untrue. The animal represents all our biological needs and responses which include: survival; hunger; reproduction; parental urges; need for exercise and rest; social drives; fear reactions; anger; urge to provide for young and mate; home/nest building; territory protection; social hierarchy, etc.

If these aspects in an individual are damaged or traumatised, the person might become a parent who has lost the natural bonding and care for their child; an individual who has no sense of social status or responsibility; criminally violent; someone with disturbed and misplaced sexuality.

Dominating or attempting to kill the animal in us can cause tension, depression and illness. The escape into dry intellectualism is a cause of internal conflict. Complete permissiveness is no answer either. Our higher brain functions need expression also. So one of the challenges of maturing is how to meet and relate to our 'animals' and perhaps bring them into expression in a satisfying way. Such drives are fundamentally a push toward *life*.

It must be remembered that where sex or sexuality is mentioned, I am not simply referring to the sex act. I mean sexuality in its overall aspect, which includes the urge toward parenthood and the love and caring connected with it. Brain damage or certain drugs or chemicals can diminish the 'human' levels of function and only the animal and lizard levels express. Below are listed some common ways animals are used in our dreams.

animal situations   Neglect, mutilation or killing our 'animal': a common theme. In the example below, Lynda's feelings show how she senses what she is doing to her inner nature, but she dismisses this by convincing herself such feelings are not 'true'. We have a responsibility to care for our animal drives, to see our sexual, nutritional and body needs are met.

> *Example: 'I am given an animal to look after, usually somebody's pet while they are away on holiday. I then completely forget the animal, go away and when I return the animal is either dead or very dried up or has been got at by another animal and is in the throes of dying. When I wake from the dream I feel most dreadful and it is only when I am fully awake and realise it is not true do I feel better.' Lynda E.*

Eating the animal: integrating our natural wisdom and energy. Hiding from or trapped by an animal: see the *wolf* entry. Animal with its young: parental feelings; one's basic childhood needs. Baby animal: oneself when young; baby feelings; desire for babies. See example in **eating**. Talking, shining, holy or wise animals: important intuitive information; a meeting with the gathered wisdom we have unconsciously. This is one of the sources of religious inspiration. Many older cultures represent their origin of great learning or holiness as animals or animal-headed beings. See: *ape* below; **birds**; **pets**; **reptiles – lizards**, **snakes**; **unconscious**.

ape   Can represent a world of experience human beings have lost and feel sorrow at its absence. In developing self-consciousness, with its labyrinth of ideas and decisions, humans lost a sense of oneness with life around them. Animals have enormous remembered wisdom; remembered through instincts and complex social codes. Without it humans can feel alone in the world, a meaningless existence in the midst of uncaring circumstance. This wisdom is still accessible to humans who know how to listen to the unconscious and thus discover the enormous wealth of information they have about such things as social behaviour and body language. The ape can depict this wisdom, especially if it is white haired. Or it might show the personal folly of trying to let instincts dominate us now we have self-awareness. Idioms: he is just aping.

ass The basic life processes in the body, which uphold or carry us through the years; the plodding, long-suffering body.

bear Power of our feeling reaction and traits; possessiveness, as or by a parent or lover; the 'animal' side of our relationship with our parents. Maybe a play on the word 'bare', such as bare facts or overbearing.

bull With Taureans may depict their innate characteristics and how they are dealing with them. Sex drive; the basic drives toward parenthood, and caring and providing via sex. The aggressive bull often shows the frustration arising from these basic drives being taunted or thwarted. For instance a person may wish for a family, yet be frustrated by a form of sexuality in their partner which does not care for the instinctive drive for children. The killed bull is a killing of these drives. If sacrificed though, it may show self-giving. The ridden bull in dreams shows a harmony between self-awareness and its decision making, and the basic 'animal' drives. Idioms: like a bull at a gate; bull in a china shop; red rag to a bull; score a bull's eye; take the bull by the horns.

cat Because a cat is often an easy source of physical contact and affection it depicts the need to be cared for and for warm affection. For some women, cats are a substitute baby. It is therefore used in many dreams to represent a woman's urge or need to care for someone, or directly her need to reproduce. Also refined female sexuality unless the cat is markedly a tom; or it can be our intuition, warning us through its sensitivity to moods or unseen dangers; cattiness – showing one's 'claws', jealousy, anger in a relationship.

Example: 'I went to the fridge to get out some minced meat to feed the cat. It came in, as it fed I had a strong urge to touch it, such strong feelings of love were pouring out of me. The animal looked up at my face as I wanted to kiss it. The lips had pink lipstick on. I kissed it, it's paw came up around my arm, I could see the black claws. We were rolling around on the floor, it felt very sexual.' Monica

*Example: 'My husband died over a year ago and I live alone,
no pets. Yet I dreamt I opened my front door and there was a
cat waiting to be let in. It was my cat and I knew I hadn't fed
it for ages or looked after it. I felt awful that I had neglected it
for so long. The strange thing was that the next day as I walked
around the supermarket, I kept wanting to go to the cat-food
section to buy food.' Winnie P. (Exeter).*

In losing her husband, Winnie has lost her source of given and
received affection. Idioms: copy cat; bell the cat; cat and mouse; cat's
whiskers; cat out of the bag; cat and dog life; cat on hot bricks;
something the cat brought in; a cat's paw; cat among the pigeons;
while the cat's away.

cow Similar to the bull, but representing the female side of one's
nature, especially the easy, self-giving of oneself and one's body to
others, or a baby; one's mother or the mother role. Idioms: sacred
cow; milch cow; till the cows come home.

dinosaur Exploring dreams is like uncovering different strata of
human psychological history – history we all share. The dinosaur
represents our very basic urges of survival such as fear, reproduction
and survival reactions to situations. This does not make these
'brutal'. They are fundamental and necessary in today's life. Because
these aspects of ourselves are so old and have survived so long,
there is often great wisdom in them to be made conscious. Such
urges also need to be integrated in a way that socialises them,
otherwise they exist in a primitive form still, perhaps in conflict with
our personality.

dog Easy expression of such aspects of ourselves as aggression –
maybe because they show their teeth easily – sexuality, friendship;
our easy flowing natural feelings; devotion, perhaps to a lover or
child. For some people a dog was the only source of expressive love
in their childhood, so may well depict this. Like the cat, the dog can
be a substitute baby for childless women, or represent affection or
caring. See: *cat.* Dog on lead: restrained or controlled urges. The dog
appears more often than other animals in dreams. Black dog: the

black dog figures in quite a lot of people's imagery. Bernard Levin uses it to represent depression. For some people it is death. The sense or meaning the dog gives in relation to depression or death is that it is a living energy in us which has gone 'bad' which causes the depression or death. <u>Idioms</u>: Die like a dog; dirty dog; dog eared; dog eat dog; dog in the manger; gay dog; go to the dogs; let sleeping dogs lie; etc.

> *Example:* '*I continue on my path, and suddenly the nettles disappear and the path is clear. Ahead the wall has curved round to face me, but there is a gate in it and I can see my dog waiting for me on the other side.*' *Mrs M.G.*

In the dream of this elderly woman, the dog is leading the way through the experience of meeting death. Mythology has often shown the dog in this light, as an inner sense of knowing how to find transformation through death – or as the ravaging threat of death.

elephant The enormous potential power we have in growth and activity. If we run from the elephant we are afraid of our own strength or inner drive. Sometimes represents the collective unconscious. <u>Idioms</u>: white elephant; pink elephants; rogue elephant. See: *the self* under **archetypes**.

frog The deeply unconscious psycho-biological life processes which transformed us from a tadpole/sperm into an air-breathing frog/adult. The enormous information such symbols hold if we explore them gives them their power.

goat A Capricornian's basic traits. Rutting sexuality; ability to climb socially; tough ability to survive difficulties. Sometimes connected with repressed natural drives which become reversed or evil/live.

hare Intuition; creative ideas; the crazy, irrational notions we sometimes call intuition. The hare occasionally appears as a supernatural figure giving advice; or as a sacrificial animal. As such it depicts our ability to make great changes in life.

horse Pleasurable energy and exuberance; dynamic sexual drive; the physical energy and life processes that 'carry' us around. It is human instincts that have been harnessed or socialised for generations.

But they have perhaps been let slide into non-use. It is also survival drive, sexuality, love, all yearning toward service, toward metamorphosis. See: example in **rescue**.

Controlling the horse or fear of it: fear of feelings of love and sexuality, of our own natural drives. If the horse dragged the dreamer along: impetuosity of such feelings; feelings dragged along by natural urges. Running away from a horse or horsemen: fear of sexuality, which includes responsibility for parenthood and relationship; fear of life drive. The winged horse: shows how our life or drive is not limited to sexuality or survival, but can lift into wider activities – a woman turning her love of her children into social caring. A horse race: one's life; everyday competition and where you rate yourself in it. A sick or dying horse: loss of health, energy, enthusiasm. Black horse: unaccepted passions; threat of death. White horse: changing sexual drive into love and wider awareness; a meeting with an expanded awareness of ourselves. The mare: femininity, receptiveness, fertility. The stallion: masculinity, power and virility. Idioms: back the wrong horse; from the horse's mouth; horse sense; you can take a horse to water; wild horses. See: **dream as spiritual guide**.

> *Example: 'As I talked to the pale, golden horse it felt more and more as if I were talking to a male companion who was in union with me.' Alison B.*

Alison's horse is obviously portraying her feelings for a man. The dream shows how easy and integrated she is with these.

> *Example: quoted from* Dreams and Dreaming *by Norman Mackenzie, page 23: 'I dreamed that I was awakened by the sound of horse's hooves in the street. I saw a white horse, with no rider, stopping at midnight in front of our house. I knew it came for my younger sister. I went to the door and opened it to call her, when suddenly I saw her coming down the stairs, all dressed in white. She did not say a word to me, but walked with stately steps down the stairs, through the hall, and out of the door. She mounted the horse and rode away. I woke up crying.'*

The woman who had the dream thought it foretold the death of her sister (which, in fact, occurred about a month later) whom she hated for marrying the man that she herself loved.

lamb   The childlike, dependent, vulnerable part of self; innocence; Christ.

lion   The power of our physical strength, of our temper, of our emotions or sexuality; love that has become anger through jealousy or pain. The story of Androcles and the lion shows how the pain felt by our 'animal' life process, if tended by the conscious personality, brings a loving relationship between conscious and unconscious.

Many children experience recurring dreams of a lion chasing them through their house. This is most likely caused by a developing struggle with their natural feelings of anger and aggression. This because their parents might attempt to quieten or control the child's temper, or criticise it as 'bad'. Idioms: brave the lion's den, lion's share; head in the lion's mouth.

monkey   Foolishness; thoughtlessness; being ruled by impulse. But sometimes same as *ape*. Idioms: make a monkey of; monkey business; monkey with; monkey tricks.

mouse   Minor irritations; fears and worries; the mousy or timid part of self; the activities within us – our house – which go on unconsciously, which might be important though small, or gnaw away at one; the sexual organ which goes in and out of a hole.

pig   Physical appetites; life directed only by physical needs; sensuality. The sow represents giving of oneself and sustenance; lack of spiritual directive. Idioms: pig in a poke; happy as a pig in shit; make a pig of oneself; pig in the middle; pigs might fly; pig-headed.

rabbit   Sexuality – because of human associations with its rapid breeding; softness and non-aggression, sometimes to the point of depicting us as a victim, or foolishly passive – may thus represent unwordly idealism. Perhaps because of its tendency to be the victim of predators, it is often used as a sacrifice in dreams, which suggests the hurt we might experience to the soft, vulnerable parts of our nature as we experience the pain of meeting reality in the maturing process. Rabbit hole: Alice down the rabbit hole illustrates this – a going within the self; into the unconscious; the womb.

rat What the dreamer senses as sick or negative inside self; physical sickness or anxieties about health; feelings of sexual repulsion, or using sex to gain material aims; intuitions about a person being a 'rat' – doing things behind one's back or under-handedly – or deserting a relationship when difficulties arise; seeing the underhanded side of oneself; time gnawing away at our life. Idioms: rat on someone; rat race; smell a rat; feeling ratty.

sheep Conformity; feeling or being 'one of the flock'; the aspects of oneself that are the same as in other human beings. Sheep may depict the way me may be led into situations, sometimes awful ones by conforming to prevailing attitudes and social pressures.

> *Example: 'I walked past a married couple who were walking up the hill too. As I passed I heard them say something about a shepherd. Looking up the hill I saw the sheep, then The Shepherd. A beautiful aura of many colours surrounded The Shepherd. I looked and felt joy and exuberance rise in me, and I ran to the couple saying it was The Shepherd.' Brian C.*

In the example Brian is not only aware of the sheep, but also *The Shepherd*. The sheep represent his experience of being one of the crowd and The Shepherd is his sense of his own unique potential or love transforming his ordinariness. Caring for sheep: helping people to grow spiritually.

wolf Although the wolf can depict a feeling that 'things' are out to get us, the wolf is often just fear. Fear is one of our instinctive reactions to situations, so it is depicted by an animal. We may find ourselves a prisoner of such feelings, as Anna is the following example.

> *Example: 'I was in a caravan in the middle of a field and in this field was a large, black wolf. Every time I tried to run from the caravan to the edge of the field, the wolf chased me back, so I was a prisoner in the caravan. It all sounds so simple now, but at the time I was truly terrified.' Anna S.*

This next example from Oliver, a boy of six, illustrates how such fears can be met with a little courage. It is a dream which recurred several times, so his description is of a series of dreams.

> *Example: 'I am in my bed in my own room and I hear what I know to be a wolf wearing the sort of clogs worn in Lancashire. When the wolf gets to a certain point, there is a bang and I wake terrified. My mother's reassurances do not help. Each night he gets a bit nearer before my panicky awakening. The night came when I knew he would reach me. Sure enough he arrives and the bedroom door – in my dream – is flung wide open with a tremendous bang. There is no one there. I never dreamt it again.'*

Idioms: wolf at the door; wolf in sheep's clothing; cry wolf; throw to the wolves.

antique   See: **old**.

anxiety dreams   One of the most frequent dream themes is that of anxiety in some form. This may not be because most dreams are about things we fear, but simply because we remember those more than bland dreams. In our dreams, all that exists to disturb us are our memories, disturbing images and our own emotions. Of course, the dream may be about a snake or car accident – frightening things which do not appear to be inside us. Even so, it is our emotions about the image of the snake or situation which disturbs us, and these can be changed. If we can recognise what an enormous power our imagination has on our emotions and body, this can start the process of lessening anxiety. If we cannot meet our feelings of fear or emotional pain we are controlled or trapped by them. Sometimes we need the help of a professional therapist to meet what we fear, but many anxieties can be met by using the simple techniques explained in dream processing. See: *wolf* in **animals; dream processing; premenstrual tension**.

apparitions   See: **ghost**.

appointment   Reminder of something our unconscious feels we are about to meet, or something we ought to meet.

applause Desire for acclaim or giving self-acclaim.

archetypes Although the word archetype has a long history, Carl Jung used it to express something he observed in human dreams. He said the archetypes are a tendency or instinctive trend in the human unconscious to represent certain motifs or themes. As our instinctive urge to reproduce may show itself in consciousness as sexual fantasies, so archetypes show themselves as certain dream, fantasy or story themes. Just as each individual animal does not create its own instincts, we do not create our own collective thought pattern. The influence these archetypes have upon our conscious self is varied. Partly they are supportive, as instincts are to an animal.

Some ancient cultures erected a pantheon of gods and goddesses. Many of these gods were expressions of archetypal themes, such as death, rebirth and womanhood. A sheep dog has in itself unconsciously a greater propensity to herd animals under direction than any other dog breed. Through the worship of gods, perhaps ancient people touched similar reservoirs of strength and healing innate in them. Without such strength, the individual might find it more difficult to face the fact that death waits at the end of life, or to allow sexuality to emerge into their life at puberty.

The dream of a girl suffering from anorexia shows her cutting off her own breasts with scissors. It portrays her developing sexual traits and urges as unacceptable to her. Perhaps she 'cuts them off' by not eating and thus preventing her body and psyche from maturing. In the past, it would have been recommended that she give offerings to a goddess, thus aligning her with the unconscious archetype or power to become a woman.

Some of these archetypal patterns of behaviour, such as territorialism and group identity, are only too obviously behind much that occurs in war, and their influence needs to be brought more fully into awareness. But we must be careful in accepting Jung's description of the archetypes. In more recent years, through the tremendously amplified access to the unconscious made possible in psychiatry through such drugs as LSD, a lot more information about unconscious imagery has been made available. It is possible that certain synthesising aspects of the mind produce images to represent huge areas of collected experience, i.e. the Mystic Mother or Madonna representing our collected experience of our mother.

The propensity for human beings of widely separated culture, language, age or gender to meet with the same symbols in their dreams, fantasies or religious feelings does suggest a collective level of consciousness. We each sink into this collective region of experience during sleep and our dreams depict aspects of our individual relationship with it, or what we have harvested from it. Such dreams suggest that nature stores the essence of all experience. Such collective experience forms a dynamic, ever-moving and developing process that interacts with one's conscious and apparently independent personality. This is so like our relationship with language, in which we ourselves did not develop the words we use. Language is a reservoir of past thought and endeavour. From it we gain personal self-awareness and interpersonal communication. We may add to it and use it, but it is never limited to our personal self.

If we could encompass all of one language, we would see it emerging out of an immense history, an amalgamation of all human experience, constantly shifting. We would have a vision of the extraordinary mind, love, pain and multifaceted nature of human life. If such language was expressed as a person, they would be like a god, having all human experience. It is perhaps the sense of such huge and *apparent* reservoirs of human experience that we sense unconsciously and erect a god image around.

Whatever may be the explanation of these archetypal themes, they are important because they illustrate how we as individuals, and human beings collectively, have been able to develop our sense of conscious identity amidst enormous forces of unconsciousness, collectivity and external stresses.

Below are some common archetypal symbols and their associated images. Remember that most images in your dreams are expressions of personal feelings and associations. It is only occasionally they connect your conscious self with the great pool of the collective experience. When they do, drink the waters.

anima   The female within the male, shown as a woman in a man's dream. Physically a man is predominantly male, but also has nipples and produces some female hormones. Psychologically, we may only express part of our potential in everyday life. In a man, the more feeling and caring side may be given little expression. Apart from this some functions such as intuition and unconscious creativity may also be latent. These secondary or latent characteristics are depicted by the female in male dreams. In general we can say the woman represents the man's emotions, his nurturing and caring quality. It also holds in it an expression of his complex of feelings about women, gained as experience mostly from his mother – or lack of mother – but also from a synthesis of all his female contacts. So the whole realm of his experience of the female can be represented by the woman in his dream and is accessible through the image.

Good relationship with or marrying the woman: shows the man integrating his own real emotions, sensitivity and intuition. This makes him more whole, balancing his exterior male qualities. He would then be less dependent upon an external female to feel whole. It also shows the man meeting his experience of his mother in a healing way. This enables the man to have a realistic relationship with an actual woman. It also brings a sense of connectedness between his conscious self and what he senses as Life or as Bucky Fuller calls it, Universe. See: *mystic mother* below.

To be in conflict with the woman or unable to make real physical and pleasurable contact with her: suggests difficulty in meeting what may have been a painful or threatening experience of mother. This can lead to becoming an intellectual but emotionally barren man. Or being possessed in a negative way by the female traits, becoming emotionally unstable, opinionated and illogical. Actual relations with women will be difficult. Actual emotional or intimate merging is threatening because it brings the man close to the pain of fear connected with mother. Sex may be possible but not a close feeling union. See: **woman**.

animus   The male within the female, shown as a man in a woman's dreams. Physically a woman is predominantly female, but also has a clitoris and produces some male hormones. Psychologically, we may only express part of our potential in everyday life. In a woman, the more physically dynamic, intellectual and socially challenging side of herself may be given less expression. Apart from this some features such as innovation and creative rational thought may be latent. These secondary or latent characteristics are depicted by the male in female dreams. In general we can say the man represents the woman's mental and social power, her ability to act creatively in 'the world'. It also holds in it an expression of her complex of feelings about men, gained as experience mostly from her relationship with – or lack of – father, but also from a synthesis of all her male contacts. So the whole realm of her experience of the male can be represented by the man in her dream and is accessible through the image.

Good relationship with or marrying the man: shows the woman integrating her own ability to be independent and capable in outwardly active terms. This makes her more whole, balancing her 'female' qualities. She would then be less dependent upon an external male to feel whole. It also shows the woman meeting her experience of her father in a healing way. This enables the woman to have a realistic relationship with an actual man. It also brings a sense of connectedness between her conscious self and what she senses as the 'commercial' world. See: *Father* below.

To be in conflict with the man or unable to make real physical and pleasurable contact with him: suggests difficulty in meeting what may have been a painful or threatening experience of father. This can lead to lack of ability to make clear judgements and lack of decisiveness in areas outside of feeling values. She is prone to acceptance of collective or long-held social norms without question; family or national attitudes not applicable to present situations; and 'reasoning' which actually arises out of emotions connected to such family or social norms. Actual relations with men will be difficult, or entered into simply as a duty. Emotional or intimate merging is threatening because it brings the woman close to the conflicts and pain connected with father. Sex may be possible but not a close feeling union. See: **man**.

blood   It is something we all have in common and we all depend upon for our life. It therefore represents the process of universal life in us. It may be shown as red wine, the drinking of which, in some dreams, is realised to be wine and blood at the same moment. This wine/blood depicts the life and pain, the genius and despair of all that has lived. In the form of Christ's blood it depicts all human experience, which we can share in and meet death and rebirth through, by allowing personal awareness to be open to the collective. In other words it flows into our life through some measure of acceptance of ourselves as an integral part of life *and* human society. It touches us when we accept or love our fellows in a non-judgemental way and are ready to live our life as part of the whole. This leads to our old sense of self as a separate being dying. Born from this death is a greater certainty of life within the whole.

Christ Although people generally think of Christ as a historical figure, in dreams he is not this at all. He is a powerful process in the human unconscious.
Christ may represent:

- The denied force of joyous life within – denied through attempting to live social or religious rules and regulations.
- Social pressure to conform.
- A personal sense of connection and oneness with all life, or a sense of living within eternity now.
- An awareness in our unconscious, of the forces of symbiosis – or co-operative existence – operative in human life and the cosmos.
- Christ is to humanity, what our personality is to the billions of cells of our body – the collective personality of humanity.

In the West we call these processes within the human psyche Jesus or Christ. But the process or archetype is universal and has various names in different cultures – Krishna for instance. Sometimes represented in dreams as a fish or a big man. There are at least four aspects to Christ as depicted in dreams.

The Sunday school or church Christ: depicts social norms; the generally accepted morals and social rules. This 'Christ' comes about because the church tends to represent traditional values and national history, and attempts to press people to live these values. The dreamer may have a child-like relationship with this Christ, or if attempting to be self-responsible, be in conflict with it. Some people find this Christ has a castrating role in their life and flee in horror. In fact this aspect of social indoctrination may lead to such a burden of guilt and suppression that it can create psychic cripples. Trying to do all the 'right' things may lead us to the point where 'we can't say no to a glass of water without a pang of guilt'.

Two of the great forces which push at the human soul or psyche are social pressure such as the moral norm and biological pressures such as the sex drive. Individuals may fight a life-long battle with one or the other of these. The social criminal typifies battle with the first; the ascetic battles with the second.

The positive aspect of this 'Christ' is that prior to taking realistic self and social responsibility, people need guidelines for behaviour. They often yearn for security or certainty. Religion, in the form of powerful positive declarations of 'truth', supplies this need.

The ideal Christ: the psychological process which causes us not to take responsibility for our own highest ideals; our own yearnings for the good; our own most powerful urges arising against what we see as evils in the world. This influences us to wait for a sign from Christ in our dream in order to gain authority or to overcome the anxiety associated with the drive. We want God to say we should act in a certain way because we are not willing to be self-responsible.

> *Example: 'I stood outside a castle. It was closed and guarded by soldiers in armour. Wondering how to get in I thought that if I dressed and acted as a soldier I would be allowed entrance. It worked and inside Christ met me and said he had important work for me to do.' Sonia.*

The closely guarded secret is Sonia's own impulses to do some sort of socially creative work. She doesn't want to own them as her own. It is much easier if she can say 'Christ told me to do this.' In this way she avoids direct encounter with opposition.

The unofficial Christ: Peter, whose dream appears below, had a debilitating psychosomatic illness at the time of his dream, causing pain where the tentacles ran. The shell is his defence against feeling his own hurts and inner conflicts. The dream shows him contacting a strength which is not afraid of his internal battlefield of conflicts and can show ways of healing real human problems. The healing rests upon the dreamer's conscious action, not Christ's, suggesting the dreamer taking responsibility for his own situation. Peter realised he had been avoiding his own internal battlefield, but felt he had found a strength – in the Big Man – which would support his efforts to find healing. In fact he met his conflicts and grew beyond his ailments.

> *Example: 'A fierce battle was raging with bullets flying. I immediately fell down and "played dead". It wasn't that I was*

*hurt in any way, but I didn't want to be at any risk in the fight.
As I lay there I saw a tall, well-built man in soldier's uniform
walk to me. He gave no sign of any fear concerning the bullets
and quietly knelt beside me. I felt he was Christ, but was
confused by him being a soldier. He placed a hand on my back
and gradually worked his fingers under the shell of a large
limpet-type creature that I had never before known was
parasitically attached to my back. I could feel him pull it away,
but knew its tentacles still ran right into my chest. He then sat
me up and told me how I could rid myself of the tentacles and
so be healed.' Peter Y.*

Peter's conflicts were between his love for his children and his
sexuality. This Christ was Peter's undammed life, the flood of loving
sexuality, the strength to burst through social rules and regulations
because love or life pushes. When we find it in ourselves we don't
give a hang about bullets, death, right or wrong, because we have
a sense of our own integral existence within life and our own
rightness and place in eternity.

The integral or cosmic Christ: each of us have a sense of
connectedness with the whole, with the cosmos. We may be little
aware of this sense. Our scepticism may deny it as Lester's was doing
in the example below. But finding it can enrich the rest of our nature.
The awareness of connectedness brings with it a realisation of taking
part in the unimaginably grand drama called life. It gives a feeling,
no matter what the state of our body – crippled or healthy – that we
have something that makes any faults in body or achievement
insignificant. It doesn't take all the difficulties out of life, but it is a
good companion on the way.

*Example: 'I am a journalist reporting on the return of Christ.
He is expected on a paddle steamer going upstream on a large
river. I am very sceptical and watch disciples and followers
gather on the rear deck. The guru arrives, dressed in simple
white robes. He has long, beautiful auburn hair and beard,
and a gentle, wise face. He begins to tap a simple rhythm on
a tabla or Indian drum. It develops into complex inter-
mingling of orchestral rhythms as everyone joins in. I now
realise he is Christ and feel overwhelmed with awe as I try to*

play my part in the music. I'm tapping with a pen and find myself fumbling. A bottle or can opener comes to me from the direction of Christ. I try to beat a complementary rhythm, a small part of a greater, universal music.' Lester S.

In dreams and religion, Christ is also represented as the son of the Cosmos or God. This aspect of Christ possibly comes about because of a sense many people have that the origins of their personal life is from beyond the Earth. This powerful urge to see oneself as more than a physical body is symbolised by Christ, a being who transcends physical boundaries. Human beings of all ages have, when opening to the influence of the unconscious during meditation, trance, prayer, or drug use, experienced awareness of a love existing behind the creation of things, a love that is the source of the big bang itself, that willingly died that we might exist. Humanity became aware of this at a particular stage of the development of self awareness. The arrival at this stage of self-awareness was expressed in what we know as the historical Jesus. See: **Religion and Dreams**; *the Self* under **Archetypes**.

death and rebirth   The symbols of death or the fear of death can be: sunset; evening; a crossed river or falling in a river; a skeleton; snarling dogs; sleep; anaesthetic; grave stones; a cemetery; blackness or something black; an old man or woman, or father time with a scythe; ace of spades; a fallen mirror; stopped clock; a pulled tooth; an empty abyss; the chill wind; falling leaves; a withering plant; an empty house; a lightning-struck tree; a coffin; struggling breaths; a dead animal in the gutter; a rotting carcass; underground; the depths of the sea – the *void*.

What lies beyond death is conjecture, but the archetype of death we are considering is not completely about physical death. It is about our observation of it in others; our conceptions of it gained from our culture and our impressions gained from seeing dead animals, rotting corpses; the feelings which generate around our experiences and thoughts of it; our attempts to deal with our own ageing and approach to death – *plus* what material the deeper strata of our unconscious release regarding it. It is about how our sense of conscious personal existence meets the prospect of its disintegration.

Unless we can come to terms with what is behind the haunting images of death we meet in our dreams, we will fail to live fully and daringly; we are too haunted by death lurking in the shadows of injury and the unknown. Images of death and the associated emotions, carried within for years, can have a negative influence on our health. Coming to terms means the courage to feel the emotions of fear or chill and discover them for what they are – emotions. They are certainly not death, only our feelings about it. The differences shown in the two following examples illustrate the avoiding and the meeting. The first can be called an experience of the 'death pit'.

Example: 'Disturbed by an unusually vivid dream last night – unable to sleep afterwards for almost two hours.

I went out for the evening to see some friends. Golden beer spilled as one of my friends doubled up and the room sprang open with a Death's Head shrieking behind him. As if a skin had been peeled back to reveal the bones of life crackling in a gigantic electric chair. It burned my brain. With a great effort I managed to wall up the apparition behind the bright fabric of the evening, leaving only a blurred after-image of the hole, like the torn edge of a strip of wallpaper that has been ripped and glued back into place.

It happened again. At first it was the result of a form of irritated curiosity, like picking at a scab, or scratching an itch irresistibly, in spite of the inevitable pain. This hurt far too much though. My whole frame shuddered, as if my bones were lines being ridden by a hundred express trains, or an electric current, a force field of limitless indifferent energy.

I sealed it up again, but the wound had been weakened by my curiosity, and burst open at the slightest agitation: as soon as I tried to lose myself in the happy group, my laughter triggered the catch, and I saw my friends' faces twisted by laughter, with their own deaths crowing scornfully behind their backs. As if Death couldn't wait to show He had the last laugh, pointing it out obscenely, obvious as a schoolboy's joke. I was denied the temporary relief of friendship by the hideous mockery that was audible to me alone.

When I realised that I couldn't control it, I was speechless and dizzy with fright and pain. I couldn't stand properly, and vainly tried to stop falling against people and things like a drunk. Either my appearance or something I was unaware of saying had upset V. as I could see her crying, and from the snatches of conversation I caught, I realised that I had spoilt everyone's evening. Eventually I was picked up and carried out by the bouncers and left on the opposite side of the street. As I struggled, I became vaguely aware that I was dreaming, a fact which glimmered like a pinprick of light seen from the foot of a mine shaft. I groped desperately towards it, even as I realised that the multifarious shapes of memory and imagination were materialising in the very street around me. I averted my gaze as a squat, malformed figure limped by, unwilling to acknowledge it as the progeny of my own brain. I clawed my way desperately in the shaft, as I felt visual imagination solidify into sound and the threat of touch. Liquid splashed on the ground behind me, as if a bucket had been emptied from a half-remembered opening in the building above.

With a desperate convulsion of mental energy, I deliberately tore my way out of the dream. I opened my eyes with relief to see my room unchanged and still lit by the street lamp outside, opposite the school where the children would arrive in a few hours' time. In spite of the heat of the June night, I was not even sweating and felt surprisingly calm, apart from a raging suspicion about the means of my escape from my own imagination and its absurd but terrifying creations.' A.J.

Example: 'Suddenly I was in a huge underground cavern. It was hundreds of feet high and as wide. It had two great statues in it, both to do with death. The whole place overpowered me with a sense of decay and skeletal death, darkness, underground, earth, the end. I cried out in the dismal cave, "Death, where is your sting! Grave, where is your victory!" I immediately had the sense of being a bodiless awareness. I knew this was what occurred at death. Fear and the sense of decay left me.' Andrew.

Summarising these and many other dreams, it is not only the accumulated images of death, but also bodilessness and loss of power and identity which bring so much fear. There are two antipodes of human experience. At the tip of one is focused, self-determining self-consciousness. At the tip of the other is unfocused void without identity. Strangely enough we experience both each day to some degree. The first while awake; the second when we sleep. Yet to face the second with consciousness feels like all the horrors of death and loss. But facing it is important, especially to the second half of life. Although the unconscious carries the dark images we have of death, it also provides what feels like certainty to those who experience it, an awareness of existing eternally as part of the very fabric of life. Those who dare to confront the dark images find this.

The symbols of rebirth are: the cave; an egg; spring; the tree; the cross; dawn; emerging out of the sea; the snake; the bird; a seed; arising from the Earth or faeces; green shoot from a dead branch; phoenix; drinking alcohol or blood-red wine; flame; a pearl; the womb. Rebirth is as difficult to face as death. It holds within it not just the memories of the struggles and difficulties of our own physical birth and growth, but also the challenge of becoming the unknown future, the dark possibility, the new. The dream of Andrew in the underground cavern, in the section on Death above, is an example of positive rebirth. After realising himself as bodiless awareness he emerges from the cave and finds himself near a tree.

> *Example: 'A tremendous jolt of power poured into me from the tree. I saw that we had arrived at a place where a line of trees, about a 100 yards in length, stood very close together in a slight semicircle on the top of a bank. The trees had great spiritual power and the place was a holy temple. Two spiritual beings were there – an ancient Earth Being and Christ.' Andrew.*

The next example is of a dream typical of meeting memories of physical birth. As can be seen, the experience is powerful enough to cause physical shaking.

> *Example: 'All I can see of what I enter is a very narrow space with a light showing through. But immediately I enter I realise I have made a mistake for I am being forced swiftly through a dark, very narrow tunnel. I feel pain as I am dragged along and I hear loud banging noises which frighten me, but*

*although they are loud they seem to come from inside my head.
I feel terrified and breathless and very relieved when I wake
before reaching the end of the tunnel. In fact as I write this
account I am shivering.' Female, anon.*

devil   Usually repressed natural drives, particularly sexual feeling –
one can express physical sex, yet still repress sexual longing and
connected emotions of tenderness. It is what is unlived in us – 'devil'
is 'lived' spelt backwards. Any code of conduct, whether accepted
from parents or peers, leaves aspects of our total self unlived. The
struggle with paternal authority or power within oneself is often
represented as the devil. If we change our code of conduct, we may
meet the devil because we release the previously unlived area of
self. As Pan: the same, except that Pan represents losing oneself to
the natural urges.

father   The dream images representing father are many: God; a
god; a giant; a tyrant; executioner; devil; Pan – and of course father.
A child is, figuratively, like a growing plant. It takes in lumps of
external material and transforms them to its own being. A child
unconsciously either takes father or mother as its main model for
structuring its behaviour and aims. But huge areas of our basic self
also revolve around mother and father. Even not having an available
father leaves an enormous imprint in this archetypal area. Our father
in our dreams therefore is most often the overall effect, habits, traits,
which arise from our experience – or lack of it – of our father. Father
is also the great figure of original authority and strength in our life.
He therefore depicts our relationship with outside authority or
power. Struggle with or seeking to placate father: may show how we
deal with authority.

   Our baby or child self has no restraints, and in its relationship with
father at times felt urges which as an adult we might find hard to
believe or accept. In our dreams we frequently release these urges.
Killing father: expressing anger; getting rid of him so there is no
competition for mother; gaining our own ability to make decisions
and be independent. At some point we need to kill him inside us to
claim whatever strength we can from our experience of him and
become independent. Sex with father: for the woman fulfilment of
childhood desires to possess; for a man desire to receive his love.

The father may not easily have shown his love, so the child becomes desperate to receive. <u>Burying father</u>: most likely same as killing; or facing his death and one's own independence.

the great mother   The symbols are: Virgin Mary; sometimes one's own mother; a divine female; an old or ageless woman; the Earth; a blue grotto; the sea; a whale; a cave. Whatever the image it often contains great religious feeling or spiritual uplift. After all, our mother was the most powerful being in our early world. 'Did she admire hunters; then we would kill dragons and cleanse the world. Did she feel the weight of the world; then we would be the peace maker and bring her joy.' (W.V. Caldwell.)

The symbols of mother represent not simply our relationship with her, but also how it influences our own growth toward independence. As a baby our consciousness of self does not feel separate from mother. The gradual separation of the sense of self is difficult. In some people it is never managed, even though they separate physically. Their mother, or their sense of their mother within them, still directs their decisions. The old joke about 'My mother wouldn't like this' is true.

In many older cultures this break was worked out in ritual custom. Today we have to manage these subtleties of our psyche alone. A woman must find a way of transforming the pleasure – or absence of it – of her mother's breast into a love for a male. If she cannot she may wish to return to the breast of another female, or be the man her father never was for her. A man must find a way of transforming his unconscious desire for his mother into love of a woman which is more than a dependent or demanding baby or youth. If he cannot he may seek his mother in a likely woman, ignoring who that woman is as a real person. And the acceptance of our mother as she really is – a human being – precedes the acceptance of ourselves as we really are.

The symbols of the great mother hold in them our awareness, unconscious as it may be, of the forces of nature active in us. These forces, in the guise often of a beautiful woman dancing or beckoning, are both wonderful and dangerous. The dance of nature is unconscious. If we get in its way we will be ground under its heel, as it dances on its beautiful way. To meet this aspect of ourselves we must be both admiring and resourceful. The danger for a man might be that he loses himself in desire for all women or one woman. For a woman, that she becomes a spiritual whore, thinking she can uplift all through her womb.

hero/ine   The archetype of the hero has fascinated, taught, even ennobled human beings for thousands of years. Appears as Christ; Athena; Krishna; Mohammed; Mary; Ulysses; Superman; Florence Nightingale; a great game hunter; Hercules; or any film or TV hero such as Captain Kirk or Dr Who. We are the hero/ine of our own life. We brave great dangers, face monsters, pass through difficult initiations. Fundamental to the whole drama of the hero/ine is the evolution of our own identity from the depths of unconscious in the physical process of conception, through to developing self-awareness as an adult. To do this we face death and rebirth several times when we metamorphose from baby to child; from child to adolescent; from adolescent to adult; from adult with youthful body to ageing body. It is such an incredible journey, so heroic, so impossible of achievement, so fraught with dangers and triumphs, that it is the greatest story in the world.

We find it told over and over symbolically in all the 'holy' books as the birth of the holy child; the journey of the hero/ine; the creation of the world – our consciousness; the journeys of Moses. All pertain to the difficulties and means we use to *be*; to the art of keeping balance amidst the multitude of forces acting on our human psyche. The hero/ine is the one who dares even though they feel afraid and in pain. The avoidance of fear and pain in our society, where chemical anodynes or tranquillisers are sought to remove any tiny discomfort, is a great tragedy. Not that we need to become masochists, but we miss our own wholeness through fear of our own power of experiencing. In other cultures, the ability to meet pain and fear were considered spiritual strengths. They still are. The following example shows one dreamer meeting his own fear and uncertainty. See: *Christ* above.

> Example: *'I was in an ancient room. It had the feeling of being an old church. Then my wife and I were in bed in the room. A middle-aged woman was in the room. She was a ghost. I felt afraid of her, but to meet the fear I tried to confront her. I reached out my hand to her. I was crying out in my sleep from*

fear. As she took my hand I was amazed and shocked to feel it as physically real.' Desmond.

the Self   Our conscious self or ego is only a tiny part of our totality, as is obvious when we consider how much of our memory or experience we can hold in mind at any one time. The Self, as defined by Jung, is both what we are consciously aware of, and the massive potential remaining unconscious. The Self has no known boundaries, for we do not yet know the end of what the mind is capable of, or what consciousness is or touches out of sight of waking.

The mass of experience and awareness which lies behind our waking awareness is like an inner guiding factor which, apart from expressing precise information in the form of remembered facts and events, guides us, if we listen, through intuition, feeling states, dreams or illumination. When we meet this inner guiding or healing principle, we may have a powerful experience of meeting Christ, Buddha or Krishna. Gradually our meetings go beyond form and cultural imagery into a direct awareness of existing throughout all time and space; of being involved in all living forms.

This involvement in all things is not in the end a mystical experience, it is the recognition, sometimes with awe, sometimes with shock, of an existing reality. It is so much a part of everyday life we fail to see it – as perhaps the fish might not know it is living in water. For instance, none of us grows all our food, makes our own clothes or their material, produces the energy of gas or electricity in our homes – neither did any one of us form the language we exist within and which forms the very structure and self-awareness we identify with as our Self. We exist constantly as an integral and dependent part of this huge web of interactions; we cannot exist outside of it or without it, yet we may fail constantly to *realise* our integral existence. We may never see we are part of *one* huge organism. Dreams frequently depict this situation with such symbols as the sea, or symbols of the Self.

The symbols of the Self are: a ring; a square area; a great tree; Christ; a shining being or animal; a talking animal; a strange stone or rock; symbols like the cross or mandala; a round table; God; a guru; an elephant; a crowned or shining snake.

Here are some examples of the Self in dreams.

Example: 'I am climbing a tree to get a stone. This stone has special powers that flower. I'm nearly there when I look down and notice that there aren't any branches on the left side of the tree. This causes me to consider the possibility of falling and that in turn leads to a fear of climbing any higher. I wake with my heart beating strongly, but little feeling of fear.' Alan J.

Example: 'I am standing in the toilet peeing into the water. This creates lots of bubbles. As I look at these bubbles I notice each one has an eye looking at me. Fascinated I bend lower to look back at these eyes. When I do so I see they are not "eyes" but "I's". Each is a tiny reflection of myself looking back at me. Amused I ponder this multitude of me. Each tiny being, with its own individual sense of self, its own eyes and legs and fingers, feels it is separate from its fellows – and it is. But what they don't realise is that their awareness, their consciousness is a reflection of me. I am their god. Out of me all have their being. Then suddenly I realised I am myself a bubble. I too have a sense of being independent, with my own eyes, fingers and legs. Yet in reality I am only a reflection of one great life, One Self, existent in all diversity and multifarious forms. I felt afraid.' Tony.

Example: 'I look into the third square, it was filled with an iridescent blue colour, shining and beautiful to look at, a beautiful substance. I felt it had to do with religion, but I couldn't quite grasp it.' Hyone C.

Example: 'I watched an insect emerging from what appeared to be its chrysalis – shaped a little like a mermaid's purse. As it emerged it was vibrant with life, movement and colour. In fact it shifted its shape so quickly I was amazed at how it moved in and out of shapes as it adjusted to its final form. It had a beautiful gold barred design on its back, like a symbol – perhaps a bit like one of the zodiacal symbols. I watched another insect doing the same thing and began to realise how life was bursting forth in the garden. Looking up in the hedge I noticed a large pod expanding on top of a stalk. It was visibly getting larger, like a balloon. Suddenly it opened, forming many stalks with leaves and small, rose-like buds. Another pod was doing the same. As I watched I noticed a young woman nearby. I called to her to witness this extraordinary explosion of growth and life – a dynamic extravagant springtime of activity. She didn't appear to really see. I was very moved though, and stood leaning against what felt like a wall, perhaps the wall of a house, and wept at the beauty. I started to restrain my emotions as the woman did not share them, but then thought I wouldn't hold back because of her.' Andrew.

Awareness of the Self is important. It contains what is our own personal wisdom and insight regarding life in general and particular. It is not full of creeds and dogmas and conflict as are organised attempts to express the spiritual. But it does have its dark side. To grasp the stone with special powers, understand the significance of the iridescent blue square, or realise we are a bubble, as these dreams depict, we need a clear rational mind which allows intuition and feeling but is not relinquished or lost in the immensity of the Self. Touching the vastness of our being we may ourselves feel vast, all knowing, a guru. In this state Jung says a person loses all sense of humour and drops ordinary human contacts.

Functionally what happens is that as a defence against meeting our pain and childhood trauma as we enter this vast storehouse of our being, or as a way of escaping the self-responsibility for our condition, one might fly off into feelings of loving all things, of knowing the mystery of it all, of being the Buddha. The problem is that while it might be true we are in essence the Christ, or have wisdom, these realisations are distorted by the undealt with childhood traumas and longings. See: **aura**; **mandala**.

the Shadow   <u>Depicted as:</u> a shadowy figure, often the same sex as the dreamer; a zombie or walking dead; a dark shape; an unseen 'Thing'; someone or something we feel uneasy about or in some measure repelled by; what is behind one in a dream; anything dark or threatening.

The Shadow is any part of ourselves which we reject and so do not allow expression in our life. We may so dislike aspects of our nature we fail to see them altogether and instead see them in other people and criticise them. Nations as well as individuals do this. The Nazis projected all problems onto the Jews. The Americans have not wished to see their own social sickness and looked instead at the Russians. No doubt the Irish blame the English, and the English use the class system, with its projections between employee and employer. It is easier than looking at one's own Shadow.

If you can think of the characteristics you loathe in others, that is a fair picture of what you repress in yourself. The great 'ladies' man' may hide a Shadow which feels inadequate sexually. The loving Christian mother might meet a Shadow full of resentment and anger at how she has been taken for granted. Meeting the Shadow through our dreams is a meeting with our own reality, which in turn enables us to look at the world realistically. The shadow can be met – it leads to wholeness.

Fraser Boa tells the story of a man who told his analyst he had dreamt of Red Rooster – a cartoon character used in American national parks. Red Rooster is bossy and tells people to keep their litter and cigarettes. The analyst asked the man if he recognised Red Rooster in himself. After some thought he said no, he couldn't see he was like that. The analyst suggested he go ask his wife if she could see Red Rooster in him. He did this and was astonished when she said she could. After a few minutes of trying to suggest she was mistaken, she suggested he ask each of his three children. He took each one aside and was amazed when each said that of course they could see Red Rooster in him. He was always bossing people around and being authoritative. Red Rooster was his shadow. Other archetypes can be seen under: **games**, **gambling**; **god**; **guru**; **king**; **queen**; **sea**.

arena, **amphitheatre**   A focus of attention; a mental capability to bring an unimaginable number of associated bits of information and experience together in considering something; area of conflict.

armour   The emotional and intellectual rigidity we use to protect ourselves from hurt. Can depict muscular tension which blocks free-flowing sexuality and feelings.

army   See: *soldier* in **roles**; **war**.

arrested   Suggests a restraint of one's easy expression by moral judgements or questions of right and wrong. See: *policeman/woman* in **roles**.

art   See: **painting**.

artist   The aspect of oneself which is in contact with the irrational, creative side of the unconscious; the desire or ability to be creative.

ascending   General: the rising feelings of passion or sexual pleasure; the transition from expressing our energy genitally to expressing it in self-awareness is often shown as ascending. See: **flying**. Climbing stairs, going up in an elevator or lift: movement toward waking or becoming more aware; the mental; or an escape from anxiety or being 'down to earth'; sexual pleasure. If the lift goes out the top of the roof, or the connection with base is missing: can show a critical situation of the mind being split from body awareness; schizoid. Ascending a hill or mountain or tree: often shows having a more inclusive view or understanding of one's activities and place in the scheme of things.

ascetic   Conflict with natural drives; desire to be less dominated by same; avoidance of sex; an attempt to find the spiritual, which may be an inverted fear of one's unconscious or a bid for power to control; development of will. See: **religion and dreams**.

Asclepius   A Greek god of healing, especially in relationship to dreams. The people of Epidaurus claimed their city was the birthplace of Asclepius. L.R. Farnell suggests he was a hero who was elevated to a god-like status. See: **dreams and ancient Greece**.

Aserinsky, E. and Kleitman, N.   In 1953, Aserinsky, while working under Kleitman in a sleep study laboratory, was the first to observe the rapid eye movements (REM) now known to occur during dreaming. As Aserinsky had observed this in the sleep of babies, it was first assumed only to occur with infants. Later investigation proved it to occur with all people observed. See: **science**, **sleep and dreams**.

ashes   What remains in our experience, perhaps as memory or wisdom, after the event or person has gone; purification; something that once moved us, but the feelings have burnt themselves out; death. Idioms: rake over the ashes.

astral travel   See: **out-of-body experiences**.

atom bomb   Anxiety regarding external world, political forces etc., that the dreamer feels at the mercy of. Often coupled with dreamer's survival strategies; the end of a particular world or way of life for the dreamer; i.e. the end of school life; divorce; loss of spouse. It can also be a fear of the irrational forces of life and the unconscious which may destroy all we have built – our conscious Self.

attack   Being attacked: feeling under threat from external events or internal emotions, impulses or ideas; feeling a victim in relationship to others and the Self; taking a defensive attitude. Attacked by animal: introverting one's own aggression or sexuality; fear of one's own natural urges. Bird attacking: fear of ideas, ideals or opinions; verbal attack by others; fear of the Self. Being the attacker: positive self-expression; defending oneself against something one feels threatened by; attempt to destroy some urge or feeling in oneself or others. The word attack is also used in many ways, so might refer to an 'attack' of an illness, or 'heart attack'. Can express the difference between feeling threatened by a work/relationship/sex problem, or feeling challenged by it in a way to stimulate creativity or research. Someone else being attacked: anger or aggression toward another. See: **fight**; **war**.

attic   See: *attic* under **house**, **buildings**.

audience   Standing in front of: you might be dealing with an important issue in your life which attracts the attention of many associated ideas and feelings – thus audience participation or attention; desire for attention; baring one's soul. In the audience: witnessing some emotion or process in yourself; considering some aspect of your life.

aura   An expression of the Self. What this means is that some parts of our consciousness, such as the memory of our address, or emotion about our dog, will have many interconnections with other ideas and related feelings. We can associate the idea of address with home; room; family; food; rent; bed – and each of those with other connected ideas and feelings. Sometimes we touch a concept of feeling which has massive connections, so vast they begin to build up beyond usual levels of realisation. We might call it a mega-concept, which goes on building and generating realisations we have never made before – that is we have never made those connections before. An aura around an object, person or animal depicts this mental function. See: *the Self* under **archetypes**.

automobile   See: **car**.

autonomous complex   Many of the characters or elements of our dreams act quite contrary to what we wish ourselves. This is why we often find it so difficult to believe all aspects of a dream are part of our own psyche. Some drives or areas of the Self do act or express despite what we consciously wish. These are named autonomous complexes. Recent research into brain activity shows that, in fact, the brain has different layers or strata of activity. These strata often act independently of each other or of conscious will. Sensing them, as one might in a dream, might feel like meeting an opposing will. Integration with these aspects of the Self can be gained.

autumn   Mrs C. had the following dream at a time when she started her own business against her husband's wishes, and one week before he walked out on her. Autumn here depicts the sense of something coming to an end. Can also be 'the autumn of one's life'; mellow feelings.

> *Example: 'My husband was in a wheelchair, I was pushing him along a promenade. At the end of the promenade was a path which we took. The path went along the top of a cliff. The sea below was pretty rough, a typical autumn day at the seaside. All of a sudden the path came to an end and there was a steep slope to the right which led down to the beach. I decided to turn right and go down the slope. When we got halfway down the slope the path started to give way on the left and I found myself*

without enough room for the four wheels of the wheelchair. I was desperately holding on, tilting the wheelchair to the right to keep it balanced on the two right wheels when my husband got panicky in the chair and moved. The chair tilted to the left and fell down onto the rocks. I started running down the path towards the beach, towards my husband and the wheelchair. I never reached the wheelchair or my husband because I awoke and that was the end of the dream.' Mrs C.

avalanche   The power of frozen emotions. We can freeze sexuality by anger or jealousy, etc., and the build up of tension might then release in a dangerous way.

awake   See: **wake up**.

axe   See: **weapons**. <u>Idioms</u>: axe to grind; to be axed – lose one's job.

baby <u>General</u>: one's own feeling urges at that level of development – such as possessiveness, joy, curiosity, innocent love, infant trauma; dependence; feelings of helplessness; vulnerability; lack of responsibility; being cared for. Also a new phase of life; a new idea; new activity – as when we say someone has a new baby, meaning new project or business. <u>When with a couple</u>: the marriage – what is created in a relationship; the life process in us, based on reproduction.

<u>In woman's dream</u>: oneself at that age; desire for a baby; responsibility of caring for a baby; worries about having a healthy baby; worries about a baby's welfare. <u>In a man's dream</u>: oneself at that age; desire for parenthood; weight of responsibility; fear of inability to produce. <u>In child's dream</u>: themselves at that age; feelings about a baby sibling.

> *Example: 'I have my own baby who is lying in a cot in a bedroom looking very weak and pathetic with eyes closed. I know that he or she is getting weaker and weaker through lack of food and care. In fact the baby seems to be dying. The feelings of guilt are terrible because I know it is my responsibility to do something to make it well. I keep saying to myself I must go and feed that baby – but I don't. I just keep worrying and feeling guilty.' J.C.*

Because of circumstances we may not have been able to satisfy all our babyhood needs – we may have been weaned earlier than we wanted; our need for attention may have been unsatisfied – and these are shown as a baby in our dreams, as with J.C. Dreams such as the above show how we sense the need of this part of us to be cared for and nourished. If any of these earliest needs are not met in some way, the development of our enthusiasm, our pleasure and ability to be involved and self-giving may be diminished, giving rise to dreams suggesting the need for nourishment, as above.

Example: 'I am forty-eight, have two children in their late teens and definitely do not want another baby. Nevertheless I have a recurring dream in which I am always in labour, experiencing no pain, and although there are nursing staff I am in some sort of laboratory, although everything is very pleasant. I never actually give birth and when I wake I always have a vague feeling of disappointment.' V.I.

This dreamer's conscious decision to have no more children is in conflict with her biological urge for another baby.

Example: 'My mouth was full of what looked like liver. It was also coming out of my left ear. When I turned away from the mirror I saw medical people in caps and gowns who kept telling me to bear down. I then gave birth to a baby out of my mouth. I am an invalid and very sick at present.' Mr M.S.

This man's dream is about his preparation for death. The baby is the extraction of all that can live on after his present life is left behind in death.

bachelor Man's dream: oneself if unmarried; desire for freedom, or comparison with present if married. Woman's dream: possible hope for sexual partner; husband prior to marriage.

back Back of house, etc: more private; intimate; less formal; surreptitious; out of sight; second best. Behind: repressed urges; one's past and memories; what is 'behind' one, or is in the past, but may be influencing one again; one's inner feelings; inferior. Idioms: at the back of; at the back of one's mind; back-room boys; by the back stairs/door; behind one's back; take a back seat. See: **front**; **left behind**.

bag   Sometimes represents vagina, female sexuality. More often, as in the example, it depicts the dreamer's identity. Our sense of identity is often dependent largely on social contacts and recognition. The bag, with all one's personal belongings and money, represents this social ability to get places and cope. Occasionally it shows the loss of child-bearing function. Idioms: bag and baggage; in the bag; pack one's bag. See: example in **clothes**; **knapsack**; **luggage**.

> *Example: 'I am in a strange town – usually where there are shops and lots of people. I don't know where I am or how I got there, but I suddenly realise I have lost my handbag. I know no one and do not know what to do. When I panic I wake.'* Mrs R.

baker   Creative ability; ability to alter one's approach to make experience more acceptable – such as when comments, instead of being taken as criticism, are taken as information.

ball   See: *sphere* or *ball* under **shapes**, **symbols**.

balloon   Party mood; breasts; desire for sex; similarity to condom; the womb.

banana   Male penis. Taking one or handing one to someone: desire to receive or have sexual relation. Man eating one: may be homosexual tendency.

band   Team work; sense of different parts of the Self working harmoniously; work for a musician.

bandage   Hurt feelings; past emotional injury; healing process; death.

bank   Resources – financial, mental and spiritual; one's internal sense of security; emotional resources such as confidence and sexual certainty; social power. River field or canal bank: minor difficulty or obstruction; a boundary, such as the border of what you might permit sexually. *Idioms*: bank on; break the bank.

baptism   New influence entering your life, cleansing away old attitudes; opening to one's inner possibilities; life pervading and healing; an influx of what had been latent or potential in the Self; birth. See: *Christ* under **archetypes**; **religion and dreams**.

bar   Strength; male sexuality; rigidness; energy; symbol of power. What we do with the bar: how we are expressing energy or power at that time. If barring way: obstacle; block against our self-expression. Idioms: prop up the bar; colour bar.

bar room   Often indicates how we relate to groups; our feelings about society; can be difficulties regarding alcohol; one's technique for avoiding confrontation with loneliness, anxiety, sense of failure, etc.

barber   Change of attitudes, thoughts or opinions about oneself. Because we can change our social appearance by a haircut or style, it depicts changes of mind, change of image. Also being in someone else's hands or influence.

basement   See: *basement* and *cellar* under **house**, **buildings**.

bat   Thoughts or influences emerging from the unconscious; fear of the unconscious. Cricket or baseball bat: male sexuality; positive aggression; defensiveness.

bath, bathing   Relaxation; cleansing wanting to 'come clean' or be rid of guilt. Such cleansing could depict a change of heart or forgiveness where old feelings are washed away. Also need to cleanse the body internally. See: **baptism**.

bay   Similar to **beach**, but the crescent shape sometimes depicts a woman's sexuality and openness to mating; receptiveness. Idioms: at bay; keep at bay.

beach   Family gatherings or relaxation and intimacy; state of mind in which you are open to inner intuitions and emotions. Also a boundary, or threshold, between our individual Self and effort, and our potential in the universal processes of life and death. To go further we would have to swim to take a boat – so a change is needed, new qualities must be developed. The threshold is a great tester of confidence and daring. It confronts us with the vastness of life processes, space, eternity, which we stand on the brink of. How we deal with changing from one environment – school, work – to another such as parenthood or retirement is shown by the beach. The beach might be the place where aspects of the unconscious meet us – out of the sea. It thus illustrates how we draw on, or avoid our own potential. See: **sea**.

bed See: *bed* under **furniture**.

bed wetting Possibly to do with allowing yourself freedom of expression, but with worry about social condemnation or propriety; anxiety that reduces you to childhood feelings with lack of self-control over emotions.

beer See: **alcohol**.

beggar The emotions, drives and thoughts you seldom allow into expression. Feelings of failure. Desire to 'drop out'; avoidance of involvement in society.

behind See: **back**.

bell Warning; signal; calling for attention.

Bible Traditional moral standards; religion; one's most inclusive realisations, in which case like **aura**. See: **dream as spiritual guide**; **religion and dreams**.

bicycle Personal effort or motivation which gets you somewhere. For many people a bicycle was their first experience of mastering a body skill and gaining greater freedom. Might be youthful freedom without responsibilities.

big See: **size**.

biological dream theory J.A. Hadfield, in his book *Dreams and*

Nightmares (Pelican 1954) puts forward what he calls a Biological Theory of Dreams. He says the function of dreams is that by reproducing difficult or unsolved life situations or experiences, the dream aids towards a solving or resolution of the problems. He gives the example of a man climbing a cliff who slips fractionally. He then may dream of actually falling and waking terrified. Subsequently the dream recurs, but in each the dreamer tries out a different behaviour, such as clasping for a branch, until he manages to act appropriately to avert the disaster. Hadfield sums up by saying dreams stand in the place of experience. They make us relive areas of anxious or difficult experience. They thus help problem solving. But they not only look back at past behaviour, they act just like thinking in considering future plans and needs.

birds The life cycle of a bird has so many similarities with important human stages of maturity we frequently use it to represent ourselves.

General: imagination; intuition; the mind; freedom from restraints; thoughts or hidden wishes or hopes; our spiritual longings; expanded awareness – in this form, perhaps a large bird which can fly high, because wider, or spiritual, awareness is like a higher, overall view of things. This may be painful.

A huge bird: the power of the collective mind or unconscious. It may uplift or be felt as threatening. Bird in house: hope that something interesting or new will enter one's life; a wish for new love. Dead bird: threat to ideals. Feeling life is only material. Flying: rising above something; independence; freedom; self-expression. Hatching from the egg: our birth and infancy. Leaving nest: gaining independence. Making nest: home building; parental urges. The baby bird our own childhood, as in the following example. The old lady is once more a reference to the mother, who the bird is first connected with before moving on to the difficulty of independence. The bluebird: especially represents the spirit or soul after death. The nest: home; family environment; security; even the womb.

Freud said the bird represents the male phallus and flying means the sexual act. Many languages use the word 'bird' to mean woman. In Italy it alludes to penis. The bird is also used to denote a sense of death and survival.

The example shows Pauline using the bird to depict her own urge to be independent of her mother's influence, opinions, likes, dislikes and decisions. Later in the dream her mother hands Pauline the ribbon to hold, suggesting an offer of independence.

> *Example: 'I was standing outside the house of my teens, with my mother. She had a very young bird on a long ribbon and the bird was flying very high in the sky.' Pauline.*

As soon as she lets go of the ribbon, a huge blackbird attacks the ribboned one. The ribbons are a reference to Pauline's own girlhood. When she lets go of her girlhood, moving toward independent womanhood, she feels threatened by her internal feelings of guilt – i.e. a child feels guilty if it acts differently to what its mother wants. This is the blackbird. To become independent we have to find a way of doing what we wish despite this internalised mother. (Internalised means all the standards, self-controls she learned from her life with her mother, which she now carries within her even if absent from her mother.)

> *Example: 'An old lady made room for me to sit at the end of one of the three seats of a bus. As we drove away a very large chicken-sized baby bird flew in. It had short stubby wings and yellow down, but flew expertly. I believe it first landed on the lady and chirped squeakily. But in its squeaks it actually spoke, saying it had lost its mother. It sounded as if it were crying.' Andrew.*

blackbird Unconscious drives; death; the negative aspect of mother.

chicken Nourishment; the female in a male; being 'chicken'. The cock: a male or the male sexual characteristics; confidence. The hen: mother. Idioms: chicken feed; chicken hearted; she's no chicken; cock of the walk.

crow, rook, raven Being carrion birds, and so often seen near corpses, they are linked with death; bad news; fear; unconscious feelings. The negative aspect of father.

cuckoo   Wanting to, or feeling your partner is, having sex outside your relationship.

dove   Peace; awareness of one's potential; religious experience; relatedness. See: **religion and dreams**.

eagle, buzzard, hawk   Sometimes the hunting, providing parent; dominance. Often the ability to develop an integrated vision or perception out of a wide range of experience. This is because the height of the bird and its steady gaze give it unusual perception and wide awareness. See: **aura** as it relates to mega concept.

owl   Because the owl sees in the dark, it represents our intuitive sense which 'sees' into our unconscious. This sense 'feeds' by watching or acting as an integrating function the many dark or hidden aspects of our experience and behaviour. Because this part of our mental process is aware of the hidden activities in the depths of our body and mind, it can initiate our conscious Self into the mysteries of life and death. If one can imagine having a council of all living things, we would all have in common the drive to reproduce and there would be huge links of understanding regarding care and rearing of young and perhaps of love for mate. The unconscious seems to have a sense of this synthesis of all life, and the owl, representing it, speaks with this sort of collective wisdom. See: **aura**; **dream as spiritual guide**; second example in *wife* under **family**.

peacock   Pride; self display; sometimes the same as phoenix.

phoenix   The ability to find a new impulse, new strength, new growth even in death.

swan   The side of human nature usually hidden because unconscious, often referred to as the spiritual – meaning the consciousness of connection with all life. Also the ideal in sexuality, and as such may represent virginity or a blend of male and female.

vulture   A relative waiting for you to die – or vice versa; people around you trying to live on you – or vice versa; difficult feelings about dependents.

Idioms: charm the birds from the trees; a bird told me; bird has flown; bird in the hand; bird of ill omen; free as a bird; odd bird.

birth Woman's dream: desire to have a baby. Man's dream: envy of the creative ability of women. General: when we were born, one world of experience ended for us and another began. Birth in a dream has the same meaning. The beginning of a new way of life; new attitude; new ability; new project. But also the death of the old. Can be about our own physical birth, its difficulties and trauma. But most difficult birth dreams are about coming to terms with our existence. Many of us are still wondering whether we wanted to be, or want to be, born. 'To be or not to be, that is the question.' Lots of us live at a remove from life because of this.

Birth of a shining, talking or holy child: the beginning of awareness not intellectual knowledge of how the conscious Self is interwoven with the forces and beings of the cosmos. Birth pains: the creative process; pain of arriving at a wider vision. Giving birth to a more mature self, is a struggle. The new in our life is born out of such pains. Recurring dreams of giving birth: the drive to have a child doesn't stop just because one has one or more children. Many women, even past childbearing age, dream this over and over as in the example below. The urge to care, to love, to give birth, exists despite one's age. The dream may also be, as with Pamela below, an urge to have a child of the sex dreamt of. See: **baby**.

> *Example: 'For years I have dreamt I am pregnant. I go into labour in different surroundings, not always hospitals, with different people. I never see the child but I think it might be a girl, and the labour is different each time. I stop dreaming as the birth is completed. I have one thirty-three-year-old son – my only pregnancy.' Pamela B.*

bite Aggression; the desire to suckle the breast hidden under aggression – this applies to women equally as to men. The following example shows another aspect of bite.

> *Example: 'I had to get a large spider into a small dwelling. At one point it was like trying to get the spider into a narrow-necked bottle, the spider was unwilling, and bit my finger. I was worried the bite might be poisonous, but it seemed all right.' Alan P.*

The large spider, small dwelling and finger refer to sexual intercourse. Alan feels fear of introducing his finger into the bottle
because he might be bitten. So here the bite refers to the injection
of fearful emotions, unwillingness, into his sexual impulse – but of
course also into his ability to get emotionally close to a woman. The
spider often refers to the mother, and in fact Alan's mother made him
fearful of sex. So the bite is clearly to do with feeling attacked by
anxieties or one's urges.

black person   Depends which skin colour one has. If white: one's
natural drives; feelings about coloured people; or if person is
known, what you feel about them. If black or brown: one's own
cultural feelings; same as any 'person' dream.

> *Example: 'I was in a cubicle or small toilet with a very black
> coloured woman. She told me there was something wrong with
> her vagina. She was undressed. I rubbed her vagina and we
> both felt enormous passion. I then awoke but couldn't at first
> remember the dream. I have refrained from sexual intercourse
> for some weeks, as I always feel shattered/tired afterwards.
> Anyway I awoke very wet yet couldn't remember any orgasm.
> I could remember some question of sex as I awoke. Then I
> remembered the dream and continued it in fantasy. I experi-
> enced powerful urges to find a woman to have a non-
> committed sexual relationship with. But in the end I wanted to
> share my feelings with my wife, but she seemed deep asleep and
> unresponsive. When I slept again I dreamt I was in London,
> had got off one bus, but was not at my destination. I was
> standing about not making a move to find my direction. Then
> I began to look.' Alfred C.*

To understand the above dream in some depth it is helpful to think
of the sexual drive as a flow, like a river. As such it can be blocked,
in which case it will seek an alternative route. Sexual energy or flow
is not simply a mechanical thing though, it is also deeply feeling in
its connection with the most profound sides of human life such as
parenthood and the caring and providing for young. In the history
of white people a great deal of sexual frustration has arisen out of the

ideas of sin and guilt in their religion. A view arose for the white race that the black races had an easier and less frustrating relationship with the *natural* – which includes not only sexuality but the body as a whole, and nature also. So when Alfred dreams of the black woman, he is meeting what is natural and flowing in himself, but which he has blocked by his will because he feels shattered after sex. The part about the bus shows him trying to find a direction in which his sexual feelings could move satisfyingly in connection with other people.

Unfortunately, as Jung points out in *Man and His Symbols*, people in modern society, whether black, yellow, brown or white, have lost their sense of nature and the cosmos as being anything other than processes without consciousness or living feeling. Jung says, 'No river contains a spirit, no tree is the life principle of a man, no snake the embodiment of wisdom . . . No voice now speaks to man from stones, plants, and animals, nor does he speak to them believing they can hear.'

The importance of dreams such as Alfred's is that it shows the passionate relationship between our personality and the primitive and natural. A black person born and bred in a modern setting would most likely dream of a black bushman to depict their own natural drives. See: **Africa**; **identity and dreams**; sex in dreams.

blindness   Unwillingness to 'see' something; losing sight of something; not seeing traits which we don't like about ourselves. <u>Idioms</u>: blind impulse; none so blind; turn a blind eye; blind leading blind. See: *eye* under **body**.

blood   See: *blood* under **archetypes**; *blood* under **body**.

boat, **ship**   <u>General</u>: our journey through the seas of life and how we meet the rough and smooth experiences, as with following example. The dream occurred a few weeks before a breakdown centering on the dreamer's wife leaving him.

Example: 'I am in a large glass boat with my wife. The sea is very rough and I am afraid the boat will sink.' Ron D.

<u>Many boat/ship dreams depict something else</u>: a situation we are

involved in with other people or person, such as marriage, business partnership, armed forces; this is the relation-'ship', a shared journey in which we 'are all in the same boat'. Keel: basic personal strengths. Bows: one's strength to meet life's changes. Rudder: sureness about direction in life. The ship sinking: fear of relationship ending; could be children leaving mother, so the collective 'boat journey' has finished; illness; death. Leaving boat but leaving bag on it: lack of identity alone – perhaps when children have gone or job ended. Lots of small boats: other people's relationships. Small boat with one other person: one's relationship with that person. Going on a cruise: desiring relationship with others; or to be a part of other people's lives. Boat journey by night: classic archetype of searching for one's roots in life; the journey into the unconscious. Missing a boat: missing opportunity; not grasping significance of events. Anchored boat: security; stable relationship; opposite if drifting. Motor boat: similar to **car** but more sense of isolation or aloneness. Ferry boat: if across a river, death; end of a relationship; transition from one phase of life to another; the emotional connections in a relationship. Disembarking: leaving a phase of life, such as motherhood or marriage. Embarking alone: independence or loneliness. Idioms: burn one's boats; in the same boat; miss the boat; rock the boat; ships that pass; ship comes in; a tight ship. See: **submarine**.

body   It refers to oneself, as in the word somebody. Although it includes the totality of our experience, it seems to be most pointedly referring to our sense of identity. From this sense of ourselves we project meaning onto the rest of the world to some degree. Thus many symbols are stylised body forms. The cross is a standing figure with arms outstretched; a church's structure, a representation of the body, and the miracle of sexual reproduction – the mystery enacted within it; a maypole is the penis. Therefore various things can represent our body or aspects of oneself. Seeds, swallowed teeth can be sperm; anything long and pointed, even a finger, can be the penis; anything hairy, a male; anything receptive like a bottle, bowl or cave, a woman or vagina.

A body, or our body: physical life and the processes of life in our body; potentials of personality, such as artistry, love, etc., depending on body; material existence; the process which causes growth and ageing. A dead body: our skin or shape is felt as our boundary, the edge of our universe. The dead body depicts a whole set of personality traits or attitudes, very often potentials, which have been denied life by us. We have not allowed them expression. A person hurt in love might kill any feelings toward the opposite sex. This 'dead' part of them can be shown as a body. May also be the way we meet feelings about death. Sickness in body: can refer to an awareness of illness in part of the body shown. Most often depicts psychological problem symbolised by part of body – see body parts below. Maggots in body: possible need to cleanse body to toxins or infection; sense of dis-ease emotionally in that area of self. Injuries: hurts; or events that may have led to emotional scars. See body areas below. Appearance: how you or others appear in a dream gives a lot of information. Most of this can be taken literally. So smiling would be referring to confidence and happiness, frowning to the reverse. See: **dead people dreams**; **hiding**.

Bodiless: the 'noises' around us, sensory impressions, other people's expressed feelings and actions are building bricks for our sense of Self. In a real sense we create each other by believing in each other. With prolonged absence of other people and events, and especially if we lose our 'noises' and body awareness, we feel we – our sense of identity – is dying. Bodilessness may therefore show us feeling unrecognised, unnoticed. May also be feelings of loneliness; being cut off from sexuality and body drives. In its positive side it is exploration of the unconscious and void. As such, bodilessness is a great realisation of freedom. Often a sense of survival of bodily death. See: second example in *death and rebirth* under **archetypes**; **identity and dreams**.

> *Example: 'I felt as if I was going very deep inside myself. It was dark but at first there were noises of the world around me. I seemed to go in much deeper and it was very dark, but with the feeling of great space. Everything was all right until I didn't hear any noise at all, all that space and no noise was too much and my whole body freaked out and then pulled out very fast before I could stop it.' Kate P.*

If you are right handed, the left of the body represents: inner feelings which support outer action – such as confidence; our less used or supportive functions. If we are an intellectual, the left might depict one's feelings and vice versa. The left may represent our mother's influence in our life and body. The right of the body: our outer activity and dominant functions; expressed abilities; our father's influence in life and body. If father is an anxious man there might be a lot more signs of stress on this side of the body. See: **left**, **right**. Top half of body: thinking feeling. Bottom half: sexuality and instincts. Half a body: if top missing, lack of thinking and higher emotion. If bottom missing trauma to, loss or denial of, sexuality and sensuality. Old head on baby body: immature sexuality and emotions. Vice versa: immature personality. Dismembered body: emotional or mental stress and breakdown. May be followed by emergence of new Self.

In some cultures the areas of our body are sometimes thought of as sense organs. This may seem strange but is very simple. Without language, communication would be difficult. So language enables us to sense what another being is communicating. If we had been castrated or had a hysterectomy prior to adolescence, we would never develop sexually. Without that development we would not understand two people kissing; or what a mother was feeling when she held her baby. Out of sex drive develops a whole world of feelings and tenderness which enables us to understand many things we see in the world. It is therefore important when reading the particular descriptions below, to remember that each area of our body, through its psychological counterpart, gives us some insight into ourselves and life around us, which is missing if the area is injured or traumatised.

abdomen   Almost half the dreams on file which mention abdomen, belly or stomach, show the dreamer being shot, as in the example below. This is obviously to do with a particular type of hurt. When human beings learned to stand up, they exposed their vulnerable underbelly. If we are hurt or threatened we tense the pelvic and abdominal area. The opposite is to dream of waves of pleasure moving within us, which gives us a sense of integration within ourselves and with the world.

General: the potential of our fully active natural drives; hunger; longing to be held; desire to give of oneself. If these are hurt, we tend to hold ourselves back from active social expression or intimacy of feelings in relationships. Also our abdomen is our digestive ability, both physical and psychological. Stomach or abdominal dreams may refer to some dis-ease in the actual organs. We might not be able to stomach something we have met in the everyday world. We may not be integrating our experience. To vomit: a discharging of unpleasant feelings resulting from ingesting, hearing, reading, being told, experiencing, something unpleasant. Shot in the belly: sex; painful response to relationship; feeling a target of someone's verbal or emotional attack.

> *Example: 'The people watching are saying "Kill her! Kill her! Kill her!" Then someone finds an extra bullet, puts it in the gun and shoots me in the stomach. I wake with my body completely straight with my hands on my stomach. I feel my whole body cracking up inside.' Vanessa (LBC).*

Vanessa wakes to just such tension, with a sense of her body being fragmented. In her dream Vanessa was re-enacting a disaster in which a man rampaged and shot down many people, and feeling the fear it engendered. Idioms: belly aching; have a bellyful; eyes bigger than one's belly; have a strong stomach; turn one's stomach; butterflies in stomach.

abscess Abscess still swollen and unrelieved: emotions still repressed which may be causing psychological infection – influencing views and decisions negatively. The dream abscess may also represent a site of physical illness which may or may not be obvious while awake. In the example below, the abscess has released its pus, or painful feelings, perhaps through Hilary's prolonged crying. The emotions are, with Hilary, affecting her 'grasp'. She also uses other imaged word play in 'near the knuckle'. Washing up shows her clearing away the influence of her 'evening meal' of experience. See: *individuation.*

> *Example: 'Was looking at my knuckle and saw that I had a nasty boil which had come away as I did the washing up and all that was left was a big hole, pink and healthy-looking skin around. It felt very close to my knuckle bone. My lover had told me he was leaving me for good and going back to his children. That evening, I cried most of the night.' Hilary K.*

ache Indicates where we may be holding back the energy relevant to that part of the body. A man who dreamt of an ache in his throat later discovered in therapy that he had been holding back emotions about his father who had died suddenly. On release he was able to say how much he loved his father. In chest: withheld emotions. Lower back: sexual energy blocked. Idioms: my heart aches; a pain in the arse.

anus General: babyhood self-expression and pleasure. Basic and perhaps rejected feelings. Also our *will*. If relaxed: easy self-expression. If tense: not letting go of feelings you might be judging as 'shitty'. If playing with or being entered by penis or finger: introverted sexuality; self-pleasure; narcissism. Excrement: the negative emotions and ideas we might not want to let go of; sometimes money; worry over something judged unclean; a cleansing or need for cleansing of inner feelings, such as guilt, inhibitions, resentments, hate, worry, or fear. Holding or letting go: how we give of ourselves; whether we can 'let go'; our generosity or lack of it. Idioms: talking out of arse; pain in the arse; an arsehole; head up the arse; disappears up; all tits and arsehole – no ability to reason. See: **excrement**.

arms General: our ability to love, give, take, create, defend, reach out. Injury to: loss of confidence; not able to reach out or create; inability to reach out to others; a feeling of helplessness or paralysis connected with helping oneself or being active externally. Left is the supportive feelings. Right is extroverted activity. Tied up: sense of restriction to activities. Bicep: strength; sense of being capable. Idioms: chance one's arm; give one's right arm; arm twisting; keep at arm's length; with open arms; one arm tied behind back, babe in arms; strong-arm tactics.

back Strength; particularly moral fibre; confidence physically; decisiveness, ability to stand in face of opposition; power to endure without being overcome. A psychiatrist once told me that many men in a tramps' home were diagnosed CWB. It meant 'congenitally without backbone'.

> *Example: 'I was looking across a hedge at a bull. I seemed to be just looking at its back.' Andy.*

Andy was a teenager, uncertain of himself. In this dream he was looking at his strength.

Somebody on one's back: feeling dominated by someone else; carrying one's parents' wants and decisions instead of one's own. Idioms: back breaking; back to the wall; behind one's back; get off my back; put somebody's back up; rod for one's back; pat on the back; stab in the back; turn one's back on; scratch my back.

blood   One's energy and sense of existence. Bleeding: being hurt – such as hurtful remarks, being told we are not loved – these can sap our motive to live and may be depicted as blood; injury, often from past trauma, which is causing us to lose energy or motivation; our fundamental biological, evolutionary life – thus a link with all life, so seen as a sacrament. This is portrayed not as injury but nourishment, wine or bloody meat. In sexual dreams: may refer to loss of virginity, menstruation or fertility; or hurt to sexual drive. See *blood* under **archetypes**.

brain   Intellect; thinking; insight; creativity; what someone really thinks. Idioms: brainstorm; brainchild; pick someone's brains; hare-brained; scatter-brained.

breasts   General: self-giving. In woman's dream: in many women's dreams the breasts figure prominently in a generally sexual way. Woman's breast in a man's dream: return to infant dependence; sexual desire. Kate in the example gives of herself, even though frightened, and feels whole – the circle.

> *Example: 'I was about to lie down naked near my grandmother as I was caring for her, when she started to suckle my breast. For a short time I was very frightened that she would hurt me or even suck my breast right off, but she didn't and it felt very good as I fed her. It felt as if we were one, our bodies forming a circle.' Kate*

chest   Like wooden chest – a place to store emotions. General: our emotions; pride. Man's dream: sense of social confidence. If healthy: positive sense of social recognition. Woman's dream: ability to give of oneself; good feelings about womanhood. See: **breath**.

ears   Subtle information; rumours. Idioms: an ear for; all ears; reach one's ears; flea in the ear; gain the ear of; ears burning; long ears; lend an ear; hear from; will not hear of; hearing things.

eyes How we *see* the world and ourselves. Although eyes are not mentioned much in the collection of dreams used for data in this book, *saw, see, seeing, look* and *looking* constitute the highest number of mentions. In a computer word count of 1,000 dreams these words were mentioned 1,077 times. Feel, feeling, felt came second with 855 hits. So dreams are predominantly a looking at and seeing activity, in the sense of insight and awareness.

Eyes are used in many ways in dreams. As these quotes from dream descriptions show, eyes can represent the soul or psyche in its many moods – dark, deep eyes; desperation in its eyes; shining eyes; impersonal eyes; staring eyes; eye to eye.

> *Example: 'I saw a young soldier with a gun, but as our eyes met we were attracted to each other, and he put his arm round me.'* Pauline B.

As the example shows, eyes can represent the state of a relationship. Lack of eye contact: avoidance of intimacy. Closed eyes: introversion or avoidance of contact; not wanting to see.

> *Example: 'I was dimly aware of a biggish blackbird that came down close beside us on the step and pecked at the baby's eye, then it flew off. The eye was gone completely.'* Heather C.

Heather's dream shows the eye depicting the 'I' or identity. In fact her sense of Self was damaged in infancy. Therefore can often be a play on words meaning 'I'.

In many dreams the eyes represent our understanding or how we 'see' the world, our view of things or other people. Also intelligence; our attention; our boundaries of awareness. Blindness: not being aware, not wanting to see something – usually about oneself. Loss of sight in right eye: not seeing what is going on in the outside world. Loss of sight in left eye: not seeing what you are really thinking or feeling; not aware of Self, motives, behaviour; no 'in-sight'. Idioms: I see; can't you see; you must be blind; I saw it with my own eyes; all eyes; eye opener; evil eye; sheep eyes; one in the eye; turn a blind eye; keep your eyes open; easy on the eyes.

face Self-image: concerns about how others see you; expression of or hiding of inner feelings and attitudes. Something wrong with face: sense of not being adequate; fear of how others see you. Idioms: face the facts; face the music; face value; flat on one's face; face lift; long face; poker face; blue in the face.

feet Foundation; to have 'one's feet on the ground'; to be well or badly 'grounded'; fundamental issues in our life. Barefooted: to be in contact with reality. Might also suggest rough going if walking is hard. Idioms: put one's foot in it; feet of clay; grass grow under.

hair General: thoughts; self-image; attitudes. Changing hair style: changing attitudes; a change of mind. Cutting right off: less thinking; denial of sensual and physical drives, as monk. Tight style: discipline; self-restraint. Plaited or pony tail: girlhood; socialised thoughts and feelings. Long: freedom; permissiveness; girlhood with woman. Long matted: not caring about social image or self; drop out. Dishevelled hair: mental confusion. Brushing hair: clarifying attitudes or thoughts. Wig: false attitudes or thoughts; an assumued social front. Fair hair: awareness; 'light-headed'. Dark hair: unconscious area of thoughts and attitudes; 'dark' thoughts or attitudes. Genital or armpit: sexuality. Woman's dreams – armpit or leg hair: social expression of sexuality or physicality. Head hair: may be expression of female sexuality, as Paul's suggestion women should cover hair in church. Hair on chest of female, even child: the male side of the woman; might be parents' desire for a boy generated male characteristics. Man's dreams – beard: might represent uncertainty, so hiding behind the beard; male sexuality. White beard: wisdom or experience. Very long beard: sense of eternal. Baldness: ageing; feeling obsolete; lack of thought. Chest hair: masculinity, virility. Idioms: keep your hair on; hair raising; have us by the short hairs; let one's hair down; make you hair curl/stand on end; didn't turn a hair; put hairs on your chest; tear one's hair out; split hairs. See: **shampoo**.

hand Most frequently dreamt of part of body. General: self-expression; grasp – of life, of ideas, of opportunities; our hold on people; our children; situations. Extension of our power – to give, take, wound, heal, support or do. Fingers: manipulation; penis;

dexterity. Handshake: contacting an aspect of Self, friendship. Fist: anger; restrained anger. Dirty hands: dirty work; unclean activity. Rough hands: marks left by difficult experience; roughness in handling others. Claw-like hands: clawing, wounding ability. Idioms: second hand; in the hands of; bite the hand that feeds; hands are tied; soil one's hands; hand to hand; hand to mouth; hands off; hard hand; helping hand; open-handed; lend a hand; upper hand; burnt fingers; at one's fingertips; snap one's fingers; green fingers; have a finger in; itchy fingers; sticky fingers; fingers crossed; lay a finger on; point the finger at; get one's finger out; fingers to bone. See also: example in *sweets* under **food**.

head General: thoughts; opinions; intellect; decisions; intentions; self-image. Fairly understandable from the huge number of idioms about head and face, such as 'lose one's head/face', so one might literally dream of a headless figure. Idioms: above one's head; enter one's head; get something into one's head; go off one's head; over one's head; swollen or big head; head above water; head in sand; egg head; square head; off the top of my head; hold your head up high; come to a head; head over heels; over your head; get it through your head; turn one's head; heads up.

heart Emotions; pity; sympathy; likes and dislikes. Idioms: lost your heart; have a heart; have no heart; heart like stone; change one's heart; done one's heart good; from bottom of heart; sick at heart; don't let your heart run away with your head; wearing your heart on your sleeve; the heart of the matter; heavy heart; after your heart; break your heart; my heart's in my mouth; open-hearted ... too many to list.

internal organs Often to do with concerns over health. Could be a sense of illness in that part of body. But mostly our anxiety about illness. See separate organs.

legs Support; motivation. To have one's legs knocked out from under one means loss of confidence and urge to carry on with life. Although we may depend upon someone like a partner or parent for support – or work or position for self-value – ultimately the legs represent our own emotional or conceptual support system. So we may be considering what sense we have of our own value when trying to understand legs in our dream. See: **left**, **right**; **lame**.

lungs   might relate to tension, feelings of being 'suffocated' in a relationship or situation, as one may have been with one's mother or home life. Often to do with smoking or idioms that relate to breathing, such as: catch one's breath; bated breath; hold one's breath

mouth   Pleasure area; our hungers; sexual pleasure. Also, because we speak with our mouth and tongue, they can represent what we say. A dream of our mouth being buttoned – button your lip – or sewn up could suggest that inwardly we regret having said certain things and need to hold our tongue. Chewing: considering; mulling over something. Pulling something out of mouth: trying clear emotions or attitudes not properly expressed. Perhaps one is not admitting something. Idioms: all mouth; a big mouth; nasty taste in the mouth; mouth-watering.

muscles   One's strength, therefore confidence and sense of adequacy; sense of being outwardly forceful; masculinity in its physical sense. Also may refer to physical muscle.

navel   Connection with mother; feelings of dependence; needs for nourishment at a basic baby level. See: *umbilical cord* below.

neck   Connection between body – feelings and sexuality – and head – thinking and willing; weak point. Often refers to attitudes as in idioms. Idioms: breaking one's neck; up to one's neck; risk one's neck; stick one's neck out; dead from the neck up/down.

nose   Curiosity; intuition – as with 'smell a rat'; penis. Malformed nose: might relate to the idiom, 'nose out of joint'; sense of not appearing good to others. Idioms: have a nose for; nose out of joint; rub nose in it; up one's nose.

ovaries and uterus   For many women represents their sense of validity or adequacy just as testes do for men; ability to have children, so could represent fears or feelings about this; creativity. See: **vagina**; **individuation**.

pelvis   The whole sphere of sexuality and sensuality, not just the sex act. Our unconscious often connects sex with giving oneself, a death of Self, and making connections or bonds – obviously reproduction also. In woman's dream: ability to have a child.

penis For a man the penis represents more than simply his sexual appetite. It depicts the whole drive of life through his glandular system which develops the body type he has; predisposes his body toward male sexual characteristics; brings a certain creative explosiveness to his personality; creates urges toward fatherhood and loving his woman, with connected desires to supply the needs of family if he is emotionally healthy. The positive aspect of the penis-masculinity is for him to demand his woman meets his maleness, his caring aggression, his sexual desire, with her own fiery energy and strength. In a woman's dream: one's relationship with desire for a mate; relationship with one's own male Self – ambition, work capability, aggression, intellect; depicts the relationship with genital sexuality with one's partner. As with the example of Sally's dream below, the events in the dream define the problem or relationship.

General: direct reference to sexual feelings, fears or problems. As these can be quite complex, several examples are given below. Penis replaced by vagina: could be feeling inadequate as a man; contact with the female receptive in oneself; loss of male drive in sexuality. Loss of penis: see castration. Penis turns into a snake: feeling the intense instinctive drive of sexuality. This is a realisation of the drive as existing beyond one's personality; an expression of what the sex drive is doing, depending what is happening to the snake. Bleeding from penis: emotional hurts or fears that are interfering with expression of healthy sexual feeling.

> *Example: 'So for the third time I held the woman and made love. The woman's vagina was like a flower; I don't mean to look at, but in physical sensation. My penis felt like it was penetrating petals of flesh and touching with great pleasure a central receptive area. I was left with the feeling of being able to make love again and again without any negative effects. It was a very positive and healthy feeling.' John T.*

John is feeling confident about his sexual drive. Although a powerful drive, subtle feelings and fears have an intense influence not only on the pleasure of sex, but also the response of the physical organs. The relationship with the penis and sex act in one's dream shows what fears, hurts or attitudes are influencing the sexual flow. See: **castration**.

Example 'My lover Terry, myself and another woman were all on our bed. The other woman seemed very sure of herself and kissed Terry in a very intimate way, he doing the same to her as I lay very near to both of them. Then Terry stuck his bottom in the air and started to lick my chest and breast. I found myself licking around his penis, felt I was under some kind of pressure from both the other two to do so but didn't feel too shattered as I did it with love for Terry, but I had a bitter taste in my mouth.' Sally P.

In talking about this dream, Sally said she often struggled with what she wanted and what her partner wanted in sex. She might go along with his needs, but not find it palatable. Even if she did do it with some love, it might leave a 'bad taste in her mouth'.

Example: 'I felt as if I were as one with Terry and I realised he was trying to make a journey into his mother's vagina as his penis. Her vagina looked like a long, dark tunnel and was threatening to him. I said, "You haven't given your mother satisfaction and you say you will not." Then he was really smashed up in body. Withdrawing into a garden with a high green hedge. I took a leaf from the hedge and began to pull it apart with my hands. Terry said, "Look what you are doing, teasing me." I felt withdrawal wasn't the way and started to follow him, walking alongside the hedge. I said, "It feels like you are strangling me, so why don't you do it and kill me?" We have been going through a lot of sexual withdrawal, Terry saying his sexuality was his to do with as he wanted.' Sally P.

This second dream of Sally's is a shrewd summing up of Terry's sexual fears. In fact Terry suffered a great deal of anxiety about sex and later uncovered the sort of fear and desire to avoid giving his mother satisfaction in becoming a full-blooded man shown in the dream. Our unconscious is a very capable psychologist, and while Terry in Sally's dream represents her insights regarding him – and must not be seen as a statement of fact about Terry – such insights are often enormously useful in dealing with relationship difficulties.

Example: 'Was in a house with my wife. Outside the door was Something which wanted to come into her– an invisible being. We were frightened and it said "Do not be afraid, I want you to put your penis in your wife and wait for me to activate you. In that way you will form a body for me." I woke and realised the dream was moving me to parenthood. Already having three children I realised this would mean another twenty years of responsibility. Nevertheless my wife and I made love. Two weeks later I dreamt my wife was pregnant with a son. In fact nine months later she bore a son.' Nigel I.

In this interesting dream sequence the penis is Nigel's drive to be a father. See: **bed**; **castrate**; example in **flower**; **knob**; **pole**; **reptiles**; **sausage**; example in **tunnel**.

shoulders   Ability to bear or to carry what life brings. Idioms: have broad shoulders; shoulder to the wheel; shoulder to cry on; rub shoulders; chip on shoulder.

skin   One's contact with the world; what tactics we use to deal with others. Rough skin: rough exterior. Burnt skin: hurt in relationship with outside world or people. Shed skin: like a snake, changing one's old way of life; old attitudes. Idioms: under one's skin; a thick skin; skin deep; skin alive.

teeth   Aggression; ability to 'chew things over'; our 'bite' on life; words we say or swallow. Bad tooth: a painful or rotten part of one's feelings, life or relationships; angry or regretful words. A woman swallowing teeth: the throat and Eustachian tubes are like the uterus and Fallopian tubes, so can depict conception or fear of it. False teeth: lies told; false face; not keeping spoken promises; the ageing process and loss of good looks. Teeth falling out: often a sense of loss, such as death of family member or loved one; the ageing process as it relates to maturity, so worries about getting older and one's changing image. This is because we lose first teeth as we leave childhood behind, and lose teeth as we leave youthfulness behind. Spitting out lots of teeth: something you want to 'spit out' in the sense of admitting, saying or expressing emotionally.

Example: 'I felt a tooth was loose and started pushing it with

*my tongue. Then I took hold of it between thumb and
forefinger and pulled it out. I felt okay about this, but then
another tooth was loose, and another, and I pulled them out.
Running to the bathroom I looked into the mirror, horrified
and frightened. All my teeth were coming out. Not knowing
how to deal with this I ran to my mother, showing her my
mouth, empty now except for two teeth. My mother appeared
not to see my lack of teeth, or notice my fear.' Eve*

Eve was eighteen at the time of the dream. She explored it and found
a fear of ageing and death. Also apprehension about maturing and
facing independence and responsibility; loss of attractiveness.

Im Tofeeq, a Palestinian woman, told me that among the Arabs it
is believed that if you dream of losing teeth it means your brother or
son is in trouble. She had a dream in which three of her teeth fell out.
The next day she received a call from America to say her son had
been shot in the head three times by a gunman. For Artemidorus
losing a tooth meant to lose a member of one's household; to the
Africans such a dream showed that the dreamer would lose a wife
or child. Idioms: show one's teeth; get one's teeth into; gnash one's
teeth; grit one's teeth; teething troubles.

testicles   See: *penis* above. In a man's dream: what he is doing with
his sexual urge; his battery of energy and self-worth; sense of
maleness; the life process beyond personality; one's genetic connection with ancestors. A woman's dream: her feelings about sex with
a male; feelings about wanting to conceive, or wanting the man deep
in herself. What she is doing to a male or the male in herself. See:
vagina below; *penis* above.

tongue   Speech, expression of what we feel; saying what is deep
inside us, perhaps unknown to oneself; penis. Idioms: find one's
tongue; tongue in cheek; lose one's tongue; sharp tongue; hold
one's tongue; forking tongue.

umbilical cord   Dependence; connections and emotional ties of
dependence on or need for other people.

Example: 'I was looking at my belly button. There was a good three inches of cord sticking out. The end of it was red and raw.' Cassie A.

Cassie had been in a long dependent relationship which she had recently broken. She felt at the time of the dream she was having to stand alone and do things for herself. The end of her relationship felt like a ripping apart, and thus the sore cord.

vagina The vagina refers to much more than a woman's sexual feelings and drives. It depicts the urges and processes of her being which are the foundations of her waking personality. The ability to procreate; the glandular bias which connects with what the conscious personality faces in emotional, mental and physical disposition; the caring, nurturing feelings which emerge out of sexual mating when healthy; the desire for a mate; the sense of connection and identity with other women, other female creatures and female aspects of nature. In its positive aspect it may represent the sure confidence with which a woman may demand from her man that he treat her womanhood with the respect it deserves. This means meeting the full flood of her sexual need with its desire for a child, a caring and supportive nest to rear that child in, and her female creativity which may rise from that basic reproductive drive into social creativity and a personal demand for respect.

In a woman's dream: generally how one feels about one's own sexual needs, but this includes procreation as well; the health or feeling state of the sexual self and physical vagina; one's experience of motherhood or experience of the procreative relationship with one's mother and nature. One's central femininity; sexual urge; ability to have a child; concept of one's physical attraction; temple or church of life. Bleeding vagina: fears about one's sexuality and feminity; hurts to emotions connected with sexual relatedness. In a man's dream: the vagina represents one's feelings or fears about meeting a woman's full sexuality; the deep experience of the relationship with one's mother; birth and how mother met one's emerging male sexuality; one's desire for sexual expression. Bleeding vagina: his trauma, fears about a woman and sex.

Example 'He was very brown, could have been a native but he didn't feel strange to me. We were making love, I was very aware of the pleasure in my lower body. It was very slippy slidy and wet, there was enjoyment for both of us. Very intense body feelings with a child-like quality, not passion – but pleasure and joy in my vagina.' Susy I.

Susy is feeling happy and joyful about her 'native' or natural sexual feelings – particularly the sensual side of sex. Sensual pleasure, as with emotional pleasure, is as much a food for our physical and emotional Self as bread is for our physical body.

Example 'I had very little pubic hair and thought it must be because I had just had a shower, but, no, on looking again I had very little hair. I was hugging Mary, a friend, my arms around her back and one hand holding her vagina. It was then I noticed she was the shape of a man there. I drew away for a second at the discovery then felt okay as it meant I was hugging a male/female person. We were very warm together. Two days before this dream my husband had said his mother called a vagina a Mary.' Lucy R.

Lucy is 'touching' or becoming aware of what could be seen as her own wholeness, which includes her male nature.

Example: 'She was now quite naked, dead and stiff, but still bleeding from the vagina. I walked along, the dead body walked like a clockwork soldier. It was quite horrible to see its semblance to life.' Derek A.

Derek's relationship with a woman, and with his own emotions and sexuality, is 'dead' and deeply hurt – the blood. He can mechanically have sex – the clockwork soldier – but not with deep feeling bonds or satisfaction.

bomb   Explosive situation; sudden anxiety-producing events – as when we say something occurred out of the blue; one's own aggression; fear of death; remembered anxieties of war experience; social bombshells – such as being criticised in the press.

book   Memories; things you have learnt or are learning from experience; attitudes toward learning; other peoples opinions. Old books: inherited wisdom; learning; spiritual awareness.

border   See: **frontier, border**.

bottle   Vagina; feeling bottled up. If something in it: resources you have. Of wine, spirits or beer: sometimes an influence entering your life to change it; relaxation. If red wine: you may have felt there is more in life than your own ego, its worries and desires; sense of sharing life. See: **alcohol**.

boy   If known: what you feel about that boy, but referring to yourself, i.e. one might think the child cautious and anxious; so it depicts one's own childhood feelings of caution and anxiety. Male dream: oneself at that age; the difficulties faced, habits acquired, attitudes imprinted by experiences at that age – circumstances may not have permitted parts of you to mature, so your relationship with a woman and the world might still be conditioned by that age mode. So the boy could be part we need to 'father' toward maturity. Also the eternal potential for growth, openness to the new and enthusiasm about tomorrow. If older than yourself: your potential or how you feel about maturing. Female dream: your own developing ability to express in outer action. Feelings about a son. See: *son* under **family**.

boyfriend   Your emotional feelings, attachment to, the boyfriend; the difficulties, struggles with feelings and sexuality felt in connection with boyfriend or other males; your insights into his behaviour. Ex-boyfriend: any feelings or hopes still connected with him; the ex-boyfriend or lover often becomes a symbol for all the hopes for love that are not being satisfied at the moment, or in the present relationship; occasionally the past.

> *Example. 'Although married for almost nine years, I have been dreaming almost every night about an old friend. We used to date twelve years ago, but although we still meet occasionally, our relationship now is purely platonic.*
>
> *About two weeks before I found out he was getting married I had a dream where he handed me a single red rose and said*

"I love you, but the time's not right". In the latest dream I was reading a paper with the heading "Broken-hearted Babies", with a picture of both of us as babies with our names underneath.' Amanda (Teletext).

bread Fundamental nourishment; our basic emotional and biological needs. In a spiritual sense it represents our universal experience of physical or bodily life, so connection with others.

break Broken promise; shattered idealism, hope or faith; feeling broken in spirit; changes as we 'break' with the past; feelings of loss or damage. Idioms: lucky or bad break; break a habit; break down/up; break new ground; broken heart; break the ice; break the news; break through; break with.

breath Being alive; pace of life; emotional state – i.e. peaceful or disturbed. Holding the breath: expression of will. We breath-hold when repressing emotions and anxiety. Fast breathing: excitement; emotional release; experience of fear. Under water and not breathing: womb-like state; experience of level of awareness without sexual, biological drives, and without opposites; return to deep relaxation – healthy if you can easily emerge. Might be an escape from waking reality if you cannot. See: *lungs* under **body**.

bride Feelings about or desire for marriage; love; receptivity and fertility; integrating parts of personality previously not expressed. In a woman's dream: your marriage and what it means to you; feelings, fears and hopes about marriage; feelings about daughter. If getting married: integration of inner feelings and unconscious, especially if bride/groom is Oriental or coloured. In a man's dream: frequently depicts one's relationship with your own feelings and non-rational nature.

bridegroom Desire to be married or find a partner. In a woman's dream: feelings about marriage or getting married; integration with intellect and exterior capability. In a man's dream: feelings about marriage; attempt to integrate conscious and unconscious.

bridge The bridge generally has the significance of crossing from one phase of life, activity or emphasis to another. It depicts connection between yourself and another person, relationship, Self and opportunity, Self and change in life. <u>Fallen bridge</u>: lost opportunity; broken bonds and connections; parting in relationship. <u>Idioms</u>: burn one's bridges; cross that bridge when I come to it; water under the bridge.

> *Example: 'Having been enjoying ourselves with some work mates at a social club, my husband and I are travelling down a country lane in an open horse-drawn carriage. It is dark. We come to a hump-backed bridge. As we arrive at the brow of the bridge a voice says, "Fair lady come to me." I float and everything is black and peaceful. Then great fear overcomes me. I wake with terror and feelings of horror.' Evelyn K.*

Evelyn's dream paints a vivid picture of her journey through life, drawn by the natural forces within her shown as the horse. She has enjoyed life, but comes to the 'brow' of her life, her fortieth year, and feels it is all downhill now into old age, which horrifies her.

brother   See: **family**.

bubble   Illusion; delicate and easily lost; day dreams; sometimes the transitory human existence.

bud   Vagina; the penis; the unfolding of the world of sexuality, full of emotional and physical levels of experience and richness.

Buddha, **Buddhist**   Often in Western dreams associated with the denial of, or loss of, ego; liberation from thinking and desiring; in a Christian person's dream may be a threat to their belief system.

bullet   Sexual impregnation; aggression; penis; desire to hurt; pain.

burden   See: **knapsack**.

Burglar, **intruder**   <u>General</u>: fears or difficult emotions arising from the unconscious; neglected parts of oneself which if met could change one's viewpoint to a more mature or inclusive one. Female dream: repressed desire for male partner or sex; or desire for a better sexual relationship. See: second example in *door* under **house, buildings**.

burial Letting go of the past as we know it, and opening the way to a meeting with what we gained from it; repressing experience which may be painful or we do not wish to meet; feelings about death or loss. Buried alive: memories of birth and its fears. See: *death and rebirth* under **archetypes**.

burning Burning emotions; release of emotions or energy. See: **fire**.

bus Experience, undertaking or relationship with a group of people; direction taken in company with others; overweight problem. Idioms: miss the bus; big as a bus.

business and dreaming Although the world of business and the world of dreams are often considered to be incompatible, this is not so. Once one realises that dreams may be the 'printout' of the most shrewd and capable computer we have access to, we can see them as a source of useful information. If one is in business, there is information in one's own memory, along with considered projects, questions about problem areas, which have never been put on an electronic computer. Also, there is no computer program outside our own mind which can handle and manipulate all the variables, the integrating of different information sources – written words, feeling hunches, spoken information, personal observation and experience – and then sift through, explore different combinations, and reach into pure creativity by leaping into the new.

Dreams should not be seen as oracles, but if we take their information into account along with our other sources, we find them a real addition to our business equipment. See: **creativity and problem-solving dreams**.

cage, **cell**   If the dreamer is in the cage: frustration arising from a sense of social pressures restraining expression – or from one's own moral restraints imprisoning one; feeling caged by lack of opportunity or lack of developed abilities. The cell often depicts how we imprison ourselves within our own anger, resentment or depressed feelings; or we may be trapped by childhood trauma. Something or somebody else caged: desire to restrain whatever is represented by the thing or person caged.

calendar   Passage of time; reminder or suggestion of something important arising.

camera   Taking notice; memory; sometimes what we may have noticed out of the 'corner of our eye' but not processed into waking awareness. See: **photograph**.

canal   Most often the way we direct, socialise or control our emotions – therefore relates to relationships and goals.

cancer   Fear of this illness; a part of our personality or being which is out of harmony with our wholeness; expression of how we feel about other people's – especially our mother's – emotional influence on us. This influence might be eating away at our own sense of well-being. Occasionally awareness of illness in part of body suggested.

candle   Male sex organ. Lighting a candle: a birth; prayer. If lit amid darkness: finding understanding or courage amid doubts, fears, depression. Occasionally a measure of how much time we have left in life. Idioms: burn the candle at both ends; not fit to hold a candle.

cane   Aggression; sadistic or masochistic sexuality.

canyon   See: **valley**.

cap   See: *hat* under **clothes**.

capital   Capital cities such as London, Tokyo, Moscow, unless the home of the dreamer, depict: material opportunity; central issues in dreamer's life; the central sense of Self around which other issues revolve. If somewhere like Jerusalem or Mecca: then one's central religious drives and ideas.

captain   See: **roles**.

car   General: our motivating drives – sex drive, ambition, sense of failure – whatever is driving us in life; means of or desire to 'get somewhere' in life; independence; personal freedom; personal space into which you can invite other people to share your life; privacy in which you can be yourself; feelings about the particular car in dream; one's body.
   Alone in vehicle: independence; making decisions alone; feeling alone. Another driver: being passive; being influenced by the opinions or emotions of someone else, or one's own secondary characteristics; i.e. anxiety or emotional pain may lead us to make many decisions, so be the driving force in our life, rather than what might be more satisfying. Brakes: one's ability to be in control of a situation. This might be control of anxiety or sexuality or emotions. Therefore inability to brake might suggest high anxiety or losing control of a situation. Car body: dreamer's body; oneself. Car engine: energy; heart; central drive. Car on fire: stress of some sort causing 'burnout' either physically or emotionally. Car mirror: looking back on what is 'behind' you, what you have left behind, or what is approaching you from the past. Car torn apart or dismantled: stress; failure to care for one's body; self destructive attitudes. Crashing vehicle: self desired failure – perhaps to avoid stress of responsibility and change; fear of failure; failure in relationship; argument – you may be on collision course with boss or partner; occasionally

psychological breakdown threatened. If the vehicle crash has a sense of death in it, then the dream may be exploring the anxieties or feelings around death. This is not a prediction of death, but a meeting with whatever values and fears one has about it. Doors: your way of letting other people share your life. The passenger door in particular refers to the people you let near you. Driving carelessly: lack of responsibility socially or sexually; need for more awareness. Flat tyre: physical problems or injury. Fuel: feeling drives; motivation; whatever has 'fuelled one's drive'. Headlights: being able to see what is happening in your life; what lies ahead; insight. Headlights off: loss of awareness. If dreamer driving: being independent; self confidence; being responsible for one's own life direction. Old car or scrapped car: sense of old age; feelings about death. Overtaken: feeling of being left behind or not competing. Overtaking: getting ahead. Passengers: people important in your life; feelings about how you relate to others; people influencing your direction in life. Reversing: sense of not getting anywhere; feeling that one is slipping backward; reversing a decision; change of direction. Running over someone: 'killing' some part of self through misplaced drive or ambition; aggression. With one other person: relationship with that person. Idioms: back seat driver; drive at; drive away; drive somebody mad/round the bend/round the twist/to drink; what are you driving at?; taking someone/being taken for a ride.

Example: 'I get in my car which is always full of my children or relatives. Instead of driving it I put one foot inside the car and one on the road. Holding the steering wheel I propel the car forward like a child riding a toy scooter. This is extremely hard work but I somehow manage to keep it going, even up hills.' Christine K.

A clear portrayal here of the car representing Christine's relationship with the family, and how she is doing all the work in their communal journey together.

Example: Quoted from Dreams and Dreaming *by Norman Mackenzie (page 23):* 'Robert Graves, in his book The Meaning of Dreams, *cites the case of a woman who dreams that she was having difficulty turning a large car in a narrow lane. Such a dream, Graves suggests, could symbolise the anxiety of the woman, who was not a good driver, about turning her car. It could also represent a problem in her life. She was living above her income (the large car), she felt constricted by this (the narrow lane), and felt she must change her style of life (to turn round), even though such a change would be difficult for her to make. Or the dream might well epitomise the problem of checking and redirecting any powerful emotional impulse where the road of habit is a narrow one.'*

The next example was dreamt by a man who was making love to a girl and finding it difficult to stop short of sexual intercourse.

Example 'I was in my car driving along and I wanted to stop the car immediately but my brakes would not work. This went on and on until I wakened.' Anon.

cards – playing   Opportunity; sense of fate. The different suits depict different things. Hearts: emotions; relationships. Diamonds: riches, intellect. Spades: one's body, movement; sensuality. Clubs: instinctive drives, such as fear, sex, hunger. If business card: identity or opportunity. Greetings card: hoping for news; thoughts about sender. See **games**, **gambling**.

carpet   See: **colour**; **shapes**, **symbols**; *carpet* under **furniture**.

carriage   Similar to car, but because drawn by an animal, more suggestive of a direction brought about by biological drives such as sex and ageing. Can depict how you are dealing with such drives. See: example in **bridge**.

carried   General carrying: an ability being used; what 'one is carrying' in life – such as carrying a grudge or taking responsibility. Being carried: a desire to drop responsibility; a return to a childhood relationship. Carrying a person: treating someone else, or some part of yourself, as a child or invalid; feeling you are 'carrying the load' in life, work or a relationship; overzealous as depicted by idiom 'carrying things too far'. Idioms: carried away; carry a torch; carry the can.

case   See: **bag**; example in **clothes**.

castle   See: **house**, **buildings**.

castrate   General: trauma and/or fear regarding sexual drive, possibly leading to 'cutting off' full sexual flow; fear of the responsibility which develops with sexual maturity; the difficulty in facing the pains and adjustments which come with rejection by the opposite sex, competition for work and wealth, standing without parental support, making decisions, discriminating in the world of ideas and exercise of will. Doing it to oneself: denying one's own sexual drive; introverted anger at sexual drive; the conflict of choice between feminine and masculine. Done to one: trauma in sexual nature; feeling one's innate being repressed or brutalised by another person. Doing it to another: one's own sexual pains or trauma may lead to the unconscious stamping out of sexuality in one's children or others.

> *Example: 'On looking at my son I see his penis has been completely cut off. I feel terribly upset, but notice that on each side of the remaining hole, special pieces of tissue have been implanted. These are budding, just like a plant, and I know, or am told, that a whole penis will grow.' Edmond U.*

Edmond did in fact frequently 'cut off' his sexuality by abstinence. The dream graphically shows that sexual drives are like a living process.

cataclysm   See: **end of the world**; **atom bomb**.

catacomb, crypt   Usually refers to feelings connected with death as in the example. It suggests, even in this, a womb-like condition, and birth or a child may also figure in the same dream. Also a place of power or hidden forces, where a connection may be made with our unconscious, our inner link with other people and the energies of our body.

> *Examples: 'I was in some kind of cave or crypt. My father told*

*me and my family of his coming death. He was calm and
caring but my mother, sister and myself were grief stricken and
for some reason went to buy him gifts.' Clare M.*

categories of dreams   Griffith, Miyago and Tago give thirty-four
types of dream themes, from falling to being hanged by the neck. For
the lay dreamer it is more useful to put dreams into much broader
categories such as: psychological, ESP, body, sexual, spiritual and
problem-solving. In researching the data for this book, some special
clusters of dream themes were noticed. For instance a cluster was
noted in women past middle age. They dreamt of walking in a town
and losing their husband. Description of these clusters can be seen
in *son* and *husband* under **body**; **dead people dreams**; **end**;
family; **flying**; **house, buildings**; **individuation**. See also: **dream
as meeting place**; **dream as spiritual guide**; **dream as therapist
and healer**; **ESP in dreams**; **sex in dreams**.

caterpillar   Male sexuality; prenatal forces of growth; bacteria. If
moving to chrysalis stage: urge to find environment in which to
make life changes. Chrysalis: major change going on within yourself;
a new aspect of yourself getting ready to emerge; desire to retreat
from the world.

cave   Prenatal life; the vagina; the process of reproduction and
birth. Also an entrance to our unconscious; the void we face at the
end of individuation. We may experience this as an empty cave in
which we thought there would be spiritual uplifting or treasure.
Personal growth may lead us to see that beneath all our thoughts,
emotions and individual memories, lies an emptiness, a void that has
no personality. This aspect of ourselves beyond personality faces us
with our powerful urge to get something spiritual that would
enhance us personally. This confronts us with whether we can let go
of the huge effort and drive which led us through the rigors of the
spiritual adventure. Can we let the non-personal life open in us? In
some dreams a real contact with the forces of our evolutionary
journey. What we may find in the cave: a fear of madness or being
lost; a sense of meeting the divine; our own traumas or destiny; a
meeting with death and rebirth. See: **catacomb**, **crypt**, last few
paragraphs in **individuation**, **unconscious**.

*Example: 'I am in a large, airy cave-like room. I am pregnant
and wearing a white gown. I am lying on my back on a flat,
slab-like surface with my legs drawn up.' Joan D.*

Cayce, **Edgar**   Born in Hopkinsville, Kentucky on 18 March 1877.
Died at Virginia Beach, January 1945. Cayce was an uneducated man
who found he could put himself into a sleep state in which he had
access to a collective mind or universal consciousness. Cayce was a
very Christian man and couched his statements in a biblical manner.
In his sleep state, however, he could verbally respond to people's
questions, and using medical terms he did not know consciously, he
could diagnose illness in people, even at a distance; speak foreign
languages he had never learnt; get information he had no conscious
access to. Because of this he was asked to the White House twice.
At one time, a hospital was built in which he worked with six
doctors, diagnosing from his sleep condition. In this state, when
asked how he could get information about the past, about people at
a distance, etc., he replied that every person has access to what he
called the cosmic mind while they sleep, but few people can bring
this contact through to conscious expression. He also maintained
that prolonged working with one's dreams gradually made conscious this contact with our cosmic life. For Cayce, humans are
cosmic beings. A lifetime was a brief interlude of learning in an
eternal pilgrimage through time and space. The conscious personality we so often raise so high is but a temporary experience
assumed by an older larger being, the Individuality, or Self as Jung
called it. The ego dies at death, but the Individuality absorbs its
experience. Dreams are the meeting point between this older Self
and the personality it assumes but briefly. Cayce's biography is *There
Is A River* by Thomas Sugrue. Cayce dictated 14,000,000 words from
his sleep state. A record of these is kept at The Association for
Research and Enlightenment, Virginia Beach, USA.

cellar   See: *basement* and *cellar* under **house**, **buildings**.

cemetery   Depicts our thoughts and feelings regarding death; our
family heritage of attitudes or traditions; contact with the dead;
things in our life we have 'buried'; melancholy about life or feeling

'different' to other people; a relationship, which we think is 'dead and buried'.

centre, **middle**   See: **shapes**, **symbols**.

ceremony, **ritual**   Similar to initiation. In the example the girl is with her boyfriend. She may thus have been 'initiated' into sexual activity. Sex with her boyfriend has changed her image of herself. A ritual depicts: important change, such as entering puberty; deeper levels of oneself; new attitudes or skills, just as marriage is an entrance into a new type of life and social situation. From the wider sense of Self our unconscious has, things are seen as important which we consciously feel are trivial. A ceremony in a dream brings such things to our attention.

> *Example: 'A ritual began whereby a large knife was drawn and a few deep cuts were made to both our faces. I put my hands to my face and saw them covered with blood, crying and crying.' O.S.*

chain   Restriction; strength; dependence. We might feel 'chained' to our marriage partner or work. See: example in **abandoned**.

champagne   See: **alcohol**.

chased   The example shows how we can be pursued by fears or emotions and can either continue to avoid them or face them. We are, in a real sense, pursued by what we have created with our thoughts, emotions, action and inaction. What we are avoiding might be sexual feelings; responsibility; expressing what we really feel in public; our fear of death; sense of failure; guilt; emotional pain; grief; but it might be our creativity; our love; our passionate response to living; our deepest wisdom and oneness with things. We can never escape from ourselves, so such feelings may pursue us through life unless we meet them.

> *Example: 'Three men with clubs were chasing me but never actually caught me as I woke in terror. I was determined to tell myself it was only a dream and the next night as they were*

*chasing me I remembered it was only a dream and lost all fear
– stopped running – turned to face them and said "This is only
a dream, you can't hurt me." As they came closer they faded
into nothing and I never say them again.' Mr C. – Account of
dreams when six years old.*

Chased by opposite sex: afraid of love or sex; haunted by a past
relationship. By animal: one's passions; anger; natural feelings. By
thing or shadowy creature: usually past experience or trauma; a hurt
from childhood. Chasing: something you are pursuing in life;
something or someone you want; aggression. See: **follow**.

chasm   Feelings about death, sex, the unconscious or the
unknown. See: **abyss**; **falling**; **valley**.

chemist   Usually health concerns; what the body needs; healing;
can be similar to doctor – wisdom about Self, insight into Self.

chest, box   May refer to one's physical chest; more often the way
we hide in ourselves, or keep hidden, our own emotions; our most
valued ideals and hopes; our best insights; the best in us.

child   See: *boy, girl, daughter* and *son* under **family**.

childbirth   See: **baby**; **birth**.

choke   Conflict; indecision – as when we choke on our words;
repression of emotion.

chrysalis   See: **caterpillar**.

church   Religious feeling or beliefs, including moral code, or our
feelings about organised religion. Each of us have a sense of our
relationship with the forces of life within us and the world outside
of us. A church may depict this sense and what we do with it; our
sense of what is holy or fundamental to all life and therefore eternal,
such as the urge to exist; the cycles of life and growth; reproduction
and interdependence. See: *Christ* under **archetypes**; **religion and
dreams**.

cigar, cigarette   Masculinity; penis. <u>Cigarette</u>: anxiety or release from it; dependence; feeling of having a support, a friend, or help to meet stress; may associate with feelings about cancer.

city, town   One's relationship and interaction with society; one's sense of community; the mental and emotional environment in which one lives. In some dreams they represent work and opportunity. <u>Home town or town of birth</u>: the familiar way of life; the way you usually go about things. <u>Strange town</u>: the new; different attitudes or way of life. <u>Alone in a town</u>: feeling isolated and out of touch. <u>In a deserted town</u>: outmoded social attitudes or way of life. <u>Lost in a town</u>: feeling uncertain regarding your place or direction in society. <u>Idioms</u>: go to town; ghost town; man about town; paint the town.

cliff   On edge; danger; decision; taking a risk; a barrier; or the unknown, depending on dream content. In the example, we see the cliff presented as a wider view of life, one which includes death. It is shown as the uphill struggle in life, looking back or down from which one has wisdom. It is also the test of self-trust, facing fear.

Example: 'I was standing on a clifftop overlooking the ocean. By my side was a man. He had short, cropped, silver hair, gleaming and piercing blue eyes. He seemed old, but was broad, muscular and gave me the impression of having lived many lifetimes, or being very wise. He indicated the sea and I understood I should plunge into it. I did so, leaving my body behind, and became a part of the sea. At the same time it seemed I could at any time stand beside the man on the cliff again.' Debbie.

climb   We climb to avoid something; to get away; to climb out of some mess we are in – in which case it expresses effort on our part; we climb to get something, to reach it, so this can be ambition or motivation. Climbing has risks though. Attaining new heights in work or a relationship we reach the new and face anxiety, so may have a fear of failing/falling. Climbing may also depict the first half of life, and going downhill in middle or old age. The example shows a common use of climb – to see what is there, beyond, above, out

of sight. The child is exploring growth, to see what maturity and
death have in store. Idioms: climb down; social climber. See: **hill**;
mountain.

> *Example: 'We climbed this tree, the baby as well, to see what
> was at the top. The baby fell out of the tree. We climbed down
> and took the baby to a room and lay it on a bed. It seemed to
> be asleep and didn't wake up. Later we went back to the room
> to see the baby but it had gone. In its place was a bluebird. As
> we looked the bluebird flew away.' Dream of a nine-year-old
> girl.*

clock   Clock or watch: the restrictions we place upon ourselves;
our sense of duty and timing; realisation of urgency or having 'lots
of time'. Ticking clock: might be the heart; life ticking away. Big
clock: one's life – how much time one has left. Clock watching:
tension; being bored or lacking satisfaction; feelings about ageing.
Clock with hands still: death. With hands racing: time running out;
sense of urgency. Alarm clock ringing: warning. See: **time of day**.

close   To close a door, etc.: to be closed emotionally; make a
decision; protectiveness. For close as in near see **positions**. See
door under **house**, **buildings**.

clothes   Clothes can mean many things depending upon dream
context. General: the stance or attitudes we use to meet other people
or special situations such as work or danger; protection, such as
might be given by our feelings of reserve, shyness, anxiety or
aggressiveness in fending off sexual or other advances; clothes
depict self-respect and how we see ourselves in society – the
difference between what we want and what we feel others want of
us; our clothes, especially when we consider their colour, can also
express our emotional condition and moods. Constance Newland
gives the example of dressing in violet symbolising being inviolate
sexually.
   In the following example the clothes are feelings of pleasure and
confidence, and also discomfort and lack of confidence.

> *Example: 'I am packing for a holiday, surrounded by a lovely*

selection of all sorts of clothes. I am matching outfits, shoes, scarves, handbags to match. It gives me great pleasure. I am wearing an old navy blue dress which is too short for me. So short I feel panic because there will not be enough time to change. I am now on the top deck of a bus. I have one battered suitcase and an wearing the same dress, trying vainly to pull it down over my knees. Suitcase bursts open and it is full of old clothes fit for a jumble sale.' Valerie H.

Overdressed or unable to get clothes off: too cautious in relationships; difficulty in changing attitudes or self-image; self-protectiveness; avoiding intimacy. Naked or see-through clothes: Desire to be attractive and noticed as in the example below, where Miss L. is enjoying an acceptable form of intimacy; being open about what you really feel; fear of other people seeing what you really feel, think and desire; anxiety about not being adequate socially; lacking ability to conform to social norm. See: **nude**.

Example: 'I am at the doctor's being examined. It is always the same. I have all my clothes off and he examines me from the roots of my hair down to my toenails. I am just at the point where I am going to ask him for his diagnosis when he fades away.' Miss L.

Armour and protective clothing: defences against internal anxieties, past hurts, and external intimacy. Changing clothes: altering one's mode of behaviour, role or mood. Children's or teenage clothes in adult's dream: youthful or immature attitudes or behaviour. Clothing inappropriate to dream surroundings: attitudes or behaviour inappropriate to one's situation. Dirty or untidy clothes – if the dreamer's: difficult or grubby feelings; one's inner condition, such as an untidy mind, or grubby feeling values. Man in woman's clothes: unacceptability of male role, with its connection to bread winning, aggression, being cannon fodder in war; homosexual tendency; desire for mother. Old but comfortable clothes: aspects of Self we may not express in public, but is who we are when relaxed. Other people's clothes worn by dreamer: the social attitudes and responses we have adopted from others. Ragged or inappropriate clothes: feelings of inadequacy; depressed feelings; rebellion against authority or society. <u>Someone else's clothes</u>: could be feelings from that person we are meeting; their attitudes; memories. <u>Tight clothes</u>: being too restricted in attitude; being tight emotionally. <u>New clothes</u>: change in attitudes; new feeling about Self. <u>Undressing</u>: revealing one's real character; move toward intimacy. <u>Woman in man's clothes</u>: unacceptability of female role, motherhood, housewife; lesbian tendency; desire for father figure. <u>Worn-out or old clothes</u>: attitudes ready to leave behind; old habits no longer useful; feeling worn out, old or tired. <u>Idioms</u>: dress to kill; dress up.

apron Mother role; household world; getting to work on a family situation.

belt Often tightly restrained sexuality or emotions; protectiveness. <u>Idioms</u>: belt up; tighten one's belt.

blouse and shirt Feelings and emotions. <u>Idioms</u>: stuffed shirt; short sleeves – informal.

coat The general Self we use in public – we might be shy in public but very warm with a single friend. <u>Overcoat</u>: usually protectiveness; not giving any secrets away; not showing intimacy or vulnerability. Also can depict our belief system – political or religious – we use to meet the world. Such systems may be a way of allaying anxiety about decisions and self-responsibility, and without them we may feel vulnerable and exposed. <u>Idioms</u>: dragged by one's coat tails; up one's sleeve; coat of many colours.

dress Femininity; exteriorisation of feelings; how you present yourself to others. <u>Wedding dress</u>: see **marriage**, **wedding**.

gloves Protection, as in wearing rubber gloves; keeping 'one's hands clean' as in the sense of avoiding 'dirty business'; being out of touch. Also can represent someone's hand – holding their glove would be holding their hand. <u>Picking up a dropped glove</u>: similar to picking up a handkerchief dropped by a woman – an invitation to a relationship. <u>Idioms</u>: hand in glove with; iron fist in velvet glove; with kid gloves; with the gloves off.

hat or cap Opinions, beliefs, mental attitudes – for instance a Jewish skull cap would represent the religious beliefs of the wearer. <u>Idioms</u>: at the drop of a hat; brass hat; eat one's hat; hang on to one's hat; under one's hat; old hat; cap in hand; thinking cap.

raincoat   The attitudes we use to meet difficult emotions or events; often appears in dreams of dead spouse, suggesting tears or the release of emotions. See: **rain**.

shoes   Position in life; life situation; one's character or chosen way of life; the character traits developed to deal with rough life situations; the condition of one's chosen direction – i.e. formal dancing shoes in a discotheque would suggest outmoded approach; a way of life. Taking off shoes: leaving the past behind; dropping a long-established role; being open to change. Walking without shoes: going through a rough patch in life if walking is difficult; letting go of the everyday duties and responsibilities; contact with nature. Shoes from different roles i.e. nurses' shoes: may indicate our need for the qualities of that role. Sole of shoe: one's soul. Idioms: be in someone else's shoes; don't criticise your brother until you walk a mile in his moccasins; if the shoe fits, wear it; the shoe is on the other foot.

skirt   More particularly sexual than dress. Colours and length say a lot about what is being done with sexuality in a social sense.

trousers   Maleness; protection; socialised sexuality. Idioms: wears the trousers; with their trousers down.

underclothes, knickers, underpants, briefs   Intimate sexual feelings. If black: restraint or unconscious sex drives. Dirty or grubby: sex attitudes we are not proud of; difficult feelings about biological side of Self.

work clothes   Working at something; attitudes concerning work.

clouds   If bright: usually uplifting feelings or religious feelings. If dull: depression, feeling overshadowed by something.

coffee   Mostly social ritual; something stimulating. Offering or being offered: friendship, intimacy; what we thirst for or desire.

coffin   Nearly always a reminder of one's own mortality. Also death of a relationship and the feelings of loss; one's feelings about the death of someone such as husband. See: **funeral**.

cold Held-back emotions, especially fear; feeling neglected or 'left out in the cold'; sometimes connected with feelings about death. Idioms: cold shoulder; cold storage; cold feet.

collective unconscious Jung describes this as the 'inherited potentialities of human imagination. It is the all controlling deposit of ancestral experiences from untold millions of years, the echo of prehistoric world events to which each century adds an infinitesimal small amount of variation and differentiation. These primordial images are the most ancient, universal, and deep thoughts of mankind.'

Jung tried to explain his observation of a strata of being in which individual minds have their collective origin in a genetic way. This seems unlikely, and Rupert Sheldrake sees it as a mental phenomena. Dr Maurice Bucke called it Cosmic Consciousness. J.B. Priestly saw it as 'the flame of life' which synthesised the experience of all living things and held within itself the essentials of all lives. If we think of it as a vast collective memory of all that has existed, then we can say the life of Edgar Cayce exhibited a working relationship with it.

Such a collective level of mind would explain many things, such as telepathy, out-of-body experiences, life after death, which have always been puzzling because it is difficult to explain them using presently known principles. See: *the Self* under **archetypes**; **Cayce, Edgar**; **religion and dreams**; **sea**.

colours In many dreams where colour predominates there are usually strong feelings, as in the example. This suggests colours depict our emotions and feeling tones. Where a dreamer is largely intellectual or out of touch with their feelings, the colour would stand in the place of the emotion, instead of alongside it as with S.C.

White is the most frequently mentioned colour in the collection of dreams used for this book. Black is next, then blue.

Example: 'I was standing in a very beautifully carved chapel or religious place. There seemed to be shadowy nun-or monk-like figures around. But it was the exquisite colouring of the place which filled me with a sort of ecstasy. Everything was in the most delicate shell pink.' S.C.

black   The unconscious; unknown; hidden or avoided; the unaccepted side of Self; not being aware; depression; negative; secrecy; fear; death. Also the earthy, or source of life and growth. What is hidden in the unconscious or body can be powerfully transformative. Black clothes or under garments: hidden or unconscious feelings or sexuality. Black animals: unconscious drives and urges. See: **dark**.

blue   Light blues: our sense of intuition; having a wide awareness of life; religious feelings. Also coolness of nature. Often seen in visions of the womb as a blue grotto or woman with halo of blue, so connects with prenatal and infant relationship with mother. Dark blues: in many women's dreams threatening men appear dressed in dark blue or navy blue overalls; depression; negative thoughts or intuition. Idioms: blue film; blue funk; blue pencil; blue sticking; feel blue; out of the blue; vanish into the blue; blue blood; true blue; once in a blue moon.

brown   Depression; dullness; earthiness; excrement; concealment. Idioms: brown study; browned off.

green   Potential for growth; healing or positive change. Often found in dreams about heaven. Dark greens: evil intentions; growth of negative attitudes; sickness; envy; jealousy. Idioms: green fingers; green light; green – naive.

indigo, violet   Mostly religious feelings; intuition.

orange   Blending or balance of emotions and intellect. Sometimes warmth; religious feelings or insight.

red   Even where red appears quite casually in a dream, as with the hat in the example, there is frequently fear, screaming, horror or a sense of danger in the same dream. Red also represents one's basic emotions, earthy nature and sexuality. In these senses it is one's strength and down-to-earth health and power. Less frequently: blood; menstruation; the biological life force; conception; death. Red face: anger; high emotion. Red-brick building: homeliness; warmth. Red furniture or decor: plush; richness. Red flowers: love; passion; dangers of passion. Red clothes or motif: sexuality; passion; strong emotions. Red and grey often appear together: emotions connected with depression. Rose pink: love. Pale pink: baby feelings; weakness. Idioms: see red; in the red; red carpet; red-light district; red faced; red tape.

> *Example: 'An old woman with a very pink, lined face, and wearing a clashing red hat, knelt close to my face. The woman leaned forward to poke my hand, and I recoiled, screaming myself awake.' Joy S.*

white   Awareness; clarity of mind; purity; cleanness; light feelings. In certain dreams white is very threatening. Perhaps we have connections with hospitals in these dreams.

> *Example: 'There was a huge white kitchen. I was scared when I entered it and there was a door leading out of it into a white corridor with a turquoise carpet which scared me even more.'* `H.H.`

Maggots, mould, dead or sick people and shrouds can also be white, so white can depict death or sickness. White clothes: a sense of wholeness; purity or marriage. White animals: urges and sexuality which has been accepted or integrated with conscious activities.

yellow   Lightness of feeling; intellect; extroversion; cowardice; intuition; caution or quarantine; hopefulness for the future.

comb   Something you are doing or thinking about doing to tidy up your thoughts or self-presentation. Idioms: fine tooth comb.

compass   Your attempt to find a direction or activity you feel confident about.

compensatory theory   Jung, Hadfield and several other dream researchers believe the dream process is linked with homeostasis or self-regulation. See *Man and His Symbols*, Jung; *Dreams and Nightmares*, Hadfield; *Mind and Movement*, Crisp. This means that the process underlying dream production helps keep psychological balance, just as homeostasis keeps body functions balanced. Put bluntly, dreams are said to compensate for conscious attitudes and personality traits. So the coldly intellectual man would have dreams expressive of feelings and the irrational as part of a compensatory process. The ascetic might dream of sensuous pleasures and the lonely, unloved child dream of affection and comfort.

Although dreams can be seen as self-regulatory, the narrower view of compensation is only seen in a few dreams. See: **computers and dreams**; **science, sleep and dreams**; **sleep movements**; **sleep walking**.

computer Powers of the mind; personal potential or abilities; memory; looking into the unconscious or activities of the mind. See: **record**, **cassette**, **cd**, **computer disc**.

computers and dreams Because of the ease with which computers can file, sort, cross reference and present information, a great deal of work has been done in analysing the content of thousands of dreams. See *The Content Analysis of Dreams* by Hall and Van De Castle.

As computers are an everyday part of many homes, we can easily use them to gain insight into our own dreams. Two areas of helpfulness are: 1. We can enter many dreams, then with a program such as Concord or Masterfile, easily scan through them to see the frequency of dream themes. This approach to dreams – self-insight through a series of dreams – is explained by Hall in *The Meaning of Dreams*. Important issues in our life and development occur as frequent dream themes and are easily seen using a computer. 2. Programs like Nudist. Using this program, if one dreamt of a tree and wrote down one's associations, then six months later dreamt of a tree and entered this, the program instantly reminds you of the past reference to tree and can display it. Gradually a reference base of our own dreams and comments can be built up and quickly scanned. Such comparisons help us to form a personality profile of oneself or others.

contraceptive Anxiety about pregnancy; sexual responsibility; sexual standards.

Example: 'I was in my mother's bedroom with my teenage boyfriend. We were laying in my parents' double bed and he was kissing my breasts. I realised we were near to making love

*and told him I was not on the pill. Seeing him taken aback I
told him my father has contraceptives in a nearby drawer. The
dream fades as he is trying to put one on.' Julia.*

Julia, a teenager, is obviously approaching her readiness for lovemaking. She has accepted the sexual standards of her parents – their
bed.

cooking   As in the example, ways we transform 'inedible' or
'unpalatable' aspects of our life. Also nourishing ourselves; satisfying
a hunger; creativity; our ability to make something new of the varied
opportunities or experiences we have; giving of oneself. See: **food**;
kitchen under **house**, **buildings**; *cook* under **roles**.

> *Example: 'I saw piles of French loaves. On picking one up I saw
> that although the crust was crisp, the inside was runny
> wet dough. I wondered if cooking would make them usable.'
> Derek L.*

cord   May be similar to chain or rope – restriction. But often depicts
the feeling bonds we have with another person or situation; the
umbilical in the sense of dependency that holds us. Breaking the
cord represents becoming independent of parents or authority
figures – often anger or resentment is directed at the person we are
dependent upon. Also might be a play on words as in 'struck a cord';
in accord.

core   See: **centre**.

corner   General: feeling trapped or restricted; or as in the second
example, a hidden or little admitted aspect of oneself. Occasionally
such boundaries or restrictions might produce a sense of snugness
or security. When a street or projected room corner: the unexpected
or unseen; new experience; public gaze; indecision or the act of
making a decision. Idioms: drive somebody into a corner; in a tight
corner; knock the corners off someone; turn the corner; hole in the
corner affair.

Example 1: 'I was afraid the thugs would corner and attack me.' Pauline B.
Example 2: 'I went into an obscure corner of the cloakroom and hung up the coat – then I went through the pockets.' Mrs R.E.

corpse   See: A dead body under **body**.

corridor   The example may refer to the experience of birth in the birth canal. Such a corridor can also depict our sense of not being able to get out of a dissatisfactory situation. General: No-man's land; limbo; in-between state; the process of going from one thing to another. See: *white* under **colour**.

Example 'I'm trapped in a long passageway or corridor. I can't get out. I'm feeling my way along the wall – there is a small light at the end of the tunnel, I can't get to it. I'm very frightened. I wake up before I get to the end. Then I feel afraid to go back to sleep.' Margaret.

cosmetic   Desire to attract attention; our public traits; cover up.

countryside   One's natural spontaneous feelings; a relaxed state; the forces of 'nature' in us; our moods – rainy countryside would be a more introverted mood than a lively sunny scene. Country lanes: meeting what is natural in us – this may disturb the dreamer, perhaps being in the form of a wolf or other animal. See: **landscapes**; **lane**; *farmer* under **roles**, **settings**.

crab   See: *crab* and *shell fish* under **fish**, **sea creatures**.

crack   A flaw in one's thinking; a weakness in the attitudes or defences we use in meeting life; the unexpected; the irrational breaking through into consciousness; the vagina. Idioms: Cracking up; crack of doom; paper over the cracks. See: first example in *death and rebirth* under **archetypes**.

crater   Past trauma.

creativity and problem-solving in dreams   Few dreams are, by themselves, problem-solving or creative. The few exceptions are usually very clear.

Example: '*My mother-in-law died of cancer. I had watched the whole progression of her illness and was very upset by her death. Shortly after she died the relatives gathered and began to sort through her belongings to share them out. That was the climax of my upset and distress, and I didn't want any part of this sorting and taking her things. That night I dreamt I was in a room with all the relatives. They were sorting her things and I felt my waking distress. Then my mother-in-law came into the room. She was very real and seemed happy. She said for me not to be upset as she didn't at all mind her relatives taking her things. When I woke from the dream all the anxiety and upset had disappeared. It never returned.' Told to author during a talk given to The Housewives' Register in Ilfracombe.*

Example: '*I was lying in my bed and a man was beside me. Gradually he got older and older until he was dead. Then he became a skeleton in bed beside me. I felt horrible. When I woke there were still some difficult feelings but these went. I realised that things, emotions, troubling me for ages had all been cleared. Previously at church the vicar had talked about the healing of forgiveness, and in some way this had happened while I was dreaming. Now, quite a time after the dream, I am still in the state of ease.' Stephanie (Chester).*

Although in any collection of dreams such clear-cut problem-solving is fairly rare, nevertheless the basic function in dreams appears to be problem-solving. The proof of this lies in research done in dream withdrawal. As explained in the entry **science, sleep and dreams**, subjects are woken as they begin to dream, therefore denying them their dreams. This quickly leads to disorientation and breakdown of normal functioning. Therefore, a lot of problem-solving is occurring in dreams even though it may not be as obvious as the example.

This feature of dreaming can be enhanced to a marked degree by processing dreams and arriving at insights from the information they contain. This enables old problems to be cleared and new information and attitudes to be brought into use more quickly. Through such active work one becomes aware of the Self, which Carl Jung describes as a centre, but we might think of as a synthesis of all our experience and being. Gaining insight and allowing the Self entrance into our waking affairs, as M.L. Von Franz says in *Man and His Symbols*, gradually produces 'a wider and more mature personality' which 'emerges, and by degrees becomes effective and even visible to others'. This is of course a very subjective event, yet it has obvious practical results. The person arrives at a greater social connectivity through it, and this usually results in marked changes in the opportunities life presents them.

The function of dreams may well be described as an effort on the part of our life process to support, augment and help mature waking consciousness. A study of dreams suggests that the creative forces which are behind the growth of our body are also inextricably connected with psychological development. In fact, when the process of physical growth stops, the psychological growth continues. If this is thwarted in any way, it leads to frustration, physical tension and psychosomatic and eventually physical illness. The integration of experience which dreams are always attempting, if successful, cannot help but lead to personal growth. But it is often frozen by the individual avoiding the 'growing pains', or the discomfort of breaking through old concepts and beliefs.

Where there is any attempt on the part of our conscious personality to co-operate with this, the creative aspect of dreaming emerges. In fact, anything we are deeply involved in, challenged by, or attempting, we will dream about in a creative way. Not only have communities like the American Indians used dreams in this manner – to find better hunting, solve community problems, find a sense of personal life direction – but scientists, writers, designers and thousands of lay people have found very real information in dreams. After all, through dreams we have personal use of the greatest computer ever produced in the history of the world – the human brain.

1. In Genesis 41, the story of Pharaoh's dream is told – the seven fat cows and the seven thin cows. This dream was creative in that with Joseph's interpretation it resolved a national situation

where famine followed years of plenty. It may very well be an example of gathered information on the history of Egypt being in the mind of Pharaoh and the dream putting it together in a problem-solving way. See: **dream process as computer**.

2. William Blake dreamt his brother showed him a new way of engraving copper. Blake used the method successfully.

3. Otto Leowi dreamt of how to prove that nervous impulses were chemical rather than electrical. This led to his Nobel Prize.

4. Frederich Kekule tried for years to define the structure of benzene. He dreamt of a snake with its tail in its mouth and woke to realise this explained the molecular formation of the benzene ring. He was so impressed he urged colleagues, 'Gentlemen, learn to dream.'

5. Hilprecht had an amazing dream of the connection between two pieces of agate which enabled him to translate an ancient Babylonian inscription.

6. Elias Howe faced the problem of how to produce an effective sewing machine. The major difficulty was the needle. He dreamt of natives shaking spears with holes in their points. This led to the invention of the Singer sewing machine.

7. Robert Louis Stevenson claims to have dreamt the plots of many of his stories.

8. Albert Einstein said that during adolescence he dreamt he was riding a sledge. It went faster and faster until it reached the speed of light. The stars began to change into amazing patterns and colours, dazzling and beautiful. His meditation on that dream throughout the years led to the Theory of Relativity.

To approach our dreams in order to discover their creativity, first decide what problematical or creative aspect of your life needs 'dream power'. Define what you have already learnt or know about the problem. Write it down and from this clarify what it is you want more insight into. If this breaks down into several issues, choose one at a time. Think about the issue and pursue it as much as you can while awake. Read about it, ask people's opinions, gather information. This is all data for the dream process. If the question still needs further insight, before going to sleep, imagine you are putting the question to your internal store of wisdom, computer, power centre, or whatever image feels right. For some people an old being who is neither exclusively man or woman is a working image.

In the morning note down whatever dream you remember. It does not matter if the dream does not appear to deal with the question. Elias Howe's native spears were an outlandish image, but nevertheless contained the information he needed. Investigate the dream using the techniques given in the entry **dream processing**. Some problems take time to define, so use the process until there is a resolution. If it is a major life problem, it may take a year or so. After all, some resolutions need restructuring of the personality, because the problem cannot disappear while we still have the same attitudes and fears. See: **dream processing**; **secret of the universe dreams**.

cricket   See: **games**, **gambling**.

crossing   General: a change, but often with much vulnerability; an obstacle usually of a feeling nature to overcome. Maybe fear or uncertainty causes us to be unable to make the change, so we dream of a bridge giving way. Such changes often are to do with major life junctures, such as from youth to adulthood; pre-puberty to adolescence; single to married; young to middle age. Sometimes a trial or test such as initiation. Crossing a river or chasm: often depicts death. See: **bridge**; **individuation**; **river**; **road**.

crossroad   Decision – as in the example; union of opposites; conflict. Crossroads also have a certain amount of anxiety involved, as with crossing.

> *Example: 'I keep in touch with an old boyfriend who I have not seen since I was eighteen, which is fourteen years ago. In my dream I was on holiday on a coach which stopped at a crossroads. I met my old boyfriend who had come from the other direction and we walked together. I felt enormous pleasure being in his company again. A hearse passed us slowly with a child's coffin.' Mrs R.*

In trying to decide what direction to take, Mrs R. still finds emotions tie her to the past, but the dead child shows she really knows the relationship has ended.

crowd   Feeling crowded out; public opinion; one's feelings about people in general; anonymity; camouflage. Lost in a crowd: feeling without personal direction; confusion on meeting many opinions; desire not to stand out. Attacked by crowd: fear of public opinion; feeling one's own angry urges as threatening. Talking to, leading, or part of crowd at a central event: an impulse or idea which unifies many parts of one's own nature – as the many aspects of our own being, such as visual impressions; sensuality; thoughts; musical sense; religious feelings; sexual drive; intuition; fear; ambition; hunger; our desire for acclaim; the sadist in us and so on, constitute a crowd. How we relate to the crowd: suggests our relationship with our own inner community and the external public. Being unable to tolerate parts of oneself leads to intolerance toward external people with those traits.

crown   Success, either desired or achieved; realisation of expanded awareness. See: **dream as spiritual guide**.

crucifixion   Masochism; guilt; feelings of being a scapegoat; frequently connected with the pains of being born. Also parts of us may have been 'killed' and if they are coming alive again – being felt once more – the pain of their emergence is shown as crucifixion. In some cases the dying of an egocentric Self as it gives way to a wider awareness emerging from unity of unconscious and waking Self. See: **religion and dreams**.

crystal   The human sense of the eternal; the Self; rigid views or emotions; crystallised opinions, thus habits.

cuckoo   See: *cuckoo* under **birds**.

cul-de-sac   Sense of efforts leading nowhere; a woman's legs – vagina at the end.

cup Offering oneself; a woman offering herself and her sexuality; a receptive state of being which can receive intuitively from the unconscious.

dam The way we attempt to 'bottle up' our emotions and drives such as ambition or sexuality. There is often tremendous power or energy waiting to be used or directed.

dancing General: feeling at one with someone or aspects of yourself; unity, as seen in the cells working as a harmonious whole. Also happiness; sexual mating dance; getting closer or more intimate. If the dance is awkward: lack of harmony connected with what is depicted. Animals dancing: harmony with unconscious drives and sexuality. Skeletons or dark 'things' dancing: developing a relationship with what we fear – meeting it; dancing with death – in life we always dance with death, meaning we have an intimate relationship with it, but might not be ready to recognise who our partner is.

> *Example: 'We were both shy of each other but as the dance went on I found I could move so well to his steps that we felt like one, it was so effortless that it felt like floating.' Heather.*

danger Most often anxiety. We may fear the danger of allowing our sexual urges – the danger of falling in love with its possible pain – the danger of failing if we take a risk. Even ideas, such as those of future peril cause enormous anxiety. These may be depicted as impending danger in a dream. In such cases the real danger is of taking our anxieties as reality, instead of seeing them for what they are, a feeling reaction to a situation. A relative or loved one in danger: the temptation is to believe the dream is presaging a real event. Our concern for children and loved ones, but more often our fears regarding them, create most of such dreams. A woman told me a dream in which her daughter was strangled while at university. In processing her dream the woman wept strongly as she met feelings of fear about her daughter leaving home and living independently at university. See: **attack**; **precognition**.

dark   General: what is unknown; not defined by the intellect or conscious Self; unconscious; depression; confusion; terror; secrets we hide from Self or others; things we do 'under cover of darkness'; age; the womb: death. Dark water: emotions which are felt and are powerful but have not been defined or their source understood. Dark colours: feelings emanating from unconscious sources; depressed or unhappy feelings. Idioms: a dark horse; in the dark; keep it dark.

Darkness has many meanings depending on what else appears in the dream. In the example the feeling is of being lost and trapped in depressing feelings.

> *Example: 'I ran down very dark streets, like a maze, and could not find a way out of them.' Mrs N.*

The following dream depicts particular aspects of darkness.

> *Example: 'It was a festival in this strange world in which everything had a rather dark, dilapidated look.' Tom.*

Dark here is ancient; things dating from times past. This may refer to our sense of our own childhood which feels like the ancient past; or to our unconscious knowledge of family and cultural attitudes and experience. In general the 'strange' world of the unconscious or sleep.

> *Example: 'I was overwhelmed by terror, as if the very darkness of the tunnel was a living force of fear which entered and consumed me. I screamed and screamed, writhing in uncontrollable fit-like contractions. Nevertheless a part of me was observing what was happening and was amazed, realising I had found something of great importance.' Andrew P.*

Because the dreamer explored this dream with me, I know the darkness was depicting fear Andrew experienced while a nine year old in hospital. He was given a rectal anaesthetic because he was about to have a nose operation. He fought and begged for the nurses to stop, but to no avail. This led to a very real feeling that humans were terrifyingly dangerous animals who would not respond even if you were on your knees begging. So trauma was the fear in the darkness. Darkness here is the forgotten area of experience.

> *Example: 'I am back in time looking at an old cottage. I see the windows, walls and doors, everything about the place. It is dark and old and warm. I see the curtains and bedrooms, all the ornaments and I feel safe and comfortable.' Mrs R.*

Here dark is comfortable, perhaps because it is undemanding; one is not in any glare of attention or activity. It is the relaxed quiet of evening. This woman has a relaxed relationship with her unconscious.

> *Example: 'I met a woman I know in a long, dark underground tunnel. She was waiting for me. We had sexual intercourse. She had a very formed vagina mouth, and a very large clitoris, like a small penis. I masturbated this.' Norman.*

Norman has no fear of the tunnel. It is his secret desire and pleasure which he admits to no one, often not even to himself. Dark here is one's secret Self.

daughter   See: *daughter* under **family**.

day and night   Mostly our mood. In the example Kim feels bright and cheerful. An overcast day would be the reverse. Also being conscious; 'seeing' what we are doing; our waking experience. See **light**; **time of day**.

> *Example: 'It was a beautiful hot sunny day and I was in a children's playground talking to a woman I knew vaguely.' Kim B.*

night   Similar to dark. Usually the unconscious, dark, or a little sensed area of oneself. Also loneliness; areas of subtly felt urges or feelings. Sometimes freedom. We may be constrained by the social or moral rules we apply to ourselves during the 'day' or waking consciousness. But on the edge of consciousness, or in sleep, we find a wonderful freedom which allows us escape. Sometimes shown by escaping from a house at night and running away. See: **dark**.

In the example below the secrecy occurs because parts of Tom's childhood experience were 'hidden' behind the forgetfulness or unconsciousness of emotional hurt.

> *Example: 'I was creeping through a field at night. In darkness I and others were trying to accomplish some secret act, rather as spies or underground agents might.' Tom.*

dead end   See: **cul-de-sac**.

dead people dreams   Most dreams in which dead people appear are expressive of our attempts to deal with our feelings, guilt or anger in connection with the person who died; or our own feelings about death. <u>General</u>: when someone close to us dies we go through a period of change from relating to them as an external reality to meeting and accepting them as alive in our memories and inner life. <u>Dead husband or wife</u>: many dreams of dead people come from women who have lost their husband. It is common to have disturbing dreams for some period afterwards; or not be able to dream about the husband or wife at all; or to see the partner in the distance but not get near. In accepting the death, meeting any feelings of loss, grief, anger and continuing love, the dream may become as in the third example. In the first example the dreamer is feeling fear about being carried off by death.

> *Example: 'My husband's mother, no longer alive, came and slid her arms carefully under me and lifted me up. I shouted "Put me down! Put me down! I don't want to go yet." She carefully lowered me onto the bed and disappeared.' E.H.*

> *Example: 'A dark grey sugar loaf form materialised. This pillar*

*lightened in shade as I watched. It didn't move. I began to
think it was Mrs Molten who died in 1956. The feeling grew
stronger but still the colour lightened. Then it bent over and
kissed my head. In that instant I knew it was my mother. An
ecstatic joy and happiness such as I have never known on
earth suffused me. That happiness remained constantly in
mind for the next few days.' Mr M.*

Here the dreamer has not only come to terms with his mother's and
his own death, but also found this inner reality.

*Example: 'A couple of months ago as I was waking I felt my
husband's arm across me and most realistically experienced
my hand wrapping around his arm and turning towards him,
which I had done so often in his lifetime, and saying "I thought
you had died. Thank God you have not." Then I awoke alone
and terribly shaken.' Mrs I.*

This example shows both the resolution of the loss, but also the
paradox felt at realising the meeting was an inner reality.

A critic might say this is only a dream in which a lonely woman
is replaying memories of her dead husband's presence for her own
comfort. Thus her disappointment on being disillusioned. Whatever
our opinion, the woman has within her such memories to replay.
These are a reality. The inner reality is of the experience that was left
within her from the relationship. Her challenge is whether she can
meet this treasure with its share of pain and draw out of it the
essence which enriches her own being. That is the spiritual life of her
husband. The 'aliveness' of her husband in that sense is also social,
because many other people share memories of the same person.
What arises into their own lives from such memories is the
observable influence of the now dead person. But the dead also
touch us more mysteriously, as in the next example. See: *husband*
under **family**.

*Example: In a recent news programme on television, a man who
survived the Japanese prisoner of war camp in Singapore had been
given a photograph of children by a dying soldier he did not know.*

The man had asked him to tell his family of his death, but did not give his name. The photograph was kept for forty odd years, the man still wanting to complete his promise but not knowing how. One night he dreamt he was told the man's name. Enquiries soon found the family of the man who had an identical photograph.

death   Some aspect of our outer or inner life is fading, or being superseded by a changed approach, so may be shown as dying. Our drive to achieve something might die and be shown as a death in our dreams. Changing from adolescence to puberty, maturity to old age, are also shown as oneself dying. Lost opportunities or unexpressed potentials in oneself are frequently shown as dead bodies. All of us unconsciously learn attitudes or survival skills from parents and others. If these are unrecognised they may be shown as dead. Sometimes we have killed the child or teenager in us because of difficulties or trauma at those ages, and these may be seen as a dead person in one's dream.

Some death dreams may show the awakening of new life in the dreamer. For instance, Sue worked on a dream in which she was told her baby had died. She woke shaking with grief and tears. The dream and emotions appeared to show her becoming alive enough to feel the grief of her past pain and death of her hopes, love and ideals. She had suppressed her pain for so long. In now coming alive enough to feel her emotions, she was feeling at last that something had died in her.

If the death is someone we know: frequently, as in the second example, desire to be free of the person; or unexpressed aggression; perhaps one's love for that person has 'died'. We often 'kill' our parents in dreams as we move toward independence. Or we may want someone 'out of the way' so we do not have to compete for attention and love. Death of oneself: exploration of feelings about death; retreat from the challenge of life; split between mind and body. The experience of leaving the body is frequently an expression of this schism between the ego and life processes. Also death of old patterns of living – one's 'old Self'. The walking dead or rigor mortis: aspects of the dreamer which are denied, perhaps through fear. Dancing with or meeting death or dark figure: facing up to death.

Example: 'My son comes in and I see he is unwashed and seems preoccupied and as if he has not cared for himself for some days. I ask him what is wrong. He tells me his mother is dead. I then seem to know she has been dead for days, and my two sons have not told anyone. In fact my other son has not even accepted the fact.' Anthony.

Anthony is a divorcee. Processing the dream he realised the two sons are ways he is relating to the death of his marriage – the children's mother.

Example: 'During my teens I was engaged to be married when I found a more attractive partner and was in considerable conflict. Consistently I dreamt I was at my fiancé's funeral until it dawned on me the dream was telling me I wanted to be free of him. When I gave him up the dreams ceased.' Mrs D.

Example: 'I dream I have a weak heart which will be fatal. It is the practice of doctors in such cases to administer a tablet causing one painlessly to go to sleep – die. I am completely calm and accepting my fate. I suddenly realise I must leave notes for my parents and children. I must let them know how much I love them, must do this quickly before my time runs out.' Mrs M.

This is a frequent type of 'death' dream. It is a way of reminding ourselves to do now what we want to – especially regarding love.

Although the unconscious has a very real sense of its eternal nature and continuance after physical death, the ego seldom shares this. Unconsciously we realise that collective humanity carries living experience from the life of those now dead. The farmer today unconsciously uses the collective experience of humanity in farming. What innovation he does today his children or others will learn and carry into the future. <u>Idioms</u>: dead and buried; dead from the neck up/or neck down; dead to the world; play dead. See: *death and rebirth* under **archetypes**.

deep   Usually we live on the surface of our mind. In sleep we dive down deeper but lose sense of Self. If we maintain some awareness in these 'depths' of the mind it is somewhat like snorkelling in deep sea. We realise what immense and unbelievable depths lie beneath us. Dreams often portray this as depth – a hole; deep water; a chasm; space. Also our non-verbal life in the womb or early childhood, which is remembered as patterns of feeling reaction rather than verbal utterance. In the depths we may find gems, skeletons, archaeological objects, and these relate to the memory of our evolutionary past, family influences we carry within us unknown. Deep cuts: suggests a hurt which penetrates us; or emotions which affect us powerfully. Idioms: in deep water; in the deep end; deeply troubled; deeply hurt.

defecate   Self-expression; release of tension; getting rid of negative experience or emotions; creative expression; permitting the natural in oneself. See: **excrement**.

defence mechanisms   Although the dream process attempts to release difficult emotions, trauma and past experience, most people have inbuilt mechanisms which prevent this spontaneous healing activity. It is natural to pull our hand away from a hot surface because of the pain. We do this 'without thinking', unconsciously in fact. Similarly, we unconsciously pull away from any painful or frightening emotions, even though it may be in our best interests to release or integrate them. The non-release leads to physical tension, a massive use of energy to contain such emotions and even the development of physical illness. Resistance may also be in the form of not wanting to change; fear of the new; feeling threatened by fresh views of life or any questioning of the values one has long lived by. To free oneself from such resistances needs a positive motivation and the learning of new psychological and even physical skills, as presented in current forms of psychotherapy.

déjà vu   Many dreamers say they find a connection between a place they dream of – especially a house – and a place they later see while awake. Most of these descriptions appear to be attempts to find connections obvious to no one but the dreamer. A strong desire to have the inner world connect with the real world seems to be the motivation. This may be through a need for human life to have meaning and connection with a wider, invisible life. The evidence of thousands of dreams suggests that searching for meaning in this direction is misplaced. Meaning arising from a love or acceptance of the many aspects of oneself, and thus the expansion of awareness into what was unconscious.

Déjà vu literally means seen before. The valid cases of it are rare. Nevertheless people do have dreams and experience in which they can demonstrate they have been to a place before, yet not physically. The most common explanation is that of reincarnation.

The Bralorne's, on tour to India for the first time, stepped off their tour boat into Bombay for the first time. Within minutes Mr Bralorne knew what street they would shortly arrive at, giving its name. This continued, until he had a memory of a house that he thought should be at the foot of Malabar Hill with a big banyan tree in front of it. The couple asked a policeman if such a house existed. He said such a house had been on that very spot. His father had been a servant in the house and it had belonged to the Bhan family. This really amazed the Bralornes as they had called their son Bhan Bralorne.

demolition   Major changes in dreamer's inner or outer life have been, or are being, undertaken; breakdown of old attitudes and approaches.

departing   A breaking away from old or habitual patterns of behaviour; leaving a situation, such as a relationship, a financial set-up or work; the struggle to become independent as in leaving home. Sometimes desire to get away from responsibility or difficulties. Can also refer to death, perhaps when we see a spouse walking away from us, or departing on journey. This is not necessarily a prediction, but confronting the situation. Idioms: new departure; the departed dead; leave in the lurch; leave someone to it; left holding the baby.

Example: 'I was leaving some people, like at a junior school. Some of the children tried to detain me with the attitude that I was defying teacher's authority, and they restrained me with the rules they restrained themselves with. I broke free and walked off.' Timothy.

depression and dreams   Some 140 dreams were collected from a group of patients suffering from depression. The same number of dreams were collected from people similar in age and social background but not suffering depression. The dreams were given code numbers, mixed and given to an independent judge. He was asked to look for any evident themes of self-punishment such as 'I was waiting for my friends all night but they never turned up' or 'My fiancé married somebody else.' Such self-punishing themes occurred with greater frequency in the depressives' dreams. These self-punishing themes can be changed using such techniques as outlined under **dream processing**.

descending, down   <u>Something below us</u>: as in Rita's dream below, where there is fear, can depict past trauma which is not being faced. Literally run away from; something we have left behind or we feel 'above'. <u>Descent, going down stairs or in a lift</u>: getting more down to earth or practical; a return to difficulties after living in our fantasies or escapism; depression; sexual restraint; a return from meta conception, see: **aura**. <u>Descending into cave, cellar or hole</u>: meeting unconscious content such as repressed fears or wisdom carried unconsciously from family or culture; experience of womb existence. <u>Going down a hill</u>: can mean loss of status, ageing, failure or death, but is also, as shown in the second example, a positive sense of life within us. <u>Idioms</u>: feel down; down and out; down in the dumps; down to earth.

> *Example: 'I look down and the stairs and banister rail are swarming alive with a black moving wave of crawling things, like some awful insects; and in the hallway is a swamp with crocodiles and other hideous things. My terror is terrible and I cry out to stop dreaming this nightmare. The person who actually lives in this part of the house was the owner's mother. She treated me badly but no one knew as she was artful in her abuse. She pulled me along by my hair, locked me in a cupboard, and once locked me in the orchard – four high walls and a hidden door.' Rita.*

> *Example: 'Then I was climbing down a steep hill. Arriving at the foot I found rippling sparkling water. I stopped and looked*

*around and found everything incredibly beautiful – the green
fields and the pebbles in the water, the soft fresh air; then I
looked up and the sky was a glorious picture, the sun so warm
and the clouds fluffy and soft and pretty. I felt at peace and so
happy, and thanked God with all my heart for giving us so
much beauty.' Mrs R.E.*

desert, **wilderness**   Loneliness – literally being deserted; lack of
emotion or satisfaction; no creativity or growth in one's life; dry
intellectualism; social isolation; sexual barrenness. Occasionally as
the symbol in the Bible of wandering in the wilderness which
depicts both the human sense of having no real meaning or direction
and of being a wanderer in the infinity of time and decision. It shows
the difficulty of being self-responsible and making decisions in the
infinity of choices, and of honouring the Self in such decisions.

desk   Work; authority; discipline.

destination   Because the unconscious has a powerful faculty for
synthesising our experience, it frequently arrives at a sense of what
we most wish for, or want to create through our life. Yet we may not
have become aware of what has been realised. It may be depicted
by a place we are heading toward, or a goal; a destination we do not
remember. Also our conscious ambition and desire; our hopes; what
we have struggled long for.

devil   See: **aboriginal**; **active/passive**; **evil**.

devour   Being eaten by dogs or creatures: losing our sense of
identity, or what we think or want, in meeting other people's will,
anger or ideas; being 'consumed' by fear, emotion or a drive; fear of
death. Swallowed by large creature or fish: opening to awareness of
unconscious content. Devouring: being possessive; hungering for
something.

diamond   See: **jewels**.

digging, **excavation**   Digging usually depicts delving into hidden
or buried areas of ourselves. We may uncover feelings from our

childhood, creative realisations, features of the unconscious, even dead bodies or ancient creatures. Also digging can represent our work on renovating our attitudes, personality structure or habits. See: **garden**.

> *Example:* '*I entered a neglected garden adjoining a house I had formerly lived in. I was astonished that I had never noticed this garden before. I took a spade and hoe and began to work vigorously in order to put things right, digging like a navvy. But wherever I put my spade I turned up live shells and hand grenades – highly explosive and very dangerous. I was terrified I would be blown to pieces and hurried away.'* From Organism of The Mind, *G.R. Heyer (Kegan Paul, 1933).*

The dreamer was a man in his forties who had taken up meditation at the suggestion of a friend. It shows him discovering and uncovering a part of himself he had not known before. In doing so he meets explosive emotions and conflicts he is not used to dealing with.

dinosaur   Our personality is a young new thing. It grows throughout our life, but its roots reach into the processes of life and consciousness active in our own being, which are as ancient as life on this planet. Life on the planet is also only an extension of processes active in the cosmos. So in dreams we often sense this primordial past out of which our present Self has grown, and frequently depict this meeting as a prehistoric animal. Also extinct; outmoded; clumsy; instinctive.

dirty   Actions or feelings which we feel are grubby or immoral. The unconscious has a natural morality based on its sense of connection with the universal principles of mating, birth, growth and death. Where our social life does not align with this or our own consciously accepted principles, we may dream of being dirty.

disappearance   Depicts the way our conscious Self relates to the unconscious. Memories, emotions or ideas suddenly appear in awareness, but can disappear just as rapidly, sometimes never to be seen again. See: **vanish**.

displacement Displacement of aggression from a threatening target to a less threatening one is a common human and animal practice. If we are angry at our partner we may kick the cat or nag at the children instead of confronting the real target. Freud stated that in dreams we express what we usually censor, or would be censored socially, in terms of behaviour or sexuality, but often in a displaced way. What appears to be most important and full of emotion in the dream may, according to this theory, be really of least significance.

Areas of a dream that one might judge as having little feeling value or importance, when explored can certainly unfold into powerfully felt emotions, insights and memories. This need not mean these emotions have been displaced.

diving Taking a chance; facing anxiety. Diving underwater: delving into one's mind or unconscious. Exploring the meaning of a dream, or an eventful meditation, might be depicted as diving underwater in dreams. See: **swimming**.

divorce May be an expression of anger towards one's spouse; fear of or hope for break up of marriage. In a man's dream: difficulty with one's feelings. In a woman's dream: difficulty with social extroversion and intellect.

doll Many 'doll' dreams are, as the example, using the doll as a target for violence. This may refer to how the dreamer felt as a child when smacked or attacked emotionally – like a helpless doll. Also childhood states of feeling; a means of displacement for anger or feelings the dreamer would like to discharge on another, a feeling of wanting to be a precious 'doll' to someone; wanting to be loved. See also: **toy**.

> *Example: 'She continues to attack him and to my horror and feeling of helplessness, his head comes off. But the neck is made of some sort of material with a string hanging off it, and I realise it is a doll's head.' Mr R.H.*

dolphin See: **fish**, **sea creatures**.

door   See: *door* under **house, buildings**.

dragon   Because the part of our mind we name 'the unconscious' is so ancient and huge, we sometimes depict contact with it as a dragon or monster. Also the untamed or unsocialised sexual drive which can overpower or trap a girl emerging into womanhood, or threatens a youth facing manhood. The overcoming of it means facing one's fears of the vast power of such natural drives and finding satisfying expression.

drama   See: **film; theatre**.

dream analysis   Analysing dreams has a very long history. Very clear examples of it are given in the Old and New Testament of the Bible. Prior to this, however, other cultures had looked at dreams and tried to fathom their meaning. See **dreams and ancient Greece; dreams as spiritual guide; religion and dreams**.

Sigmund Freud was the founder of modern therapeutic analysis of dreams. Freud encouraged clients to relax on a couch and allow free associations to arise in connection with aspects of their dream. In this way he helped the person move from the surface images – manifest content – of the dream, to the underlying emotions, fantasies and wishes – latent content – often connected with early childhood. Because dreams use condensation – a mass of different ideas or experiences all represented by one dream image or event – Freud stated that the manifest content was 'meagre' compared with the 'richness and variety' of latent content. If one succeeds in touching the feelings and memories usually connected with a dream image, this becomes apparent because of the depth of insight and experience which arises. Although ideally the Freudian analyst helps the client discover their own experience of their dream, it can occur that the analyst puts to the client ready-made views of the dream. Out of this has occurred the idea of someone else 'analysing' or telling us about our dream.

Carl Jung used a different approach. He applied amplification, helped the client explore their associations, used active imagination, and stuck to the structure of the dream. Because amplification also presents to the client the information and experience of the therapist, again the dream work can be largely verbal and intellectual, rather than experiential. See: **amplification**; **active imagination**.

The approach of Fritz Perls (Gestalt therapy) and Moreno (psychodrama) to dream analysis is almost entirely experiential. The person exploring the dream acts out or verbalises each role or aspect of the dream. If one dreamt of a house, in Gestalt one might start by saying, 'I am a house' and then go on to describe oneself just as if one is the particular house in the dream. It is important, even if the house were one existing externally, not to attempt a description of the external house, but to stay with the house as it was in the dream. This is like amplification, except the client gives all the information. This can be a very dramatic and emotional experience because we begin consciously to touch the immense realms of experience usually hidden behind the image. When successful this leads to personal insights into behaviour and creativity. See **amplification**; **dream processing**; **Gestalt dream work**; **psychodrama and dreams**.

dream as a meeting place   Any two people, or group of people who share their dreams, particularly if they explore the associated feelings and thoughts connected with the dream images, achieve social intimacy quickly. Whether it is a family sharing their dreams, or two friends, an environment can be created in which the most profound feelings – painful and wonderful – can be allowed. Such exposure of the usually private areas of one's feelings and fears often presents new information to the dreamer, it also allows ventilation of what may never have been consciously expressed before. In doing so a healing release is reached, but also greater self-understanding and the opportunity to think over or reconsider what is discovered.

Herbert Reed, editor of the dream magazine *Sundance* and resident of Virginia Beach, USA, initiated group dreaming experiments. It started because Reed noticed that in the dream groups he was running, when one of the group aired a problem, other members would subsequently dream about that person's problem. He went on to suggest the group should attempt this purposely and the resulting dreams shared to see if they helped the person with the problem. The reported dreams often formed a more detailed view of the person's situation. In one instance the group experienced many dream images of water. It aided the woman who was seeking help to admit she had a phobia of water and to begin thinking about learning to swim. In another experiment, a woman presented the problem of indecision about what college to transfer to and what to study. Her group subsequently said they were confused because they had not dreamt about school. Several had dreamt about illicit sex though, which led the woman to admit she was having an affair with a married man. She went on to realise that it was the affair which was underlying her indecision. She chose to end the affair and further her career.

Whatever may be underlying the results of Reed's experiments, it is noticeably helpful to use the basic principles he is working with. They can be used by two people equally as well as a group, by a parent and child, wife and husband, business man and employee. One sets out to dream about each other through mutual agreement. Like any undertaking, the involvement, and therefore the results, are much more pronounced if there is an issue or reasonable importance behind the experiment. It helps if one imagines that during sleep you are going to meet each other to consider what is happening between you. Then sleep, and on waking take time to recall any dream. Note it down, even if it seems far removed from what you expected. Then explore its content using the techniques in **dream processing**.

> *Example:* '*My wife and I decided to attempt to meet in our dreams. I dreamt I was in a room similar to the back bedroom of my previous marriage. My present wife was with me. She asked me to help her move a wardrobe. It reminded me, but did not look like the one which had been in that bedroom. I stood with my back to it and reached my hands up to press on the top, inside. In this way I carried it to another wall. As I put it down the wood broke. I felt it ought to be thrown away.*'
> *Thomas B.*

Thomas explored the dream and found he connected feelings about his first marriage with the wardrobe and bedroom. In fact the shabby wardrobe was Tom's feelings of shabbiness at having divorced his first wife. In his first marriage, represented by the bedroom, he always felt he was married for life. In divorcing, he had done something he didn't like, but was carrying about with him. He says, 'I am carrying this feeling of shabbiness and second best into my present relationship and I need to get rid of it.' See: **peer dream work**.

dreams as spiritual guide   Dreams have always been connected with the spiritual side of human experience, even though today many spiritual leaders disagree with the consideration of dreams. Because dreams put the dreamer in touch with the source of their own internal wisdom and certainty, some conflict has existed between authoritative priesthood and public dreaming. A lay person finding their own approach to God in a dream might question the authority of the priests. No doubt people frequently made up dreams about God in order to be listened to. Nevertheless, despite opposition, Matthew still dreamt of an angel appearing to him; Joseph was still warned by God to move Jesus; Peter still dreamt his dream of the unclean animals.

The modern scientific approach has placed large question marks against the concept of the human spirit – an eternal aspect to human life. Study of the brain's functions and biochemical activities have led to a sense of human personality being wholly a series of biological and biochemical events. The results of this in the relationship between doctor and patient, psychiatrist and client, sometimes results in a communication of human personality being of little consequence. It may not be put into words, but the intimation is that if one is depressed, it is a biochemical situation or a brain malfunction. If one is withdrawn or autistic, it is not that there is a vital centre of personality which has for some reason chosen to avoid contact, but that a biochemical or physiological situation is the cause. It's nothing personal – take this pill to change the biochemistry, because you are not really a person.

Of course we have to accept that human personality must sometimes face the tragedy of biochemical malfunction, but we also need to accept that biochemical and physiological process can be changed by human will and courage, and particularly by the transformative influence of the spiritual dimension of experience.

In attempting to find what the human spirit is by looking at dreams, the simplest definition is that when a dream enables us to go beyond the limitations of our personal memories, our learning, our body and our sense of what life is, it opens our spiritual life to us. Certainly one of the sources of the spiritual is that we have a sense of something, or an experience, which shows us a very different view of our life and the objective world than we usually arrive at through our sense impressions or our inherited cultural views. Common experiences of the spiritual are as follows:

- Tragedies in our life are suddenly seen from a much more inclusive view, or one's personal situation is seen as a part of a continuing and cosmic process. This dignifies and integrates our life into a greater whole and removes the sense of tragedy.
- The spiritual might also be felt as experiencing our own wholeness. This meeting might be an encounter with Christ, or a holy being.
- We experience ourselves as part of one great life, existing throughout time and space, and the variety of living creatures and inanimate matter are all manifestations of that one life. The oneness behind multiplicity is experienced as self-existent.
- A great experience arises in us of the essential part of us streaming back throughout all time. Our personal life connects with all that has existed and all that will exist.
- A realisation of oneself as existing apart from and more than one's thoughts, emotions and body sensations. This direct experience of being is called illumination and cannot be described as it is outside of the thinking process and its definitions.

Example: 'I had got hold of a book of photographs of Japan. It was printed in the thirties or earlier and was externally worn and dog-eared. I opened the book to look at the pictures. They were all black and white. The first one was spread over the two open pages. It was of a beach, taken from a hillside. The day was cloudy but bright. One could almost feel or see the breeze blowing because there was a sense of movement. The beach was slightly curved, bay-like, with the hill rising from near the edge of the sea. Here and there trees growing, not big. On the beach the rollers were breaking, quite big surf. A large rocky shelf ran into the sea from the beach, and this caused the

*breakers to roll up and around at one point, turning back
toward the sea again. In the middle of this, quite small in the
photo was the figure of a man sitting in the lotus position
facing the land. Waves were breaking around and slightly
over him, but he sat at peace, undistracted, in Zen meditation.
It was so simple, so beautiful. I realised I had read somewhere
of the man who sat amidst the waves.' Anthony.*

Anthony worked on the dream and realised he was the man on the
beach. He was finding a realisation of his connection with the great
ocean of life. This was not making him turn away from everyday life
– shown as facing the land. It gave Anthony an experience of a
radiance within him existing beyond effort – just being. Whenever
he relaxed he experienced this gentle radiance bathing him. This
removed from him a great sense of struggle that had dogged him
nearly all his life. He also felt his life was meaningful and part of a
great wonder. He was filled with a radiance from within.

*Example: 'I felt myself rushing upwards in blackness. Then a
sense of release followed, like a cork coming out of a bottle and
I could see. I was floating above my bed, near the ceiling of the
room. Below I could see myself asleep. Terror overcame me. In
hindsight I think I was afraid I was dying. Then I realised I had
read about people doing this, and the terror became uncon-
trollable laughter, perhaps release of the awful tension
moments before.*

*Next I was flying through space with my knees up to my
chest. I was in the RAF in Germany at the time, and I could see
the land underneath. It was still a light summer evening. I
started to pass over the sea and could see a few ships, but was
suddenly at my home in London. I couldn't believe what was
happening, it was so real. I noticed I was in my clothes, not
pyjamas. My mother was sitting knitting. My dog was asleep by
the gas fire. I called excitedly to my mother. She paused but
didn't see me. I couldn't understand this as I experienced
myself as totally real with full self-awareness. I shouted to her
in an attempt to break through what I felt must be a barrier.
She carried on knitting, but I had an immediate experience of
there being two levels she operated at. There was the level of*

*herself that was knitting but not aware of me; then there was
a level her everyday waking self wasn't in contact with. This
level knew I was near her. There was a merging of consciousness and a sharing of love – a becoming 'one'. At the same
moment my dog was awoken. He 'saw' me and rushed to me
barking and howling, as he usually did when he saw me after
an absence. Then I woke in Germany, feeling as heavy as lead.
I found out that my mother had been alone knitting on that
evening and the dog had unaccountably rushed to the back of
the sofa howling.' Tony C.*

An aspect of the human spirit demonstrated by dreams is consciousness of massive integrated experience. The unconscious mind, if its
function is not clogged with a backlog of undealt-with, painful
childhood experience and non-functional premises, has a propensity to form gestalts. It takes pieces of experience and fits them
together to form a whole. This is illustrated by how we form gestalts
when viewing newsprint photographs which are made up of many
small dots of different shades. Our mind fits them together and sees
them as a whole, giving meaning where there are only dots. When
the human mind is working well, when the individual can face a
wide range of emotions, from fear and pain to ecstasy, this process
of forming gestalts can operate very creatively. This is because it
needs conscious involvement, and if the personality is frightened of
deep feeling, the uniting of deeply infantile and often disturbing
experience is cut out. Yet these areas are very rich mines of information, containing our most fundamental learning experiences.

If the process is working well, then one's experience is gradually
transformed into insights which transcend and thereby transform
one's personal life. For instance, we have witnessed our own birth
in some manner, we also see many others appearing as babies. We
see people ageing, dying. We see millions of events in our own life
and in that of others. The unconscious, deeply versed in imagery,
ritual and body language out of which it creates its dreams, picks up
information from music, architecture, traditional rituals, people
walking in the street, the unspoken world of parental influence. The
sources are massive, unbelievable. And out of it all our mind creates
meaning. Like a process of placing face over face over face until a
composite face is formed – a synthesis of all the faces. So the

unconscious scans all this information and creates a world view – a concept of life and death. The archetypes Jung talks of are perhaps the resulting synthesis of our own experience, reaching points others have met also. If so, then Christ might be our impression of humanity as a whole. If we dare to touch such a synthesis of experience it may be searing – breathtaking. It breaks the boundaries of our present personality and concepts because it transcends. It shatters us to let the new vision emerge. It reaches, it soars, like an eagle flying above the single events of life. Perhaps because of this the great hawk of ancient Egypt represented the human spirit.

Beyond this is another way of finding wisdom when we realise our own spiritual dimension. It is that within the one great life in which our personal existence merges like water in the ocean, is all experience, all history, all knowledge.

Example: 'I thought about the dream that I had about L., the dream was that L. was heavily pregnant, she had a very red face, she told me that she was pregnant but I didn't think that I could have made her pregnant and I told her so, she then changed her mind and said, "OK I'm not pregnant then". I became L., entered into her pregnant body and felt her sexuality and understood the dream. She had offered herself to me, her sexuality and her body but I hadn't recognised it, I couldn't see it and so she withdrew. L. wants another child and she had offered herself to me but I couldn't give myself to her, I have never given myself before. In the dream I felt I was not responsible for her pregnancy which represents the denial of my own sexuality and of all that results from it.

This is when I entered into the house of God. At first I saw the image of a huge cathedral or church with a magnificent domed roof and I knew that I was in the house of God. I felt the utopia, I felt like I have never felt before, so very good, so excellent. I knew all things, I didn't have to read the Bible or any kind of teachings because the answers are all here in the presence of God. In this state I could ask any question and know the answer. I knew God, yet I was God because there was no separation.' Neal C.

Lastly, humans have always been faced by the impossible. To a baby, walking and not wetting its pants is impossible, but with many a fall and accident it does the impossible. It is a god in its achievement. To talk, to fly heavier-than-air planes, to walk on the Moon, were all impossible. Humans challenge the impossible every day. Over and over they fall back into defeat. Many lie there broken. Yet with the next moment along come youngsters with no more sense than grasshoppers, and because they don't know what the difference is between right and left, do the impossible. Out of the infinite potential, the great unknown, they draw something new. With hope, with folly, with a wisdom they gain from who knows where, they demand *more*. And it's a common everyday sort of miracle. Mothers do it constantly for their children – transcending themselves. Lovers go through hell and heaven for each other and flower beyond who they were. You and I grow old on it as our daily bread, yet fail to see how holy it is. And if we turn away from it, it is because it offers no certainties, gives no authority, claims no reward. It is the spiritual life of people on the street. And our dreams remember, even if we fail. For this is the body and blood of the human spirit.

dream as therapist and healer   There is a long tradition of using dreams as a base for both physical and psychological healing. One of the earliest recorded incidents of such healing is when Pharaoh's 'spirit was troubled; and he sent for all the magicians of Egypt and all its wise men; and Pharaoh told them his dream, but there was none who could interpret it'. Then Joseph revealed the meaning of the dream and so the healing of Pharaoh's troubled mind took place (Genesis 41). The Greek Temples of Asclepius were devoted to using dreams as a base for healing of body and mind. See: **dreams and ancient Greece**. The Iroquois American Indians used a social form of dream therapy too. See: **Iroquoian dream cult**. The dream process was used much more widely throughout history in such practices as Pentecostal Christianity; Shaktipat Yoga in India, and Anton Mesmer's groups. See: **sleep movements**.

Sigmund Freud pioneered the modern approach to the use of dreams in therapy, but many different approaches have developed since his work. Examples of the therapeutic action of gaining insight into dreams are to be found in the entries on **abreaction**; **recurring dreams**; **reptiles – lizards, snakes**. The entry on **dream process-**

ing gives information about using a dream personally to gain insight and healing. See also: **dream as a meeting place**.

A feature which people who use their dreams as a therapeutic tool mention again and again is how dreams empower them. Many of us have an unconscious feeling that any important healing work regarding our body and mind can only be undertaken and directed by an expert. The expert might be a doctor, a psychiatrist or psychotherapist or an osteopath. Witnessing the result of their own dream process, even if helped by an expert, people feel in touch with a wonderful internal process which is working actively for their own good. One woman, who had worked on her dream with the help of a non-expert friend, said, 'It gave me great confidence in my own internal process. I realised there was something powerful in myself working for my own good. It was a feeling of co-operating with life.' One is frequently amazed by one's own resources of wisdom, penetrating insight and sense of connection with life, as met in dream work. This is how dreams play a part in helping one toward wholeness and balance. The growing awareness of one's central view of things, which is so wide, piercing and often humorous, brings developing self-respect as the saga of one's dreams unfold.

There may be no hint of this, however, if a person simply records their dreams without attempting to find a deeply felt contact with their contents. It is in the searching for associated feelings and ideas that the work of integrating the many strands of one's life begins. Gradually one weaves, through a co-operative action with the dream process, a greater unification of the dark and the light, the painful and transcendent in one's nature. The result is an extraordinary process of education. See: second example in **creativity and problem-solving in dreams**.

dream deprivation   See: **science**, **sleep and dreams**.

dream dictionaries   See: **interpretation of dreams – history of**.

dream eating   Recent findings show that quite a few people go on eating binges while they sleep. The food eaten at such times may be extraordinary mixtures of foods and sauces. The cause of this behaviour is not yet understood, but may, like sleep-walking, have its roots in anxiety experienced during the day. Some individuals use food as a means of comfort and stress management, in the same way others use alcohol or nicotine.

dreamer What we are doing in our dreams is an expression of how we see ourselves at the time of the dream, our stance or attitude to life, or what could be generalised as our self-image. It typifies what aspects of our character we identify with most strongly. To define what self-image is portrayed in your dreams, consider just what situation you have created for yourself in the dream and what environment and people you are with.

> Example: 'My husband and I are at some sort of social club. The people there are ex-workmates of mine and I am having a wonderful time and am very popular. My husband is enjoying my enjoyment.' Quoted from article by the author in She magazine.

The dreamer in the above example describes herself as 'a mature forty-one-year old'. The dream, and her description of it, sum up her image of herself in just a few words. She sees herself as attractive, sociable, liked, happily married. She is probably good looking and healthy. But the dream carries on. She and her husband 'are travelling down a country lane in an open horse-drawn carriage. It is very dark and is in the area we used to live. We come to a hump-backed bridge, and as we arrive at the brow of the bridge a voice says, "Fair lady, come to me." My body is suddenly lying flat and starts to rise. I float and everything is black, warm and peaceful. Then great fear comes over me and I cry out my husband's name over and over. I get colder and slip in and out of the blackness. I wake. Even with the light on I feel the presence of great evil.'

From a very positive sense of Self, she has moved to a feeling which horrifies her. How can such a confident, socially capable woman, one who has succeeded professionally as well as in her marriage, meet such feelings? The answer probably lies in the statement of her age. At forty-one she is facing the menopause and great physical change. The image of herself she has lived with depended, or developed out of, having a firm sexually attractive body and being capable of having children. Losing whatever it is that makes one sexually desirable must change the image others have of one and that one has of oneself. The hump of the bridge represents this peak of her life, from whence she will start to go downhill towards death – certainly toward retirement. So she is facing a mid-life crisis in which a new image of herself will need to be forged.

Example: 'I am a shy sixteen-year-old and am worried about my dream. In it I am walking along the school's main corridor. I try to cover myself with my hands as a few people go by, not noticing me. Then a group of boys pass, pointing and laughing at me – one boy I used to fancy. A teacher then gives me clothes. They are too big but I wear them because I have nothing else.'
H.M.

Adolescence is a time of great change anyway, when a lot is developing as far as self-image is concerned. H.M.'s nakedness shows how vulnerable she feels, and how she has a fear that other people must be able to see her developing sexuality and woman-hood. It is new to her and still embarrassing, particularly with boys she feels something for. She tries to cover up her feelings and uses attitudes she has learnt from parents and teachers – but these are not suitable. So we might summarise by saying that the situation she places herself in within the dream shows her present uncertainty and sense of needing clothes – attitudes or confidence – of her own. See: **identity in dreams**; **individuation**.

Our current 'self-image' is displayed by what we do in our dreams. If we are the active and central character in our dreams, then we have a positive, confident image of ourselves. The role we place ourselves in is also the one we feel at home with, or one which is habitual to us. If we are constantly a victim in our dreams, we need to consider whether we are living such a role in everyday life. Dreams may help us look at our self-image from a more detached viewpoint. We can look back on what we do in a dream more easily than we can on our everyday waking behaviour. This helps us understand our attitude or stance, a very growth promoting ex-perience. It is important to understand the viewpoint of the other dream characters also. Although they depict views not habitual to us, they enlarge us through acquaintance. See: **identity in dreams**;

individuation; *Have a dialogue between two characters or objects* under **dream processing**.

dream interpretation   Once you understand a dream, its images can be seen as a clear expression of personal information. For instance a woman dreamt she was standing alone on a plateau and she could see two worlds hanging in the sky. In talking about the dream she said her husband had died and she had met another man. This new man was very different to herself and her past husband. The world he lived in was new to her and she was cautious. This helped her to see she had the choice between two worlds and her dream was simply illustrating her situation – she was alone, on a plateau facing choices.

From this point of view dreams are not strange or coded. They are not trying to hide information, but express it in much the same way we use imagery in our everyday speech. In the above example 'worlds' is the imagery used. But it might also be: 'that was a close shave', 'barking up the wrong tree', 'got the sack', etc.

Dreams also use other things that we take for granted as everyday parts of our mental life – word play and puns for example, and the drama we understand so easily in films and plays, but say we are mystified by in our dreams. Such dream statements as 'I was in a dark and lonely house', 'The dark water moved slowly between the stones', 'It was a beautiful bright sunny day and I was in a children's playground' are immediately understandable as expressions of mood.

What may confuse us in looking at dreams, especially our own, is these factors are used all at once and all put into imagery. Even so, if we look at them as if they were all a sort of mime – where speech may occur but the main message is expressed by dramatic mood, substitution of an image for words, word play and puns in image form – then we can begin to grasp what the dream is communicating. See: **dream processing**; **interpretation of dreams**; **language and dreams**.

dream process as computer   The brain is not a computer, but it has the power to compute. The word *computare* is Latin and comes from *putare* – to think. Neither is a computer anything like a human brain. But there are parallels. Christopher Evans, a psychologist, computer scientist and world authority on micro-processors, says the brain and computers are both information handling devices – taking impulses which in themselves mean nothing, like sound waves, and processing them. It is also his theory that both computers and the waking brain function are taken 'off line' to reprogram. Our behaviour responses and information bases need bringing up to date with new experience and information received. In the case of the computer, 'off line' means having modifications made to programs. In the human it means sleeping and dreaming – the dream being the powerful activity of review, sifting and reprogramming. Thirdly, the brain and computer use 'programs'. In humans, a program means a learnt set of responses, values or activities, such as walking or talking, but including more subtle activities such as judging social or business situations.

If, as Christopher Evans believes, dreaming is partly a period of revising and updating responses, insights and skills, then by working with the process one can make it more efficient. The background for this statement is that many people have recurring dreams which change very little. Looking at this from the 'programming' view, the attempt to revise is thwarted. But individuals can free such 'stuck' dreams by using dream processing.

Also, as some dreams are obviously a synthesis of experience and information gathered over a lifetime, the dream process is much more than a computing function which sorts new information and updates. It is also capable of creative leaps through synthesis and conjecture. J.B. Priestley's dream of the birds – see **religion and dreams** – appears to be a massive synthesis of things observed over a lifetime. It also depicts a brain function like computer simulation, which takes information and forms it into an experimental view of possibilities arising from the thousands or millions of separate bits of gathered data. See: **creative and problem-solving dreams**; **dream processing**; **ESP in dreams**.

dream processing   Below are described simple techniques which make it possible to gain information from dreams quickly. They have been presented as a series of questions.

What is the background to the dream?   The most important aspect of your everyday life may have influenced the dream or feature in it.

Briefly consider many aspects of your life which connect with what appears in the dream.

> *Example: 'I have a plane to catch. I get to the plane but the suitcase is never big enough for my clothing which I have left behind. I am always anxious about stuff left behind. I wake still with the feeling of anxiety.' Jane (LBC).*

When asked, Jane said plane flights had been a big feature of her life. She had moved home often, travelling to different parts of the world, leaving friends and loved ones behind.

What is the main action in the dream?   There is often an overall activity such as walking, looking, worrying, building something, or trying to escape. Define what it is and consider if it is expressive of something you are doing in waking life. Activities such as walking or building a house need to be seen as generalisations. Walking can simply represent taking a direction in life or going somewhere, and building can be seen as creating something new. When you have defined the action, look for further information under the other headings in this book, such as **swimming** or **sitting**.

What is your role in the dream?   Are you a friend, lover, soldier, dictator, watcher or participant in the dream? Consider this in relationship with your everyday life, especially in connection with how the dream presents it. Where possible, look for the entry on the role in this book. See: **dreamer**.

Are you active or passive in the dream?   In this context, passive means not taking the leading role, being only an observer, being directed by other people and events. If you are passive, consider if you live a similar attitude in your life. See **active/passive**.

What do you feel in the dream?   Define what is felt emotionally and physically. In the physical sense are you tired, cold, relaxed or hungry? In the emotional sense did you feel sad, angry, lost, tender or frightened anywhere in the dream? This helps clarify what feeling area the dream is dealing with. It is important also to define whether the feelings in the dream were satisfyingly expressed or whether they were held back. If held back they need fuller expression. See: **emotions**, **mood**.

Is there a 'because' factor in the dream? In many dreams something happens, fails to happen, or appears, because! For instance, trapped in a room you find a door to escape through. All is dark beyond and you do not go through the door 'because' you are frightened of the dark. In this case the because factor is fear. The dream also suggests you are trapped in an unsatisfying life situation through fear of opportunity or the unknown.

Am I meeting the things I fear in my dream? Because a dream is an entirely inward thing, we create it completely out of our own internal feelings, images, creativity, habits and insights. So even the monsters of our dream are a part of ourselves. If we run from them it is only aspects of ourselves we are avoiding. We can never escape ourselves, so we might as well find a way of internal ease. Through defining what feelings occur in the dream you may be able to clarify what it is you are avoiding. See: **dream as spiritual guide**; **nightmares**.

What does the dream mean? We alone create the dream while asleep. Therefore, by looking at each symbol or aspect of the dream, we can discover from what feelings, thoughts or experience, from what drive or what insight we have created the drama of the dream. In a playful relaxed way, express whatever you think, feel, remember or fantasise when you hold each symbol in mind. Say or write it all, even the seemingly trivial or 'dangerous' bits. It helps to act the part of each thing if you can. For instance as a house you might describe yourself as 'a bit old, but with open doors for family and friends to come in and out. I feel solid and dependable, but I sense there is something hidden in my cellar.' Such statements portray oneself graphically. Consider whatever information you gather as descriptive of your waking life. Try to summarise it, as this will aid the gaining of insight.

When doing this remember that dreams are multidimensional in a certain sense, just like words in a sentence. Morton Hunt, in his book *The Universe Within* illustrates how words have an unusual dimension. For instance, what do you make of the following sentence? 'Mary heard the ice-cream truck coming down the street. She remembered her birthday money and ran into the house.'

You have probably already formed an image of Mary – her age, skin colour, an approximation of what she is dressed in, and what she is doing. You believe she is going to buy an ice-cream and she is young. But where does it say this in the sentence? And if you change any of the words – say 'truck' for 'bus' or 'money' for 'gun' – an entirely new image of Mary arises.

The factors relating to how we extract meaning out of words and images is crucial when considering our dreams. In our dreams any one factor – such as Mary – alters enormously in its meaning because of its context with the other dream factors, such as objects, people, setting and plot or theme. Get a sense of this overall connection when looking at the various parts of your dream.

Can you amplify the dream?   You will need the help of one or two friends to use this method. The basis is to take the role of each part of the dream, as described above. This may seem strange at first, but persist. Supposing your name is Julia and you dreamt you were carrying an umbrella, but failed to use it even though it was raining, you would talk in the first person present: 'I am an umbrella. Julia is carrying me but for some reason doesn't use me.' Having finished saying what you could about yourself, your friends then ask you questions about yourself as the dream figure or object. These questions need to be simple and directly about the dream symbol. So they could ask: Are you an old umbrella? Does Julia know she is carrying you? What is your function as an umbrella? Are you big enough to shelter Julia and someone else? . . . and so on.

The aim of the questions is to draw out information about the symbol being explored. If it is a known person or object you are in the role of – your father for instance – the replies to the questions need to be answered from the point of view of what happened in the dream, rather than as in real life. Listen to what you are saying about yourself as the dream symbol, and when your questioners have finished, review your statements to see if you can see how they refer to your life and yourself.

If you are asking the questions, even if you have ideas regarding the dream, do not attempt to interpret. Put your ideas into simple questions the dreamer can respond to. Maintain a sense of curiosity and attempt to understand – to make the dream plain in an everyday language sense. Lead the dreamer toward seeing what the dream means through the questions. When you have exhausted your questions ask the dreamer to summarise what they have gathered from their replies. See: **postures**, **movements**, **body language** for an example of how to work with body movement to explore a dream meaning. See: **peer dream work**.

Summary To summarise effectively, gather the essence of what you have said about each symbol and the dream as a whole and express it in everyday language. Imagine you are explaining to someone who knows nothing about yourself or the dream. Bring the dream out of its symbols into everyday comments about yourself. A man dreamt about a grey, dull office. When he looked at what he said about the office, he realised he was talking about the ·grey, unimaginative world he grew up in after the Second World War and how it shaped him.

Further information on using these techniques can be found in my book *Instant Dream Book* (published by C.W. Daniel). See: **adventure of the dream world**; **amplification**; **dreamer**; **peer dream work**; **plot of dream**; **postures**, **movement**, **body language**; **settings**; **symbols and dreaming**; **word analysis of dreams**; **wordplay**, **puns**.

dreams and ancient Greece Antiphon, a Greek living in the fourth century BC, wrote the first known descriptive book of dreams. It was designed to be used for practical and professional interpretations. He maintained that dreams are not created by supernatural powers but natural conditions. In the second century AD, a similar book was written by Artemidorus, a Greek physician who lived in Rome. He claimed to have gathered his information from ancient sources, possibly from the Egyptian dream book dating from the second millennium BC. He may have used works from the Assurbanipal library, later destroyed, which held one of the most complete collections of dream literature. Artemidorus classified dreams into dreams, visions, oracles, fantasies and apparitions. He stated two classes of dreams: the somnium, which forecast events, and the insomnium, which are concerned with present matters. For the somnium dreams Artemidorus gave a dream dictionary. He said Abyss meant an impending danger, a dream of warning. Candle: to see one being lighted forecasts a birth; to exhibit a lighted candle augers contentment and prosperity; a dimly burning candle shows sickness, sadness and decay. This latter is taken from folklore of the times and, because dreams tend to use commonly used verbal images, was probably true. He maintained that a person's name – that is their identity and the family, national and social background from which they arose – has bearing on what their dream means.

Plato (429–347 BC) said that even good men dream of uncontrolled and violent actions, including sexual aggression. These actions are not committed by good men while awake, but criminals act them out without guilt. Democritus said that dreams are not products of ethereal soul, but of visual impressions which influence our imagination. Aristotle (383–322 BC) stated that dreams can predict future events. Earlier Hippocrates, the 'father of medicine' discovered that dreams can reveal the onset of organic illness. Such dreams, he said, can be seen as being illogically representing external reality.

Hippocrates was born on the island of Kos. On the island was the famous temple dedicated to Aesculapius, the god of medicine. There were about 300 such temples in Greece alone, dedicated to healing through the use of dreams. Hippocrates was an Aesculapian and learnt his form of dream interpretation from them. In such temples the patient would have to ritually cleanse themselves by washing, and abstain from sex, alcohol and even food. They would then be led into what was sometimes a subterranean room with harmless snakes in – these were the symbol of the god. In the morning the patients were asked their dream and it was expected they would dream an answer to their illness or problem. There are many attestations to the efficacy of this technique from patients.

dreams are more than dreams   A dream is not simply a mental image. It is fully physiological as well. The dream process creates full *physical, emotional, visual, sensory* and *sexual* experience. It is *not* simply a mental visionary thing. The whole brain sends out impulses to the body to move, to feel, to experience. One may take this for granted while it happens in sleep. This may be because one might think of dreams as a fantasy or mental image. They are not. They link with full physical process and sensation.

dream within a dream   A dream presents us with emotions or information we may be avoiding while awake. Usually a dream within a dream is a ploy one uses to explain away the impact of the feelings met – which is all the more reason to understand the dream.

drink To absorb or take something subtle into oneself. This may be taking in feelings such as pleasure; absorbing a mood; 'drinking in' our surroundings. When connected with thirst: suggests needs or longings being met. If in company with someone of the opposite sex, or a group: taking in the pleasure or otherwise of the relationship or group. Sometimes connects with childhood emotional need. See: **alcohol**.

driving See: **car**.

drowning Because of the water, drowning depicts fear of being overwhelmed by difficult emotions or anxieties. Dreamt about someone else: may occasionally show our apprehension about their health or well-being, having the suggestion of death or breakdown.

> *Example: 'I fell into a pond. My brother was frightened to be by himself so he jumped in. We were both drowning in the water and we shouted out for Mum. My brother drowned.' Poppy S.*

Poppy dreamt this while feeling insecure and anxious because her father was ill.

drugs In general they relate to whatever we associated with the particular drug. For instance aspirin would connect with our attempts to deal with pain; hallucinogens to the meeting with unconscious material, or the attempt to avoid reality.

drum May represent the heart; sexual tension; intercourse; masturbation, depending on context in dream. Can be our awareness of the natural rhythms of our own life processes, such as heartbeat, menstruation, circulation and the feelings arising from our depths such as primitive urges. See: **music**.

drunk Loss of control; lack of reason; having no soul or self-control; abandonment to the irrational or natural urges. Thus freedom from the burden of self-awareness, responsibility and decision making. Occasionally means we are filled with power from our spirit, or connection with the one life. See: **alcohol**.

dwarf, malformed figure   A part of our personality left undeveloped or not integrated. For instance we may have musical ability which was suppressed by the need to bring up children. Also a part of Self malformed by painful childhood experience or lack of emotional nourishment. It may therefore be a link with our unconscious.

earth   General: the things we take for granted which act as the supportive background to our lives and activities, such as parental love, our own reality as a person, social order, the thousands of things which constitute 'reality' for us; the basic 'taken-for-granted' aspects of one's nature – for instance, language and culture. They give us the very basis for our personal and unique personality, yet we stand upon them just as the earth supports us. Also the 'ground we stand on'; attitudes and relationships we have taken for granted; everyday life; the past. The ground, like earth, holds in it all past experience, summarised as it is in culture and language. Soft earth or fields: mother; the fundamental processes of life out of which we have our being and which continually nurture us. Under the earth, or swallowed by the earth: the unconscious habits, drives and psycho-biological processes which existed before our emergence as a conscious Self and in which we might lose Self in death. Off the ground: losing connection with one's roots of family or culture. This may also be occasionally shown as being on a high building. Idioms: down to earth; go to earth; like nothing on earth. See: **unconscious**.

earthquake   Insecurity; the breakdown of opinions, attitudes or relationships which seemed so dependable. May also show great inner change and growth which makes us feel uncertain of our 'ground'. The growth from youth to puberty may be felt as an earthquake, as also maturity to middle age. See: **earth**.

east   Personal connection with source of life; birth; the mysterious or religious aspect of Self.

137

eating   General: satisfying one's needs or 'hunger'. This can be any area of need, such as emotional, mental, sexual, depending on dream context.

> *Example: 'I am putting four of our puppies under the grill and cooking them.' (LBC).*

Although Maureen hasn't eaten her puppies yet, her dream illustrates how food is used to represent her emotional needs. Maureen is childless, has a lot of mother love, planned the pregnancy of her bitch, and gets enormous satisfaction from rearing the puppies. She is literally hungry for the exchange of love and care she finds in dealing with her puppies.

Occasionally eating shows information about actual nutritional needs or physical allergies. Also to eat is to continue involvement in the fundamental processes of life, a celebration of interdependence. To not eat: shows a conflict with the physical reality of one's body and its needs; an avoidance of growth or change; an attempt to be isolated from others, reality, the whole. Avoiding certain foods: expression of decision making in dealing with needs; food allergy. Giving food to others: giving of oneself to others, or nurturing some aspect of oneself. Eating objects or repulsive food: meeting objectionable experiences; trying to 'stomach' things which make you 'sick'.

> *Example: 'I ran into a house and came face to face with a huge stag. I noted the open back door, whereupon he started eating my leg. I was pushing against his horns and managed to stop him chewing me.' Jasmine C.*

Being eaten: the first part of Jasmine's dream not quoted is obviously sexual. Being eaten therefore suggests she is being consumed by her sexual drive. Being eaten, especially if it is the face, also shows how our identity or our fragile sense of Self is feeling attacked by emotions or fears, other people, or internal drives. The classic story of Jonah illustrates this and shows how the conscious personality needs to develop a working relationship with the unconscious. Eaten by dogs or maggots: feelings about death. See: *dog* under

animals; **food**; **individuation**. Idioms: eaten away; eat dirt; eat humble pie; eat like a horse; eat one's heart out; eat one's words; eat out of one's hand; eat out of house and home; what's eating you?; proof of the pudding is in the eating; dog eat dog. See: **food**.

egg   Potential; parts of Self as yet unrealised or not fertilised by our conscious action or quality; the female ovum; a sense of wonder regarding life; our prenatal life; feelings about wanting to retreat from life.

Egypt   Usually the hidden side of Self; the riches of the unconscious. In the biblical symbolism, life dominated by material values.

ejaculation, **emission**   The example under **black person** shows how our sexual needs attempt to satisfy themselves even though we may make a conscious attempt to deny them. The ejaculation, male or female, shows the sexual nature of one's dream, even if the symbols seem to have no obvious connection. The attitudes in one's dream also show something of one's relationship to sex. This may be mechanical, fearful, loving, guilty, etc. Alfred in the example mentioned sees sex as a problem to be solved and has difficulties with commitment.

embryo   An extremely vulnerable aspect of us; our own prenatal experience; or our feelings connected with our prenatal life – for instance we may have been told our mother tried to abort us. Even if this is not so, the idea acts as a focus for our feelings of rejection and infantile pain. The embryo or foetus would therefore symbolise such feelings. See: **baby**.

emotions, **mood**   There is a level of human experience which is typified by intense emotional and physical responses to life. Such emotions and bodily drives may remain almost entirely unconscious until touched by exploring our dream content in the right setting. When such feelings and bodily movements arise, as they do in dreams, we may be amazed at their power and clarity. See: **dream processing**; **sleep movements**.

If we take away the images and events occurring in a dream and simply look to see what feelings or emotions are evident, the dream is often more understandable than if we try to interpret the symbols.

Feelings in dreams are nearly always undistorted. We therefore do not need to interpret them, simply to recognise them and see if we can recognise where they occur in waking life.

The images in a dream may be the way we unconsciously pictorialise our flux of feelings and the play of internal energy flows. For instance love or sexual drive can give rise to physical movement as in sexual intercourse. Repression of sex or love also represses such physical movements, leading to tension and conflict, which might be presented in the drama of a dream.

> *Example: 'I was with my wife, walking along a street, on holiday with her. But I felt awful tension. It was the sort of stress I feel when I have turned off my sexual flow – as I have at the moment.' Brian V.*

Brian can easily see the connection between the dream feelings and his everyday life. Making such connections may take practice. But the situation could as easily be expressed as a dream image of a blocked river. The underlying feelings would then be less easy to grasp.

> *Example: 'I was in a very ancient crumbling building, confronted by a large stone door, deeply engraved with many designs and creatures. I began to open the door and felt high feelings of anxiety. I realised this was an initiation and I must calm my feelings in order to pass beyond the door – i.e. if I were controlled by my feelings I would run away.' Derek F.*

How we meet the emotions in our dreams illustrates our habitual method of dealing with them. The feelings of anxiety in Derek's dream were met and moved beyond, but this is unusual. This is because most of us change our direction as soon as there is a hint of fear. The amount of nicotine and alcohol human beings consume suggests how poorly we meet anxiety. Going beyond fear or pain is an initiation which opens doors for us. We might now apply for the job; ask for the date; raise the issue; express the creativity; make the journey abroad, which anxiety previously kept us from. We see this in the next example. Angela is not married and feels obvious anxiety about the commitment.

Example: 'I had a ring on my marriage finger. It was a thin band of gold. I woke up frightened.' Angela (LBC).

Dreams give us a safe area to express emotions which might be difficult or dangerous to release socially. Anger in a dream may be expressing what we failed to discharge in a waking encounter, or it might be our habitual response. It may also be directed against oneself.

Dreams also contain many positive emotions. Sometimes they present a new aspect of feeling which is life enhancing. In the example below, the dreamer overcomes the feeling of defeat and death and in imagery expresses a sense of rebirth.

Example: 'While heavily pregnant eleven years ago, I dreamt I and thousands of Japanese-like soldiers had been at war and lost. Our punishment was beheading. Not wanting to see my comrades killed I went to the front. I felt the cold blade hit my neck, then was dead, outside my body. Dressed in golden armour with a lion symbol I told my comrades they out-numbered the enemy. They won and took my baby from my dead body.' BMW (Southport).

Some feeling states in a dream are subtle and may be more evident in terms of the symbols than the feelings. A grey, dreary environment suggests depression and lack of pleasure. A sunny light environment with flowers and colour shows pleasure and good feelings. A country landscape depicts quite a different feeling state to a smoky, busy city street. We can define these for ourselves using the techniques described under **dream processing**.

Whatever feelings or emotions we meet in our dreams, many of them are bound to be habitual responses we have to life. Where these habits are negative we can begin to change them by working with the dream images as described in **dream processing** under *Can I alter the dream to find greater satisfaction?* See: **hostility**; **love**.

emperor   See: **king**.

empty <u>General</u>: lack of – pleasure, enthusiasm, good feelings; loneliness; lack of relationship; sense of isolation. Or one's potential; opportunity; space to be oneself. Depends on feeling quality in the dream. <u>Empty house, buildings, shell</u>: outgrown habits or ways of life; old attitudes; death; and/or potential. See: **house**, **buildings**.

> *Example: 'I was down in a low bit of a village, trying to get to a road high up on a hill where the sun was shining and was walking through dark, empty houses.'*

The use of empty in this dream can be understood by the comparisons existing between the 'down low, empty houses' feeling, and the 'high up sunny hill' feeling.

enclosed, enclosure   The defences we use, such as pride, beliefs, anger, to protect ourselves from deeply feeling the impact of the world, relationships, love, anxiety or pain. These are often felt as traps or restraints, even though they are parts of our own personality. For instance one may feel trapped by one's own feelings of dependence upon family.

> *Example: 'I am trapped in a bricked room with no way out and I shout for somebody to help me. Then either a big bird or a creature with long arms tries to catch me, and I scream.'* Karen S.

Karen had previously lost a baby, been divorced, had an unsatisfying relationship with a man. She feels trapped by the defences she has herself built 'brick by brick', but is frightened of the opportunity of change represented by the bird. What encloses or traps us in our dream gives a clue to what constrains us in waking.

> *Example: 'As I go through a tunnel it either gets smaller so I can't get through, or it goes on so far there is no end to it. I am trapped and terrified.'* Don M.

This sort of enclosed dream is typical of trauma relating to a difficult birth. In fact Don's mother was in labour for four days and never had another child because of the pain.

end   Used in many different ways, depending on context. General: goal; point of change; release; death. End of path or road: the end of one's life; the boundary of what one already knows or has done; end of a relationship especially if walking with person. End of tunnel or cave: finding the way out of a difficult or depressed stage of life. End of table or queue: feeling left out, unconsidered, forgotten; putting oneself last. End of garden, room or road: can be used to show polarity or opposites, as in the following example in which the end of the tunnel suggests an opposite to the fear she is experiencing.

> *Example: 'I'm trapped in a long passageway or corridor. I can't get out. I'm feeling my way along the wall – there is a small light at the end of the tunnel, I can't get to it. I'm very frightened. I wake up before I get to the end. Then I feel afraid to go back to sleep.' Margaret C.*

> *Example: 'I was due to be executed – what for I don't know. I was not especially afraid of this, but my most vivid feelings were of great sadness at the people I was leaving behind, and for all the things I wanted to do in life, but would not now be able to. Then at the end I was watching myself being hanged.' D.K.*

Many people dream this 'end of life' theme. In virtually every one of these dreams, there is a highlighting of 'things to do'. Such dreams are a way of deciding what is of most value in the dreamer's life.

> *Example: 'I found myself alone in the garden at the far end of the house near the stables.' M.M.*

Here 'the end' relates to being alone, as opposed to being in the house with people. Idioms: at an end; end of one's tether; wit's end; end of the day; be the end of; a sticky end; dead end; the deep end; end it all; end of the line; both ends meet; not the end of the world; loose ends; to no end; light at the end of the tunnel. See: **cul-de-sac**.

engine   One's motivating drive or energy; the body's energy and mechanical or automatic functioning; the sexual or natural urges; sometimes the heart. See: **machine**.

enter, entrance   New experience or new area of experience. A secret entrance: an attitude of psychological 'stance' which opens a new experience of Self, or allows access to parts of oneself usually inaccessible. See *door* under **house, buildings**.

erotic dreams   See: **sex in dreams**

escape   Finding a way of moving beyond restrictions, perhaps caused by anxiety or past pain. We often use 'escape', as in the example below to avoid difficult feelings. This is like reading an exciting novel because it distracts our attention. The problems remain. Something escaping from us: a realisation, emotion or opportunity eluding awareness. See: **enclosed, enclosure**.

> *Example: 'I often dreamed I was being chased by boys or men. I would suddenly take off like a helicopter and fly away. Sometimes narrowly escaping from my pursuer.' M.C.*

> *Example: 'I dreamt I was a prisoner with many others. Myself and other men were outside the prison working. Then a tremendous explosion blew a hole in the prison wall. I knew prisoners were trying to escape. I saw some wardens and shouted or signalled to the prisoners to be careful.' Terry D.*

Terry worked as a therapist without academic qualification. He represents his attitudes to authority as the prison, because he had felt second rate due to his lack of scholarship. The escapees are his potential that had been trapped by those attitudes.

ESP in dreams   Many dreams appear to extend perception in different ways.

dreaming the future   Just before his title fight in 1947, Sugar Ray Robinson dreamt he was in the ring with Doyle. 'I hit him a few good punches and he was on his back, his blank eyes staring up at me.' Doyle never moved and the crowd were shouting 'He's dead! He's dead!' He was so upset by the dream Robinson asked Adkins, his trainer and promoter, to call off the fight. Adkins told him, 'Dreams don't come true. If they did I'd be a millionaire.' In the eighth round Doyle went down from a left hook to the jaw. He never got up and died the next day.

The problem is that many such dreams felt to be predictive never come true. Often dreamers want to believe they have precognitive dreams, perhaps to feel they will not be surprised by, and thereby anxious about, the future. When the baby son of Charles Lindbergh was kidnapped, and before it was known he had been murdered, 1,300 people sent 'precognitive' dreams concerning his fate in response to newspaper headlines. Only seven of these dreams included the three vital factors – that he was dead, naked and in a ditch.

Out of 8,000 dreams in his Registry For Prophetic Dreams, Robert Nelson, who was sent dreams prior to what was predicted, has found only forty-eight which bear detailed and recognisable connections with later events.

dreaming together   The Poseidia Institute of Virginia Beach, USA, have run a number of group 'mutual dreaming' experiments. Although the Institute suggests very positive results, a critical survey of the dreams and reports reveals a lack of hard evidence. Like other areas of ESP dreaming, it can seldom ever be willed. But the dreams did show themes related to problems regarding intimate meetings. Also, some of the dreams were directly about the goal of dream meeting, as in the following example. See: **dream as a meeting place**.

'I find the group of people I am looking for. There were maybe six or more people. They were asleep on mattresses except for two or three. These were awake and waiting for me, and wearing small pointed hats such as Tibetan Lamas wear. In the dream I realised this meant they had achieved sufficient inner growth to remain awake in sleep. We started to communicate and were going to wake the others.' Tom C.

There are 'meeting' dreams, however, although these seldom occur under test conditions.

Example: 'I dreamt my sister was attacking me with a pair of scissors. She backed me against a wall and stabbed me. During the day after the dream my sister phoned me at work and said she had an awful dream in which she stabbed me with scissors.' D.

Example: 'My husband is in the navy, serving on a ship in the Gulf. We've always been close, through twenty-two years. I dreamt we were making love and could even smell him. It ended as lovemaking always does for us, with orgasm and a cuddle into deep sleep. I woke surprised he wasn't next to me. He phoned the next day to say he had the same dream, same night.' Mrs E.H. Gosport (Teletext).

the dream as extended perception   Even everyday mental functions such as thought and memory occur largely unconsciously. During sleep, perhaps because we surrender our volition, what is left of self-awareness enters the realm where the nine tenths of the iceberg of our mind is active. In this realm faculties can function which on waking seem unobtainable. A list of these would include:

1.   Extending awareness to a point distant from the body, to witness events confirmed by other people. This is often called out-of-the-body experience or OBE, but some of these experiences suggest the nature of consciousness and time may not be dualistic having to be either here or there. See: **out-of-body experience; dreams as spiritual guide**.

2.   Being aware of the death or danger of a member of family. Kinship and love seem to be major factors in the way the unconscious functions. See: **dead people dreams**.

3.   Seeing into the workings of the body and diagnosing an illness before it becomes apparent to waking observation. Dr Vasali Kasatkin and Professor Medard Boss have specialised in the study of such dreams. In a recent dream told to me a man looked back into a bedroom and saw a piece of the wall fall away. Waves of water gushed from a main pipe. The dreamer struggled to hold back the piece of broken pipe. Within two weeks his

colon burst and he had to have a major operation. See: **meditation**.

4. Access to a computer-like ability to sort through a massive store of information and experience to solve problems. These dreams are often confused with precognitive ability. Prediction does occur from these dreams, but it arises, as with weather prediction, from a massive gathering of information, most of which we have forgotten consciously. Morton Schatzman, in an article in *New Scientist*, showed how subjects can produce answers to complex mathematical problems in their dreams. See: **creativity and problem-solving in dreams**; **dream process as computer**.

5. Tapping a collective mind which stores all experience and so is sensed as god-like or holy. See: **dream as spiritual guide**.

6. It seems likely that before the development of speech, the human animal communicated largely through body language. Some dreams suggest we still have this ability to read a person's health, sexual situation, intentions and even their past, through body shape, posture and tiny movements. See: **postures**, **movement**, **body language**.

See: **Cayce, Edgar**; **collective unconscious**; *wife, dead husband* and cannot find husband under **family**, **hallucinations**.

Evans, Christopher In his book *Landscapes of the Night*, Dr Evans puts forward a new theory of dreaming. He states that our brain has 'programs' for dealing with survival. We have basic behaviour programs for walking and talking, rather like a computer might have. We also have programs for social interaction and skills. In the different roles such as lover, parent, breadwinner, employer, we need such different skills. But also, to deal with our own process of change, our internal urges, anger, drive to succeed, we also need learnt skills to handle them well. A person who doesn't handle anxiety or stress can easily fail in work or in relationships, despite being highly intelligent. Many people do not enter a relationship because of the problems it poses. Dr Evans suggests that dreams are the means by which we both practise and update our programs of survival. Our experience of the day may question or enhance our behaviour strategems for work success or relationships. Without the reprogramming occurring in dreams we would be stuck at one level of behavioural maturity. 'As we gain in experience, as our input gets richer and more diverse, we modify our programs rather than replace them with a completely fresh set.' See: **Humphrey, Nicholas**.

evening   Relaxation; quiet peace; time for oneself; nearness to the 'shadows' of the unconscious, the parts of Self we do not like. Sometimes the last years of life; old age. See: **autumn**.

evil   Usually refers to some of our own urges which we have judged as wrong because of moral or social values and have thus denied expression. Charles, in the example below, probably feels that what he identifies with as himself – his established values and beliefs – is threatened by what he senses beyond the door. Whatever threatens our 'I' or ego is often felt to be evil, even if they are natural urges. The unbalanced and real evils in the world, such as terrorising of individuals and minority groups, can of course be shown as the feeling of evil.

> *Example: 'At the top of the stairs is a small door, half opened as if inviting me to go up. I get an overpowering sense of something evil beyond the door just waiting for me.' Charles M.*

> *Example: 'I am lying on the floor in my bedroom with a towel over me. I am trying to hide and protect myself because I am terrified. There are four devils trying to get into my body and take over. My bedroom is going like a whirlpool around me, like evil all around me. I wake in a hot sweat and am terrified to go back to sleep.' Joanna (LBC).*

Joanna is most likely to be in conflict with her sexuality – the bedroom. When we fight with our own urges they often feel like external agencies – evil forces – attacking us. See: **aboriginal**; **active/passive**; *devil* under **archetypes**.

exams, being examined   Self-criticism or attempts to live up to moral or intellectual standards; habits of concern over accomplish-ments; worry about some coming test of self-value, such as a new job or new sexual partner. Examined by doctor: concern over health; desire for attention. See: **test**.

excrement   Feelings of repulsion; emotions or parts of experience which need to be let go of; infant level of self-expression and self-giving; physical need to have a healthy bowel. Like digested food, faeces can represent experience that was relevant and enjoyable at the time of consumption, but needs to be let go of; release of tension. Sometimes personal creativity; being able to let go of what you don't need – so can link with money and generosity; the primal level of our being; sensuality and infant sexuality. If shitting on someone or something: expressing desire to belittle them or to feel one's superiority; heaping unjust accusations on someone; bringing something which appeared powerful into perspective. Idioms: in the shit; feeling shitty; talking a lot of shit; being shat on. See: **toilet**.

exercise of the psyche   Just as our body can become stiff and unstimulated by lack of exercise, so our soul – our mind and emotions – can become atrophied through lack of use. Often everyday life may not challenge us enough, may not face us with fears or be such that we encounter new environments. Dreams are an area of human experience where a phenomenal range of experience can be allowed. Because dreams contain deeply felt emotions and fresh experience, such as mentally stimulating envir-onments and situations, they can truly be thought of as exercise for the soul.

explosion   Anger; dramatic release of energy in making chan-ges in self-expression; social upheaval; fear; orgasm.

eyes   See: *eyes* under **body**.

face See: *head* under **body**.

faeces See: **excrement**.

failure Comparison; competitiveness; sometimes depicts alter-natives – failure is the alternative to success. So the failure might be 'because'. See: *because factor* in **dream processing**; **falling**.

> *Example: 'I was in a race riding a horse but couldn't get to the starting gate in time. The others were way ahead of me jumping the fences. I couldn't catch up, and one fence I came to grew to a huge height and was like a steel barrier. I couldn't get over it and felt a failure.' Ron S.*

Ron had not done well at school, had not taken any particular training, had no steady relationship or children. In his late twenties Ron looked at his friends with steady jobs, married with a family, and felt a failure. From the dream he realised he was viewing life as a competitive race to succeed. This was stopping him from following his real interest – psychotherapy – which his family viewed as playing games. He could ride his horse into the fields and explore. He did, by going to America, training, and raising a family.

fair See: *hair* under **body**.

fairground One's public activity; the range of human fate – rich to poor, midgets to giants; 'swings and roundabouts' of life. <u>Carnival or fiesta</u>: dropping social or moral restraints; letting go; creativity;

social connections. See: **marketplace**.

falling   Some dream researchers suggest falling is one of the main themes in dreams. But in the sample used for this book, the words fall, falls, fell, falling, occur seventy-two times in a 1,000 dreams. The words find, finds, finding, found, occur 297 times. Whereas the words connected with looking and seeing occur 1,007 times.

During our development of growth we 'fall' from our mother's womb when ripe; being dropped by a parent must be our earliest sense of insecurity; we fall many times as we learn to stand and walk; as we explore our boundaries in running, climbing, jumping and riding, falling is a big danger. At times it could mean death. Out of this we create the ways falling is used in dreams. By learning to meet our insecurities, perhaps by using *Can I alter the dream to find greater satisfaction?* in **dream processing** we can dare more in life. This is in essence the same as meeting the fear of falling off our bike as we learn to ride. If we never master the fear we cannot ride.

General: loss of confidence; threat to usual sources of security such as relationships, source of money, social image, beliefs; tension. Sometimes loss of social grace; losing face; moral failure – falling into temptation; coming down to earth from a too lofty attitude; sexual surrender. Occasionally if we use fantasy and thought to get away from the 'real' world, or if we use entertainment, alcohol, socialising, to escape from inner pain and conflict, when these distractions are taken away the reality breaks through again there is a sense of falling and threat. So falling may depict this fear of being faced with our own inner feelings. Going fast to an edge and falling: could mean overwork and danger of breakdown of health. A person falling: wish to be rid of them; or anxiety in regard to what they represent. A child or son falling: see: *baby*; *son* and *daughter* under **family**. House falling down: personal stress, illness; personal change and growth due to letting old habits and attitudes crumble. Seeing things fall: sense of danger or change in regard to what is represented.

Example: 'I am sitting in a high window box facing outwards, with my son and a friend of his on my left. I feel very scared of falling and ask my son and his friend to climb back into the building. I feel too scared to move until they shift.' Trevor N.

At the time of the dream, for the first time in his life, Trevor was working as a full-time freelance journalist. His wife was out of work and his frequency of sales low enough to cause them to be running out of money. The building behind felt like a place he had worked from nine to five – security. Falling was fear of failure, getting into debt, dropping into the feelings of self-doubt and being incapable.

> *Example: 'I was on a road which led up to the hospital I was put in at three. I felt a sense of an awful past as I looked at the road. Then I was standing on the edge of a precipice or cliff. My wife was about four yards away near the road. I stepped in an area of soft earth. It gave beneath my weight and I sank up to my waist. I realised the cliff edge was unstable and the whole area would fall. I was sinking and shouting to my wife to help me. She was gaily walking about and made light of my call for help. I cried out again. Still she ignored me. I shouted again for her help. She took no notice and I sank deeper, the ground gave way and I fell to my death.' Barry I.*

Through being put in a hospital at three without his mother, Barry had a deep-seated fear that any woman he loved could desert him. His fall is the loss of any sense of bonding between him and his wife out of this fear. His death is the dying of his feeling of love and relationship, and the pain it causes. Understanding these fears Barry was able to leave them behind in later dreams and in life.

> *Example: 'Near where I stood in the school gymnasium was a diving board, about twenty feet off the ground. Girls were learning to dive off the board and land flat on their back on the floor. If they landed flat they didn't hurt themselves – like falling backwards standing up.' Barry I.*

The school is a learning situation. Once we learn to fall 'flat on our back' – i.e. fail – without being devastated or 'hurt' by it, we can be more creative. Dreams like this take falling into realms beyond fear. The following examples illustrate this.

> *Example: 'As I prayed I realised I could fly. I lifted off the*

ground about three feet and found I could completely relax while going higher or falling back down. So it was like free fall. I went into a wonderful surrendered relaxation. My whole body sagging, floating in space. It was a very deep meditative experience.' Sarah D.

Sarah has found an attitude which enables her to soar/dare or fall/fail without being so afraid of being hurt or dying emotionally. This gives a form of freedom many people never experience. This does not arise from denying or suppressing fears.

Example: 'I was standing outside my mother's house to the right. The ground in front had fallen away. The house was about to cave in. I felt no fear or horror. Instead I was thinking about new beginnings and the possibility of a new house.' Helen B.

Helen is here becoming more independent and leaving behind attitudes and dependency. See: **abyss**; **chasm**; **flying**; **house**.

family   From our family we learn most of the positive and negative patterns of relationship and attitudes toward living which we carry into daily events. Father's uncertainty in dealing with people, or his anxiety in meeting change, may be the roots of our own difficulties in those areas. If our mother is unable to develop a feeling contact with us, we will lack the experience of being able to love.

Our maturing process calls us to meet and integrate in some way our childhood desire, which includes sexual desire, for our parent of the opposite sex and rivalry mingled with dependence with the parent of the same sex. Even a missing parent, the mother or father who died or left, is a potent figure internally. An absence of a father or mother's love or presence can be as traumatic as any powerfully injuring event. Our parents in our dreams are an image, full of power and feeling, of the formative forces and experiences that created our identity. They are the ground, the soil, the bloody carnage, out of which our sense of Self emerged. But our identity cannot gain any real independence while still dominated by these internal forces of our creation. Heraclitus said we cannot swim in the same river twice. Attempting to repeat or compete with the virtues of a parent is a misapprehension of the true nature of our own personality. See: **individuation**.

brother General: oneself, or the denied part of Self, meeting whatever is met in the dream; feelings of kinship; sense of rivalry. In woman's dream – younger brother: outgoing but vulnerable Self; rivalry. Older brother: authority; one's capable outgoing Self. In man's dream – if younger brother: vulnerable feelings; oneself at that age. Older brother: experience; authority; feelings of persecution. Idioms: big brother; brothers in arms; blood brother. See: **boy**; **man**.

children and siblings Whether *brother, sister, daughter* or *son* (see each separate section), the most general use in our dreams is to depict an aspect of ourselves! It is almost universal to believe with great conviction that our dream is about the person in our dream. A mother seeing a son die in her dream often goes through great anxiety because there lurks in her a sense of it being a precognitive dream. Virtually everyone at some time dreams about members of close family dying or being killed. Lots of mothers dream this and their children live until they are eighty. But occasionally children do die. Is the dream then precognitive or is it coincidental?

> *Example: 'I was walking along a rather dusty track carrying my younger son who would be around ten months old and I was feeling rather tired. Suddenly I met a man who stopped to talk to me and commented I looked rather weary carrying the baby. He said, "Come with me and look over this wall and you will see such a sight that will gladden your heart." By standing on tiptoe I could just see over the wall and the sight I beheld took my breath away, it was so beautiful.' Johan E.*

Here Johan's son depicts the weight of responsibility she feels. The beauty is her own resources of strength in motherhood.

> *Example: 'I have just given birth to twins and they lay on the floor. We started to care for them. My mother took them to the doctor for his advice while I went to see my married sister who has two children. I met them there with the twins so that my sister could give her opinion on the babies. She had recent*

experience of childbirth and could tell us if the babies were good specimens.' Miss E.

Miss E. has no children of her own, so she is uncertain of her own capacity to have and raise them. The mother depicts her own mothering abilities which seek confidence from an authority figure. Her sister is her own nearest experience of childbirth. So out of what she has learnt from observing her sister, she is assessing her own qualities.

Most often the family member depicts the qualities in ourselves which we feel are part of the character of the person dreamt of. So the passionate one in the family would depict our passions; the intellectual one our own mind; the anxious one our hesitations. Use the questions in **dream processing** to define this. Having done this, can you observe what the dream depicts? For Miss E. it would be questions regarding motherhood.

> *Example: 'My daughter told me the only positive part of my work in a helping profession was with a woman who had turned from it to religion. There followed a long and powerful interchange in which I said she had as yet no mind of her own. She was dominated by her mother's anxiety and the medical rationalism of her training. When she had dared to step beyond her own anxieties to integrate the lessons of her own life, then I would listen again.' Desmond S.*

Desmond was divorced and struggling with his own pain and guilt about leaving his daughter while still a teenager. His daughter depicts this conflict between his feelings and his rational Self.

daughter One's relationship with the daughter; the daughter, or son, can represent what happens in a marriage between husband and wife. The child is what has arisen from the bonding, however momentary, of two people. In dreams the child therefore is sometimes used to depict how the relationship is faring. So a sick daughter might show the feelings in the relationship being 'ill'. In a mother's dream: often feelings of support or companionship; feelings of not being alone in the area of emotional bonds; or one's feeling area; responsibility; the ties of parenthood; oneself at that age; one's own urges, difficulties, hurts, which may still be operative. Also a comparison. The mother might see the daughter's youth, opportunity, and have feelings about that. So the daughter may represent her sense of lost opportunity and youth, even envy; competition in getting the desire of a man. <u>In a father's dream</u>: one's feeling Self; the feelings or difficulties about the relationship with daughter; the struggles one's own feeling Self goes through to mature; how the sexual feelings are dealt with in a family situation – occurs especially when she starts courting; sister; parental responsibility; one's wife when younger. <u>Someone else's daughter</u>: feelings about one's own daughter; feelings about younger women.

> *Example: 'I am standing outside a supermarket with heavy bags wearing my Mac, though the sun is warm. My daughter and two friends are playing music and everyone stops to listen. I start to write a song for them, but they pack up and go on a bus whilst I am still writing. I am left alone at the bus stop with my heavy burden of shopping, feeling incredibly unwanted.' Mrs F.*

Such dreams of the daughter becoming independent can occur as soon as the child starts school, persisting until the mother finds a new attitude. See: **child**; **woman**.

family group   The whole background of experience which makes up our values and views. This background is made of thousands of different obvious and subtle things such as social status; the number of books in the home; how parents feel about themselves; how they relate to life outside the family; whether dominant roles are encouraged; what nationality parents are; what unconscious social attitudes surround the family i.e. the master and servant, or dominating employer and subservient employee roles which typified England at the turn of the century, still colours many attitudes in the UK. Simply put our internal 'family' of urges and values; the overall feeling tone of our family life – security, domination, whatever it was; the unconscious coping patterns of the family. <u>Parents together in dream</u>: our general wisdom; background of information and experience from which we make important decisions or gain intuitive insights – negative or positive. Parents also depict the rules and often irrational disciplinary codes we learnt as a child which still speak to us from within, and perhaps pass on to our own children without reassessment. These include everything from 'Don't speak with your mouth full' to the unspoken 'masturbation is unholy'.

Hurting, burying or killing parent: in the example below, Audrey's height shows her as a child. She is releasing anger about the attitudes and situations her father forced 'down her throat'. To be free of the introverted restraints and ready-made values gathered from our parents, at some time in our growth we may kill or bury them in our dreams. Although some people are shocked by such dreams, they are healthy signs of emerging independence. Old myths of killing the chief so the tribe can have a new leader depict this process. When father or mother is 'dead' in our dream, we can inherit all the power gained from whatever was positive in the relationship. Seeing parent drunk, incapable or foolish: another means of gaining independence from internalised values or stultifying drives to 'honour' or admire father or mother. Dead parent in dream: either the beginning of independence from parent; repression of the emotions they engendered in us; our emotions regarding our parent's death; feelings about death. See: **dead people**.

Example: 'My father was giving me and another woman some medicine. Something was being forced on us. I started to hit and punch him in the genitals and when he was facing the other way in the backside. I seemed to be just the right height to do this and I had a very angry feeling that I wanted to hurt him as he had hurt me.' Audrey V.

Sometimes a dream about our family is a literal statement in symbols of what we sense is happening in the family.

Example: 'I was on a train with my family – wife and two daughters. The train was derailed but nobody was hurt and we got off the train. I was walking in a field near the train. I thought my wife and daughters had got back on the train. Then suddenly another train smashed into the rear of the derailed train making it concertina into a heap. I wasn't sure if my family were still on the train.' Roger.

Roger associated the theme of derailing with a change in direction – the change that was coming about through his children becoming independent. Some months later his wife and daughters left him. Divorce followed.

father General positive: authority; ability in the external world; family or social conventions; how we relate to the 'doer' in us; physical strength and protectiveness; the will to be. General negative: introverted aggression; dominance by fear of other people's authority; uncaring sexual drive; feelings of not being loved. See: *father* under **archetypes**; **man**.

grandparents Personal feelings connected with the grandparent; family traditions, such as established values or unconscious attitudes; spiritual values; old age; death.

husband General: depicts how you see the relationship with your husband; your relationship with your sexuality; sexual and emotional desire and pleasure; how you relate to intimacy in body, mind and spirit; habits of relationship developed with one's father.

> *Example: 'My recurring dream – some disaster is happening. I try to contact the police or my husband. Can never contact either. I try ringing 999 again and again and can feel terror, and sometimes dreadful anger or complete panic. I cry, I scream and shout and never get through! Recently I have stopped trying to contact my husband. I managed once to reach him but he said he was too busy and I would have to deal with it myself. I woke in a furious temper with him and kicked him while he was still asleep.' Mrs G.S.*

The husband here depicts Mrs S.'s feelings of not being able to 'get through' to her man. This is a common female dream theme, possibly arising from the husband not daring to express emotion or meet his partner with his own feelings. For Mrs S. this is an emergency. Although the dream dramatises it, there is still real frustration, anger and a break in marital communications.

Cannot find husband: many middle-aged women dream of 'losing' their husband while out with him, perhaps shopping or walking in a town somewhere. Sometimes the dream portrays him actually being killed. Mrs A.D. wonders if her dream was a premonition. It is more likely a form of practising the loss so it does not come as such a shock. The greatest shocks occur when we have never even considered the event – such as a young child losing its mother – an event it has never practised, not even in fantasy, so has no inbuilt shock absorbers. As most of us know, men tend to die before women and this information is in the mind of middle-aged married women. Mrs A.D. may have unconsciously observed slight changes in her husband's body and behaviour and therefore readied herself.

> *Example: 'I dreamt many times I lost my husband, such as not being able to find the car park where he was waiting and seeing him go off in the distance. I wake in a panic to find him next to me in bed. These dreams persisted and then he died quite suddenly. He was perfectly healthy at the time of the dreams and I wonder if it was a premonition of me really losing him.' Mrs A.D.*

dead husband: your memories and remaining emotions about your husband. The example below illustrates the 'psychic' meeting some women experience. In anything of an apparently psychic nature, we must *always* remember the unconscious is the great dramatist. It can create the drama of a dream in moments. In doing so it makes our inner feelings into apparently real people and objects *outside of us*. While asleep we lightly dismiss this amazing process as 'a dream'. When it happens while our eyes are open or we are near waking, for some reason we call it a ghost or psychic event. Yet the dream process is obviously capable of creating total body sensations, emotions, full visual impressions, vocalisation – what else is a dream? On the other hand, the dream process is not dealing in pointless imaginations. Many women tend to believe they have little sexual drive, so it is easier for G.L. to see her drive in the form of her husband. But of course, her husband may also depict how she felt about sex in connection with his 'sexual appetites'. It is a general rule, however, that our dream process will dramatise into a past life, or a 'psychic' experience, emotions linked with trauma, or sexual drive, which we find difficult to meet in the present.

> *Example: 'My dead husband came into my bedroom and got*

into bed with me to make love to me. I was not afraid. But owing to his sexual appetites during my married life with him I was horrified and resisted him with all my might. On waking I felt weak and exhausted. The last time he came to me I responded to him and he never came back again. This happened three times. The last time I don't think it was a dream. I was not asleep. I think it was his ghost.' G.L.

Other woman's husband: one's own husband; feelings about that man; desire for a non-committed relationship with less responsibility.

mother   General positive: feelings; being given to, looked after and fed; protection; feelings of dependence; ability in relationships; uniting spirit of family; how we relate to feelings in a relationship; strength to give of Self and nurture; intuition. General negative: will based on irrational likes and dislikes; opinion generated by anxiety or jealousy; domination by emotions; lack of bonding. See: *great mother* under **archetypes**; **woman**.

relatives   including uncle, aunt, cousin, nephew, niece etc. Usually an aspect of oneself relevant to the character of the person dreamt about. Sometimes represents one's family traditions – unconscious attitudes, conventions or even talents which are part of the unique psychological and social environment a family provides.

sister . General: feeling Self, or the lesser expressed part of Self; rival; feelings of kinship. In man's dream – younger sister: vulnerable emotions; rival for love of parents. Older sister: capable feeling Self; feelings of persecution. In woman's dream – younger sister: one's experiences at that age; vulnerable feelings; rival for parents' love. Older sister: capable feeling Self. Idioms: sisters under the skin. See: **girl**; **woman**.

son   General: extroverted Self; desires connected with self-expression; feelings connected with son; parental responsibility. Mother's dream: one's ambitions; potential; hopes; one's marriage – see example. Father's dream: oneself at that age; what qualities one sees in one's son; one's own possibilities; envy of youth and opportunities; rivalry. Someone else's son: feelings about one's own son; feelings about younger men. If dreaming of dead son: see: **dead**

people. See: **boy**; first example in **falling**; **man**.

Example: 'My wife and I were walking out in the countryside. I looked around suddenly and saw my four-year-old son near a hole. He fell in and I raced back. The hole was narrow but very deep. I could see water at the bottom but no sign of my son. I didn't know whether I could leap down and save him or whether it was too narrow. Then somehow he was out. His heart was just beating.' Richard H.

Richard had argued with his wife in such a way he feared for the stability of their marriage. The son represents what they had created together – a child, a marriage. The marriage survived, as his dream self-assessed it would.

Death of son: a mother often kills off her son in her dreams as she sees him make moves toward independence. This can happen from first day of school on as in the example below.

Example: 'I am on a very high bridge over an extremely wide and deep river with steep banks. My son does a double somersault over the railing, falls into the water. I think he is showing off. I am unable to save him. My son is eighteen and has started a structural engineering course at University.' Joyce H.

The showing-off suggests Joyce feels her son is doing daring things with his life, and the relationship in its old form dies.

the triangle   The example shows a typical flow of feeling toward another male. The other male here depicts Joan's desire to be attractive to other men. This is a danger signal unless one fully acknowledges the impulse.

Example: 'There were three of us. My husband, a male friend and I, all riding small, white enamel bikes. My husband proceeded slowly first with his back to us. Then my friend followed. Suddenly my friend ahead of me turned and gazed fully at me. He gave a glorious smile which lit up the whole of his face. I felt a great sense of well-being surge through me.' Joan B.

wife   General: depicts how you see the relationship with your wife; your relationship with your sexuality; sexual and emotional desire and pleasure; how you relate to intimacy in body, mind and spirit; your feeling, intuitive nature; habits of relationship developed with one's mother.

> *Example: 'My wife was trying to get me out of her life, and out of the house. It was as if she were attempting to push me into a feeling of tension and rejection which would make me leave.'*
> *David P.*

Out of childhood experiences in which his mother repeatedly threatened to give him away, David was finding it difficult to commit himself emotionally to his wife. In the dream his wife represents these feelings, so he sees her – his anxiety and pain – pushing him to break up the marriage. David 'broke up' the relationship with his mother by breaking his emotional bond with her.

> *Example: 'I was standing with my wife at the end of the garden of the house I lived in as a child. We were looking over the fence to the rising meadow beyond. She said, "Look at that bird in the tree there." On our right, in a small ash tree, an enormous owl perched. It was at least four feet high, the biggest bird I have ever seen. I recognised it in the dream as a greater hooded owl which was not native to our country. I was so excited I ran into the house to telephone someone – zoo, police, newspapers? – to tell them about the bird. I cannot remember contacting anyone, but felt the bird was there in some way to meet me. Also it was hungry and looking at next door's bantams. So I wondered what I could give it to eat.' David P.*

This shows the positive side of David's relationship with his wife. The garden represents the behaviour boundaries which arose from his childhood. But he is growing – the garden – and looking beyond them through his marriage. The amazing bird is the deep feelings he touches because he has a mate like any other natural creature. Out of his mating he becomes aware of drives to build a home – a nest – and give himself to his mate. These are natural and are a part of his unconscious or spiritual nature. The bird is a hooded owl which can see in the dark – the unconscious – meaning David is realising things he had never 'seen' before. The bird is masked because David through loving is learning to put his ego aside, which is a necessity for touching the wider dimension of life or the unconscious. The hunger of the bird shows an intimate detail of what David has learnt from his wife. She had been working as a waitress and bringing home pieces of chicken for him, saved from her own meal. The spiritual side of David wants to develop this quality of self-giving, which his wife's love had helped him see.

Example: 'I have been a widower since January 1979, having married on October 1941. I continually dream I am in London where my business was. I am walking the streets with my wife and suddenly I see her ahead of me in a yellow raincoat and hat. I call her and try to catch up, but suddenly she vanishes. In spite of calling and searching I cannot find her.' Douglas G.

This is a common theme dreamt by widowers or widows – disappearance of spouse. Douglas has 'lost' his wife. His dream shows the paradox of love after death of a partner. His love is still there years after her death. He is possibly still trying to love his wife as an externally real person, so his feelings can make no connection. To meet what actually remains of his wife, within himself, he would need to face his own internal grieving, emotions and *all the feelings, memories, angers and beauty* which make up the living remains of his wife within him.

The first wife: The dreamer in the example below is now feeling easier about her husband's first relationship. The first wife represents her sense of competing for her husband's affections, even though his 'first woman' was dead.

Example: 'I was with my husband and our three children. About two or three yards to our right stood my husband's first wife – she died about a year before I first met him. I remember feeling she no longer minded me being with him, so I put my arms around him from the back and felt more secure and comfortable with him.' Mrs N.S.

famous people   General: one's own potential, often unacknowl-edged, and projected onto dream character; a parent; depending on how you relate to the famous person – your own ability to accept yourself as respected; desire for success. Sometimes the person may, because of their life or role, represent a particular quality such as courage, love, 'ruling' drives in life, authority, etc. Actor/actress: one is acting a role; wanting attention; deception. Queen: often one's mother; a feeling or drive ruling your life; wanting approval. King: father; thinking; authority; power to command. See: **king**; **queen**.

Famous people can be seen as social guinea pigs. Collectively we expose them to enormous amounts of money, sexual opportunity, drugs, alcohol and tremendous social and commercial pressures. Then we examine every part of their life to see how well they cope. Millions then identify with the image they portray of how to deal with reality at its best and worst. The famous person in our dream might therefore represent our coping mechanism.

> *Example: 'A film star I admire came and lay beside me in the night. He told me he loved me and would stay with me. I knew he was living with a woman who had borne his child, but he told me he was going to tell her he was leaving her. In the morning we walked along the road where I live to tell the woman.' Sharon.*

Sharon processed her dream and saw the film star as her own strength and determination to further her career as a dancer. Being eighteen she was faced with the decision of whether to become a wife and mother – the other woman – or put those urges into her work. In her dream she chose to be fully involved in her dancing.

fantasy and dreaming   The world of dreams is sometimes thought of as purely a fantasy world, irrelevant to the so-called real world. Fantasy, whether in dreams or in waking, is not of course disconnected from the rest of our life. When we imagine a fight scene our glandular system responds, along with our muscles. While dreaming this is even more deeply true, so fantasy has great physical reality in this way.

Unconsciously we are continually controlled by our fantasy. Our ideas and concepts of ourselves for instance have no physical reality at all. They are a sort of massive fantasy with reality only at a human emotional and mental level. Yet people kill themselves out of such feelings. They strut or cringe out their life because of this internal fantasy of who they are and what life is. Thus fantasy is of enormous importance in our lives. It has wonderful or terrible power, depending upon how we relate to it. We certainly need to know something of how to use it wisely.

What I am calling fantasy is the greatest disease and killer of our times – perhaps of all times. AIDS, cancer, heart disease and cholera all rolled into one kill fewer people than the war arising from the fantasy or mental illness of tribal and national identity; the mental mirage and illness of religious intolerance; the dream of ethnic cleansing. This is the great killer humans face – the killer in the mind. The fantasy monsters that fasten on the human soul and destroy it. These are the nightmares we meet in our dreams.

fare   The price one pays to achieve a goal; getting the right attitude or stance. See: **ticket**.

farm, **farmyard**   Care or expression of our natural drives such as sexuality, parenthood, love of fellowship; the down-to-earth side of Self; area of our animal propensities where territorial fighting, fighting over mate, etc., are expressed. See: *farmer* under **roles**.

fat person   Defences used against anxiety or feelings of inadequacy; healthy, jolly feelings; sensuality. Becoming fat: pregnancy; carrying 'more weight'.

fax machine, **fax**   May represent things, ideas, messages, imagery, emerging out of the unconscious; the previously unexpected arising out of one's unconscious contact with other people and society; communication with someone. See: **telephone**.

fear   See: **emotions**, **mood**.

fence   The fence often depicts our sense of social barriers or class barriers; need for privacy; territorial feelings; also our boundaries in relationships which might prevent us daring to express ourselves or be creative. Idioms: rush one's fences; wrong side of the fence; sit on the fence. See: **wall**.

> *Example: 'I saw that we had got into a fenced-off area where the gentry landowners parked their cars while they went shooting. I could see the landowner and his car beyond the fence looking angry that I was on his property. I thought I would break through the fence with the elephant, but then saw a low area which the elephant easily stepped over.' Arthur P.*

ferry   General: movement toward change; connections in a relationship; often associated with ferry across the River Styx and death. If ferry you know: consider why you use the ferry, what you associate with it. See: **bridge**.

field   fields often appear with animals and suggest the dreamer's contact with what is natural in themselves. Also freedom from social pressure; one's sense of oneself when away from other people, with one's own natural inclinations; field of activity or study; feeling states – depending on condition of field, cloudy, bright, overgrown. Field across river or very green fields: death or the dreamer's conception of spiritual realm. See: **landscapes**.

fight   Usually, as in the example below, the dreamer's anger or frustration; may express difficulties in regard to independence or self-confidence; desire to hurt another person or damage their reputation.

A fight also depicts, as in the second example, fighting for our space; our values of honour; we may fight for survival or for our health, fight crime, resist criminal impulses; we may also feel attacked by another person's opinions; assaulted by sexual desire; fight against depression; have a conflict over moral issues. Idioms: fight it out; fight like cat and dog; look for a fight. See: **attack**; **war**.

> *Example: 'Some three years ago I had constant dreams with my mother. We were nearly always in some sort of argument or fight.' Marjorie B.*

> *Example: 'I realised a door had been left open that should have*

been locked and I felt very vulnerable. Suddenly a sword of light appeared in my hand and a voice told me that it was my weapon to fight the evil.' Mrs D.B.

film An aspect of our own past or character which we do not wish to acknowledge – it is easier therefore to view as not about oneself. An attempt to view oneself objectively; images of Self and behaviour projected from the unconscious; one of our means of escaping from reality.

film star See: **famous people**.

find, found Usually, as in the first example, to discover, realise, become aware of some aspect of oneself and gain access to or use of it. One might be living with constant resentments about one's past or present situation, and then 'find' release from this for a day, yet not be conscious how it was achieved. The dream might attempt to define this. Or it might be a new idea you realise unconsciously in sleep.

Example: 'I went into a cellar. It was rather cave like. I had to scramble to get into it. The entrance was difficult to find, but I had discovered it many years before and been in lots of times. I found objects in the cellar and was looking for something.' Tony C.

Example: 'Then I was with my dead father and was showing him a handful of exotic bank notes I had found in the building. They were £100 notes. I wasn't sure if the money was legal tender or not. The notes had unusual design.' Andy (LBC).

Andy has found a sense of his own value – the money – but is not sure if other people also value him. The dream illustrates the attempt to 'find a place' in society. The effort to search and find it frequently to do with one's own identity and what one is searching through is one's experience, as in Tony's cellar above, or the example below.

Example: 'I was looking into the crowd in the film to find me

*and it was like looking at a snapshot, it felt very important that
I find me, I saw my green slacks just showing, right at the back
of the crowd.' Trudy K.*

<u>Idioms</u>: find oneself; find fault; find out; find one's bearings. See:
look; **see**.

fire   <u>General</u>: passion; sexuality; anger; desire; burning feelings
such as resentment or frustration; our desire to destroy. Also our life
process, often described as a flame which burns forever through
different generations but leaves only ash behind; our vital energy;
occasionally refers to physical illness. <u>The fireplace</u>: homeliness; the
womb, <u>Underground flames</u>: unconscious emotions or desires
which one may need to face for real growth. <u>Fire in the sky</u>: great
changes in viewpoint; meeting the next step in maturity. Artemidorus said fire in the sky meant war or famine. For the Africans a
bush fire meant war.

> *Example: 'I was in a small terraced house with a friend I had
> known years earlier. It was her house, there were two or three
> children in it. Suddenly, it caught fire. I wanted to stay and
> put the fire out but she did not. She dragged me outside and
> down the street. We saw the house burn down. I had this
> dream the day I got home from hospital, after undergoing a
> hysterectomy.' Mrs G.*

Here the fire depicts the consuming feelings of loss regarding Mrs
G.'s childbearing function. Also the loss of an area or era of life.

> *Example: 'I found quite a large, old fireplace. I asked my
> husband if he would like a fire. I thought it would be cosy if we
> both enjoyed the fire together. Woke up with warm feelings
> towards my husband, he reached out to me.' Dinah Y.*

Here fire is not only homemaking and human warmth, but also
sexuality.
<u>Idioms</u>: too hot to handle; you burn me up; baptism of fire;
between two fires; fire up; go through fire and water; play with fire;
under fire; the burning bush.

fish, sea creatures General: when we will to speak or move, unconscious physical and psychological impulses and processes occur to produce the response. These deeply unconscious processes are often depicted by fish. Also the attitudes and urges we have in common with humanity – the collective unconscious – and the impulses or insights arising therefrom can therefore represent the Self or Christ; sexual drive in connection with reproduction, the many little fishes being sperm. In this sense we are the fish which swam the incredible journey and grew into a human, but is still on the odyssey of life and death. The fish may be the wisdom we have not yet brought to consciousness regarding our personal journey in time and eternity.

Fishing: creating a receptive state of consciousness which allows the deep insights or processes to become known; trying to find spiritual nourishment. Eating fish: integrating our inner realisations; partaking of Christ. Eaten by fish: feeling threatened by the unconscious; threat of losing conscious or rational direction of life. Dead fish: non-expression of basic urges. Many little fish in round container: could be sperm or depict becoming or wanting to become pregnant.

Example: 'Last week I suddenly started having a recurring dream. In it I woke, walked downstairs, went into the kitchen and looked in the kettle. It was full of little fish.' Karen (LBC).

The fact that Karen goes 'downstairs' suggests the lower part of her body and the shape of the kettle, which is a round container, make it likely this dream is about pregnancy.

crab The shell of brittle emotions we guard ourselves with; grasping or hurtful attitudes. Being nipped by crab: physical or psychosomatic pain or even illness caused by being too tight or self-protective.

dolphin Because dolphins are wild creatures of the sea that actively develop a relationship with humans, they are often taken to represent the contact and relationship we have with the deeply unconscious natural forces within. Such dreams suggest life is not simply operating blindly, but reaches out to us if we reach out to it.

<u>General</u>: powerful unconscious energies in us; conscious awareness of one's link with all life; contact with the one life within all things.

Example: 'About a month ago I decided to terminate a relationship which had lasted more than twenty years. Two nights after making this decision my body took over at night and started rocking, banging, pushing, the back arching. These alternated with rest and floods of soothing energy pulsating through my whole system. In the morning my back felt totally open and vulnerable. Soon after this event I had this dream – I was swimming in a broad river of clear, warm water full of life energy. It was deep and the river had rock cliffs rising either side of it, forty metres high. Above that I could see the green of some trees in the sunlight. Further upstream the walls of rock joined and formed a tunnel.

I was swimming on my back when suddenly I saw a huge fish. It was about four metres long, coming out of a cave towards me. I panicked. Then I thought it might be harmless and went on swimming quietly. It was a dolphin, and very gently it swam behind my back and covered it, hugging me from behind. I lay absolutely quiet embraced by the powerful and gentle energy of this being. Energy was pouring into my back. Finally I reached round and touched the fin of the dolphin. It was like thick velvet.' Rhea.

jellyfish   Feelings arising from the unconscious which might be painful/sting the dreamer, bring a sense of helplessness/spinelessness, or are from a non-verbal level of memory.

octopus   Feeling trapped by one's mother; dependence upon mother; one's own possessiveness. Hadfield (*Dreams and Nightmares*) says that a baby often seizes upon its mother's breast with this feeling. The octopus can also symbolise any unconscious fear which may drag us into its realm of irrational terror.

shark   Fear of death; fear of the collective unconscious, or loss of Self in the impersonal Whole or All; the power of the unconscious – so its protectiveness; someone who is a 'shark' or unscrupulous.

shellfish   Often the defensive shell we use to avoid hurt or sexual or emotional involvement; the female sexual organs. <u>Oyster</u>: also defensive shell, but may link with sexuality through common association; tight-lipped; secretive; frigidity. See: *crab* above; *pearl* under **jewels**. <u>Lacking shell</u>: our naked vulnerability.

whale   The powerful evolutionary drive involved in reproduction which lies behind individual male or femaleness; the beneficent power of the collective unconscious.

> *Example: 'I was leaning over the settee with my hands cupped under my chin looking out of the window. The view was spectacular, in that it was as if the house was situated on top of a cliff overlooking a huge bay, shaped like a horseshoe, with the house in the middle. From the sea suddenly, coming into the bay I could see three enormous whales making their way toward me. As I was staring in amazement they began to transform themselves and come up out of the water as three giant Viking-like figures. They were so huge that the water only came up to their knees and everything was moving so slowly as they waded toward me. It was the most awe-inspiring thing I had ever seen in my life.' Sue B.*

The bay, the beautiful sea, the sperm? Whales/men, show Sue touching the most primordial yet inspiring aspects of her own womanhood and urge to love.

<u>Idioms</u>: big fish; big fish in a small pond; cold fish; fish for compliments; fish out of water; queer fish; smell something fishy. See: *Christ* under **archetypes**; **religion and dreams**; **sea**.

flames   Life itself – our life as it moves through experience leaving only memories; passion or anger. <u>Idioms</u>: add fuel to the flames; old flame; the old illness/love flared up. See: **candle**; *fireman* under **roles**.

floating   <u>On water</u>: relaxation; opening to power beyond the ego; being indecisive; being carried along by events. See: **flying**.

flood   Depression could be seen as an inundation of negative emotions; anxiety a flood of fear; an overflow of usually unconscious or uncontrolled feelings and urges into consciousness. The flood can of course be of positive feelings like love. In any case, floods can be enriching to growth if handled well. In many flood dreams it is positive energy the dreamer is anxious about.

A flood dream for Artemidorus indicated misfortune in litigation or ill-tempered masters, and it has virtually the same meaning for the Africans.

flowers   General: sense of beauty; flowering of a feeling quality or ability; the sexual organs, depending on shape.

> *Example: 'So for the third time I held the woman and made love. The woman's vagina was like a flower – I don't mean to look at, but in physical sensation. My penis felt like it was penetrating petals of flesh and touching with great pleasure a central receptive area. I was left with the feeling of being able to make love again and again without any negative effects. It was a very positive and healthy feeling.' John T.*

Also feelings of pleasure; youthfulness; time of flowering. Bud: penis or vagina in the sense of growing male or female qualities. Giving flowers: giving love and tenderness. Many flowers growing: feelings of well-being and relaxation. Dead flowers: death or old age; dying love or abilities. Giving dead flowers: wishing someone dead or out of one's life; dead feelings. Lotus and lily: as these grow from mud, through water to the air and light, they sometimes represent our wholeness and growth, showing our connection with the universe as we develop individually. Rose: love; femininity. When the shape or number of petals is featured: a flowering of a new aspect of the Self. See: **castrate**; **colours**; **growth**; **plants**; **shapes**.

flying   The example below illustrates how much will, effort and learning can be involved in flying in dreams. This aspect of flying connects with the gaining of independence and the expression of one's potential. We are all born into a certain paradigm or 'reality'. At one time, part of the 'reality' for most Britons was that anyone without a white skin was a heathen or savage. At other times the 'reality' has been that anything heavier than air could not fly. Meteors did not exist because theory discounted them – and so on. To break free of such paradigms and from the 'gravity' or hold our parental and social authority has on us, to find a measure of emotional and intellectual freedom takes the sort of will, effort and learning depicted.

Example: 'During childhood I learnt to fly in a long sequence of dreams, each linked very clearly to the last. I would go to the nearby churchyard and in the beginning I would run along as fast as I could then jump and just manage to extend the jump by a great effort of will. In subsequent practices I managed gradually to extend the jump for many yards; and eventually I could skim along indefinitely. The next stage though was to extend my height, and this took enormous effort of will and body. I made active swimming motions and climbed, but only held altitude with great and constant concentration. With further practice still, this clumsy mode of flying was left behind as I learnt to use pure motivation or will to lift me into the air and carry me easily and gracefully wherever I wished. At this stage my flying was swift, mobile and without struggle.' Jason V.

Flying expresses also the dealing with other internal influences which hold us down, such as self-doubt, anxiety, depression.

Example: 'I was flying. I felt nervous at first that I would fall down, but not afraid. I soon became confident and felt very happy and wanted the sensation to continue. I was flying over a building, could have been a small church, crematorium or graveyard but did not feel afraid or upset. When I woke I lay in bed and tried very hard to keep the feelings with me and, for reasons unknown, I do not wish to forget it.' Mrs S.M.

In flying, Mrs S.M. is finding a way to look at death – the graveyard – which gives her a different viewpoint, a different feeling reaction to it, and she doesn't want to lose that precious newly learnt view. In their maturing process, some people learn to see their thoughts and emotions as things they experience rather than what they are. For instance, I might feel a failure and thus believe I am indeed a failure. Or I might recognise the feeling of failure as simply an emotion I sometimes have which I can choose a reaction to. This brings the sort of new viewpoint and freedom seen in the above example.

> *Example: 'I was in a building with a group of people. I was being chased and suddenly I fly up in the air to escape my pursuers.' Michael O.*

Learning independence and the ability to make decisions despite what others feel may be done by ignoring our own feelings. This may be achieved by always keeping busy; never having quiet moments alone; filling empty periods with entertainment or company; smoking, drinking alcohol, taking sedatives or tranquillisers; rigid positive thinking. Then, as Michael does in his dream, we fly from issues we are pursued by instead of resolving them. This may lead us to the extremes of being either rigidly materialistic or as rigidly ethereal. In either case we lose contact with everyday human issues and may begin to have the 'escape'-type flying dream, or out-of-body experiences.

> *Example: 'I knew I could fly. I picked up one of the young women I felt love for and flew with her. Laughingly I felt like superman, and flew easily.' Simon W.*

Flying alone occurs most frequently, showing the independent aspects of flying. But because it often involves our positive feelings of pleasure, flying may depict our sexuality as above, especially aspects of it expressing freedom from social norms and restraints.

> *Example: 'I was floating atop a tree near houses and a rising walkway. I was saying to people around the tree that I had found something wonderful. Reaching out my hand I told them they could join me if they accepted this possibility in themselves. Some thought it was a publicity campaign, but were enjoying the spectacle. A few reached out and were immediately with me, until there were about six of us, men and women. We joined hands, experiencing a most amazing sense of well-being. Then we slowly and effortlessly flew to a great height, leaving a trail of coloured smoke which could be*

seen for miles. It was to demonstrate the triumph of the human spirit. We then descended and were going somewhere else to show others.' Margareta H.

Transcendence is also depicted by flying. The tree is Margareta's personal life. She is at the growing tip, transcending, leaving behind her past. Being high in flight or on a hill or mountain also represents the action of seeing our life as a whole, having a sense of our overall direction and destiny, our essential Self. This frequently gives rise to the drive to give of one's best to others, as Margareta does in leaving behind a sign – the spire of colour.

Some researchers believe flying dreams often precede lucid dreams. Idioms: fly by night; flying high; send flying. See: **hill**; **lucidity**, **awake in sleep**; **out-of-body experience**.

flying saucer   See: **UFO**.

fog   Confusion; indecision; inability to see the real issues in yourself and your environment. Idioms: not the foggiest.

follow   To follow: is to be influenced by; have an attraction to; pursue; seek something; look for. Nearly always suggests we are being led by an attitude, hope or habit and not consciously assessing present needs. Following animal: led by basic drives, intuition or instinct. Following opposite sex: led by desire for satisfaction in love. Being followed: taking the initiative; pursued by memory, pain, guilt; ambition or a continuing sense of hope, doom, hunch, instinct. Followed by opposite sex: memories of old love. Followed by animal: see: **chased**.

Example: 'The group I followed on the Underground got off. I followed them. An elderly woman friend told me they were going home, not to my destination.' Debbie T.

Debbie processed her dream and realised she was following old habits – the friend – which weren't taking her where she wanted.

food   There is food for the mind; food for thought; food for the body; and spiritual nourishment. We can digest information or experience, the latter being food for our growth as an individual. Food can represent any of these. General: something we might take or are taking into ourselves – such as experience of a relationship, qualities of another person, sexual pleasure, social pleasure; warning about health in regard to what is eaten. Frequent dreams about eating: suggesting a great hunger for something; perhaps a compensation for dieting or problems with eating. Food in connection with a particular person: being nourished by or hungry for relationship with them; enjoyment of sexuality with them. Giving food: giving of oneself, time, love, work, sex. Stealing food: dishonest about needs in a relationship; feelings of being parasite.

bread Experience; everyday life. Given a slice of bread: sex; generosity.

cake Sensual enjoyment.

fruits Fruits of experience or effort and what emerges from them. Soft or luscious fruits such as fig or peach: may represent female genitals. Long fruit such as banana: may depict male sexuality. Apple: temptation; breast.

meals Social pleasure; acceptance; social intercourse. If alone: independence; loss of family ties; lack of social relationships or outside stimulus.

meat Physical or worldly satisfaction or needs. Raw meat: quoted from *Dreams and Dreaming* by Norman Mackenzie: 'It was found that some themes not only appeared in widely separated cultures, but that they also evoked very similar responses. C.G. Siligman, for instance, found that dreams about raw meat occurred in Ireland, Switzerland, China, Greece, the Ukraine, Nigeria, Tanganyika, Borneo, and Achin in Sumatra – and that in all these places such a dream was associated with some impending misfortune. In the Ukraine it presaged a burial; in the Zungeru district of Nigeria, the death of a friend; in Tanganyika, it was a symbol of a funeral feast. The origins of this common belief may be simple: for many poor societies, the consumption of large quantities of meat would be limited to funerals and similar occasions and the association would therefore be direct.'

milk   Self-giving; baby needs.

olive   Peace; kindness, because the oil can be pressed from the olive.

sweets   Sensual pleasure; pleasures in life; special love.

> *Example: 'A lot of sweets, brightly wrapped, were being put into my open hands. All I saw of the giver were his hands. Beautiful, big, gnarled hands of a working man.' Alex U.*

Alex saw the hands as the holiness of everyday human experience, especially regarding self-giving, as in parenthood, love and work – the hands of Christ we forget. Alex doesn't eat sweets, so they represent pleasures he seldom allows himself, the pleasure of everyday life and love.

vegetables   Basic needs; material satisfaction. If long like a carrot: male sexuality. If a woman's dream – feelings about sex with a male. If a man's dream – his own sexuality. Onion: something to cry about; also the different layers of oneself – inner Self, outer Self.

See: **eating**; *wife* under **family** second example; **restaurant**; **salad**.

foreign countries   Different attitude; different mental or emotional 'climate' than one's norm. One's personal associations or ideas about any particular country need to be explored. Use the questions in **dream processing**.

foresight, **foreseeing death of relatives**   Many people report dreaming of events before they occur. Such foresight is often about problems such as death or illness, but can also be about positive things.

> *Example: 'I have dreams that come true. I foresaw the birth of my cousin's triplets and named them correctly – when everyone expected twins. I foresaw my father's death from heart failure two weeks before it happened. At the time of his heart attack – daytime – I kept hearing a phone that didn't exist ring, and knew it was to call me to him.' A.*

Such dreams portray us as like fingers. We move about independently and believe we have nothing to do with the other fingers and are different to the toes. But when we take our awareness below the surface, we discover a great body of mind and experience that links us all. This one life behind our separate lives seems to know a great deal about the unconscious state of our body and personality.

Love and care links us with this knowledge, so occasionally we see where someone's life is taking them. It is better called foresight than prediction. Some people feel afraid of the experience, but those who touch it deeply have an awareness of great love for all living things and a sense of existing always. See: **ESP in dreams**; **precognition**.

forest   See: **tree**.

forgetfulness of dreams   See: **science of dreams**.

fortress   See: **house**; **buildings**.

fountain   The process of life; flow of consciousness into awareness; joy of collective life. <u>Drinking from and bathing in</u>: the separate sense of Self experiencing wider awareness arising from the unconscious.

Freud, Sigmund (1856–1939)   When Freud, as a qualified doctor and neurologist, became interested in psychology, it was still a branch of philosophy. He gave to it a geography of the human mind, showed the influence the unconscious has upon waking personality, and brought dreams to the attention of the scientific community. His book, *The Interpretation of Dreams*, was a turning point in bringing concepts on dreaming from a primitive level to alignment with modern thought. With enormous courage and against much opposition he showed the place sexuality has in the development of conscious self-awareness.

Freud defined dreams as being:

• 'Thoughts in pictures' – a process of thinking while asleep.
• 'Ego alien'. They have a life and will which often appears to be other than our conscious will. This led older cultures to believe

they were sent by spirits or God.

- 'Hallucinatory'. We believe the reality of the dream while in it.
- 'Drama'. Dreams are not random images. They are 'stage managed' into very definite, sometimes recurring, themes and plots.
- 'Moral standards'. Dreams have very different moral standards than our waking personality.
- 'Association of ideas'. In dreaming we have access to infant or other memories or experience we would find very difficult to recall while awake.

Freud originally said that two of the main functions of a dream were wish fulfilment and an expression of the 'primary process of human thinking' unaffected by space, time and logic. Later, in considering recurring dreams which re-enact a recent traumatic incident, he agreed that dreams were not only an expression of the 'pleasure principle'. W.H.R. Rivers, studying dreams connected with war neuroses, saw such dreams as attempts to resolve current emotional problems.

Although there is still controversy regarding whether there can be a valid 'dream dictionary', Freud himself saw dream symbols as having consistent meaning so frequently that one could attribute an interpretation to them independently of the dreamers' associations. See: **abreaction**; **Adler, Alfred**; **birds**; **displacement**; **door**; **dream analysis**; **dream as therapist**; **Fromm, Eric**; **hallucinations, hallucinogens**; **hypnosis and dreams**; **Jung, Carl**; **lucidity**; **plot of dreams**; **secret of universe dreams**; **unconscious**; **wordplay, puns**.

frog   See: **reptiles – lizards**, **snakes**.

Fromm, Erich   A New York psychoanalyst who stands between Jung and Freud in his view of dreams. In his book about dreams, *The Forgotten Language*, he says they express both the biological drives and urges which are the substructure of our self-awareness, as well as the wisdom and spirituality that transcends waking thought.

front   The more public or expressed part of one's nature, or attitudes used to meet 'the world'; a 'font' or façade, used to create an impression; the point of stress where we as people contact others and meet impacts, and so are more vulnerable. Also what is in front can mean the future. Sometimes, as with the front of a car or the front door of a house – especially if bonnet or door is being opened – depicts sexual nature. Idioms: a lot of front; in front of; putting up a good front. See: **back**.

frontier, **border**   Making great changes in life; decisive changes; meeting a very different Self and thus a new experience of life.

frozen   See: **ice**.

functions of dreams   Over the years many theories to explain the 'why' of dreams have been put forward. These range from dreams being messages from spirits; being results of food eaten prior to sleep; the mind freewheeling nonsensically; the garbage disposal system of the mind; suggestions from waking experience; a computer reprogramming for the brain; to Freud's wish fulfilment and Jung's compensation theory.

If we do not argue any particular theory, however, then perhaps we see dreams as having a much wider function. The most primal drives observable are *survival, growth, reproduction.* Other urges, such as eating, social position, curiosity, are secondary. The human animal appears to have survived and reproduced more capably after the development of self-awareness, language and reasoning. With or without these, we remain an animal with a psycho-biological nature. All animals are known to dream. All animals share a certain situation. They have an internal world out of which arises impulses to eat, to mate, to avoid danger and feeling reactions, anger, fear, anticipation. They have an external world which confronts them with real survival dangers, sources of food, a mate, changes in environmental conditions. A dream lies somewhere between these two worlds.

We can think of the human personality as being like a special sort of cavity or organism into which all these influences are dropped or are thrown. Physical sensations, internal drives and emotions, language, social rules; religious ideas; prompts to make decisions; news of war; massive media and advertising information, are all dropped in. The cavity/organism has to deal with it, but as it is a mixture of things, many of which are in opposition, some sort of balance has to be kept. But how? And it cannot be simply a matter of throwing out all of one sort or aspect of things. Eradicating the memory of criticism might make us more calm, but it would limit the process of psychological growth which has survival value.

Dreams can be seen to be connected with our survival and self-regulating process. Because this involves all aspects of oneself and one's experience, one cannot give dreams a single definition. They probably have many secondary functions, such as: an interface to balance the internal and external influences. To compensate between the inner needs and outer reality – a baby may miss its feed, to cope with this primal need, it may dream of being fed. Traumatic or exterior dangerous events, which cannot be processed imme-diately, can be stored and dealt with, experimented with or abreacted while asleep. In higher mammals, infant traumas can be stored and dealt with in sleep when or if a stronger ego develops. To meet 'the loneliness and isolation of consciousness' or fears of death, the dream can link the waking Self with its unconscious sense of unity or God. To meet survival needs of primitive human beings prior to rational thought, the dream probably acted as a computer synthesising experience and information, giving rise to creative solutions to hunting or social situations, presented as sleeping or waking imagery. This may explain why many primitive people say skills such as farming, weaving, writing, were told them by a vision of a god/goddess.

If we realise that the dream is an end result of a process which produces it, we are able to see that the 'process' – the survival function which regulates, compensates, links, problem-solves – can be accessed without meeting the dream. See: **Adler**; **dream process as computer**; **Freud**; **Jung**; **sleep movements**.

funeral   General: feelings about one's own death; very occasion-ally warning about health of person buried; wanting the buried person out of one's life. One's own funeral: it is a common dream to watch one's own funeral. It depicts your own philosophy about your end. May also remind you of what you want to do while alive; desire for sympathy from family; retreat from the world; a feeling of deadness in life. Burying yourself: leaving an old way of life or old Self behind. Someone else's funeral: a wish they were dead; a wish to be rid of them. It is often unconsciously used as an easy way out of a relationship – to fantasise that they are dead. It avoids the responsibility of making your wishes known. See: second example under **death**. Parents' funeral: difficulties with or move towards independence; exploring the feeling of their loss; repressing or letting go of the painful past. See *death and rebirth* under **archetypes**; **buried**; **death**.

furniture, furnishings   General: attitudes or habits developed from family or home life, especially if it is a piece of furniture from family home or past dwelling; the attitudes, beliefs we 'furnish' our mind with; notions about Self; self-image.

bed, mattress   Bed is an important symbol to understand. It so often shows exactly what we are doing in our subtle areas of relationship; our close relationship; intimacy; sexual pleasure; rest; a desire to get away from the world, to withdraw into oneself; passivity; sensual rather than sexual contact; sickness; privacy. Sometimes it represents sleep and meeting our unconscious – or torture – because in bed we may be tortured by insomnia, worries, physical pain. Also our life situation – made your bed, now lie on it. Bed is one of the commonest symbols in dreams.

In the example below the man is wrestling with his desire for pleasure and his sense of commitment; but also, whether he will keep his pleasure for himself or share it with his wife. Idioms: bed of nails; bed of roses; go to bed with; make one's bed and lie on it. See: example in **bed wetting**; **contraceptive**.

> *Example: 'I sit on a bed. Near me, looking at a book I am holding is a woman I know, Jane. I realise as we talk that her foot is touching mine. As my wife is on my left across the room I feel uncomfortable about this. Now Jane has her left hand on my penis. I have only underpants on. The contact is pleasant and undemanding, but I feel more and more ill at ease. I feel Jane is not having any respect for my relationship with my wife and start to tell her so.' Mr B.S.*

carpet   Sometimes depicts one's financial state, bare floorboards being poverty; can be the colour or design which are important; comfort or lack of it in life – do you feel satisfied with Self; a cover up; feeling of being walked on. Idioms: sweep something under the carpet; on the carpet; roll out red carpet.

chair   Passive, relaxed attitude; inactivity; receptivity or openness; escapism. Placing of chair in group: sense of status. Wheelchair: an in-valid situation; a sense of weakness. If pushing someone else: seeing Self as carrying an invalid. See: example in **autumn**.

cupboard or wardrobe   Memory; resources; different roles you play or attitudes and emotions expressed if wardrobe; hidden memories and emotions – such as skeleton in the cupboard; womb. Open or closed or trapped in cupboard: whether we are 'open or closed' to other people; trapped in old feelings; sense of isolation.

table   General: social connection with others; communal activity; everyday certainties which support our activities such as confidence you will get paid at the end of the week; one's attitude toward the inner and exterior community; an altar or self-giving – if table is bare, perhaps not giving much of Self. Quality of table: the quality of your relationship with others. Place at table: self-image of your status. Dressing table: one's attempts to create a good social image.

> Example: *'Then I was in a place where we were having a staff party. Not very big but people were sitting at tables eating, a party mood. I sat with my child, maybe youngest son, no one else at the table. I felt I didn't wish to get involved with the others, the feeling I often get at parties, just alone in a crowd.'* Simeon T.

Simeon's dream table shows him not feeling inclined to connect with others. So it shows how he relates socially.

games, *gambling* In some games there are real prizes like money, but in many there is the sense of success or feeling of defeat, so dreaming of games can indicate these. But in dreams, games are often used to represent life, where chances we take can have very direct connection with real events. Such adult 'games' as making a record, developing a business, starting a job, bring us into direct interaction with the world with an incredibly wide range of responses. Such games are extremely satisfying because of these interactions, but like racing driving can be fatal because of their reality. What we do in our dream game will indicate how we are playing the 'game' of life. We may be playing recklessly, by the rules, skilfully, caringly etc. These indications can be seen as comments on our real life activities.

General: stances used to meet life; not taking life seriously – making a game of it; competitiveness; sense of winning or losing; team work; life skills. See: **playing**.

Particular games suggest different 'stances'. Ball games and athletics: competitiveness; conflict within the dreamer – the two sides; sense of win or lose, success/failure; the game of love. Cards and chess: use of strategies and observation. Gambling: taking risks with your life, health, family; work, money – whatever is indicated in dream. Games like darts, billiards, etc.: your aims and ambitions; aiming at a goal and trying to achieve it; the difficulties of achievement. Opponents: what you are meeting or in conflict with. This may be a part of your nature, such as self-awareness, sexuality, even your body. You might be in conflict with life itself or 'God'. Idioms: beat somebody at their own game; deep game; dirty game; fair game; game of chance; game to the end; give the game away;

know what someone's game is; mug's game; name of the game; on the game; waiting game; game is up. See: *ball* under **shapes symbols**; **doll**; **toy**.

football, baseball, rugby matches   These are generally the same as the above, but have another side to them. They also represent for many people the strong drive to identify with a tribe, a group. They are therefore ways the person gains identity and a sense of connection with people around them. In growing internationalism, such games may be of vital importance to maintaining a sense of identity within what may feel like being lost in a multitude.

tennis   Relationship and the sometimes battle for who is going to dominate that goes on in it; competition; the game people play in approaching sex, i.e. veiled remarks, casual telephone calls, verbal clues to readiness, etc.

garage   General: reserves of drive, energy, motivation; abilities, personal 'tools' to meet life; resources; things you do not need but can't let go of. See: **car**. Personal home garage: depends how you see a garage. It may be a tool shed, workshop, frozen food store, storeroom, as well as a car park. Car repair garage: need for personal attention or 'repairs' to your ambition, drive or ability to motivate yourself.

garbage   Parts of your experience or feelings no longer useful. Occasionally one discards, or considers as useless, some aspect of Self or an ability which is actually valuable.

garden   General: the inner life of the dreamer; the area of growth or change in your life; what you are trying to cultivate in yourself; feelings of peace; being near to one's natural Self; meditative attitude. See: second example in *wife* under **family**.
   Beautiful garden: suggests satisfaction at time of dream; depicts the beauty of your inner feelings. Overgrown or weeds in garden: awareness of particular parts of your personality which need working on. Perhaps negative habits need 'weeding out'. Square or circular garden: holds a lot of your gathered wisdom and insights which would be useful if made conscious. Garden pool: childhood, or early stage in the evolution of one's self-consciousness, during

which there was a sense of communal awareness; sense of unity with life. <u>Idioms</u>: bear garden; up the garden path. See: *the Self* under **archetypes**; **digging**; **dream processing**.

> *Example; 'I was working in quite a large garden by my house. A part of the garden was like a little alcove by other buildings. The garden was kidney shaped. I had dug this small plot and was considering how I might relax and sunbathe there. My daughter said I should have worked harder on it – dug it better. I felt intense emotions of resentment and anger at her criticism. I started telling her what a bad time I had in the past. How difficult it was even to work, let along work hard.'*
> *Beatrice G.*

This shows the garden as depicting what one has 'worked on' or produced in life. This could mean externally or one's own nature. The daughter is Beatrice's own self-criticism which pushes her on, though she has a tendency to want to relax in the sun. This aspect of garden suggests how 'fruitful' one's life has been socially and spiritually.

gardener   The down-to-earth but wise aspect of Self; the wisdom or insights gathered through life experience from which we can direct our own growth and life to integrate the many parts of our nature; the process in each of us – the Christ – which synthesises our life experience and considers what love, what resonance with all life there is in it. See: **digging**; **garden**.

gate   A threshold, like that between conscious self-awareness and our total experience. Such a gate needs to open and close. Open to allow selected memory – close to prevent massive flooding of impressions. The gate can also portray the passage from one period of life, or level of maturity, to another. Therefore, to stand before adolescence, parenthood, death, might be shown as facing a gate in a dream. Also similar to a door – an entrance to something different – or to someone else's life, as in marriage; change. See: example in *dog* under **animals**; *door* under **house**, **buildings**.

geese   Freedom; our soul. See: **birds**.

genitals Direct reference to sexual aspect of Self; often used to represent gender. In such dreams a man might dream of having female genitals, suggesting he is experiencing the female aspect of himself. See: *penis* and *vagina* under **body**; **castration**.

Gestalt dream work Fritz Perls (1893–1970) was the main influence in an approach to dream work that was not interpretative. Unlike the Freudian or Jungian work that includes a lot of interpretative comment on the part of the analyst, Perls encouraged the dreamer to explore and express their own sense of each character and object in the dream. This developed a sense of personal ability and insight in the dreamer. It enabled the dreamer to arrive at a direct perception of how they had unconsciously formed their own dream. The insights into their own behaviour arising from this enabled them to make decisions about action more wisely. It also opened a door of direct experience regarding the enormously potent emotional content of their dreams.

Gestalt work lends itself to peer dream work in which there is no external authority to judge the dreamer's insights or to tell them how to work. This has great benefits in that dream exploration can be made by many people who cannot afford or do not wish to undertake psychoanalytic work. Its drawback is that the dreamer may easily avoid uncovering deeper material and conflicts or fears. See: **dream processing**; **peer dream work**.

gestures See: **postures**, **movement**, **body language**.

ghost Memories, feelings, guilt, which haunt us; part of the wider awareness of the unconscious which attempts to communicate; the husks of influences from past traumas or events which have been emptied of hurt and real influence, but still affect us as habit patterns; fantasies, hopes, longings we have given time to and so filled with our life and sexual energy and which now influence us. Ghost of a living person: a sense of their thoughts or presence influencing us; haunted by desire for them, or a resentment of feeling about them. A ghost which feels solid: the dreamer is 'touching' aspects of their own mind or awareness existing beyond preconceived ideas and beliefs.

Example: 'While I was engaged to be married I had a dream in which I was looking at thick velvet curtains, very rich in texture. The curtains parted and my dead mother walked through. She came to me with such a look of love and said, "My darling I am so sorry, but this marriage is not to be." The dream then ended.

I was due to meet my fiancé at a hotel as he was working travelling around the country and this would be our last meeting before our wedding. I travelled to the hotel and when I got there the manager took me to one side and told me my fiancé had been killed in a car accident. My mother's warning had saved me from a terrible shock.'

Some people believe that in their dreams the living haunt a place. Seeing a ghost while awake can still be considered as connected with the dream process. See: **hallucination**, **hallucinogens**; third example under **husband**.

giant   Childhood feelings about grownups, especially the frightening side of parents.

gift   General: intuition; unconscious knowledge; what is received in a relationship such as support, a sense of worth, acceptance. Giving gift: giving of Self; hoping receiver accepts or likes one. Receiving unwanted gift: difficulties in accepting someone or something from within; pregnancy. See: **giving**.

girl   General: feelings; emotional Self; young sexuality; vulnerability. In a man's dream: emotions; sexual feelings; daughter. In a woman's dream: oneself at that age – whether older or younger; feelings about sister or daughter; the aspect of oneself portrayed by the girl – as in following example. Another girl with your man: how you deal with your sense of being unwanted; anxiety about not being attractive or lovable; suspicion; a side of yourself which relates you differently to your man.

Example: 'I was watching and at the same time I was a young girl sitting on a lawn.' Honey J.

Example: 'I was away from home somewhere and was helping and encouraging a young Japanese girl, who was pregnant, to come back to England to have her baby here. I felt a lot of care for her.' Dave L.

Dave processed his dream and discovered a lot of sexual pleasure in connection with the girl. He had held himself back in this area most of his life, and as he was learning to allow his sexual feelings, and not simply genital sex, he found a deepening in his caring also.

girlfriend   Your emotional feelings, attachment to, the girlfriend; the difficulties, struggles with feelings and sexuality felt in connection with a girlfriend or other males; your insights into her behaviour. *Ex-girlfriend*: Any feelings or hopes still connected with her; the ex-girlfriend or lover often becomes a symbol for all the hopes for love that are not being satisfied at the moment, or in the present relationship; occasionally the past.

giving   General: relatedness; the sort of exchange or give and take which goes on in a relationship, even the internal relationship with oneself, or the environment. Giving: one can give affection, support, sex, ideas, as well as wounds. One needs to see what the interaction is by looking at what is given. Received: consider what is received to define what you are accepting or rejecting in oneself or from others.

The idioms show the many ways this action can be used. Idioms: don't give me that; give and take; give as good as one gets; give away or give-away; give oneself away; give somebody away; don't give a brass farthing; give place; give a piece of one's mind; give them enough rope; give someone the evil or glad eye; give someone the elbow; give one's notice. See: **gift**.

glass   The sort of invisible yet tangible barriers we may erect or feel around others, such as natural caution, emotional coldness, disinterest, fear of being hurt or pride; social barriers; invisible aspects of oneself which nevertheless may trap us, such as fear, lack of self-respect; self-doubt. Frosted or smoked glass: desire for privacy; keeping parts of oneself hidden; an obscure or unclear view of a situation; occasionally relating to death – the very real yet obscure experience we all face. <u>Breaking glass</u>: breaking through a barrier; shattered emotions. <u>Breaking something made of glass</u>: breaking a relationship; shattering an illusion; broken hearted. <u>Empty drinking glasses</u>: past events; memories. <u>Full glasses</u>: present or future experience. See: **break**.

glasses, **spectacles**   Ability to see – understand – or lack of it; a way of hiding oneself, as behind sunglasses. Terms like 'short-sighted' or 'long-sighted' help to understand the use of glasses in a dream.

glove   See: **clothes**.

gnome   See: **dwarf**.

goal   May refer to the external goals we have set ourselves, but dreams often use the image to refer to the internal sense of where we are going in our life as a whole, and not just what job we might achieve. After observing the symbol forming action of the unconscious, Jung came to the conclusion that the unconscious itself was purposive and had certain goals. Such goals arise out of the connection the unconscious has with all life and its sense of wholeness.

God   Jung says that while the Catholic church admits dreams sent by God, most theologians make little attempt to understand dreams in relationship to God.

   <u>God in a dream can depict several things</u>: a set of emotions we use to deal with anxiety – i.e. our own belief that a higher power is in charge, so therefore we are okay in the world and are not responsible – thus an escape from responsibility; a parent image from early infancy; a set of moral or philosophical beliefs we hold; self-judgement; something/one we worship; a feeling of connection with humanity; an expression of the fundamental creative/destructive process in ourselves.

   The powerful emotions we sometimes experience about God may well be connected with our tremendous childhood need for love and approval from parents.

Example: 'When I explored the emotions that had surfaced in recent dreams about God, I came across something totally unexpected. I had decided I would treat the image of God like a dream image and 'get inside it', find out what was behind it. When I managed to do this I found with amazement that my desperate need for my father's love, a love he found difficult to express, had been transported into my internal sense of God.

At this point I suddenly saw that my urge for God is actually the urge for my father. My unsatisfied urge to receive love from my father became a power to create an image of a loving God, an image of a cosmic father who can love – and from this inner creation of the psyche I can get the love I wanted. I create a loving God because that was my need. But others may create an avenging God to deal with their feelings of guilt; or a mysterious, beautiful, ever-present God to deal with a sense of parental loss, and so on. The image takes the place of real human love – a second best. I see also that it is much more honest to say, not God loves me, but I love myself. I have become the father. I am the God. I have dared to take on the role of father and God.' Tony C.

There are at times direct experiences of 'God' beyond the symbols of the divine, not as expressions of parental need but as an experience of the very core of one's existence, beyond words, symbols, emotions or body sensations. See: *the Self* under **archetypes**; **individuation**; **religion and dreams**.

goddess   In a woman's dream: the unconscious connection one has with all women and all female creatures; the power of the collective psyche underlying one's personality; the mysterious connections with nature and the forces of nature the woman is in tune with through menstruation, childbearing and mothering. In a man's dream: one's collective sense of women as a whole and not as individuals; personal fear of female power, usually relating to early experience of one's mother; one's capacity to love in a transcendent way.

gold   The best or most valuable in oneself or in opportunity; the eternal; what stands the 'acid test' or does not tarnish with time in terms of personal qualities, such as love, patience or care in work; something you value or want in your life. If cheap or false: something you valued but does not deserve respect. If tarnished: something beautiful and valuable in yourself, perhaps your spirit, that you have let become soiled. See: *gold* under **colours**.

grave   Feelings or concepts of death; feelings about someone who is dead; realisation a part of yourself is dead, buried or killed. See: **cemetery**; **tomb**.

graveyard   See: **cemetery**.

green   See: **colours**.

grey   See: **colours**.

ground   See: **earth**.

group   See: **people**.

growth of something   The changes in us which bring about new ways of relating to other people, ourselves and activity. The change or personal growth may be mental, emotional or physical. Sometimes the change is one of achieving new realisations. There appears to be a drive from the unconscious to gather and integrate experience to thereby expand the sense of Self. This expansion can lead to an awareness of existing in an ocean of being in which all things live.

guillotine   Losing one's head, or threat of it; killing out one's ability to think and reason – so perhaps becoming irrational.

guilt   Feeling guilt in a dream is a direct experience, but what you are feeling guilty about may well be in symbols and need clarifying. See: **emotions**, **mood**.

gun   See: **weapons**.

guru   The wisdom of the unconscious. The essence of what one has learnt from life and the collective unconscious becoming known to your conscious Self. See: *the Self* under **archetypes**; **God**.

half   General: part of; divided; incomplete; in between; conflict. Half open: opposing feelings about whether to 'be open' or not; can I, can't I – will I, won't I. Halfway up/down: indecision; faltering motivation; sometimes between the opposites, or outside of one's everyday experience. Half full: may refer to half one's life used up. Cut in half: conflict between intellect and body/sexuality. Half buried: something you are only partly aware of.

> *Example: 'I could see an older woman watching me from the road. I felt very scared at her being there. I walked to the front door, I started to walk past the front door, felt great fear and hung back, half behind the front door, for protection from her.'* Pamela H.

Hall, Calvin   Author of *The Content Analysis of Dreams* and *The Meaning of Dreams*. Hall's work with content analysis – which is looking at the personality of the dreamer through a series of dreams rather than a single dream – is expressed in a popular form in *The Meaning of Dreams*. With the entrance into home life of computers, easy content analysis has become much more available. See: **computers and dreams**.

hallucinations, **hallucinogens**   An hallucination can be experienced through any of the senses singly or all of them together. So one might have an hallucinatory smell or sound. To understand hallucinations, which are quite common without any use of drugs such as alcohol, LSD or cannabis, one must remember that everyone has the natural ability to produce such images. One of the definitions of a dream according to Freud is its hallucinatory quality. While asleep we can create full sensory, vocal, motor and emotional experience in our dream. While dreaming we usually accept what we experience as real. An hallucination is an experience of a 'dream' occurring while we have our eyes open. The voices heard, people seen, smells smelt, although appearing to be outside of us, are no more exterior than the things and images of our dreams. With this information one can understand that much classed as psychic phenomena and religious experience is an encounter with the dream process. That does not, of course, deny its importance.

Example: 'I dream insects are dropping either on me from the ceiling of our bedroom or crawling over my pillow. My long-suffering husband is always woken when I sit bolt upright in bed my eyes wide open and my arm pointing at the ceiling. I try to brush them off. I can still see them – spiders or wood lice. I am now well aware it is a dream. But no matter how hard I stare, the insects are there in perfect detail. I am not frightened, but wish it would go away.' Sue D.

Sue's dream only became an hallucination when she opened her eyes and continued to see the insects in perfect clarity. There are probably many reasons why Sue should experience an hallucination and her husband not. One might be that powerful drives and emotions might be pushing for attention in her life. Some of the primary drives are the reproductive drive; the urge towards independence; pressure to meet unconscious emotions and past trauma and fears – any of which, in order to achieve their ends, can produce hallucinations. An hallucination is therefore not an 'illusion' but a means of giving information from deeper levels of Self. Given such names as mediumship or mystical insight in some cultures or individuals, the ability to hallucinate is often rewarded socially.

Drugs such as LSD, cannabis, psilocybin, mescaline, peyote and opium can produce hallucinations. This is sometimes because they allow the dream process to break through into consciousness with less intervention. If this occurs without warning it can be very disturbing. The very real dangers are that unconscious content, which in ordinary dreaming breaks through a threshold in a regulated way, emerges with less regulation. Fears, paranoid feelings and traumas can emerge into the consciousness of an individual who has no skill in handling such dangerous forces. Because the propensity of the unconscious is to create images, an area of emotion might emerge in an image such as the devil. Such images and the power they contain not being integrated in a proper therapeutic setting may haunt the individual, perhaps for years. Even at a much milder level, elements of the unconscious will emerge and disrupt the person's ability to appraise reality and make judgements. Unacknowledged fears may lead the drug user to rationalise their reasons for avoiding social activity or the world of work. See: **ESP and dreams**; *dead lover* in *husband* under **family**; **out-of-body experience**.

hammer　See: **tools**.

hand　See: **body**.

harbour　See: **quay**.

hare　See: **animals**.

harness　Directing our energy or potential; control; restraint.

hat　See: **clothes**.

hearing　See: *ear* under **body**.

hearse　Feelings about death; reminder of time left to live. See: **funeral**.

heaven　Compensatory feelings for difficulties in life; intuition about life after death; retreat from life; meeting one's religious concepts; one's own sense of harmony or integration. See: **dream as spiritual guide**.

hell　If threatening: emotions, anxieties of which one is fearful; one's self-created misery, perhaps arising out of such things as anger or resentment we cling to or a sense of being different or unwanted; feelings which burn in us. Sometimes people reverse the roles of heaven and hell. Hell becomes attractive, full of excitement. Heaven becomes an insipid place. See: *devil* under **archetypes**; **dream as spiritual guide**.

hermaphrodite   Being both sexes: might suggest feeling uncertain about our own gender or having problems in the role of our own sex; finding a balance and wholeness in oneself.

> *Example: 'I was outdoors in my underpants teaching a group of people. Looking down I saw my genitals were exposed and I had female organs. I felt okay.' Bill S.*

Although Bill works in the building trade, he finds it easy to cook, look after his children, cry and accept his 'female' characteristics.

hero/ine   If we are not the hero/ine of our own dream, we are probably still not accepting responsibility for all our own drives, potentials and weaknesses. The hero/ine frequently depicts our initiative and unexpressed potential. We might see our highest ideals as coming from an exterior figure such as Christ, and so miss touching the depths of our own being and avoid responsibility for our urges or actions. What happens to the hero/ine shows how one's own creativity and expressed love fare. See: the ideal Christ, *the hero/ine* and *the Self* under **archetypes**; **religion and dreams**.

hiding   General: hiding from feeling; avoiding awareness of something we don't want to see; being protective – hiding how we really feel about someone or our sexual feelings about someone; not knowing. Hiding from something dangerous, or dangerous thing hidden: feeling threatened either by unconscious contents or exterior situation. Hiding a body or object: not facing difficult feelings connected with the body or thing. See: **dead people dreams**.
   The example below illustrates how we may use one emotion or situation to hide what is really important.

> *Example: 'I was in my bedroom, I looked up and saw the top of some long curtains were on fire. I thought "My God, now my sister is setting fire to the house to hide the evidence".' Ms A.T.*

high   Being high: as in the example below, can depict having a very wide view of one's situation in life; feeling isolated, alone, or away from the known and secure – as one might in starting a new job, losing one's job or moving to a new town; apprehension; anxiety. Looking at something high: above one's head; feeling impressed or awed; challenge. Being on a high building: being cut off from one's emotions and thus feeling isolated; achievement; fear of losing control. Also one's aspirations and widest view of life, therefore the spiritual. Idioms: high and mighty; high as a kite; high flown; high-flyer; high-minded; high places. See: **descend**; **hill**; **mountain**; **positions**.

> *Example: 'I must have climbed up this fire escape okay, but the building was incredibly high up and when I reached the platform I looked down and saw everything miles below. At this stage I was gripped with panic and I lay on the floor, clinging to the metal grid it was made of, and couldn't move. I was so panic-stricken it immobilised me completely and I couldn't move up or even get back down.' Helen B.*

hill   On a hill: a clear view of our situation; achievement; something we have made an effort to attain; expanded awareness. Going up hill: difficulties; hard work or effort; the first half of our life; or life itself if it feels like an uphill struggle. Going downhill: feeling as if circumstances are pushing you; feeling you might, or have, lost control; the second half of your life or old age. A hole at the bottom of a hill: especially if surrounded by shrubs, depicts the vagina. Green sunny hillside: feeling whole; a sense of heaven. Also hill or hills sometimes represent breasts or the belly. See: **descending**; last example in **flying**; **high**; **mountain**.

> *Example: 'I am riding through thick fog. I feel I should turn back. But then I see a pale golden white glow and know that if I continue to the top of the hill I will emerge from the fog into a most beautiful place.' C.B.*

historic   In some dreams we find ourselves in the past with the feeling of those times. This nearly always depicts, not a past life, but our own feelings. So a cowboy scene might depict our pioneering spirit or sense of adventure. We need to define what feelings we derive from reading about or seeing films about such periods of history. Also our past; the person we were at some period in our life.

Hobson, J. Allan   In his book, *The Dreaming Brain*, Hobson presents a well-researched theory of dreaming based on biological and psychological processes. Closely examining historical dream theories and measuring them against present-day findings, he unfolds his new theory that dreams are not disguised urges, but transparent though sometimes scrambled hallucinations.

In this theory, internally generated brain signals excite the visual and motor senses, but cannot be checked against external reality. This gives rise to bizarre imagery and discontinuities in the dream which are integrated into meaning by the brain. Hobson is not saying dreams do not hold information about the dreamer, but that such information is as straightforwardly expressed as is possible given the nature of the brain's activity during sleep.

holding   There are five aspects to holding. On<u>e</u>: to control, as in controlling or 'holding one's breath'; to be able to manipulate, kill or do something with what is held – this includes holding on to something for support or protection. <u>Two</u>: ownership – this is mine to share or not. <u>Three</u>: in touch with; knowing; having a 'grasp' of. <u>Four</u>: responsibility; left holding the baby; one's situation. <u>Five</u>: intimacy; taking to oneself, taking hold of oneself as in masturbation; as in following example.

> *Example: 'I am a prisoner in a room with three boys aged three, five and fourteen. They seem to be my children. There are two prison warders – a man, a woman. The man was subservient to the woman who holds the keys and keeps control.' Carol J.*

> *Example: 'I was in a large removal van with a woman sat on my lap. I held her breasts with pleasure.' Tony C.*

<u>Idioms</u>: get hold of; have a hold over someone; hold back; hold in.

hole   <u>General</u>: difficulty or tricky situation in life; a situation you might 'fall into'; a place to hide or feel protected in – therefore womb-like feelings; an escape route; a way of 'seeing through' something; the vagina; death. Going in hole: meeting feelings, urges or fears we usually keep unconscious; confronting aspects of Self buried beneath our surface awareness; memories of womb existence; death – burial. Holes in clothes, objects: faults; weaknesses; illness; 'full of holes'. Holes in body: sense of weakness; emptiness in one's life such as loneliness; illness; negative feelings about that part of Self; see **body** for appropriate part. Hole in head: letting everyone know what you think; gossiping. Hole in road: often represents death or death of person falling down the hole. Occasionally used as word play meaning whole. See: third example in **dark**; first example in *son* under **family**; **tunnel**; hole in hand dream in Introduction.

holiday   Sense of relaxation; being independent; satisfying one's own needs; reaching a period in one's life in which one can rest on one's laurels. See: example in **clothes**; example in **crossroad**.

hollow   Feeling of emptiness in one's life; womb feeling or memories; feelings about the vagina. See: **hole**.

homosexuality   Each of us has some element of homosexuality in us unconsciously. In one's dreams it may suggest a desire for the father's or mother's love, perhaps because they were not demonstrative. So one was led to crave the love of a man/woman; conflict or anxiety about one's own gender; feelings of sexual inadequacy or inadequacy in one's own gender; unconscious pain in regard to the opposite sex – this may be rationalised into reasons for being homosexual rather than being experienced and made conscious; depicting an introversion of one's sexual drive.

honey   The essence of one's experience; pleasure; sweetness.

horns   Protectiveness; desire to hurt; the animal in the human – as in the form of Pan; sexuality or the penis. Idioms: pull in one's horns; lock horns with someone; take the bull by the horns; on the horns of a dilemma. See: second example in **eating**.

horse   See: **animals**.

hose   Intestines; penis. <u>Hosing</u>: sex play. See: **garden**; **water**.

hostility   Direct expression of that feeling. It is worthwhile considering who or what the dream suggests you feel hostile toward. In general the most powerful hostile feelings are those generated in our infancy toward parents. As an adult these feelings of hostility project on to any person we make a close emotional bond with, so need to be met if one is to become an adequate sexual person in a relationship with an adult of the opposite sex. This also influences our relationships with social authority. Unconscious hostility may cause one to remain at a mystic or idealistic level in a relationship with the opposite sex, causing difficulty in meeting the real individual. Often in dreams however there is an expression of anger we have witheld in our daily life.

> *Example: 'As I talked about my mother, she was standing before me in full anger and blaming me for bringing out the witch in her. She said "look at my eyes", they were horrid to see, all red and angry and she was dark.' Hy.*

> *Example: 'My father was giving me and another woman? some medicine? something was being forced on us. I started to hit and punch him in the genitals and when he was facing the other way, in the backside. I seemed to be just the right height to do this and I had a very angry feeling that I wanted to hurt him as he had hurt me.' Barbara G.*

Hostility toward society or authority may be directed inwards and become self-destroying. Social hostility leads to an inability to express adequately in the world. Introverted hostility can cause illness and lack of self-value. Meeting anger, aggression and hostility does not mean suppressing it or expressing it socially.

Many of us have become, in the words of W.V. Caldwell, the author of *LSD Psychotherapy*, 'hostility cripples'. As human animals, anger and aggression are natural, but growing in a society which, although it practises the most terrible aggression at a national level, suppresses individual aggression, makes it difficult for us to lead these urges toward maturity. Maturity in love is often talked about but not maturity in hate. It helps if we can recognise whether we are repressing aggressions or hostility in our dreams. If anger is felt but not expressed in a dream, then use the technique explained in **dream processing** in which you carry the dream forward and express in the imagination the held-back emotions. This should begin the process of more expressive anger in one's dreams, allowing the maturing of the aggression to begin. See: Sunday school Christ under **archetypes**.

hot   Pleasurable, 'warm' feelings; passion for someone. Very hot or burning: potentially painful emotions or passions which may leave their mark. Idioms: be hot on; hot and bothered; hot-blooded; hot-headed; hot stuff; in hot water; in the hot seat; make it hot for someone; get the hots; hot air. See: **fire**.

house, **buildings**   A house nearly always refers to oneself, one's body and attributes of personality. Thus if we take a large house with its many functional rooms, the library would represent the mind; the bathroom cleansing or renewal of good feelings; the bedrooms one's sexuality or intimacy; the roof one's protectiveness or 'coping mechanisms'. Large public buildings such as hospitals, factories, blocks of flats, depict particular functions suggested by their nature, such as work or healing. But of course, if the house or building has a personal connection – the house you live in, or place you have worked – then you need to define what is the essential feeling about such. Or see **dream processing**. If a house or building has a quality of some other type of construction, such as a library feeling like a factory, or a house feeling like a church, both aspects should be accepted as important.

attic   The mind, ideas, memories, past experience. If trapped in an attic: a purely intellectual approach to life. Finding an attic: pleasure at new ideas, discovering potential or wisdom from past experience. Threat from attic: disturbing thoughts. Window or turret looking out from attic: our sense of connection with the cosmos; wider awareness; intellectual view. Hiding in attic: escape from other people; retreat from everyday life. See example below.

Example: 'I was sleeping in an attic. A large dog was with me – a wolfhound like I used to exercise a few years ago. I and the

*dog would go out together. The dog was wild and free. I
enjoyed being with it. Together we did things like hunting
which felt very real in the sense of not being artificial
behaviour. Although I never washed I felt clean and healthy.'
Leon.*

When Leon explored his dream he felt the attic was a place where
he could exist but not be involved with people. The attic reminded
him of the attic in a childhood house, where his mother never went
because of the steep ladder. So he could go there and be alone, free
of other people's presence and influence.

basement, cellar Usually the things we have hidden from awareness in our unconscious. The example shows how Mrs L. has killed
or repressed a part of herself. We might 'kill' ambition, love, sexual
drive, and these be pushed into our unconscious. But the basement
or cellar also is the entrance to personal and transpersonal memories, our biological 'unconscious' functions, archetypal patterns of
behaviour, subliminal or psychic impressions, the collective unconscious. Frequently it is the place where we keep memories of
traumatic events in our life. So a dark shape or intruder might
emerge from 'downstairs'. Our dark deeds or guilty memories are
also in the basement. A snake in the cellar or cave: our psycho-
biological drive; the energy behind our growth and motivation
which includes sex drive. This connects us with an awareness of our
evolution. Bad smell: emotions which could cause depression or
illness.

*Example: 'I know I have killed somebody and their body is
walled up in the cellar. The strange thing is I haven't a clue
who this person is. Various people visit my home and I am
terrified the body will be discovered. In one of these recurring
dreams the police actually investigate the disappearance of
'the person' and go into the cellar. When I wake from these
dreams I always have the most terrible guilty feeling.'
Mrs P.L.*

castle Feelings of security or insecurity; our defensive attitudes; the
way we defend ourself against 'attack'; past attitudes which may

have been necessary in childhood to defend ourselves while strengthening our identity.

chimney smoking; the birth canal; sign of inner warmth. Belching black smoke: the grim, mechanised side of our culture centred on production instead of humanity.

church, chapel, temple General: as in the example below, the powerfully regenerative side of our inner life or feelings; the world of experience we have created inwardly by our thoughts, meditation, actions; our sense of contact with *life* itself. Also the moral rules we make decisions from – such rules may at times kill much of our inner life; moral authority; our relationship with the community. Occasionally baptism, marriage, death, the mother or refuge. Walking past the church: not entering into contact with the best in us, or our anger toward dogma.

> *Example: 'It was like an English church with several great spires. The whole building seemed to be built in a white and gold design. The gold parts shimmered in the sun. I gazed at this wonderful sight for some time and felt such a wonderful feeling of upliftment, my tiredness gone.' Johan E.*

> *Example: 'The priest was going to question and assault my friend in connection with some opinion he had offended the church with. I went to stand near him to give him moral support and physical help if necessary. I hated seeing anybody degraded. The priest saw my move and sent three thug-type men to shoulder me out. They surrounded me to knock me down. I went berserk and knocked them all over the place with kicks and punches.' John P.*

In the example John sees the dogmas of the church as an assault and degradation of human qualities of love and moral support.

door Freud felt that a door, a keyhole, a handle, a knocker all depicted sex and sexual organs. The first example shows this clearly. Knocking refers to the sex act, the cul-de-sac is the woman's legs. But the image of a door has so many other ways of being expressed in dreams and is used very frequently. In the next example it represents the experience of discovering a new feeling state. For instance if one had always been apologetic and now became affirmative, 'new doors' of experience could well open.

General meanings depending on dream: a boundary; the difference between one feeling state and another, such as depression and feeling motivated; the feelings or attitudes, such as aloofness, we use to shut others out of our life to remain independent or private; being open or inviting; a sense of leaving an environment or relationship – escape; entering into a new work or relationship situation. Someone at a door: opportunity; the unexpected; new experience. Front door: public Self; confidence; our relationship with people in general; a vagina. Back door: our private, family life; our more secret activities; the anus. Side door: escaping from a situation or being indirect. Shutting a door: privacy; trying to find 'space' for oneself; the dismissing attitudes or tension we use to shut others out of intimate contact; repressing memories or feelings. Door to strange landscape or world: finding entrance to unconscious. Door knob: see: **knob**.

> *Example: 'I find my way to a door and knock. It is at the end of the cul-de-sac. An old woman of about sixty comes to the door. Although old she is healthy and well-preserved. Without a word I grab her in my arms and have sex with her.' Patrick S.*

> *Example: 'I came up to a door which I'd never seen before, and on opening it, I came across another house fully furnished.' Mrs R.F.*

> *Example: 'I am being strangled from behind by a faceless man! I had gone down to lock my flat door for the night when I noticed the door was open. I hastily bolted it and ran upstairs, but unknown to me the intruder was already in the flat.' Miss H.*

Here the door represents the censorship the dreamer places between her conscious Self and her sexual drives. In 'strangling' our own life drive, we ourselves feel cut off from life.

fortress See: *castle* above.

hall, hallway Public or dance hall: how you relate to groups or the public; the attitude or function in oneself which connects the many different aspects of oneself; meeting sexuality; a place of initiation – maturing beyond old habits, ways of life and views – perhaps because civic ceremonies such as marriage, trials, social rewards, take place in hall-like environments. Hallway: the way one meets other people or allows them into one's life or intimacy; the receptive female reproductive function; connecting link with aspects of oneself.

> *Example: 'I find myself in the entrance hall of a very large house. The hall is very large with a curved staircase either side meeting at the top to form a balcony. There is nobody about and I am frightened. I start to walk up the stairs but then find myself hiding in the roof with very little space above my body.'*
> *Mrs B.*

The hall is probably Mrs B.'s childbearing ability and her image of herself as a woman. The words 'little space above my body' suggest her main area of life has always been her childbearing function or physical attractiveness as a woman, and she has not developed her mental self. See: *white* under **colour**; **corridor**.

home General: one's basic needs such as shelter, warmth, nourishment – but usually in the sense of what we have created as our basic way of life; the values, standards, goals we have accepted as normal or are 'at home' with; as in the first example – the situation or feeling state in our home, which here means family atmosphere; the state of feeling relaxed, being oneself because away from other people and what we need to be in our relationship with them. Thus a sense of being oneself or absence of concern over other people's criticism. In a past home: depicts the parts of our character or experience which developed in that home environment. Someone else's home: what we sense as the attitudes and atmosphere or the situation prevailing in that home. So a young woman going to the home of her lover and his wife shows her facing the fact of her lover's home situation and commitment in marriage. Future home: the direction you would like your life to take, or fear it might take. Idioms: bring something home to someone; close to home; come home to roost; home and dry; broken home; home truth; home is where the heart is. See: *house* below.

> *Example: 'I was sitting in the living room at home and my mum was sitting there; like we do when we're relaxing in the evening. From nowhere in particular my dad was there. He held his girlfriend in his arms and displayed her in front of us. She was stark naked. My mum tensed up, tightened her lips and tried to look away. I felt acutely embarrassed for me, Mum, Dad and his girlfriend.' Lynsay S.*

> *Example: 'I am walking down a busy street when I realise all I have on are my bra and pants. Everyone is staring at me and I try to appear unconcerned but feel more and more embarrassed as I go on. Eventually the street and the people fade and I am alone in my own home and a great sensation of relief comes over me. I do not bother to put any more clothes on but wander about the house secure in the comfort people are no longer looking at me.' Mrs S.C.*

This depicts the home as an absence of demands made on us by other people or social rules – so the ability to be oneself.

hospital   Hospital represents needing or being involved in a healing process of body or mind; worries about one's health.

> *Example: 'I was a prisoner in a hospital, although there were no locked doors or bars. It was a psychiatric hospital, but we were allowed to believe we had a physical illness. I had been very ill, but was trying to escape.' Joan P.*

At the time of her dream, Joan was feeling trapped in depression and also attending a therapy group.

hotel   Temporary attitudes or way of life; a short-term situation; relaxation; escape or separation from family or home situations; sexual activity outside home life; for people such as businessmen/ women or media people, the hotel can represent work or the pursuance of work.

house   If the house is one we know, live in now or in the past, what is said about *home* applies. If it is a house created by the dream: one's body and personality in all its aspects. Inside the house: within oneself. Outside the house and garden: extroversion or one's relationship with environment. Ground floor: practical everyday life, sexuality; hips and legs. Basement: unconscious. See: *basement and cellar* above. First and other middle floors: internal needs, rest, sleep, hungers; the trunk. Top floor or attic: thinking; the conscious mind; memory; the head. See: *attic* above. Front of house: our persona; façade; social Self; face. Things in the house: aspects of one's feelings and makeup. Other people in house: different facets of dreamer. Windows: one's outlook on life; how you see others. See: entry on *window* below. People or things coming from downstairs: influences, fears, impressions from unconscious or passions – or from everyday worries. People or things from upstairs: influence of rational Self. Attackers or intruders from outside: social pressures or response to criticisms. Repairs, enlargement or renovation: reassessment or change of attitudes or character; personal growth. Damage or structural faults: faults in character structure; hurts such as broken relationship; bodily illness. House falling down or burning: big changes in attitudes; leaving old standards or dependencies behind; sickness. See: last example in **falling**. Cramped house: feeling of need for personal change; feeling restricted in home environment or in present personal attitudes. Kitchen: creativity; nourishing oneself; mother role; diet. See: **cooking**. Living room: personal leisure; 'space' to be oneself; everyday life. Dining room: appetites; social or family contact; mental or psychological diet. Bedroom: privacy; sex; intimacy; rest. See: *bed* under **furniture**. Study or library: mental growth; mind. Larder: hungers; sensual satisfaction. Toilet: privacy; release of tension; letting go of emotions, fantasies or desires which we need to discharge. See: **toilet**. Nursery or child's bedroom: feelings about your children; one's own childhood feelings and memories. Floor: basic attitudes and confidence; what supports you, such as health and goodwill of others. Ceiling: boundary of ideas of awareness. Row of houses: other people. See: entries on *attic*; *roof*; *room*; *stairs*; *wall*.

hut Childhood family feelings; basic uncomplicated situation or relationship.

housework The cleaning out of non-functional – negative – attitudes, thoughts and experience; keeping our internal house in order, perhaps by taking time to clarify or define motives, opinions and feelings about others.

lift Mood shifts or movement of attention – as when we move from being involved in physical sensation and shift to thinking; rise or drop in status or work situation; our emotional highs and lows – the lift going out through the roof could show tendency toward being manic whereas going underground could be a meeting of influences from the unconscious; being 'uplifted' or feeling 'down'.

> *Example: 'I was in a lift with a young woman. She intimated there was some difficulty about getting the lift to work. I felt this was not so and pushed the button. The doors closed and the lift began to ascend. As it did we moved close together and kissed. But the main feeling was of being accepted and liked. This moved my feelings so much I felt a great melting feeling in my abdomen, and a lot of body sensation against her body.'* Anthony F.

Here the lift shows Anthony 'being moved' emotionally and sexually – the lift can depict sex and the energy flowing up the trunk in love or meditation.

mansion Although a house represents all the aspects of Self in which our identity lives – a body, emotions, creativity, etc. – a mansion is depicting the same thing with a different emphasis. It is ourselves as we are plus features still latent, possibilities not yet developed or explored. See: *house*.

public house Social, free and easy side of Self; one's ability in relating to the public; alcohol dependency.

roof The philosophy, beliefs or coping strategies we use to protect ourselves from stress. Standing on a roof: heightened awareness. See: **dream as spiritual guide**. Mending roof: developing new coping strategies; feeling vulnerable. Leaking roof: need for new coping strategies. No roof: if not a threatening dream, suggests no barrier between personality and psychic or spiritual awareness; a sense of connection with life or wider awareness. If threatening, feeling invaded by forces outside oneself. Roof garden: spiritual or mental growth or flowering of new ideas, insights or abilities. See: last example in *window*.

room   A particular feeling state – for instance the room might feel sinister, warm, spacious, cold, etc., and so depicts such. Sometimes a room, because of its spaciousness represents the amount of potential or opportunity one has. The 'containing' quality of a room may also depict involvement with one's mother. The finding of extra rooms: a common dream theme – recognition or discovery of previously unnoticed aspects, abilities, fears or traits in oneself.

> *Example: 'There was a room in my house I had never been in before. It was filled with water and had three kittens submerged in it. While in the room I didn't need to breathe.'*
> *Audrey P.*

The room here represents Audrey's childbearing function – her womb. The room can therefore depict mother or qualities of mothering. See: description of various rooms under *house*.

stable   The natural urges you have; birthplace of Christ – i.e. where we meet the influence arising from our innate link with all life.

stairs   Taking steps toward something; going up or down in life in your own estimation. Running up: escaping from urges arising from lower down in the body – so a movement of attention towards the abstract or mental away from fears arising from the unconscious or sexuality; lack of confidence, a fear of failing or not being capable is also a common feeling in connection with stairs.

> *Example: 'I go up the first flight of stairs, then the next, and there is my ex-husband's Nan who is dead and whom I have never met. I don't see her face but I know it's her. She is a blinding white light and I run down the stairs.' Mrs H.*

The example shows how going upstairs can be an opening or

widening of awareness to include areas of experience usually avoided. In fact Mrs H. takes her awareness down to more everyday levels to escape meeting the light.

> *Example: 'I climb a few flights of stairs. As I go up, the stairs start wobbling and breaking up. At the top the last flight breaks away from the landing and I am left to cross a gaping hole with a few bits of debris to cling to. It is very frightening, but I see other people passing me on the caved-in stairs and onto the landing as if nothing has happened.' Maureen.*

In the last dream, Maureen sees life as full of pitfalls.

wall   Codes of behaviour, belief systems, attitudes – often unconscious – you live within or are protected by; the boundaries of behaviour or thought you keep within, are fearful of extending beyond, or are trapped by – thereby what one feels to be barriers or restrictions; one's feelings of confidence which protect against anxiety or social 'knocks'; fears that keep you limited in your activities; the feelings or attitudes you keep people away with – the walls we put up between us to maintain privacy, stop being hurt, or to maintain a role or status; a special feeling situation which you have created, such as developing a sense of one's own value.

Sometimes what the wall depicts is obvious as in the example below, where it is shown as the way Cyril maintains his separation from others and thus is a private individual. The fall of the wall shows how 'exposed' one might be. The description of private areas of our life in a newspaper might be an example of just such a wall coming down. Idioms: drive up the wall; go to the wall; writing on the wall; back to the wall; knock one's head against a wall. See: **fence; wall**.

> *Example: 'I realised T. had been in Bill's room and not respected his need for privacy, so Bill had torn down the wall as a protest and made the room, which now appeared about four times its usual size, into a public sitting room.' Cyril A.*

warehouse   Memories; past experience; aspects of Self put in storage, such as ambition while bringing up children.

window In general one is either looking out of, looking into, or going through a window. This makes them largely connected with what we see in the sense of perception or being aware of things, either within ourselves – as in the example – or in regard to other people. So they can depict our eyes or awareness also. Looking out of a window: your 'view' of or feelings about what you perceive in your environment or life; looking for a way out of a situation. Looking into a window: what you feel or 'see' in regard to someone else if you see another person; what you are aware of when 'looking' at or giving awareness to yourself. Climbing out of a window: possibly your way of avoiding difficult feelings, i.e. by giving attention to exterior things – television, a book – rather than what we feel. Climbing in a window: looking within oneself or seeing what makes someone else 'tick'. Opening window: letting others see your feelings or opinions; allowing other people's influence into yourself. No windows: not seeing what is going on around you; introversion; attention held by internal feelings, thoughts or concerns. Height of windows – such as first floor: suggests what area of your experience you are looking at the world through. You may only look at life through a basement window, which suggests being influenced by one's sexuality or unconscious feelings. See mention of levels of house above. Domed window or window in roof: depicts our head or mind. We each have a cosmic sense – a synthesis of experience in which we develop a personal view of what life is about in the largest sense – and so looking through the domed or roof window depicts the vision provided by this cosmic sense. See second example. Idioms: window dressing; window on the world; a room with a view.

Example: 'I was looking at a little matchbox-shaped thing and one looked into it like a window. I looked at my arm through the window, then my vision was full of patterns of my energy going up and down my arm. It was very beautiful, leaf-like shapes with glass-like balls and clear liquid but even the liquid making patterns on the move up and down.' Wendy O.

Example: 'Presumably I come to another domed window and stand looking at sea and sky. I am filled with serenity and peace.' J.D.

Humphrey, Nicholas   Sees human beings as needing to learn and modify strategies for social survival and interaction. He says of the human animal, 'It depends upon the bodies of other animals not merely for immediate sustenance in infancy and its sexual fulfilment as an adult but in one way or another for the success – or failure – of almost every enterprise it undertakes. In these circumstances the ability to model the behaviour of others in the social group has paramount survival value.' We know that cats, while dreaming, practise stalking and hunting. Humphrey speculates that in dreams humans practise and modify social behaviour.

hunger   Our needs or demands physically, emotionally and mentally. We may feel the need for success or fame just as acutely as the need for sex or food. See: **eating**; **food**.

hunter, huntress   The aspect of ourself which is either killing our 'animal' or gaining sustenance from it; the urge to get away from everyday responsibility; our bread-winning qualities.

hypnosis and dreams   Many experiments have been done using hypnosis in connection with dreams. In the early part of this century, Carl Schroetter hypnotised Miss E., a pharmacist, in an attempt to test Freud's theory of symbol formation. He suggested Miss E. would dream of having homosexual intercourse with a female friend, L. The dream she subsequently reported was: 'I sit in a small dirty café holding a tremendous French newspaper ... A woman with a strong Yiddish accent – L. is Jewish – asks me twice, 'Don't you need anything?' I don't answer ... she comes a third time ... I recognise her as my acquaintance. She holds a threadbare suitcase with a sticker on it that reads: 'For ladies only!' I leave the café with her ... she hangs on to me which I find unpleasant but suffer it ... Before her house she pulls out an enormous bunch of keys and gives one to me. 'I trust only you with it; it is the key to this case. You might like to use it. Just watch that my husband doesn't get hold of it.'

The dream contains several of the classic Freudian symbols of sex, such as the suitcase, the key and the phrase 'For ladies only'. Miss E. had not, according to Schroetter, heard or read of Freud's ideas.

Roffenstein, suspecting Miss E. may have known something of

Freudian ideas, chose 'a twenty-eight-year-old, totally uneducated nursemaid of lower than average intelligence, who grew up and still lives in an uneducated milieu'. He suggested she dream of intercourse with her father. She reported: 'I dreamt about my father, as if he had presented me with a great bag ... and with it he gave me a large key. It was a very large key. It looked like the key to a house. I had a sad feeling. I opened the bag. A snake jumped out against my mouth; I shrieked aloud.'

More recent experiments are reported by Woods and Greenhouse in *New World of Dreams*. The suggestion was made to one subject that as a child she had wet the bed and her mother scolded her. That night she dreamt she fell into a pond in winter and her mother was angry. An interesting aspect of these experiments is that another subject under hypnosis was told the dream and asked what it meant. Without hesitation she said, 'Oh, that girl must have wet the bed.' This and other experiments suggest humans have an inherent, although perhaps unconscious ability to understand the language of dreams.

I   See: **dreamer**; **identity and dreams**; **individuation**.

ice   Being cold emotionally or sexually. It depicts what is meant by the term cold shoulder, where we shut off any display of warmth or compassion. It also therefore shows the dreamer as having 'frozen assets' in a personal sense. <u>Icicle</u>: frozen male sexual feelings. <u>Iceberg</u>: similar to ice, but may suggest frozen potential. <u>Body locked in ice, perhaps dead</u>: deadening of all our feeling reactions and enjoyment or motivation. <u>Idioms</u>: break the ice; cut no ice; put on ice; tread on thin ice. See: **cold**.

identity and dreams   To have a sense of personal existence distinct from others may be unique to human beings and in large measure due to the learning of language. Jung and Neumann's studies of the historical development of identity suggest, in an evolutionary sense, that having an 'I' is still a very newly acquired function. This makes it vulnerable. It is also noticeably something which develops during childhood and reaches different levels of maturity during adulthood. Although it is our central experience, it remains an enigma – a will o' the wisp which loses itself in dreams and sleep, yet is so dominant and sure in waking.

In dreams, our sense of self – our ego, our personality or identity – is depicted by our own body, or sometimes simply by the sense of our own existence as an observer. In most dreams our 'I' goes through a series of experiences just as we do in waking life, seeing things through our physical eyes, touching with our hands and so on. But occasionally we watch our own body and other people as if from a detached point of bodiless awareness. If we accept that

215

dreams portray in images our conception of Self, then dreams suggest that our identity largely depends upon having a body, its gender, health, quality, the social position we are born into, and our relationship with others. In fact we know that if a person loses their legs, becomes paralysed, loses childbearing ability or is made redundant, they face an identity crisis. But the bodiless experience of Self shows the human possibility of sensing Self as having separate existence from the biological processes, one's body, one's state of health and social standing. In its most naked form, the 'I' may be simply a sense of its own existence, without body awareness.

Dreams also show our sense of Self, either in the body or naked of it, as surrounded by a community of beings and objects separate from the dreamer, and frequently with a will of their own. If we place the dreamer in the centre of a circle and put all their dream characters, animals and objects around them, and if we transformed these objects and beings into the things they depicted – such as sexuality, thinking, will, emotions, intuition, social pressure, etc. – we would see what a diverse mass of influences the ego stands in the middle of. It also becomes obvious that our 'I' sees things as outside itself in nearly all dreams. Even its own internal urges to love or make love may be shown as external creatures it has a multitude of ways of relating to.

If we take the word psyche to mean our sense of Self, then in our dreams we often see our psyche at war with the sources of its own existence, and trying to find its way through a most extraordinary adventure – the adventure of consciousness. In this adventure – very like the Odyssey – the psyche meets all manner of creatures, people, demons, temptations. It travels into dark places, climbs to the heights of wondrous experience, discovers magical powers. One of the functions of dreams can therefore be thought to be that of aiding the survival of the psyche in facing the multitude of influences in life – and even in death.

Another aspect of Self which is depicted so vividly in dreams is the way we create our own heaven or hell in life. When we realise each aspect of the dream, each emotion, each landscape and environment are materialisations of our own feeling states, we begin to see how we live in the midst of a world – thoughts, feelings, values, judgements, fears – largely of our own making. Whatever we think or feel, even in the depths of our being, becomes a material fact of experience in our dream. In the world of the psyche we are the creator for we shape with the magical powers of the mind, with the streaming energy of sexuality and with the colours of our emotions, whole worlds and multitudes to fill them. From this experience we might say that our life is a dream. This is not saying our life is an illusion or unreal, but that the great loves we feel, along with their jealousy and passion, the sense of our own success or failure, the struggle and pain we strive to survive, all emerge out of our feeling states. The feeling and mental states are our own private universe like a dream. They are our own private 'dreams' we colour our life with, weave an intense story about ourselves with and live within and feel have enormous reality – and yet are as insubstantial as a thought. It is almost certainly this inner universe which religion speaks of as heaven or hell. Finding some degree of direction, mastery or harmony within this world of our own being, is the great work of individuation or maturity. See: **dreamer**; **individuation**.

idol   See: **statue**.

igloo   A cold and perhaps unloving home environment. Also the womb; frigidity; a sense of uncaring parental influence. See: **ice**.

illness   If one has painful memories which are never cleared, or feelings of anger or resentment which are held within, these will often be shown in a dream as an illness or infection; a collapse of one's confidence, or the uprising of fears and depression can also be shown as illness. Also occasionally depicts the way we attempt to get love or attention – by being ill; sometimes relates to our actual physical body, but quite rarely; also may show our intuitions about the physical condition of someone else.

Strangely, for both the Africans and Artemidorus, the dreams of illness and death signified the opposite – recovery. See: **body**; **infection**.

imprisoned   We are often imprisoned by a state of mind, by a fear or by ignorance. In attempting to develop a relationship, we may be trapped by feelings of dependence upon what our parents want us to do. If we fear failure we will not meet the challenge of the new, so we are imprisoned by the fear. Such feelings as being an outsider, unwanted, resentful, can also imprison us in particular situations. See: **escape**; **trapped**.

incest   Such dreams very seldom refer to physical incest, but to the desires we carry from infancy to possess or be in control of the love and body of our parents. As a baby we have a sense that nothing exists outside of ourselves – therefore everything should obey our desires. That it does not, that parents do other than what we need of them is a shock that is a part of maturing. Our infant emotions, uncensored by social rules and self-consciousness, are enormously powerful, and wherever unsatisfied or unresolved are stored unconsciously. If we are to integrate the potential energy locked in these areas, we must meet some of the incestuous desires and transform them into adult love.

incubation   As can be seen from the entry on **hypnosis**, the dream process is quite amenable to suggestion and conscious influence. It is probably most helpful to think of this action as similar to the process of memory. In seeking information from memory we hold a question or idea in consciousness, the resulting associated memories or information are largely spontaneous. The question held directs what information is taken from the enormous pool of memory. A question might even call together scattered pieces of information which are then put together into a new composite, a new realisation. So the process is not only recall of existing memory, but creative. It may also access skills such as the ability to subtract one number from another.

Because of these factors our conscious queries can influence the process of dreaming, causing them to respond. As dreams have access to our full memory, our creative potential as well as learnt skills, such response to concerns or queries are often of great value.

To make use of this, first consider the query as fully as possible while awake. Look at it from as many viewpoints as you can, talk it over with others. Make note of the areas that are already clear and what still remains to be clarified. Just before going to sleep, use imagery to put your question to your unconscious resources. Imagine standing before a circle of gentle light – a symbol of one's total Self – and asking it for the information sought. Then, as if you have asked a question of a wise friend, create a relaxed state as if listening for the considered reply. In most cases, dreams which follow will in some way be a response to what is sought, though not necessarily in the way imagined. See: **creativity and problem-solving in dreams**; **dream process as computer**.

Indian   An aspect of your own desires or needs which you do not usually identify with or acknowledge. See: **aboriginal**.

individuation   One of Carl Jung's most interesting areas of thought is that of individuation. In a nutshell the word refers to the processes involved in becoming a self-aware human being. The area of our being we refer to when we say 'I', 'me' or 'myself', is our conscious self-awareness, our sense of Self, which Jung calls the ego.

The autobiography of Helen Keller has helped in understanding what may be the difference between an animal and a human being with self-awareness. Helen, made blind and deaf through illness prior to learning to speak, lived in a dark unconscious world lacking any self-awareness until the age of seven when she was taught the deaf and dumb language. At first her teacher's fingers touching hers were simply a tactile but meaningless experience. Then, perhaps because she had learnt one word prior to her illness, meaning flooded her darkness. She tells us that 'Nothingness was blotted out.' Through language she became a person and developed a sense of Self, whereas before there had been – nothing.

The journey of individuation is not only that of becoming a person, but also expanding the boundaries of what we can allow ourselves to experience as an ego. As we can see from an observation of our dreams, but mostly from an extensive exploration of their feeling content, our ego is conscious of only a small area of experience. The fundamental life processes in one's being may be barely felt. In many contemporary women, the reproductive drive is talked about as something which has few connections with their personality. Few people have a living, feeling contact with their early childhood, in fact many people doubt that such can exist. Because of these factors the ego can be said to exist as an encapsulated small area of consciousness, surrounded by huge areas of experience it is unaware of.

To a different degree, there exists in each of us a drive toward the growth of our personal awareness, toward greater power, greater inclusion of the areas of our being which remain unconscious. A paradox exists here because the urge is toward integration, yet individuation is also the process of greater self-differentiation. Also this is a spontaneous process, just as the growth of a tree from a seed is – the tree in dreams often represents this process of self-becoming – but our personal responsibility for our process of growth is necessary at a certain point to make conscious what is unconscious.

Because dreams are constantly expressing aspects of individuation it is worth knowing the main areas of the process. Without sticking rigidly to Jungian concepts – which see individuation as occurring from mid-life onwards in a few individuals – an aspect of some of the main stages are as follows.

Early babyhood   The emergence of self-consciousness through the deeply biological, sensual and gestural levels of experience, all deeply felt. The felt responses to emerging from a non-changing world in the womb. Also the emergence from a feeling of deep unity with the mother, and of being undifferentiated life awareness. The need to reach out for food and make other needs known. Learning how to deal with changing environment and otherness in terms of relationship.

Childhood   Learning the basics of motor, verbal and social skills. The very basics of physical and emotional independence. One faces here the finding of strength to escape the domination of mother – difficult because one is dependent upon the parent in a very real way – and develop in the psyche a satisfying sexual connection. In dream imagery this means, for the male, an easy sexual relationship with female dream figures and a means of dealing with male figures in competition – father. See: **sex in dreams**. The dream of the mystic beautiful woman precedes this – a female figure one blends with in an idealistic sense, but is never sexual. The conflict with father – really the internal struggle with one's image of father as more potent than Self – when resolved becomes an acceptance of the power of one's own manhood.

Women face a slightly different situation. The woman's first deeply sensual and sexual love object – in a bonded parent–child relationship – was her mother. So beneath any love she may develop for a man lies the love for a woman. Whereas a man, in sexual love which takes him deeply into his psyche, may realise he is making love to his mother, a woman in the same situation may find her father or her mother as the love object. In the unconscious motivations which lead one to choose a mate, a man is influenced by the relationship he developed with his mother – a woman is influenced by both mother and father in her choice.

At these deep levels of fantasy and desire, one has to recognise that the first sexual experience is – hopefully – at mother's breast. This can be transformed into later fantasies/dreams/desires of penis in the mouth; or penis in vagina; or penis as breast, mouth as vagina.

> *Example: 'I have recently gained a new girlfriend. We used to look forward to going out together and going to bed. Since she moved in with me my feelings have changed. I dreamt about her with real hatred. I woke up shouting "I hate you!" Just before I woke her face and hair changed to look like my mother.' John (Teletext).*

For most of us, however, growth toward maturity does not present itself in such primitively sexual ways, simply because we are largely unconscious of such factors. In general we face the task of building a self-image out of the influences, rich or traumatic, of our experience. We learn to stand, as well as we may, amidst the welter of impressions, ideas, influences and urges which constitute our life and body. What we inherit, what we experience and what we do with these create who we are.

Puberty In a real sense, one has already undergone radical transformations before reaching puberty. The loss of the womb, the death of babyhood with it delicious or terrible dependence, the falling away of early childhood, have all been journeyed through. But now there is greater self-awareness, self-consciousness than ever before, and this makes puberty a transition and a death with many more difficulties. The major changes here are the meeting of the sexual drive that urges one toward the opposite sex; the finding of a sense of Self that enables one to meet other adults in a world of action and interaction; the success or failure to let the flame of one's life forge action in the world sufficient to satisfy one's urge to power, to creativity, toward recognition and acknowledgement by one's fellows. Failure to achieve these may lead to some level of remaining dependence upon parents for money, emotional support and even housing – lack of full heterosexual adaptation and so a remaining in adolescent homosexuality – a partial passivity in the world or a difficulty in initiating change.

One of the great areas of learning for this period connects with how to meet other adults outside our family. We begin to turn toward strangers for important reasons such as looking for a mate; finding others to work with or acknowledge our own ideas such as music, writing, etc. We try to make things happen in human society and so meet the co-operation and antagonism of others more fully than protected childhood and its groupings allowed.

During the change from adolescent to adult, one of the greatest of our childhood needs becomes apparent in the way we meet situations and the choices we make. The need is for parental enthusiastic love and recognition of oneself as a unique person. If we have not received this love we carry in us such pain and need, it influences all our decisions. Even without any maltreatment, the lack of love traumatises us. There are so few of us who have actually received this love to the degree we needed that the dealing with this inner lack is one of the major tasks before us if we are to reach our full potential. This is often worked out in our relationships and the tribulations that arise out of our desperate need for, or pain regarding, intimacy.

Example: 'I am a sixteen-year-old girl. In my dream I wake up in bed with the boy I am in love with beside me. He wakes and we start kissing. My parents come in and throw us out. I am pregnant and he stands by me. When the baby arrives another boy, who is a close friend, says it is his.' Jordan (Teletext).

Example: 'I'm an eleven-year-old girl and have fancied this boy for ages. I dream I meet him a town and he tells me he loves me. Then we are in school uniform and older boys from my school beat him up. I dream this often and wake crying. Now I'm frightened to tell him I love him in case he gets hurt.' H.M.J. (Teletext).

*Example: 'I have had this dream for about three months now.
It is about a bus driver I really like. I am only fifteen and I see
him and me making love. He is about twenty-three. The other
day he asked me when my sixteenth birthday was. I wonder if
that meant anything. Could you let me know if anything
serious could happen between us?' Debbie (Teletext).*

Our further process of maturing includes some of the major themes
of individuation such as: the journey from attachment and dependence toward independence. This is experienced as an involved
detachment with the possibility of loving independence within a
relationship. Independence is an overall theme we mature in all our
life. In its widest sense it pertains to the fact that the origins of our
consciousness lie in a non-differentiated state of being in which no
sense of 'I' exists. Out of this womb condition we gradually develop
an ego and personal choice. In fact we may swing to an extreme of
egotism and materialistic feelings of independence from others and
nature. The observable beginnings of this move to independence are
seen in our attempt to become independent of mother and father,
but dependence has many faces. We may have a dependent
relationship with a husband or wife. We may depend upon our work
or social status for our self-confidence. Our youth and good looks
may be the things we depend upon for our sense of who we are –
our self-image. With the approach of middle and old age we will
then face a crisis in which an independence from these factors is
necessary for our psychological equilibrium. The Hindu practice of
becoming a *sanyassin*, leaving behind family, name, social standing,
possessions, is one way of meeting the need for inner independence
from these to meet old age and death in a positive manner. Most
people face it in a quieter, less demonstrative way. Indeed, death
may be thought of as the greatest challenge to our identification with
body, family, worldly status and the external world as means to
identity. We leave this world naked except for the quality of our own
being.

Meeting oneself and self-responsibility   The fact that our waking
Self is a small spotlight of awareness amidst a huge ocean of
unconscious life processes creates a situation of tension, certainly a
threshold or 'iron curtain', between the known and unknown. If one

imagines the spotlighted area of Self as a place where one is standing, then individuation is the process of extending the boundary of awareness, or even turning the spotlight occasionally into the surrounding gloom. In this way one places together impressions of what the light revealed of the dark landscape in which we stand; clues as to how we got to be where we are and where we might move on.

The landscape is in fact made up of our past, the massive prior experience of the cosmos, nature, our culture and our family, and how we relate to these. This past is the basis upon which all our present experience is built. It is the fact of our physical body, our language, our family genetic history. But one may remain, or choose to remain largely unconscious of Self in connection with these. The iron curtain may be defended with our desire not to know what really motivates us, what past hurts and angers we hide, what individual, family and cultural traumas forged our likes and dislikes, our talent and ignorance. It may be easier for us to live with an exterior God or authority than to recognise the ultimate need for self-responsibility and self-cultivation. To hide from this, humanity has developed innumerable escape routes – exteriorised religious practice; making scapegoats of other minority groups or individuals; rigid belief in a political system or philosophy; search for *samadhi* or God as a final solution; suicide.

This aspect of our maturing process shows itself as a paradox, common to maturity, of becoming more sceptical and yet finding a deeper sense of Self in its connections with the cosmos. We lose God and the beliefs of humanity's childhood, yet realise we are the God we searched for. This meeting with Self, in all its deep feeling of connection, its uncertainty, its vulnerable power, is not without pain and joy. See: first example in **dreams as spiritual guide**.

The last of the great themes of individuation is summed up in William Blake's words: 'I must Create a System, or be enslav'd by another Man's; I will not Reason and Compare: my business is to Create.' A function observable in dreams is that of scanning our massive life experience. Even a child's life experience has millions of bits of information from which it can gather enormous information about *life* and *survival*. Out of this we unconsciously create a working philosophy of what life means *to us*. It is made up not only of what we have experienced and learnt in the general sense, but also from the hidden information in the cultural riches we have inherited from language, literature, music, art, theatre and architecture. The word 'hidden' is used because the unconscious 'reads' the symbolised information in these sources. It is, after all, the mastery of imagery being the creator of dreams. But unless we expand the boundaries of our awareness we may not know this inner philosopher. If we do get to know it through dreams, we will be amazed by the beauty of its insight into everyday human life.

In connection with this there is an urge to *be*, and perhaps to procreate oneself in the world. Sometimes this is experienced as a sense of frustration – that there is more of us than we have been able to express or to make real. While physical procreation can be seen as a physical survival urge, this drive to create in other spheres may be an urge to survive death as an identity. Dreams frequently present the idea that our survival of death only comes about from what we have given of ourselves to others. This creative aspect of ourselves apparently is active at the moment of death according to the many accounts of the deathbed review of one's entire life – particularly as such reviews seem to be largely about what one has 'gathered' or learnt from the experience of living.

There is a disinclination to deeply consider death in Western culture. What passes for this is the excuse that physical death ends all life when such a statement is observably not true. Nothing that we can see in the physical world exists outside of evolutionary connections with past objects or forms. Our language, our body, our personality, have all arisen out of what existed previously. The past is obviously alive in the present, so how can there be death to anything except the limited awareness people consider to be themselves – their ego?

Death is the great adventure of the psyche. The great undertaking of individuation takes us into the meeting with our birth and infant traumas. We face the monsters created by our sense of being unloved, of parental desertion or betrayal. The demons of self-doubt, of self-destructiveness, of worldly struggle and fear spring up to meet us on the journey and we have to do battle. The negative habits of our lifetime pull at us or bind us to our past unless we can break free. The instinctive hungers and drives, of reactive fear, challenge us. Can we take the tiny boat of our self-awareness across their swirling and torrential waters? Can we swim in the whirlpool of desire and use its energy to achieve a new awareness and transcendence? But after all these great feats, should we find our way through them, lies not an uplifting of our being into wonder – but death!

What a strange blow it is, after journeying so far in the psychic adventure of ourselves, after being the hero or heroine of so many battles, that when we come to the holy grail, the golden fleece, the inner sanctum of ourselves, we meet not a treasure but an empty cave. Nothing is there waiting for us – except death – the strangest paradox of all. Strangely though it is this nothing, this emptiness, this loss of Self, which holds in it the centre of ourselves. With extinction of our effort and drive, with the dying of ourselves, there comes a self-existent radiance in us. The meeting with nothing, the void, is the great treasure itself, that penetrates us and transforms us.

Dreams, when they are the great creations of high awareness, suggest the cosmos arose out of a huge death – the big bang – a death planned out of love so that we might exist. Meeting death while alive – relinquishing all we have considered to be the reason for our personal existence; dropping the urge to grasp what have been the goals of one's life, such as sex, money, power, self-expression – brings a new life in which we realise our intimate oneness with life. And although this seems like an end as we enter it, as we die to it, the vastness of it promises new and wondrous life. See: **Jung**; **love**.

infection   Ideas or thoughts which cause irritability or negative internal states. Thinking one's job is not secure might create disinterest and loss of motivation in work even if, in reality the job is secure; taking in negative attitudes from others; warning about physical health; sexual impregnation. See: **illness**; **body**.

injection   Feeling other people's opinions or will forced on and influencing one; internal influence of something exterior; social pressure to conform or be obedient; sexual intercourse. If a sedative is given: return to non-responsibility as in infancy. See: **syringe**.

insects   General: irritations or feeling something 'bugging one'; feeling insignificant – the ant in the mass of other ants; sexual urges, especially with cockroaches; as Jiminy Cricket suggests, insects can represent our conscience and guilt which reminds us of feelings we might sooner forget – perhaps insects represent these areas because they live their life in our house and garden largely unseen and so depict thoughts and feelings occurring on the edge of consciousness. Also one's children – if flying off, children leaving home. <u>Wasp or hornets</u>: painful emotions; feeling stung by remarks. <u>Lice or parasites</u>: thoughts or sexual habits which are purely selfish or carry a health risk; feeling others are parasitic. <u>Spider</u>: often the dependent emotions and conflicts one feels 'caught in' connected with mother; any emotions you don't want to 'handle', such as those surrounding a spouse leaving. See: **web**.

The example below shows memories of pain and anger are still irritating or 'bugging' Rita. The swamp shows these feelings undermine her confidence.

Example: 'I have to keep walking because there is something I am afraid of behind me. When I am pressed up against the ceiling being crushed I look down and the stairs and banister rail are swarming alive with a black moving wave of crawling things, like some awful insects. In the hallway is a swamp with crocodiles and other hideous things. My terror is terrible. The person who actually lived in this part of the house was the owner's mother. She treated me badly but no one knew as she was artful in her abuse. She pulled me along by my hair, locked me in a cupboard, and once locked me in the orchard – four high walls and a hidden door.' Rita.

Example: 'I had an awful pain in my left thumb. On going to the doctor he examined it and changed into a surgeon who operated on the thumb. As he cut it open masses of spiders poured out, releasing the pain.' Paula (LBC).

Paula's mother had died shortly before the dream. She had subsequently experienced a lot of emotional pain about undealt-with feelings between herself and her mother. These had begun to pour out into her conscious life. The dream therefore represented this as a healing process.

insomnia   See: **sleep**.

intercourse   See: **sex in dreams**.

interpretation of dreams   Although mind and body may be a total unity and the separation in language merely a convenience, despite its unity our being has a number of interacting systems within the unity. The action of the heart on the other systems is obvious, and the influence of emotions on the organs is also becoming obvious. What is not so well established is the importance of the feedback occurring when we gain insight into our own functioning through understanding a dream. Although our being is already a self-regulating system, the ability to turn consciousness inwards to make clear aspects of unconscious function appears to increase the efficiency of self-regulation. This is shown in the first example in **reptiles – lizards and snakes** where David's long-standing neck pain goes through insight into its cause. In this way we might be seen as a conscious organism which not only reprograms mental patterns or habits, but to some extent can renovate or change body efficiency as well. See: **dream analysis**; **dream processing**; **introduction**.

interpretation of dreams – history of   Most societies, ancient and modern, have professional dream interpreters. India has its Brahmin *oneirocritics*; in Japan the *om myoshi*; the Hasidic rabbis in Europe fulfilled this role; in ancient Egypt the *pa-hery-tep*; ancient Greece had the priesthood within the Asclepian temples given to dreams; among the Aztecs, dream interpretation and divination were the prerogative of the priestly class *teopexqui*, the Masters of Secret Things; in today's world the Freudian and Jungian psychoanalysts fulfil this role – I work as resident analyst for both London Broadcasting Company and television's Channel 4 Teletext.

Some of the most ancient written documents are about dream interpretation. The Chester Beatty papyrus for instance, dates from 1250 BC, from Egypt. This contains records of 200 dreams and their interpretations according to the priests of Horus.

Most social roles that survive for such long periods of time fulfil some useful purpose. The most fundamental purpose of dream interpretation is probably that of reducing tension and anxiety in the dreamer. In skilful use of dream interpretation there may also be a powerful shift in the dreamer toward greater understanding of their life situation or their internal process. With such understanding they find themselves in greater accord with themselves. As with any role, however, there is also the aspect of manipulation and control of ideas and behaviour which can occur when a lay person seeks the advice of priest or professional.

Although in some cultures the concept of dreams and their interpretation was clearly one in which dreams were seen as an expression of unconscious wishes, fears and insights of the dreamer, in some ages and cultures dreams were connected with divination, spirits and good and bad luck. This was true of periods of European history, but lights of understanding still existed. An illustration is this quote of Paracelsus rediscovered by Jung: 'That which the dream shows is the shadow of such wisdom as exists in the man, even if during his waking state he may know nothing about it; for we ought to know that God has given us our own wisdom and knowledge, reason, and the power to perceive the past and the future; but we do not know it, because we are fooling away our time with outward and perishing things, and are asleep in regard to that which is real within ourself.'

Dreams have also been linked with numerology. In 1654, *The Palace of the Curious* was published in France. It explained how algebra and the laws of chance are means by which we can interpret the most puzzling of dreams. This became a tradition and many dream dictionaries published today still explain dreams in this way. Alongside these there were many claiming to explain dreams according to ancient Egyptian wisdom. As Norman Mackenzie says in his excellent review of these books in his *Dreams and Dreaming*, these 'modern dream books represent the most degenerate form of what was once regarded as a divine art; they lack any real religious or magical sanction, and are simply an expression of popular superstition, like the belief in lucky numbers, lucky colours or birthstones. Whatever meaning may once have lain behind the symbols and the interpretation has long been lost.'

intruder   See: **burglar, intruder**.

inventor   Creative aspect of oneself; personal insights; the Self.

invisible   Becoming invisible, or appearing out of nowhere suggests something emerging from the unconscious, being forgotten, or relating to the unconscious; hidden influences – as when touching dimensions of experience states of consciousness usually unknown.

iron   Strength; the material side of life; unbending emotions. Idioms: iron fist in velvet glove; iron curtain; man of iron; rule with rod of iron.

Iroquoian dream cult   The Iroquois (Huron and Seneca) American Indians, as early as the first European contact in the seventeenth century, had developed a deeper psychological understanding than the white races of the time. They had no divinity but the dream, according to Father Fremin who studied their customs. They clearly described the conscious and unconscious, and said that through dreams the hidden or unconscious area of psyche makes its desires known. If it does not receive these desires it becomes angry. The Iroquois therefore developed a system of allowing the dreamer to act out their dreams socially. Although a moral and disciplined group, during such acting-out the dreamer was allowed to go beyond usual social boundaries. This included receiving valuable objects and making love to another person's spouse. This was to allow unconscious desires to be expressed, thus avoiding sickness of body or mind. Such hidden desires were seen as the basis of social as well as individual problems.

island   Feelings of isolation or loneliness – the loneliness could be as one might feel when retired from work, isolated from situation you once knew; feeling trapped; feeling safe from the world by introversion. Swimming or getting to an island: move to independence. Desert island: Attempt to 'get away from it all'. Island in stormy sea: personality traits which give strength amidst difficult emotions and turbulence. Large island with other people: isolating oneself by involvement with a particular belief, group of people or problem.

ivory   Something precious or beautiful, such as an insight or personal quality, which has grown out of the push and shove of life experience.

jailer May be any of a range of attitudes such as guilt, self-criticism, sense of alienation, intellect, which restrict the expression of other parts of one's nature. So attitudes or concepts you imprison yourself with, or hold yourself back with. See: **prison**.

jellyfish See: **fish**, **sea creatures**.

Jesus In a general sense, free from institutional dogma, Jesus can represent the human experience of life in the body, in which we meet conflict, temptation and death – consciousness meeting life in the body. If you have religious beliefs, Jesus would represent those beliefs. In many dreams though, Jesus depicts the link we have in our own life with what is eternally abiding in the world – with the one life existing in all phenomena. See: *Christ* under **archetypes**.

jewellery May represent the giver of the piece, or one's feelings about them; love given or received; something valuable in a 'quality of our life' sense, such as something we have learnt through hard experience and ought to value; a woman's honour, self-respect, sexuality. If the jewellery has a particular history, such as a family heirloom or the first piece of jewellery given by spouse, then it represents what we feel about family tradition, spouse, etc. See: **jewels**; **ring**.

jewels General: things we or our unconscious treasure; our integrity or sense of wholeness; the lasting parts of our nature, even the eternal aspect of Self or the essential core of ourselves. For instance, ability to creatively work with others is not just valuable in

231

general, it also expresses the powerful symbiotic force in nature. It connects one with the universal. This might be depicted as a jewel.

Because of the different colours in jewels, some of them may have slightly different meanings. Amethyst: healing; influence of dreams. Diamond: human greed; hardness of nature; what one values; the aspects of one's life that are lasting and valuable, not only in an everyday sense, but in a cosmic sense. Emerald: personal growth and awareness of connection with the natural in life. Opal: the inner world of fantasies and dreams; psychic impressions. Pearl: inner beauty and value that has arisen from the irritations or trials of life. Ruby: emotions, passion, sympathies; extending Self to others. Sapphire: religious feelings; expansion of thinking boundaries.

jokes in dreams   See: **wordplay**, **puns**.

journey   How we are feeling about our life and its ups and downs, goals and destinations, challenges and opportunities; undertakings we embark on, or experiences being met; what the overall tone of our life is may be depicted by the dream journey; the direction our unconscious is taking us; our life and what it is achieving.

In our life we have lots of journeys, such as that through schooling; marriage and perhaps divorce; work; parenthood; and the overall journey of life and death. See: where applicable **day and night**, for time of journey; **aeroplane**; **boat**; **car**; **hill**; **individuation**; **train**.

judge   Sense of guilt or self-judgement; conscience; decision making. May depict the 'shoulds' and 'should nots' we apply to ourselves or our moral code. Sometimes, the way we judge others becomes a harsh judge of ourselves. Feeling what a failure our parents were in raising us becomes a difficult judgement of our own state as a parent. Idioms: judge not, that ye be not judged; sit in judgement.

jump   See: **postures**, **movement**, **body language**.

Jung, Carl (1875–1961)   Son of a pastor; his paternal grandfather and great grandfather were physicians. Took a degree in medicine at University of Basle, then specialised in psychiatry. In early papers he pioneered the use of word association and influenced research into the toxin hypothesis regarding schizophrenia. Jung's addition to modern therapeutic attitudes to dream work arose out of his difference of view with Freud regarding human life. Jung felt life is a meaningful experience with spiritual roots. His interest in alchemy, myths and legends added to the wealth of ideas he brought to his concept of the collective unconscious. The subject of symbols fascinated him and he devoted more work to this than any other psychologist. He saw dream symbols not as an attempt to veil or hide inner content, but an attempt to elucidate and express it. It is a way of transformation where what was formless, non-verbal and unconscious moves towards form and becoming known. In this way dreams 'show us the unvarnished natural truth'. By giving attention to our dreams we are throwing light upon who and what we really are – not simply who we are as a personality, but who we are as a phenomena of cosmic interactions.

Jung recommended looking at a series of one's dreams in order to develop a fuller insight into Self. In this way one would see certain themes arising again and again. Out of these we can begin to see where we are not balancing the different aspects of ourselves. See: **abreaction**; **active imagination**; **amplification**; **archetypes**; **black person**; **collective unconscious**; **compensatory theory**; **creativity and problem-solving in dreams**; **dream analysis**; **dream as spiritual guide**; **Fromm, Eric**; **identity and dreams**; **individuation**; **lucidity**; **mandala**; **unconscious**.

jungle   Eruption of urges and feelings from the unconscious – could be negative or positive depending on dream; confusion; area of 'uncivilised' or unconscious, may be non-socialised feelings and urges, therefore may contain unmet anxieties – snakes and lions – or sexual urges – native men and women. Idioms: law of the jungle.

jury   Decision making; conscience. See: **judge**.

keel See: **boat**, **ship**.

key Any attitude, thought or feeling which opens up areas of memory, experience or motivation previously 'locked up'; realisation or information which allows solution to a problem; depicts an effective way of doing something. Also very often the penis or sexual intercourse.

kick Self-assertion; self-expression; protectiveness; aggressiveness. Idioms: for kicks; kick-back; kick over the traces; kick in the teeth; kick the bucket; alive and kicking. See: **hostility**.

kidnap If the dreamer is the victim of kidnappers: the forces of our own fears and negative feelings are often presented as an external force or organised gang who victimise us. If such feelings are recognised for what they are, self-created emotions, they lose their power. Being kidnapped also suggests loss of security or feelings of security, or someone else forcing their will on one. Kidnapping someone else: influencing someone else against their will. This may of course be about oneself, referring to forcing oneself to do something that one's feelings are against.

kill Being killed: an interior or exterior influence which you feel is 'killing' – undermining, making ineffective, strangling, choking – one's self-confidence or sense of identity. Killing: repressing or stopping some aspect of oneself – as when we kill our love for someone. Killing parents or animals: see: **animals**; **family**.

Example: 'When inside the house I dream of recurrently, I am terrified of someone, a man who is trying to find and kill me.' Barbara T.

As a young woman Barbara discovered the dead body of her father. He had shot himself in the house of her dream. Being killed here shows Barbara feeling overwhelmed by the feelings about her father – the man.

Example: 'Some two weeks before my dear wife died of cancer of the oesophagus, at about three o'clock in the morning, she shot up in bed screaming "No. No! No!" On questioning her she said her mother, who had died in November 1981, was trying to kill her.' Gerry B.

In this unusual dream the wife feels the approach of death, depicted by her mother. As dreams suggest death is as much a new area of experience as adolescence was, it would have helped to meet the mother of this dream and find a more positive relationship as described in **dream processing**. See: **death**.

king   One's father; as the father the king may depict our need for approval and loving acknowledgement; what you are ruled by; feelings of inferiority/superiority. Also in times past the king represented the group, the overall collective psyche of the people. He therefore became synonymous with God as the Pope is today. The word God was here equivalent to 'the collective psyche'. So the king or queen may represent our relationship with our fellows, our sense of identity, or depict the way we feel in relationship with the society in which we live. The acclaim or lack of notice given by the monarch in our dream also deals with this theme – of how we see ourselves in connection with the public – our public image of ourselves. See: **people**; **queen**.

Example: 'I was engaged to be married to the Emperor. I then discovered he was in love with another woman and planned to marry her. I was devastated.' Sally (LBC).

Sally felt unloved by her father and the drama of her dream works out this theme of feeling rejected.

kiss   Acceptance of what is being kissed – Pat in the example in *cat* accepts or allows her sexuality depicted by the cat; sexual agreement; tenderness; movement toward unity. Idioms: kiss of life; kiss of death; kiss something/somebody goodbye. See: first example in *cat* under **animals**.

kitchen   See: *house* under **house**, **buildings**.

knapsack   The resources and difficulties we carry in life; our past experience or karma; a burden – perhaps of nursed anger or other negative feelings – if we feel parenthood is a heavy load we may see our child as a burden.

kneel   See: **postures**, **movement**, **body language**.

knife   See: **weapons**.

knitting   Something you are concentratedly working at in your life; knitting a relationship together; consider what garment is being made and refer to **clothes**.

knob   Penis; one's hold on a situation. Door knob: Turning point in opportunity, sexual or otherwise.

knock   One's attention called to whatever is knocking. Some aspect of Self, or a realisation is asking to be let into consciousness. Knocking: trying to get attention; wanting to be allowed into someone's life; sexual act.

knot   Tangle of feelings or tension; relational tie; a problem; the ties we have to work, family, mother's apron strings, or viewpoints.

krishna   See: *Christ* under **archetypes**.

label Self-image; how you feel others see you; your view of what is labelled; definition of your feelings if labelled to someone else.

ladder Your feelings – whether anxious or secure – about reaching situations or opportunities in life which are new or not easily attained; attainment through effort and daring; the heightening of insecurity, anxiety or feelings in life or sex – getting up; getting it up. Rungs: the separate stages or efforts necessary to 'climb'. Idioms: top of the ladder. See: *stairs* under **house**, **buildings**.

lagoon, lake The inner world of our feelings and fantasies; the unconscious. Sinking into: becoming introverted; giving up on trying or expressing oneself. Looking into depth: self-awareness; looking into oneself. Dirty water: difficult feelings; being unsure of oneself; depression. See: **water**.

lamb See: **animals**.

lame Feeling uncertain about how one stands in life; loss of confidence or strength in expressing oneself or being motivated. Left leg: weakness in the feelings and ideas out of which we gain support. Right leg: weakness in our external activities.

landscapes Our moods and attitudes, but particularly the set of habitual feelings we meet life with. We create our surroundings in dreams and landscapes depict what feelings we ourselves generate and live in. Gloomy: pessimism; self-doubt; depression; a gloomy view of life. Sunny: hopeful; optimistic; something to look forward to. <u>Recurring scenes</u>: habitual attitudes with which you approach situations. <u>Recurring scenes of past residence</u>: a stance you developed from that period of your life. <u>Recurring landscapes</u>: areas of our feelings or psyche we often return to or experience. See: **countryside**.

lane See: **road**.

language and dreams People who are not acquainted with looking at their dreams often feel they are beyond understanding. This seems strange because foreign languages are equally beyond understanding, yet we can accept they can be understood or translated if we know what to associate with the presently meaningless sounds or symbols.

The language of dreams is couched in imagery, allegory, drama, suggestion, word play and innuendo. This doesn't mean it is beyond understanding. After all we understand mime and drama; we understand the wordless play and movements of animals. If we take time to put into words the dramatic scenes and themes dreams present us with we can arrive at a translation that not only satisfies our intellect but also, if we acknowledge the feeling side of dreams, our emotions.

Another aspect of language and dreams is that if we take a word such as 'allegory' it is meaningless until we take time to learn its commonly accepted definition. In this case the *Oxford Dictionary* defines the word as: 'A story, play, poem, picture, etc., in which the meaning or message is represented symbolically. The use of such symbols. A symbol.'

By considering the imagery and drama in a dream we can give them definitions. For instance if a person dreamt of digging in the ground with a spade and uncovering something old, a definition of the drama could be 'digging up the past'. The spade might be defined as the tools, mental or emotional, we use to remember the past. If the dream is of the person digging up treasure, however, the definitions must shift slightly because the 'spade' is now in context with 'treasure'.

Therefore, not only can we define the symbols and drama in dreams just as we can the words of language, but context of dream imagery is as important as the context of words. The word blue for instance changes its meaning enormously – I feel blue, the sky is blue, the blue film, the air was blue with swear words.

In considering our dreams, the definition and context must be considered just as we consider language, as in the sentences using blue. See: **dream interpretation**; **dream processing**; **interpretation of dreams**.

language – foreign or strange   One function of dreams is to bring aspects of our thinking and feeling which may be ill defined toward clarification. Foreign or strange language may therefore illustrate something which is being communicated to us from within, but is still not clear. The unconscious, as in speaking in tongues – glossolalia – and of course in dreams, frequently moves toward clear awareness in stages. The strange language is a halfway house toward focused critical awareness, as is a dream. If we bring focused attention to these, as explained in **dream processing**, the next step, clear verbal expression, can be reached. Speaking in language we are learning: the language is becoming habitual, making it possible to think in it. See: **speaking**.

larder   See: **food**; *house* under **house**, **buildings**.

large   See: **size**.

late   See: **time of day**.

laugh   Release of tension; attempt to put others at ease; ridiculing or feeling embarrassed by some aspect of Self; taking things lightly; attempt to hide the truth. Sometimes much laughter can hide tears or sadness. Idioms: don't make me laugh; laughing stock; laugh in somebody's face; hollow laugh; laugh up one's sleeve; laugh on the other side of your face.

lava   Deeply buried past experience which has pushed to the surface; heated emotions and sexuality; sometimes physical illness such as fever.

lavatory   See: **toilet**.

lead Heavy-hearted; a weighty situation; feeling burdened; materialistic attitudes.

leader See: **roles**.

leaf See: **tree**.

leak Wasted or lost energy; or something being allowed out or expressed. Idioms: leak out – be revealed.

learning while asleep There have been many claims that one can learn while asleep – possibly with the aid of a recorded series of suggestions or information being spoken from a speaker under one's pillow. Different research projects have arrived at a variety of conclusions. The major scientific conclusion is that we do not learn from what we hear while asleep. Sleep is important in the process of learning, however. If one learns a list of nonsense words, memory of them eight or twenty-four hours later is better if we have slept. Memory eight hours later without sleep is not as efficient as twenty-four hours later with intervening sleep. This suggests memory traces are strengthened during sleep.

That we do learn, in the sense of creating new information or perception while we sleep, is generally accepted. Albert Einstein suggested that the creative scientists are those who have access to their dreams. He meant that in order to be innovative we must be able periodically to leave behind the practical everyday path of common sense and rational thought. The rational tends to move in areas of thought connected with what is already known. To create something new, to find a new direction, we may need to be capable of retrieving apparently irrational ideas, sift them and reconstruct them in practical ways.

Dreams have this ability to fantasise, to look at and experience the irrational, to take an idea and move it completely out of its old setting or viewpoint. Because our mind can do this in sleep, we can touch not only our creativity but also our ability to problem solve. As a personal test of this, try the following experiment. At the end of this explanation a problem will be set. It is one that requires no special training or information to solve. The solution is simple and will be seen as correct when reached. But do not even begin to think about the problem until you go to bed! It would discount the experiment if you did. On going to bed, think about the problem for no more than fifteen minutes. If you solve the problem note how long it took. If not, stop thinking about it and go to sleep, making the resolve to remember any dreams. It is likely you will dream the answer. If not, on waking spend a further fifteen minutes trying to reach the answer. The letters 'O, T, T, F, F, –, –,' form the beginning of an intelligible series. Add two more letters which make it obvious that an infinite number of letters could be added.

left behind   Oneself left behind: feelings of rejection or inadequacy; sense of waking up to what you have not done or experienced in life, as Patience does in her dream below. Leaving something or someone behind: leaving the past behind; break-up of relationship. Idioms: fall behind; put it all behind me. See also: **bag**.

> *Example: 'In my dream I woke up and had the feeling that a lot of time had passed. I felt I had lost all this time. A group of friends I was with had gone ahead, left me behind, and I wondered if I would ever catch up.' Patience C.*

left, right   Left: if we are right handed, the left represents the less dominant, less expressed side of ourselves or the parts of our nature we try to hide or suppress. If we write or knock in a nail using our right hand, we will hold the paper or nail with our left. So left leg or arm frequently has this sense of being the supportive but less dominant functions in us. Our confidence may support our activity as a salesperson, so may be depicted as being on the left. Right: the dominant, confident, conscious, exterior or expressed side of Self; rightness; correct social behaviour; moral.

Dreams also use a play on what is right and left to illustrate polarity or opposites. Our internal world of feelings, memories and values – the left; our external world of activity and environment – the right; a secondary choice – left; the 'right' choice at the time – right; parts of Self unconscious or shadowy – left; our conscious known Self – right; the immoral, selfish, wrong action – left; the moral, right action – right.

> *Example: 'On my right are three monks, on my left sits a*

beautiful, shapely blonde. I am in the centre and I see a road which leads to the right and into a beautiful sunlit valley in the distance.' From Dreams Your Magic Mirror *by Elsie Sechrist (published by Cowles).*

Here right and left represent not only choice between sexual pleasure and religious discipline, but also the polar opposites of spiritual and material. Although in the dream there is a movement to the right, to find equilibrium we often have to take a way between the opposites. Idioms: two left feet; keep on the right side of somebody; in one's right mind; in the right; mister right; set somebody right; right-hand man; right in the head; start on the right foot; give one's right arm.

legs   See: *legs* under **body**.

lens   Focusing attention on an area of experience, realisation or intuition.

letter   Thoughts about or intuitions concerning the person letter is from; unrealised feelings about sender; hopes – perhaps to have contact with person. Opening letter: realising something; receiving news; sexual intercourse. Unopened letter: unrecognised intuition; virginity. Blacked edged: news of or feelings about death. Idioms: french letter – condom; red letter day.

library   One's life experience; the wisdom and skills we have gathered; the intellect; research. Huge library: collective unconscious; cosmic mind. See: **book**.

lice   See: **insects**.

life after death   See: **death**; **murder**; **out-of-body experience**; **philosophy of dreams**.

lift   See: *lift* under **house**, **buildings**.

light   General: being aware; being seen; waking as opposed to sleeping; being able to understand and have insight; to see; lightness of heart; confidence; release from dark feelings; becoming aware of how others might see one. Very bright light: intuition; the Self; mega-concept – see **aura**. Spot or searchlight: focusing attention on what is shown.

> *Example: 'I am alone in the house. It begins to grow dark so I switch the light on, but the light is very dim. So I go to another room and try another light, but this light is even dimmer. I carry on like this all over the house until I am in virtual darkness and very frightened.' J.W.*

J.W. was six at the time of the dream, and here light depicts feelings of sureness or confidence which gave way to anxiety. The light is the opposite to the emotions of fear which arise from within. Flickering or dimming lights: feelings about death.

Idioms: bright lights; cold light of day; come to light; hide one's light; in its true light; lighter side; in a good light; see the light; light at the end of the tunnel; throw a light on. See: **dark**; **day**.

lighthouse   Warning of danger of unconscious elements that may wreck areas of your life unless avoided. Use the light to become aware of what the danger is. See: **light**.

lightning   Unexpected changes; discharge of tension, perhaps destructively; expression of wider awareness; intuition; conscience. Killed by lightning: life changes occurring. Lightning struck tree: death in some form.

Sometimes information leading to a realisation builds up over time, but in a flash is put together forming a new, perhaps life-changing insight. The build-up toward a change in lifestyle or direction might similarly occur and so may be depicted by lightning. See: **aura**.

limp   See: **lame**.

liquid   Because feelings are often felt to flow within us – as when we listen to rousing music or notice a feeling in the chest which moves to the throat, which then may become crying or some other expressed emotion – they may be shown in a dream as fluid. Liquid in bottle: a change of feelings, as when we drink wine or medicine; influenced by exterior emotions; contained or withheld emotions. White liquid: milk of kindness, self-giving; or sperm, the magic fluid out of which life emerges.

little   See: **size**.

liver   Irritability; suggestion for health or diet changes, perhaps in connection with alcohol. See: **body**.

lizard   See: **reptiles – lizards**, **snakes**.

lobster   Male sexuality when it appears aggressive and protective; being protective or defended. See: *crab* in **fish**, **sea creatures**.

lock, **locked**   The emotions or physical tensions we use to keep others from 'getting at us', or to prevent our own urges or fears from being experienced or expressed; desire to keep something safe or protected – such as one's honour or emotions; feeling trapped; vagina; sexual tension. Occasionally a problem which needs a specific solution – the key; our ability to choose – whether to let someone into intimate relationship.

looking   See: **seeing**, **saw**, **sight**.

lorry   Similar to car – drives such as ambition, what motivates one – but usually connected with work or our more commercial relationship with people. For instance one's personal motivations meeting the influence of big unified groups such as the police or large businesses.

> *Example: 'I was a passenger in a very large eight-wheeled lorry, my husband being the driver. We stopped at a pedestrian crossing in our town and my husband got out of the driving seat and went into the local town hall near a crossing. I waited in the lorry for what in my dream seemed hours. The next thing I remember is that I was then riding a bicycle on the other side of the crossing and cycled away up the road.' Diann R.*

Her husband's involvement with social and work activities – the lorry and hall – make Diann decide to become more independent rather than wait for her husband to be 'with her'.

losing something   A lost opportunity; forgetting something which is important. Depending on the dream, may also suggest actual, or feelings about, loss of virginity; loss of health; losing a lover/partner; or whatever the lost thing depicts.

lost   Being lost depicts confusion; loss of motivation or ability to make clear decisions. Sometimes suggest issues in your life have arisen and not been noticed and you are being negatively influenced. In which case consider the environment in which you are lost. If lost in an unknown place: it suggests you are in a new area of experience, a new situation or period of your life. You need to take stock calmly and get your bearings.

loudspeaker   Something we have heard; something which is trying to gain 'a hearing'; how we receive aural information – in one ear and out of the other, or is it received and understood?

love   Like most emotions, love in a dream is usually a direct expression of that feeling or a compensation for not receiving it. So one question to ask is whether we are trying to compensate for a lack in our life. Apart from that it may be helpful to see in what way the love is being expressed in the dream. The following stages of love may help in defining this. Baby love: completely dependent upon the loved person for one's needs, physical, emotional and social. Great anger, jealousy or pain if the loved one relates to anyone else. Wants to be always with the loved one. Will have sex, but the emotional bond and cuddling is more important. Adolescent love: initial uncertainty or clumsiness concerning emotional and sexual contact. Desire to explore many relations. Still finding out what one's boundaries are. Great sexual drive. Partner will probably be loved for dreamer's own needs – for example the dreamer wants a family and loves the partner to gain that end; the dreamer loves the partner because in that way they can get away from the parental home. Great romantic feelings and spontaneous love which are difficult to maintain in face of difficulties. Adult love: growing sense of recognising needs of partner yet not denying one's own. Ability to be something for the partner's sake without losing one's own independence or will. Becoming aware of the issues which colour or influence relationship and meeting them as partners. Independence and closeness together. Caring sexual partners through discovering each other's needs and vulnerability.

lover   See: **boyfriend**; **girlfriend**.

lucidity, awake in sleep   Sometimes in the practice of deep relaxation, meditation or sensory deprivation, our being enters into a state akin to sleep, yet we maintain personal waking awareness. This is like a journey into a deeply interior world of mind and body where our senses no longer function in their waking manner; where the brain works in a different way and where awareness is introverted to a degree we do not usually experience. It can be a frightening world simply because we are not accustomed to it.

In a similar way a measure of wakening awareness can arise while dreaming. This is called lucid dreaming. During it we can change or wilfully direct what is happening in the dream in a way not usual to the dream state.

> *Example: 'I had backed my car into a big yard, a commercial area. My wife, two of my sons and I got out of the car. As we stood in the yard talking I realised there was a motorbike where my car should be. I said to everyone, "There was a car here a moment ago, now it's a motorbike. Do you know what that means? It means we are dreaming." Mark, my son, was now with us and my ex-wife. I asked them if they realised they were dreaming. They got very vague and didn't reply. I asked them again and felt very clearly awake.' William V.*

William's is a fairly typical lucid dream, but there are features which it does not illustrate. During the days or weeks prior to a lucid dream, many people experience an increase in flying dreams. The next example shows another common feature.

> *Example: 'In many of my dreams I become aware that I am dreaming. Also, if anything unpleasant threatens me in the*

dream I get away from it by waking myself.' Alan (LBC).

Lucidity often has this feature of enabling the dreamer to avoid unpleasant elements of the dream. The decision to avoid any unpleasant internal emotions is a common feature of a person's conscious life, so this aspect of lucidity is simply a way of taking such a decision into the dream. Some writers even suggest it as a way of dealing with frightening dreams. Avoidance does not solve the problem, it simply pushes the emotion deeper into the unconscious where it can do damage more surreptitiously. Recent findings regarding suppressed grief and stress emotions, which connects them with higher incidence of cancer, suggests that suppression is not a healthy way of dealing with feelings.

Another approach to lucidity is that it can be a sort of playground where one can walk through walls, jump from high buildings and fly, change the sofa into an attractive lover, and so on. True, the realisation that our dream life is a different world and that it does have completely different principles at work than our waking world is important. Often people introvert into their dream life the morals and fears which are only relevant to being awake in physical life. To avoid a charging bull is certainly valid for waking life. In our dream life though, to meet its charge is to integrate the enormous energy which the bull represents, an energy which is our own but which we may have been avoiding or 'running away' from previously. Realising such simple differences revolutionises the way we relate to our own internal events and possibilities. To treat lucid dreams as if they offered no other attainable experience than manipulating the dream environment, or avoidance of encounter, is to miss an amazing feature of human potential.

Example: 'In my dream I was watching a fern grow. It was small but opened out very rapidly. As I watched I became aware that the fern was simply an image representing a process occurring within myself which I grew increasingly aware of as I watched. Then I was fully awake in my dream and realised that my dream, perhaps any dream, was an expression of actual and real events occurring in my body and mind. I felt enormous excitement, as if I were witnessing something of great importance.' Francis P.

It is now acceptable through the work of Freud, Jung and many others, to consider that within the images of the dream lie valuable information about what is occurring within the dreamer, perhaps unconsciously. Strangely though, it is almost never considered that one can have direct perception into this level of internal 'events' without the dream. What Francis describes is an experience of being on the cusp of symbols and direct perception. Considering the enormous advantage of such direct information gathering, it is surprising it is seldom mentioned except in the writings of Corriere and Hart – *The Dream Makers*.

> *Example:* '*After defining why I had not woken in sleep recently, i.e. loss of belief, I had the following experience. I awoke in my sleep and began to see, without any symbols, that my attitudes and sleep movements expressed a feeling of restrained antagonism or irritation to my wife. I could also observe the feelings were arising from my discipline of sexuality. Realising I did not want those feelings I altered them and woke enough to turn toward her.' Francis P.*

After the first of his direct perception dreams, Francis attempted to use this function again, resulting in the above and other such dreams. Just as classic dream interpretation says that the dream symbols represent psycho-biological logical processes which might be uncovered by dream processing, what we see in Francis' lucidity is a direct route to self-insight, and through it a rapid personal growth to improved life experience. Such dreams provide not only psychological insight, but very frequently a direct perception of processes occurring in the body, as the following example illustrates.

> *Example:* '*Although deeply asleep I was wide awake without any shape or form. I had direct experience, without any pictures, of the action of the energies in my body. I had no awareness of body shape, only of the flow of activities in the organs. I checked over what I could observe and noticed a tension in my neck was interfering with the flow and exchange of energies between the head and trunk. It was also obvious*

*from what I could see that the tension was due to an attitude
I had to authority, and if the tension remained it could lead
to physical ill health.' Tony C.*

*Example: taken from Compuserve files – contributed by Mark-
ley and Oliver W. First appeared in* Whole Earth Review, *Fall
1991: 'It was as though the dream I had been watching was a
movie, and instead of looking at the screen on which it was
being projected, I somehow began looking into the lens of the
movie projector. As I did so, the energy of my gaze "melted" the
movie that was passing through, which in turn allowed my
gaze to penetrate deeper into the movie process, seeing where
the movie came from. I knew that I was about to get an answer
to some of my deepest questions about dreaming: What is the
true nature of dreams? Where do they come from? What
function do they play?*

*I was somehow able to see first the more superficial levels of
dream process within myself, and then deeper levels, until the
depth of my gaze revealed processes so alien that I was no
longer able to understand them. At this point I returned my
attention to the need to record the dream, and woke up. There
were five categories of dreams in all. The function of the first
type of dream process I saw was pure entertainment.*

*The second reviewed current concerns and unfinished
business, and the attempt to find solutions to problems therein.*

*The third process involved the reception of guidance from
higher wisdom sources within the mind. At a superficial level,
this guidance dealt with the concerns of the second type of
process; but at a deeper level, it dealt with topics that came
along with the guidance process. These topics seemed to
concern the future, and the evolution of the mind and soul
both individual and collective.*

*The fourth type answered a question about the familiar
assertion that "most of us use but a small part of our mental
capacities" (some "experts" say we use only about 10 per cent,
others that it is as small as 2 per cent). I had often wondered
about this, thinking that in nature, if things don't get used,
they atrophy. If we have all this excess mental capacity that we
aren't using, why doesn't it atrophy? The fourth mode seemed*

to be some sort of gymnasium, with a range of mental, psychic and spiritual exercises to keep the brain/mind fit.

The final type of dream content was totally surprising. As I penetrated deeply into my internal dream process, what I found can perhaps be best described as being visited by aliens. The "foreground" resembled a resort hotel, a place for sight-seeing and recreation. It was benign and human-feeling, although the visitors were anything but human! As I explored more deeply, however, things got so alien that I couldn't understand them in the lucid dream state.

As I reluctantly turned back from this journey, I realised that I had an answer to yet another question about dreams that had long puzzled me: "Why are our dreams so highly symbolised?" I now understood why the deeper reaches of dream life must be camouflaged by symbols: the self-protective belief systems which dominate waking life are simply unable to accept the alienness of deep dreaming process; symbolic camouflage artfully bridges the gap.

This last category of dream represents what I call "the L-Squared dream", a lucid dream in which the dreamer is lucid about the process of being lucid. To become lucid in this way, it is helpful to imagine having a miner's lamp on one's forehead, a metaphoric "truth beam" that reveals the under-lying truth of whatever is involved.'

An effective way to develop lucidity is frequently to consider the events of waking life as if they were a dream. Try to see events as one might see dream symbols – what do they mean in terms of one's motivations, fears, personal growth? What do they suggest about oneself. For instance a person who works in a photographic darkroom developing films and prints may see they were trying to bring to consciousness the latent – unconscious – side of themselves. A banker might feel they were working at how best to deal with their sexual and personal resources. In this way one might actually apply what is said in this dream dictionary to one's outer circumstances.

The second instruction is, on waking at a convenient moment, imagine oneself standing within one's recent dream. As you get a sense of the dream environment, realise that you are taking waking awareness into the dream. From the standpoint of being fully aware of the dream action and events, what will you now do in and with the dream? Re-dream it with consciousness. For example the things you run from in your normal dreaming you could now face. See: **dream processing** for further suggestions.

luggage   The habits of attitude or the emotional environment we have created in our life; the past we still carry with us; things we can't let go of in life; a baby or our feelings about being a parent. See: **bag**; example in **clothes**; **knapsack**.

luminous   Unity of many aspects of one's nature. See: **aura**.

machine <u>General</u>: the body's automatic functions and drives, such as breathing and ageing; the mechanical forces of nature; habitual or mechanical behaviour. <u>Intricate machine</u>: brain or the thinking process in its mechanical habitual form; the habitual, almost mechanical fantasies we have or things we do.

> *Example: 'I see a little girl humming an innocent tune, plucking daisies in a vast, lush green field. Suddenly a huge machine or monster comes ploughing through the field over the girl.' Debbie H.*

Debbie sees life itself as a machine, unfeeling, mechanical, blind in its functioning. The word juggernaut is from Sanskrit Jaganatha, lord of the world. Devotees formerly threw themselves under a huge cart as it moved.

> *Example: 'I am in charge of a life machine which keeps the world going. Unless I tend it all the time it may stop and I am terrified. I hear a pulsating noise, or imagine I do.' Mr P.E.*

Here the machine represents the heart, and the dreamer's anxious relationship with the body's functioning and processes. <u>Idioms</u>: cog in the machine. See: **engine**.

mad A dog running across a busy road to chase a bitch isn't acting rationally according to human standards. He is still acting on old drives which have not integrated fresh information about the environment – the traffic. <u>Being confronted by a mad person or</u>

<u>people</u>: meeting parts of ourselves which have not been integrated with our present situation; cultural fear we have about meeting the unconscious. <u>Being mad</u>: feeling threatened by the irrational and perhaps disintegrated aspects of the unconscious.

maggots   Impurities in body; sickness or sense of illness in the body; feelings about death. <u>Maggots in one's body</u>: the unconscious telling us that a part of our attitudes is not wholesome or 'well'. So repressed emotions causing tension in the chest might be represented as maggots. See: **body**.

magic   Might be the wish to accomplish something without effort or difficulty; desire to control situations; without knowing the underlying processes, our mind and emotions do things which appear as magic. To the child mind in us all, growth from a cellular speck to becoming a person is pure magic. Magic also represents the power of unconscious sexuality and how it can be hurt, bewitched or controlled.

magician   See: **roles**.

magnet   The influence – to attract or repel – we have on others or they have on us.

magnifying glass   Making something conscious; becoming aware of something; making something bigger than it is.

make-up   Our ability to change the impression we make on others; cover-up for our real feelings or situation.

man   <u>General</u>: an aspect of Self – even in a woman's dream – depending on the activity and character of the man in the dream. Any indication whatsoever in the dream gives a clue as to what aspect of Self. In the example below, the character of the friend, the role of the psychiatrist and the feelings of the client indicate which aspects of Bernard's character are being dealt with. Therefore a man trying to rape a woman would be her fears about sex; a homosexual would depict homosexual feelings; a businessman would be one's work or business abilities; a loving man would be one's feelings about love, and so on.

In general a person in a dream shows one of the dreamer's character resources or problems, depending upon how they relate to it. Each character trait is a part of the person's repertoire of behaviour. If they are at odds with the person in the dream or threatened by it, then the trait dominates them rather than they using it. An important point is that the dream image of the person or object summarises the trait. Through the image the dreamer can access the resources of the trait. One can call this an image of power.

Older man: father or one's accumulated experience and wisdom; perhaps even wisdom from the unconscious if man is white haired or holy. Wild, ape or half animal man: urges which have not yet been integrated and socialised, usually pertaining to sexuality in today's social attitudes or natural social feelings at odds with present attitudes. Big man: one's basic beliefs or attitudes to life which test out against reality. The bigness represents the certainties which arise from this, and therefore the sense of strength. Man in woman's dream – in general: a woman's ability to question conventional behaviour and social habits; her strength to look with insight into her own life and change it thereby – but not her feeling values, emotions and intuitions; her creative or business ability in the world and power to be competitive and challenging; her defence against 'just knowing' out of the power of her emotions and inbuilt prejudices. Man she knows or loves: feelings, worries about relationship; her summary of what is happening, or what she fears will happen in the relationship. In either case it is still information about the relationship. Dreaming the man is looking at other women or leaving: usually the fears about same. Two men: might be triangle situation.

Example: 'I was walking down the steps of a house, leading into the front area of the basement. I was with a man, perhaps a friend. At the bottom of the steps a psychiatrist was talking to a male client. They were having a session there in the open. I sensed the man's feelings of embarrassment and exposure. But it felt it was necessary to be thus exposed, i.e. the psychiatrist was purposely holding the session in the open so the man could learn to relax.' Bernard O.

Bernard, a practising therapist, is all of the men in the dream. It portrays the interaction between different parts of himself. The 'I' walking down the steps is the active, fairly adventurous person Bernard sees himself as; the man following – a friend – is a man Bernard knows who has sexual difficulties and represents Bernard's own sexual hesitations; the psychiatrist is Bernard's therapeutic skill used in his own life; the male client is Bernard's difficult feelings when dealing with groups of people – the public – which he is trying to 'expose' or get to know and transform.

Idioms: man to man; be a man; front man; hit man; make a man of; odd man out; right hand man. See: **family**; **woman**; and other entries pertaining to particular roles or age.

mandala   If one could produce a graphic image of the whole of human nature, many different forms might be integrated within an overall shape such as a circle or square. Also, if it were possible to have a visual presentation of a person's inner world of mind, weaknesses, strengths, order, confusion and quality, each person would appear differently. Some would be internally jumbled, divided and ugly; others symmetrical, integrated and beautiful.

Because the unconscious produces dreams, and because dreams are imagery which give form to the otherwise abstract elements of internal human nature, there arise in some dreams shapes or patterns which depict an overall view of one's own inner condition. Carl Jung drew attention to the circle and square designs in some dreams, calling them mandalas and seeing them as representing the nucleus of the human identity. Although we are, in our everyday life, the magical and mysterious process of life, it is difficult for us to actually answer the question 'Who am I?' or 'What am I?' with any lasting conviction.

The mysterious essence of ourselves is met in dreams as a circular or square object or design; as the sun, a flower, a square garden with a round pond in the middle, or a circle with a square or quartered design within it, a circle with cross within, a revolving or flying cross-shaped object. Classical symbols from all nations use this theme and we can find it in the Round Table of King Arthur, in the centre of which the Holy Grail appeared; the healing sand paintings of the Navaho Indians; the zodiac; circle dances; stone circles; the Buddhist wheel of birth and death; and so on.

The circle usually symbolises a natural wholeness, our inner life as nature has shaped it. The square shows wholeness we have helped shape by conscious co-operation with our inner world or the healing power of the Self. There are two main reasons why one produces this theme in one's dreams. It occurs in children or people meeting internal or external shocks and produces a strengthening of the vulnerable identity in meeting the varied influences they face. It also arises in people who are meeting and integrating the wider life of their being existing beyond the boundaries of their usual interests, or what they allow themselves to experience. The contact with the Self is then part of an extending of awareness into what was dark or unknown, not only in one's own unconscious but in external life too. In touching the nucleus of one's being in this way, one becomes aware in some measure of the infinite potential of one's life. There is often an accompanying sense of existence in eternity and the many different 'mansions' or dimensions of experience one has within the eternal. See: *the Self* under **archetypes**; *mandala* under **shapes**, **symbols**.

mansion   See: **house**, **buildings**.

manure   In some ways our personality or identity is like a plant which feeds from the most unlikely material to produce beautiful leaves and flower. The plant can transform manure into living leaves and petals. Our identity feeds on experience and information – some of which may appear uninviting, painful, or unwholesome. In fact the experience may be all of these and be depicted by manure, and if not put to our roots – our process of becoming aware of things in an intensely felt manner which links feelings with intellectual insight – remain a disintegrating influence. Learning processes which pile intellectual information on children or adults without helping them to allow their deep feeling responses are piling manure on the psyche while cutting off its roots. Personal disintegration is the result.

map   Clarification of direction in life, or how best to direct ambition or motivation.

marathon   See: **race**.

marketplace   Reality of everyday life; the push and shove, give and take of relating to people in general, but particularly 'the public'; the wide range of experience one meets in exposing oneself to more than one's close family and friends.

marriage, **wedding**   General: uniting two different aspects of the dreamer such as intellect and feelings, practical and intuitive Self; the 'marriage' between conscious and unconscious Self – any children of the marriage would be flowering of new abilities or qualities. Sometimes is about what our energy or drive is uniting us with, such as a new business venture or creative scheme – any children of this marriage suggest our intuitive assessment of the likely outcome. Also in some cultures dreaming of a wedding signifies a death in the family. Dreaming of wedding if single: as in the example below, Mary could have dreamt *she* was the bride, but being in her thirties and unmarried it is easier for her to consider or experiment with the idea of marriage using the image of her friend. Should she marry whoever offers? When single one often dreams of marriage as a way of clarifying – what it would be like? Could one succeed in it? Is the present partner okay? How shall one achieve it? Wedding dress: feelings and hopes about relationship and wedding; in a negative dream it represents anxieties about one's relationship or the future. Wedding dress given by mother: qualities and strengths absorbed from mother in regard to relationship; letting go of external mother by expressing her qualities in the present.

Example: 'I am at the wedding of my best friend. The groom doesn't turn up and she decides to marry the first person who comes along. I wonder whether this is a good thing to do.' Mary T.

Example: 'When I was engaged to my present husband I dreamt we were married and I looked down at my wedding ring. It was twisted and bent. In fact I now see it as a warning because we have not made a good marriage.' S.W.

marsh, **swamp**   Feeling bogged down, held back, losing ground, perhaps due to lack of self-confidence or emotional support; may show the emotional dependence between child and parent one gets stuck in; or feeling unable to move because of relationship with an overbearing person.

Mary – Virgin   Motherhood; positive feelings about one's mother; religious openness or receptivity. Also Mary represents the human soul or psyche and its possibility of dropping preconceptions – virginity – and thus being receptive to the unseen or unconscious side of Self – the Holy Ghost. Her child is the union between the receptive conscious Self and wider awareness.

mask   Our false Self we put on in meeting others; ego less; latent qualities we can express or don when needed – a mother might be a tigress when her children are threatened, but a meek person otherwise. Her tigress would not be 'false'.

mass   The approach of our individual Self to the sense of whole-ness, the communal whole or collective mind, or to the Christ. See: *Christ* under **archetypes**.

masturbation   This may be represented in a dream by such things as using a pump, beating a drum or any rhythmic movement. If there is a tendency to repress the sexual need, it may happen that one masturbates during sleep in an attempt to release sexual pressure. Because the person has consciously decided not to allow sexuality, this might give rise to a feeling of being possessed by another will. In fact our unconscious will to express our needs has overridden the conscious decision during sleep. Out of such a split in the person, ideas about devils and possession probably arose. Although Chris-tianity at a fundamental level appears to be teaching the love and acceptance of all sides of human nature – therefore integration through love thy neighbour as thyself, so love Self – in practice it becomes tight morality which creates devils through rejection and splits in human nature. In many white Christians, there are enor-mous conflicts between sexuality, love, work and spirituality.

mattress   Similar to bed – the situation, comfortable or otherwise, one has created in life. You made your bed, now lie on it. Also comfort; sexuality; relaxed feelings. See: *bed, mattress* under **furniture**.

maze Confusion of ideas and feelings; conflicting urges and opinions; the difficulty in finding our way through the mass of apparently irrational emotions and images arising from within, or the variety of opinions and authoritative sources of information outside. Sometimes we need to admit we are lost and need help. Occasionally the circuitous and often confusing route we take to meeting Self; the unconscious.

meal See: **food**.

measurement Might refer to wondering how long – days and weeks – something will be; comparisons; how 'big' something is in life.

meat See: **food**.

mechanic See: **roles**.

medicine Healing influence; meeting experiences we might not like but need to change a negative situation; actual drugs we are taking. Idioms: taste of one's own medicine; take one's medicine.

meditation Being self-responsible for state of mind; listening to intuition and unconscious; introverting awareness, or escaping from external world.

For people involved in any form of personal growth, they occasionally have a dream in which some form of instruction is given as an aid to their unfolding. Such dreams are worth following as the unconscious has the ability to sift and consider our collective experience and present what applies to our need.

> *Example: 'While recovering from a major operation and experiencing enormous pain I dreamt my father – dead – appeared standing at the end of the bed and he said in a very matter-of-fact voice, "Think of five pink bouquets." My father would never have used those words, so the scene impressed itself on me. I therefore woke and tried to visualise the five bouquets. I managed to get three in a row, four, but I could not manage five until I formed them into a diamond with one in*

the middle. When I achieved that my pain subsided and did so each time I used the image – why I do not know.' Ken S.

Ken's experience suggests a psychosomatic effect from his dream proposed meditation. Such meditations often show ways to alter character attitudes or help to find strength to make necessary changes in life.

medium   Intuition, but perhaps in an obscure way; contact with the unconscious or the dead in its symbolic form. See: *the dream as extended perception* under **ESP in dreams**; **symbols and dreaming**.

melt   A change; emotions softening.

menhirs   The eternal or universal aspect of Self emerging into consciousness. See: **rock**.

menstruation   Emerging sexuality; procreative drive; mystery of life; acceptance of life working in oneself if menstruating – non-acceptance of basic life drives if not menstruating. Problems with menstruating: problems with relationship between what life needs of personality and what personality wants of life; might refer to physiological problems which need attention. In man's dream: one's receptive nurturing nature; the aspect of the male Self which can 'conceive' creative ideas. If ill problems in sexuality, creativity, emotions or in letting go of 'I want'. See: **premenstrual tension**.

mermaid, **merman**   The link between the deep forces of the unconscious and the waking Self. The unconscious image or idealised sense of womanhood – mermaid – or manhood – merman; love of one's image of someone rather than the reality of them as a human being.

metal   Hardness of feelings; the restrictions of the real world or of one's own imagination; strength of will or obstinacy; reality.

microscope   Introspection; extended cellular perception; making mountains out of molehills.

milk   Human kindness; mother love; self-giving; sperm. <u>Idioms</u>: milk and water; milk of human kindness; milk somebody; cry over spilt milk. See: **drink**; **food**.

mill   Process of extracting what is useful from one's gathered experience. Can be painful as it needs intense self-awareness; crushing or painful experiences of life.

mines   For many a place of work; otherwise the unconscious and its resources; bringing to consciousness one's potential and innate wisdom. <u>Entrance to the mine</u>: feelings about the unconscious; vagina. See: **ore**.

mirror   Concern over one's 'image' or how others feel about one; self-examination; self-love, negative only if the love is not shared with others; anxiety about changing or ageing; one's view of oneself; being absorbed in oneself. Also self-awareness in the sense of insight into behaviour or character traits; the mirror is similar to water and can depict looking into the unconscious to see who one is. <u>Changed face in the mirror or multiple selves</u>: becoming aware of aspects of one's character which are usually unknown or not accepted.

> *Example: 'Getting ready for a wedding in an upstairs room, feeling a bit unsure of what to wear. I look in a mirror and see I have on stockings and suspender belt with a very short frilly petticoat. It looks very sexy. I am aware the door is open and have an urge to close it, but then feel okay about looking sexy and people seeing me.' Nora (LBC).*

Nora is looking at how she may appear to others if she allows her natural feelings to show.

miscarriage   If dreamer has had miscarriage or abortion may be an attempt to heal the experience. From the point of view of the unconscious it is at times important to name the baby; fear of miscarriage; loss of new idea, project or growing aspect of Self.

mist   See: **fog**.

moat   The 'I've got a headache' type of defence against another person's approach to intimacy. See: *castle* under **house**, **buildings**.

money   What we value; being valued by others; one's potential, energy or personal resources; personal potency, therefore links with sexuality and self-giving; what we pay for our desires or actions – 'I told my husband a few home truths last night, but he certainly made me pay for it'; opportunity because money buys time to explore or try the new. Holding on to money: feeling insecure or being 'tight' emotionally or sexually. Not enough money: sense of being inadequate or failing potency. Dud money: not giving of oneself or feeling cheated. Stolen money: feelings of guilt about gaining power; feeling cheated; loss of power if money stolen; feeling others are taking us for granted; giving oneself cheaply in sex or relationship.

> *Example: 'A small Indian boy stole a fifty pence piece from me. I had an internal struggle about whether to take it back. The hesitation was that it was "manners" to make out nothing had happened, not to blame someone for something "not nice". Because of these unspoken rules the boy could laugh at me. I decided to take the money back and accuse him of theft.'* Stephen Y.

Stephen is considering what his 'values' are, how he wants others to relate to him and whether to state his needs instead of being 'nice'.

monk   See: **roles**.

monkey   See: **animals**.

monster   Our own internal emotions or drives we are frightened of; dread of death; a monstrous deed done or lie lived; our negative relationship with our own life energy. Use the approaches in **dream processing** to change the monster into usable personal resources.

moon   Love; romance; intuitions arising from the unconscious; one's inner world of fantasy, imagination, the psychic or one's inner soul life; menstrual cycle and the female mysteries. Because of its connection with the tides the moon represents the deep inner movements caused by the subtle side of our nature, the tides of feeling, even madness; the pull and attraction of mysterious dark desires; a woman's strange, sensual, overpowering attraction. New or old moon: female sexuality; change; intuition. Moon's changes: life, death, rebirth; the tides in our affairs. Full moon: power of the inner drives. Flying to the moon: trying to escape reality or responsibility; attempting to break free of limitations. Moonlight: romantic view of the world; not seeing things too clearly; looking within Self. Two moons: decisions or indecision about something, possible relationship; conflicting sides of yourself; choices or changes occurring.

morning   See: **time of day**.

mortuary   Feelings about death; parts of Self dead but not buried – may be brought to life by being used.

mosaic   Our life, its pattern and what we manifest by it through the many separate acts and events; our view of life when we put all the pieces of experience together.

Moslem dream traditions   Islam has a foundation in dreams because of the *Lailatal-Miraj* or Night Journey of Mohammed's dream. In it he was initiated into the mysteries of the cosmos.

In some Indonesian Moslem teachings, human consciousness is often dominated by forces of the animal and vegetable kingdoms and forces resident in material objects. This means humans fail to recognise their true nature and forever feel desirous of material goods, or are led by animal urges. The spiritual force behind dreaming is a means of being delivered from unconscious dominance by these forces.

In early Islamic teachings, no distinction was made between sleeping dreams and waking visions. The world of imagery existent in dreams and visions was seen as having reality. This world, the *alam al-mithral*, exists halfway between the material world and the intellect. In today's language we might call this the world of the psyche, with its imagery. The Islamic teachings say this should not be seen as fantasy. The world of *alam al-mithral* can be entered by trained imagination and perception. Its imagery expresses truths of its nature. The reality of its landscape can be verified by others who explore its subtle territory – the territory of dreams and visions.

moth   The Self we assume in our dreams or fantasy; the unconscious urge our being has to survive personal death; the hidden side of our mind.

mother   See: **family**.

motorbike   Youthful drive and motivation; physical energy; restlessness, sexual drive; daring; independence.

mountain   Something big in one's life; reaching a wider awareness of our life or situation; something which stands above the commonplace. Also attainment achieved by facing the difficulties of life. See: last example in **flying**; **hill**.

>   *Example: 'I was on top of a mountain with my sons, but was terrified I was going to fall.' John A.*

John feels alone in a high position and fears failure.

mouse   See: **animals**.

mouth   See: **body**.

movement   Getting stuck, unable to move: often being held back by anxiety or fears, such as fear of failure. Easy, flowing movement: self-acceptance and thus easy expression of oneself; feeling in harmony with emotions and sexuality. See **postures**, **movement**, **body language**.

mud   General: the fundamental primordial, sensual, slimy basis of life and how we relate to it; emotions which cause us to feel bogged down; past experience which may hold us back, but has enormous growth potential in it; the healing possibilities of our body and its minerals. Body dirty with mud: ill health; one's life needs 'cleaning up' morally. Sinking into mud: sexual difficulties; feelings of hopelessness or despair. Idioms: mud slinging; drag somebody through the mud; one's name is mud; stick in the mud.

mummy – Egyptian   The dead; feelings we have buried about a dead person; emotions about death; our mother; a part of Self which might be reborn; attempt to preserve a way of life which is dead – mummification – instead of facing change and the new.

murder, murderer   Each of us are implicated in killing – by denying, repressing, controlling some part of our own nature. These denied areas of our own sensitivity or potential can fortunately be resurrected through self-awareness of our deed. If we flee from a murderer, it depicts a fear that is threatening our confidence or something we feel threatened by. Murderous rage in dreamer: it is observable that repressed sexuality leads to feelings of murderous rage which may not be expressed socially but do appear in dreams; may also express childhood anger linked with emotional bond with mother being damaged.

Where the dreamer imagines the death of a beloved relative: Freud believed this was because rivalry and hatred between brothers and sisters was deep rooted through the unconscious and, in adult life, concealed by apparent warm affection. One reason for this, he suggested, was that for the child the idea of death meant no more than being 'gone': to wish another dead in early childhood is simply a way of wishing him or her removed from the scene.

muscle   See: **body**.

museum   Memory; family and cultural heritage; the living past within us.

music   The play of subtle feelings and forces in our being; realisations difficult to define; the influence of wider awareness in our life. Playing music: self-expression; expressing our essential Self which might be overlooked in general activities. Idioms: music to one's ears; face the music.

musical instrument   Often one's sexual organs; one's skills in self-expression. <u>A large complex instrument</u>: the mind and its influence on the rest of our being. See: **organ**.

nail Bonding; holding power, male sexuality. <u>If nail is in body</u>: consciousness painfully bound to physical reality; pain of bonds. <u>Idioms</u>: hit the nail on the head; tough as nails; nail biting; bed of nails; nail in one's coffin.

name of person or place Our name represents our sense of Self, our essential 'I'. <u>If the name is altered</u>: suggests a sense of change in the way we see ourselves. <u>Other people's names</u>: our feelings for that person; the quality we feel in regard to someone else with the same name; or word play or associations with the name – a woman dreamt a friend asks her 'Do you know where Chris is?' and she replied he was on the back seat. On waking she realises she is being asked where's the crisis? Two weeks later she had a kidney infection – in the back seat. Names also suggest qualities – as in Peter, the rock; or one's friend Pat may be pleasure loving, so we use the name or person to represent that quality. See: **wordplay**, **puns**. <u>Place names</u>: these can represent our feelings about the place or be similar to personal names in their suggestion of something.

> *Example: 'On the other side of the road was a window with my wife's ring and watch and other trinkets. I went to pick them up but a stranger put his hand over them. I then crossed the road to get a bus to Andover.' Arthur P.*

Arthur's dream wants to make sure he gets the message by saying hand-over and handover.

<u>Idioms</u>: call someone names; clear someone's name; have a bad name; not a thing to one's name; in name alone; in the name of;

make a name for oneself; name dropper; one's middle name; name is mud; somebody who shall be nameless; or my name's not . . .; worthy of the name; name in vain; lend one's name to; name the day.

narrow   Narrow-minded; limited choices or view; feeling restricted.

natives   Natural feelings; being uncivilised. See: **aborigine**; **black people**.

navel   Dependency – especially upon mother; the way we connect our deepest Self with the outside world.

near   The nearer something is to you in a dream the closer it is to becoming conscious in a direct way rather than as a symbol. See: **positions**.

necklace   Display of special qualities; richness of feelings; feelings connected with giver; may represent 'millstone' around neck.

needle   Penetrating insight; male sexuality; power to mend ills; irritations. Needle in body: sickness in body. Needlework: what one has made of oneself. Idioms: get the needle; needle in a haystack.

negro   See: **African**; **black person**.

neighbour   One's relationship with other people; the qualities we see in our neighbour.

nest   Emotional dependence upon parents; home life; not being independent; female sexuality; nest egg. Idioms: foul one's own nest; hornets' nest; feather one's own nest; cuckoo in the nest.

nettle   Feeling stung by remarks; irritation – feeling nettled; sickness in the body; a difficult situation you may try to avoid – as in 'grasping the nettle' or 'stung into action'.

new   Whatever is new in one's life – a relationship, opportunity, scheme. If contrasted with old, an attempt to decide, contrasting what we already know from the past/old and what is arising.

newspaper   Something that is news to you; or you have just become or need to be aware of; something conscious rather than unconscious; something publicly known about yourself.

night   See: **dark**; **day and night**; **time of day**.

nightmares   Many dreams lead us to feel an intensity of emotion we may seldom if ever feel in waking life. If the emotions felt are frightening or disgusting we call the dream a nightmare. One of the common features of a nightmare is that we are desperately trying to get away from a situation, feel stuck in a terrible condition, or on waking feel enormous relief it was just a dream. Because of the intensity of a nightmare we will remember it long after other dreams – remember even if we seldom ever recall other dreams, or even worry about what it means.

As so many dreams have been investigated in depth – using such varied approaches as hypnosis, exploration of associations and emotional content, and LSD psychotherapy in which the person can explore usually unconscious memories, imagery and feelings – we can be certain we know what nightmares are. They arise from six main causes:

1.   Unconscious memories of intense emotions – such as those arising in a child being left in a hospital without its mother.
2.   Intense anxiety produced – but not fully released at the time – by external situations such as involvement in war scenes or sexual assault (this applies to males as well as females, as they are frequently assaulted).
3.   Childhood fears such as loss of parent; being lost or abandoned; fear of attack by stranger or parent; anxiety about own internal drives.
4.   Many nightmares in adults also have a similar source, namely fear connected with internal drives such as aggression, sexuality and the process of growth and change – such as encounter with adolescence, loss of sexual characteristics, old age and death. So this is fear of the future and imagined events.

5. Serious illness.
6. Precognition of fateful events.

For an example of number 1, see second example in **dark**.

> *Example for 2:* '*A* thing *is marauding around the rather bleak, dark house I am in with a small boy. To avoid it I lock myself in a room with the boy. The thing finds the room and tries to break the door down. I frantically try to hold it closed with my hands and one foot pressed against it, my back against a wall for leverage. It was a terrible struggle and I woke myself by screaming.' Terry F.*

When Terry allowed the sense of fear to rise in him while awake, he felt as he did when a child – the boy in the dream – during the bombing of the Second World War. His sense of insecurity dating from that time had emerged when he left a secure job and had arisen in the images of the nightmare. Understanding his fears he was able to avoid their usual paralysing influence.

> *Example of 3:* '*I am a detective following clues regarding some sort of crime. They lead me into a large cellar, and within the cellar I come across the entrances of two tunnels. These are nearly the size of underground train tunnels, and are side by side leading away into pitch blackness. I decide to explore the tunnels and start to walk into one. I find myself running away, having had a black-out through complete terror. I try again but once more find myself running away in terror.' Patrick B.*

Patrick explored his nightmare and discovered the terror was about being in hospital as a nine-year-old when he was forcibly anaesthetised despite his screams of protest and begging the nurses not to.

For an example of 4, see third example in *doors* under **house, buildings**.

> *Example of 5:* '*I dream night after night that a cat is gnawing at my throat.' Male from* Landscapes of the Night *(Coronet Books).*

The dreamer had developing cancer of the throat. These physical illness dreams are not as common as the other classes of nightmare.

> *Example of 6: 'My husband, a pilot in the RAF, had recently lost a friend in an air crash. He woke one morning very troubled – he is usually a very positive person. He told me he had dreamt his friend was flying a black jet and wanted my husband to fly with him. Although a simple dream my husband could not shake off the dark feelings. Shortly afterwards his own jet went down and he was killed in the crash.' Anon.*

Understanding the causes of nightmares enables us to deal with them. The things we run from in the nightmare need to be met while we are awake. We can do this by sitting and imagining ourselves back in the dream and facing or meeting what we were frightened of. Terry imagined himself opening the door he was fighting to keep closed. In doing this and remaining quiet he could feel the childhood feelings rising. Once he recognised them for what they were, the terror went out of them.

A young woman told me she had experienced a recurring nightmare of a piece of cloth touching her face. She would scream and scream and wake her family. One night her brother sat with her and made her meet those feelings depicted by the cloth. When she did so she realised it was her grandmother's funeral shroud. She cried about the loss of her grandmother, felt her feelings about death and was never troubled again by the nightmare. The techniques given in **dream processing** will help in meeting such feelings.

Even the simple act of imagining ourselves back in the nightmare and facing the frightening thing will begin the process of changing our relationship with our internal fears. It may be helpful to think of this as walking around a film set examining the parts of the drama and watching what one experiences or what memories arise.

In the UK, a nightmare clinic has been formed. See Useful Addresses on page 445.

no Unless we can say 'no' effectively, our 'yes's in life may be acquiescence rather than agreement. Therefore, saying no in our dreams is an important expression of our needs and ability to make decisions in the face of disagreement. It is important to understand what it is you are saying no to, however.

noon   See: **time of day**.

noose   Fear of getting 'hung up' on something or somebody; fear of a trap – or desire to trap. If noose around neck: feelings about death; unconscious – repressed – emotions that are causing a full expression of oneself to be held back by tensions in the neck.

north   The head, as opposed to south, the genitals; unconscious-ness; coldness, suggesting a situation which leads us to seek the light and warmth; death; frozen emotions.

nuclear explosion   Anxiety about the future; great change in the dreamer's life. See: **atom bomb**.

nude   Dropping the façade; attitudes or feelings we may mask our real emotions with in everyday life – for instance a child may scream if someone it dislikes gets near him or her, but an adult will probably tolerate the nearness, or refrain from expressing displeasure; desire to be seen for what one is; expression of natural feelings or desire to be intimate; revealing one's true nature. Anxiety about being nude: fear that others know what you really feel and desire; feeling vulnerable with one's weaknesses exposed; guilt about being a human animal with sexual characteristics and urges.

numbers   Numbers can have a personal or symbolic significance. For instance we may have had three children, so the number three in a dream about children could be connected with our feelings or fears about them. But three has generally been seen as the troublesome triangle in love, or the child, mother, father threesome. So a number may refer to a particular year of one's life; the number of a house; the months or years that have passed since an important event; your family group, or it may have a general significance.

one   One-self; a beginning; the first; unity; being alone; independ-ence. Just one left: near the end. Idioms: it's all one to me; one up; at one with; one and only; one off.

two   Duality; indecision or making a decision; balance; male and female; two sides to an argument – or a way of comparing; opposition; the opposites such as light and darkness; parents and reproductive possibility. Chased by or fighting with two people: two against one feeling, as may have happened between child and parents; feeling odds are against one. Idioms: put two and two together; two's company; two timer; in two minds.

three   Triangle; mother, father, child; synthesis; creativity – the child springing from the two opposites, therefore sometimes represents the solution to opposition. Confronting three people, or out with two others: facing collective will of others; non-sexual friendship. Idioms: three's a crowd.

four   Physicality; the earth; stability and strength; the home or house; reality; down to earth – yet at the same time the spiritual within the physical; the four sides to human nature – sensation, feeling, thought, intuition; earth, air, fire and water. Four or more people: feelings about meeting group decisions and feelings; someone's opinion or will backed by others; supportive feelings. Idioms: four square; on all fours; four-letter word.

five   The human body; human consciousness in the body; the hand; sometimes called the number of marriage because it unites all the previous numbers – 1 + 4 and 2 + 3; the five senses.

six   Harmony or balance; sex. Idioms: sixes and sevens; six of the best; hit for six.

seven   Cycles of life – 7, 14, 21, etc.; a week; spiritual meanings – seven candles, seven churches, seven chakras, seven colours, seven notes in music – so represents human wholeness. Idioms: seventh heaven.

eight   Death and resurrection; infinity; old fonts and baptisteries are octagonal because of the association with regeneration.

nine   Pregnancy; childbirth; the end of a cycle and the start of something new; cycles. Idioms: nine days wonder; nine times out of ten; nine to five; cloud nine; nine points of the law.

ten   A new beginning; the male and female together. Idioms: ten to one.

eleven   Eleventh hour.

twelve   A year; time; a full cycle or wholeness as in the zodiac or twelve disciples.

thirteen   Bad luck.

zero   The female; unconscious; the absolute or hidden; completeness. The circle or zero also represents the most profound aspect of human nature and the cosmos, that of the hidden, the invisible within all phenomena. It is the silence or void in which all feeling, thought, sound exist – the space between the notes of music that allows the heard. It is the nothingness that essentially allows existence.

big numbers   A lot; impressive; much of oneself involved.

nun   Sexual restraint; religious feelings or morals; idealism.

nurse   Healing process; someone you know who is a nurse; work situation for many; sister.

nut   Feeling a 'nut'; inner nourishment or wisdom which needs work to get at its kernel.

oak See: **trees**.

oar The personal energy and skill used to direct our way through the 'waters of life'; word play for whore; phallic because of its in and out motion. Idioms: stick one's oar in; rest on one's oars.

oasis The life-giving influence of emotions and life processes within the 'desert' of intellectualism or materialism.

oats Sexual energy; sexual satisfaction. Idioms: have one's oats; off one's oats; sow wild oats.

obelisk One's creative energy leaving its mark in the world – it is sexual in the sense the snake is sexual; how one has shaped one's basic nature through personal effort. See: **reptiles – lizards**, **snakes**.

obesity See: **fat person**.

obscene dreams It is reasonable and healthy for all of us to have a dream which surprises or shocks us occasionally. As dreams partly deal with aspects of our urges and fantasies which we do not allow in waking life, such occasional dreams are safety valves. It is healthy to be able to allow a wide range of dream experience, from the holy to the deeply sexual; from outright aggression to tender love. In fact we can gain an idea of the depth and broadness of our own soul – whether our psyche is narrow – from the range of dreams we experience. If obscene dreams assail and worry us again and again

275

however, then there is a problem in the way we are relating to ourselves and the exterior world. Psychotherapeutic counselling might help.

obsessed   We are each obsessed in some degree. Few of us could walk down our road nude or maybe even without shoes and socks. We take such obsessions for granted and accept them as norms, so we do not feel mentally unbalanced. When a similar power of feeling leads us to behaviour outside the norm we face our own doubts about ourselves. Obsession in dreams may illustrate some anxiety, drive or desire which is leading us beyond our accepted norm; or the obsession may be used to escape the real feelings, such as childhood pain or adult conflict and entrapment.

In past cultures the ideas or fears which obsess us would have been described as an evil spirit or ghost taking over the person. This is because the irrational obsession takes hold of us against our will, so is quite an accurate image. The obsessing factor may still appear in present-day dreams in the form of a spirit or demon.

obstacle   Depicts something which causes uncertainty or withdrawal of enthusiasm, creativity or love. Such might be produced by someone's criticism which evokes our own self-doubts; indecision; our own inhibitions or anxieties; maybe even a hidden form of not wanting to succeed because it would confront us with the new – and we might fail. The obstacle, obstruction, barrier or interference can be a person, a wall, a river, an animal – or it might be an internal thing like paralysis or a lump in the throat. Refer to the entry on the appropriate subject to define what it is acting as an obstacle. See: first example in **failure**; **fence**; **wall**.

Example: 'I have this recurring nightmare. I see my mother standing by my bedroom door, blocking it as if I am being trapped and stopped from getting out. I often call to her "Let me out Mum" but she just stands there staring with no expression on her face at all. I end up getting out of bed and switching my bedroom light on and then she disappears. Sometimes I will see her standing by my wardrobe. It seems as if she is always standing by a door and trying to trap me.' Natalie S.

Natalie is fourteen and the obstacle she faces in choosing her own clothes – the wardrobe – and making her own decision is her own dependence upon her mother, and the need to develop a new relationship with her.

> *Example: 'As I was driving along I turned my car over. I wasn't hurt but could not now get to my destination. I didn't feel at all upset about the car being damaged.' Tim K.*

The example shows a subtle and self-made obstacle – the damaged car. In fact Tim admitted ruining his own work opportunities – the car – because he was frightened of failure.

ocean   See: **sea**.

octopus   See: **fish**, **sea creatures**.

odour   See: **perfume**.

office   Feelings about or relationship with work; feelings about authority.

officer, **official**   Relationship with authority or officialdom; one's father; how we authorise our own activities, our sense of right and wrong; a co-ordinating or directing function in ourselves; a sense of sureness out of wider awareness or experience.

ogre   Feelings developed in relationship with one's father; lack of sympathy or understanding; being inconsiderate; feelings about authority.

oil   Attitude which removes friction in oneself or in a relationship; flattery; unctuousness; fat in one's diet. Idioms: well oiled; oil the wheels; strike oil; oil on troubled waters; burning midnight oil.

ointment   Care; healing.

old, **ancient**, **antique**
old   The past; the different lives we have lived – baby, youth, lover,

parent, provider; what is established and well-worn; tradition and wisdom of folklore. Old people: wisdom; mother or father; past experience; traditions; old age; death. Old building: past way of life; former life with family or another person. Old things or furniture: past or outworn ways of life or activities.

> *Example: 'I am standing in a book shop. It is a long-established business. As I look at the books I find two which are about the life of Christ. They are leather-bound and handwritten – quite ancient. Both seem to me to be about the author's own inner life. I believe one is written from a religious viewpoint and the other from a more occult one. I am not attracted to either.'*
> Bill O.

Bill is looking back on past attitudes, one religious, one occult, which had been big parts of his life.

ancient   Usually suggests contact with parts of our being older than the development of the conscious Self – such as cellular wisdom; life processes; accepted traditions or ways of life; wisdom of the unconscious.

antique   Elements of our past experience which might be worth keeping; wisdom of unconscious.

olive   See: **food**.

onion   See: **food**.

opal   See: **jewels**.

opera   Dramatisation of inner feeling situations. See: **arena**; **film**; **stage**.

operation   Memories regarding actual operation; a sick inner attitude which needs attention; fear of illness; physical illness.

oracle   Intuition; unconscious hopes or desires; attempt to manipulate. See: **ESP in dreams**.

orange   See: **colours**; **food**.

orchard   Efforts may be bearing fruit; one's growth. See: **garden**.

orchestra   The working relationship between the different aspects of oneself – mind, body, spirit; one's sense of social co-operation or harmony in the cosmos. <u>Conductor</u>: the Self; whatever is directing one's life. See: **music**; **musical instruments**.

ore   One's potential; new ideas or energy; resources needing work to make usable. See: **mines**.

organ   The different aspects of Self – different ideas, feelings, abilities, weaknesses and strengths which can be played or called upon; the whole range of our being as it responds to decisions and activity; sexual organs. See: **music**.

Orient   The unconscious; transcendental wisdom; intuition. See: <u>Oriental woman</u> under **woman**.

orphan   Feeling abandoned or unloved; feeling rejected or mis- understood – or part of oneself is being rejected and misunderstood; vulnerability in independence and consciousness. See: **aban- doned**.

ostrich   Because of folklore, may represent avoidance of seeing what is happening around one.

otter   See: **animals**.

out-of-body experience   Because out-of-body experiences occur while the person is apparently asleep, they can be considered as manifestations of sleep phenomena, but they do not have the same characteristics as a typical dream. Dreams are seldom verifiable observations of external events occurring at the same time as the dream. Out-of-body experiences frequently display an accurate observation of external events, not available to the sleeping person except by extraordinary means.

Example: '*At about two or three in the morning my wife Brenda and I were suddenly awoken from sleep by a noise. As we lifted our heads to hear we identified it as the handle on our children's bedroom door being turned. The house only had two bedrooms and the children's room was directly opposite ours. Both of us had the same thought – "Oh no, it's the children again." Much to our annoyance they had been waking in the middle of the night claiming it was morning and time to play. We had tried to suppress it, but here it was again.*

As these thoughts went through our minds we heard the sound of feet clomping down the stairs. This was strange as the children usually stayed in their room. Brenda got up determined to get whoever it was back into bed. I heard her switch the light on, go down the stairs, switch the sitting room light on, and I followed her via the sounds of her movement as she looked in the kitchen and even the toilet – we didn't have a bathroom. Then up she came again and opened the children's door – strange because we had assumed it had been opened. When she came back into our room she looked puzzled and a little scared. "They're all asleep and in bed," she said.

We talked over the mystery for some time trying to understand just how we had heard the door handle rattle then footsteps going down the stairs, yet the door wasn't open. Also, the door handles on our doors were too high for the children to reach without standing on a chair. There was a stool in the children's bedroom they used for that, yet it wasn't even near the door when Brenda opened it.

Having no answer to the puzzle we stopped talking and settled to wait for sleep again. Suddenly a noise came from the children's bedroom. It sounded like the stool being dragged and then the door handle turning again but the door not opening. "You go this time," Brenda said, obviously disturbed.

I opened our door quickly just in time to see the opposite door handle turn again. Still the door didn't open. I reached across, turned the handle and slowly opened the door. It stopped as something was blocking it. Just then my daughter Helen's small face peered around the door – high because she was standing on the stool. Puzzled by what had happened, I was careful what I said to her. "What do you want love?" I asked.

Unperturbed she replied, "I want to go to the toilet." The toilet was downstairs, through the sitting room and through the kitchen.

Now I had a clue so asked, "Did you go downstairs before?"

"Yes," she said, "but Mummy sent me back to bed!"' Tony C.

This is an unusual example of an out-of-body experience or OBE. Mostly they are described from the point of view of the person projecting and are therefore difficult to corroborate. Here, three people experienced the OBE in their own way. From Tony and Brenda's point of view what happened caused sensory stimuli, but only auditory. Helen's statement says that she was sure she had physically walked down the stairs and been sent back to bed by her mother. Tony and Brenda felt there was a direct connection between what they were thinking and feeling – get the children back to bed – and what Helen experienced as an objective reality.

OBEs have been reported thousands of times in every culture and in every period of history. A more general experience of OBE than the above might include a feeling of rushing along a tunnel or release from a tight place prior to the awareness of independence from the body. In this first stage some people experience a sense of physical paralysis which may be frightening – see **paralysis** – their awareness then seems to become an observing point outside the body, as well as the sense of paralysis. There is usually an intense awareness of oneself and surroundings, unlike dreaming or even lucidity. Some projectors feel they are even more vitally aware and rational than during the waking state. Looking back on one's body may occur here. Once the awareness is independent of the body, the boundaries of time and space as they are known in the body do not exist. One can easily pass through walls, fly, travel to or immediately be in a far distant place, witnessing what may be or appears to be physically real there. Sir Auckland Geddes, an eminent British Anatomist, describes his own OBE, which contains many of these features.

Example: Becoming suddenly and violently ill with gastro-enteritis he quickly became unable to move or phone for help. As this was occurring he noticed he had an 'A' and 'B' consciousness. The 'A' was his normal awareness, and the 'B' was external to his body watching. From the 'B' Self he could see not only his body, but also the house, garden and surrounds. He need only think of a friend or place and immediately he was there and was later able to find confirmation for his observations. In looking at his body, he noticed that the brain was only an end organ, like a condensing plate, upon which memory and awareness played. The mind, he said, was not in the brain, the brain was in the mind, like a radio in the play of signals. He then observed his daughter come in and discover his condition, saw her telephone a doctor friend, and saw him also at the same time.

Many cases of OBE occur in a near-death situation, where a person has 'died' of a heart attack for instance and is later revived. Because of this there are attempts to consider the possibility of survival of death through the study of these cases. In fact many people after experiencing an OBE have a very different view of death than prior to their experience.

Early attempts to explain OBEs suggested a subtle or astral body which is a double of our physical and mental Self, but able to pass through walls. It was said to be connected to the physical body during an OBE by a silver cord – a sort of life line which kept the physical body alive. This is similar to the concept that the people we dream about are not creations of our own psyche, but real in their own right. Whatever one may believe an OBE to be, it can be observed that many people in this condition have no silver cord, and have no body at all, but are simply a bodiless observer, or are an animal, a geometrical shape, a colour or sound. See: **identity and the dreamer**.

The person's own unconscious concepts of Self seem to be the factor which shape the form of the OBE. If, therefore, one feels sure one must travel to a distant point, then in the OBE one travels. If one believes one is immediately there by the power of thought, one is there. If one cannot conceive of existing without a body, then one has a body, and so on. The silver cord, from this point of view, exists simply because the 'dreamer' feels it is necessary.

In a nutshell, the world of the OBE is created by the very concepts of the 'dreamer'. This world is experienced as physically real, in a similar way to the world of dreams. The difference is that during an OBE the physical world is also experienced and witnessed. So in trying to analyse events during an OBE, we must discover what aspects are created out of unconsciously held concepts and what are witnessed physical world events or objects.

This approach explains many aspects of the OBE, but there is still not a clear concept of what the relationship with the physical world is. The many cases of OBE which occur during a near-death experience also suggest it may be connected with a survival response to death. Not necessarily as a way of trying to transcend death, but perhaps as a primeval form of warning kin of death. If there is survival of death, then the OBE may be an anticipatory form, or a preparatory condition leading to the new form. See: **dreams as spiritual guide**, **hallucinations**, **hallucinogens**.

oval   The womb; female qualities or sexuality.

oven   Because of the idiom 'one in the oven' this may depict pregnancy or the womb; the human ability to transform character qualities. From being a sulky, irritable person, one can change to being self-giving and open. Depicts this because the oven transforms inedible substances or objects into delightful food.

owl   See: **birds**; second example in *wife* under **family**.

oyster   See: **fish**, **sea creatures**.

packing   Leaving home; becoming or wanting to be independent; making changes; wanting to get away. <u>Already packed case</u>: readiness to meet change. <u>Packing and wondering what to take</u>: decisions about what stance or attitudes are suitable to meet present situation or change; sense of an end in sight; attempt to be independent. <u>Can't pack in time</u>: anxiety about details; feeling unready for change. <u>Idioms</u>: pack off; pack up; send somebody packing; pack one's bags.

paddle   <u>Idioms</u>: paddle one's own canoe. See: **oar**.

padlock   See: **lock**.

painting   <u>A painting</u>: the unconscious frequently senses things or synthesises things out of our experience, views of things we have not been consciously aware of. A dream may depict this as a painting; subtle feelings or realisations; a view we have of or about something. <u>Any form of artistic expression</u>: self-expression; expressing one's feelings or intuitions; one's inner situation; creative ability. <u>Painting as in decorating</u>: making changes in the way we live or feel about ourself; expressing feelings; the impression we give to others; what 'colour' we are painting things, in the sense of painting a very black picture; a cover-up. We can paint the town red; paint too rosy a picture. Or we might be working at changing our appearance or lifestyle. See: **photographs**.

pan, pot   <u>Cooking pot or pan</u>: receptive state of mind and feelings perhaps connected with creativity – cooking – family life· or

284

providing for one's needs. Chamber pot: feelings and values connected with excretory functions; female sexuality. Idioms: flash in the pan.

paper   Blank writing paper: unexpressed sentiments or ideas; opportunity; feeling a lack of communication with someone else. Wrapping paper: depending on the colour and quality – how you feel others see you; the exterior impression of what you are getting or giving in a relationship; the outward appearance of your own potential. Idioms: commit to paper; not worth the paper it's written on; on paper; paper tiger; pen to paper; paper over the cracks.

parachute   Depicts whatever life skill one uses to deal with anxiety about failing – falling; achieving a more down-to-earth practical attitude after flying high, or retreating into flights of fancy.

paradise   Experience of being in the womb; feeling in harmony with Self. Idioms: fools' paradise. See: **heaven**.

paralysis   Many people complain of feeling paralysed while they are partially awake but dreaming. This may be due to the fact that voluntary movements are inhibited during periods of the dream process. All brain signals to the voluntary muscles are stopped. Therefore if we become slightly awake and attempt to move at that time we feel paralysed. This is not sensed as a problem if we are unconsciously involved in a dream. If enough self-awareness arises in the dream state, then awareness of the inability to move may occur, along with the anxiety this can arouse. In fact this is probably only a problem to people who are frightened of the paralysis, as for most people, active dreams manage to break through the inhibition enough to cause mild movements and vocal sounds.

Another factor is illustrated by what Susan says in the example below – the harder she tries to move the worse it gets. Our unconscious is very open to suggestion. If this were not so we would lack necessary survival responses. In a dimly lit situation we may mistake a shape for a lurking figure. Our body reactions such as heartbeat, react to the mistake as if it is real until we gain fresh information. Whatever we feel to be real becomes a fact as far as our body reactions are concerned. The fear that one cannot move becomes a fact because we believe it. When Susan relaxes, and thereby drops the fear of paralysis, she can be free of it. This applies to anything we feel is true – we create it as an internal reality.

Dreaming one is paralysed is similar. It depicts the paralysing effects either of fears we have or what we have imagined as real in the way described; we may be 'paralysed' by feelings of guilt or inadequacy; internal conflict paralyses us. The healing of the paralysed man by Christ represents this removal of guilt, shame or fear by contact with the Self.

> *Example: 'It starts as a dream, but I gradually become aware that I cannot move. The harder I try to move the worse it gets and I become very frightened. I can neither move nor wake myself up. Sometimes I feel as if I am leaving my body. But to deal with the fear I have learnt – it's a recurring thing – to stop struggling, knowing that I will eventually wake.' Susan Y.*

parasites   Lice, fleas, bugs: things said, thought or done which make you feel uncomfortable or ashamed; feelings that one is, or someone else is a parasite in a relationship.

> *Example: 'I was practising relaxation and went into a dream state. I saw a dark shape attached to my body near my heart. I felt very frightened as I saw it. But as I watched it broke away and left me.' John W.*

John had experienced a heart attack and the dark shape was an embodiment of his fears about his heart, sucking his energy and well-being. In relaxing he was able to let go of these feelings. Because the dream process shows such internal processes in imagery, the fears are shown as an incubus or dark parasite, which falls away.

parcel, package   Something we have experienced but not explored the import of. A parent may die, for instance, but we may not 'unwrap' the feelings evoked enough to see we have taken something to heart. If we did we might find a regret of not expressing the love we felt while Mum or Dad was still alive and we now want to be more daring in giving love. Also one's potential or latent skills; impressions or 'gifts' received from others – such as support, love, their example – but not made fully conscious.

parliament   The many aspects of Self involved in decision making; one's feelings about social situations.

parrot   Repeating without judgement what others have said; accepting or copying something without evaluating it.

party   General: our feelings about groups; social skill or lack of it; social pleasure. Dreamer as the host of the party: our relationship with the different aspects of Self; exploring social relationships or our feelings about groups. Dreamer as main guest at birthday party: wanting family or social acclaim and love, or feeling loved.

> *Example: 'Then I was in a place where we were having a staff party. Not very big but people were sitting at tables, eating, in a party mood. I sat with my child, maybe youngest son, no one else at the table. I felt I didn't wish to get involved with the others, the feeling I often get at parties, just alone in a crowd. I left with my son. Some young men tried to dissuade us but I pushed away from them.' Simeon T.*

Simeon finds groups of people difficult to relate to. The dream shows this is a feeling which started in his childhood – his youngest son.

passage   A sense of being 'in-between' regarding work, love or life; change as in a 'rite of passage' – so the movement between stages or phases of life; the back passage – rectum, or front passage – vagina and so the birth passage. Idioms: work one's passage. See: **corridor**.

passenger   Being a passenger: feeling that circumstances are carrying you along, either because you are passively allowing them to, or because you feel powerless to change; sense of being carried along by the process of life such as ageing. Passenger in a car: being motivated or moved by someone else's viewpoints, opinions or enthusiasm; being dependent, perhaps on who is driving the car;

allowing a secondary part of Self such as indecision, pride, or stubbornness to direct decisions. Carrying passengers: feeling you are taking the responsibility in work or family. See: **car**.

passive   See: **active/passive**.

passport   One's sense of identity, with its connections with racial, national and family background; feelings about travel.

past lives   While there may be some evidence for reincarnation in the work of Dr Ian Stevenson, dreams which clearly state reincarnation in their theme, most likely represent present life situations.

> *Example: 'I dream of living in China a long time ago. I was married to a man with whom I had two children. He began to tire of me and brought concubines into our household. I hated him. When I woke I realised I had dreamt about a past life.'*
> *Patricia L.*

Patricia had in fact been married to a man in this life who, after her two children were born, began to bring other women home. This broke up their marriage. From Patricia's point of view, this happened because in a past life her husband and she had not resolved their difficulties, so they had to meet them again in this lifetime – Whatsoever ye sow, so shall ye reap. Where such dreams have been thoroughly explored, I have found that their imagery arises from emotions and trauma which the dreamer finds difficult to meet. Placing it in a past life setting enables one to avoid the difficulty of experiencing present life pain. Patricia says she hated her 'Chinese' husband. The dream process can create a drama to represent our present situation using any form of structure. It is, after all, the master dramatist. This function of the unconscious explains many 'past life' memories elicited by hypnotic regression. Most of them are explainable in terms of present life trauma or situation. See: **hallucination, hallucinogens**.

path   The approach or attitudes one uses regarding life in general, or in relationships or work; the direction one has decided on or is following; the way a relationship or marriage is going; a line of thought or enquiry. If well-worn path: a well-established or habitual way of doing something; the way other people do it, so following the norm. Also the path sometimes represents one's overall direction or experience of life within the process of growth and change. Losing a partner on the path: fear or intuition that the relationship will end or partner die first.

pearl See: *oyster* under **fish, sea creatures**; *pearl* under **jewels**.

pedestal To feel special or to make special; to place above other things; to idolise or worship.

peer dream work The way of working known as the Peer Dream Group came about from experience that dreams are largely self-explanatory if approached in the right way. An exterior expert or authority is not necessary for a profound experience of and insight into our dreams if certain rules are respected and used. The dreamer is the ultimate expert on their own dream, and when treated as such, and supported in their investigation of their dream drama, they can powerfully explore and manifest the resources of their inner life.

Fundamentals of practice The suggestions that follow have arisen from thirty years of dream work. They have been particularly tested with a number of small groups and are usually employed with groups of three to five people, but sometimes with just two people working together.

- The dreamer tells the dream. It is sometimes helpful if they tell it in the first person present, as if they were experiencing the dream as they are telling it. The telling of the dream can include any relevant information, such as immediate associations or events directly linked with the dream.

Example: 'This is my dream. I am driving my car, alone. I can see a female friend and stop to offer her a lift. I partly want her to be impressed by my new car. She looks at me. Now she tells me she doesn't want a lift and I am watching her walk off with a man I do not know ... I have recently bought the car I am driving in the dream. I like it very much and like to have my friends ride in it.' Joel.

• The helpers now ask the dreamer questions to clarify for themselves the imagery and drama of the dream. The questions at this point should not be to explore the dream, but simply to gain a clear image of the dream.

Example: Q: 'You didn't describe the street you were driving along. Was it a shopping centre or quiet place?'

A: 'It was quite a crowded road, with people, not so many cars. I think this was also connected with my feeling of wanting to be seen in my new car.'

Q: 'Are you attracted to your female friend?'

A: 'Yes.'

• The dreamer next chooses one of the characters or images in the dream to explore. The character can be themselves as they appear in the dream or any of the other people or things. It is important to realise that it does not matter if the character is someone known or not, or whether they are young or old. The character needs to be treated as an aspect of their dream and not as if they were the living person exterior to the dream.

In choosing an image to work with, such as a tree, cat, place, or an environment like the street in the example dream, it must again be treated as it appears in the dream, not as it may appear in real life. One can take any image from the dream to work with.

• The dreamer stands in the role of the character or image they are using. So if they chose to be the car in the example dream they would close their eyes, enter into the feeling sense and imagery of the dream, and describe themselves as the car.

Example: 'I am a car. Joel has recently purchased me and he is driving me, largely because he feels I will help him gain respect from other people. I am quite a large car and have a lot of power. But even with all this energy I do not make my own decisions. I am directed by Joel's desires and wishes, and enable him to fulfil them more readily.'

From this short description it can already be seen there is a suggestion that the car represents Joel's emotional and physical energy, directed by his desires and decisions.

- The helpers now ask questions of the dreamer who stays in the role of the dream character or image. The questions must be directly related to the role the dreamer is in. So Joel, in the role of the car, could be asked: Are you a second-hand or new car? Who was driving you before Joel? Do you feel that Joel handles you well? What does it feel like to be directed where to go all the time? Do you have places you would like to go?

  Joel should be helped to remain in role. If he slips out of it and stops describing himself as the car, gently remind him he is speaking as the car. Also the questions should be asked with an awareness of time necessary for the dreamer's adequate response. So do not hurry the questions to the point where the dreamer cannot properly explore his or her associations and feeling responses. If emotions are stimulated by a question allow the dreamer to discover what the emotion is connected to. This means that an emotion is usually a response to something and therefore gives information concerning what is moving us deeply.

- If a line of questioning is producing promising results, do not lead the dreamer off in another direction. For instance, Joel may have been asked if he wants to get out of his car and follow the woman, and show some feelings about this. A question such as 'Are there any shops in this street?' would take him completely away from such feelings.

- To help ask relevant questions it is useful to be interested in the dreamer and their dream. Have a questioning mind in relationship to the dream. So do not have already fixed opinions about it. Be like a detective gradually unfolding the information and emotions behind the dream.

- As the dreamer answering the questions, let your helpers also know what you feel in response to their questions, or what memories or associations occur when a particular part of the dream is being explored.

Example: Joel: 'When you asked me if I want to follow the woman I immediately realised that in real life I am holding myself back from letting my feelings about her show.'

- When you have come to the end of what you can ask about the dream image, the dreamer should be asked to summarise what they have understood or gathered from what they have said or felt in response to the questions. To summarise effectively, gather the essence of what you have said about the symbol and express it in everyday language. Imagine you are explaining to someone who knows nothing about yourself or the dream. Bring the dream out of its symbols into everyday comments about yourself.

Example: A man dreamt about a grey, dull office. When he looked at what he said about the office, he rephrased it by saying, 'The dream depicts the grey, unimaginative social environment I grew up in after the Second World War. It shaped the way I now think, and I want to change it toward more freedom of imagination and creativity.'

- Work through each of the symbols in the dream within the available time.
- A dream that leaves the dreamer unsatisfied, or in a difficult place, can usefully be approached by using the technique of carrying the dream forward.

The three following techniques describe how to carry the dream forward, how to use the body in dream exploration, and how to use dialogue between dream characters. These are extremely useful tools to use occasionally in peer dream work.

Carrying the dream forward   Imagine yourself in the dream and continue it as a fantasy or day dream. Alter the dream in any way that satisfies. Experiment with it, play with it, until you find a fuller sense of self-expression. It is very important to note whether any anger or hostility is in the dream but not fully expressed. If so, let yourself imagine a full expression of the anger. It may be that as this is practised more anger is openly expressed in subsequent dreams. This is healthy, allowing such feelings to be vented and redirected into satisfying ways, individually and socially. In doing this do not ignore any feelings of resistance, pleasure or anxiety. Satisfaction occurs only as we learn to acknowledge and integrate resistances and anxieties into what we express. This is a very important step. It gradually changes those of our habits which trap us in lack of satisfaction, poor creativity or inability to resolve problems.

Example: 'When my husband died, for quite a few times I had this funny dream. I was walking along a field and saw a lot of sheep guiding me, and I followed them. Suddenly they disappeared into a cave. I went in the cave and a row of mummies were there. One was wearing a medallion on a chain round its neck. The dream recurred quite often. One day Tony came to me and I told him the dream. He asked me to sit in a chair and relax, which I did. Then he said for me to go to the cave and in my relaxed state I went and walked to the mummy with the medallion. Then he said take off the bandage from the top. As I unwound it the face of my husband was uncovered. I screamed and screamed and came out of the relaxation. Tony then said now let him go. I have never had that dream since.' Betty E.

Use the body to discover dream power   The brain sends impulses to all the muscles to act on the movements we are making while in the dream, but usually a part of the brain inhibits these movements while we dream. Occasionally however the action of the dream wakes us enough for these impulses to move or cry out to break through the inhibition and we observe ourselves thrashing about in bed, or kicking and shouting.

The important factor is that a dream is more than a set of images and emotions, it is also frequently a powerful physical activity and self-expression. If we explore a dream sitting quietly talking to a friend, even if we allow emotions to surface, we may miss important aspects of our dream process. Through physical movement the dream process releases tensions and deeply buried memories that are stored in our body. These do not release and heal by simply talking about them. Exploring a dream while awake appears to avoid the inhibitory influence occurring during a dream and therefore spontaneous impulses to move can express more easily.

It is often enough to realise that this aspect of dream exploration is possible for such spontaneous movements to emerge when necessary. By being aware of the body's need to be involved occasionally in expression of dream content, we may catch the cues and let these develop. Frequently all you need to do is to let the body doodle or fantasise while exploring a dream. Jung suggested this technique for times when the person was stuck in intellectual speculation. To practise it you can take a dream image and let the hands spontaneously doodle, .watching what is gradually mimed or expressed. When you have gained skill in doing this, let the whole body take part in it. This can unfold aspects of dreams that the other approaches might not help with. See: **sleep movements**. A fuller description of this process is contained in my book *Liberating the Body*.

Have a dialogue between two characters or objects   Every part of a dream, whether an object, person or animal, is alive with our own intelligence. Each part has been created out of ourselves in some way and depicts some area of our own total being. We can therefore talk with them. Such dialogue is of great importance and very revealing.

To do this, imagine yourself as one of the characters, animals or objects in your dream. It may help at first to have two chairs – one empty and one you are sitting in. The character or object of your dream is in the empty chair. When you are ready to be that character move from your chair, sit in the empty chair and speak as that character. To answer or question the character from your own identity, move to the original chair and speak from your own character.

Be playful and curious in doing this. Question the character, and when you move to that role let whatever your feelings are as that character motivate what you say and do. Exploring your dream in this way unfolds a great deal of information that would otherwise remain unconscious. It also enables you to make real changes in unconscious attitudes or habits as you are literally dialoguing with areas of character patterning or programming and can change them.

Example: 'When I spoke as the new-born baby of my dream I really felt as if this was me, newly born. I had had a difficult birth and my reaction was that I wanted nothing to do with life. I wanted to stay curled up like an egg, not getting involved in the exterior world.

The adult observing part of me could see how this aspect of my inner life had led me to be withdrawn from social activity all my life, so I explained this to the baby me, saying – "I need you to be ready to meet the world. You are a part of me and if you continue to withdraw I lack the enthusiasm to get involved with other people."

Back as the baby I felt totally vulnerable and didn't want to take any risks: "No I don't want to come out of the egg."

As the adult again I said, "Look, if you remain curled up this is more of a gamble than actually getting out and taking risks in life. Just lying there anything can get you."

As the baby this really got to me. I felt a change in me and a readiness to begin the journey of meeting life outside the womb. This change really made a difference to my everyday activities. A lifelong habit of being introverted gradually dropped away.' Trevor P.

pegasus See: *horse* under **animals**.

pen, pencil Desire to communicate; occasionally male sexuality because of the shape.

pendant See: **necklace**.

penguin Suggests feeling isolated by cold emotions.

penis See: **body**; **castrate**.

pentacle See: *five* under **numbers**.

people Several people in a dream: not feeling lonely; involvement of many aspects of oneself in what is being dreamt about; social ability. Large crowds: enormous involvement of Self in issue; one's relationship or feelings about the social environment one lives in; in groups we have a feeling of being looked at or on view – how we relate to that may be depicted by what we are doing in the dream group. See: **party**; **roles**.

> *Example: 'I was outdoors with a group of people acting as leader. We were in the middle of a war situation with bullets playing around us. Maybe aeroplanes were also attacking. I was leading the group from cover to cover, avoiding the bullets.' Paul W.*

Despite feeling attacked, either by external events or from inner conflicts, Paul is using leadership skills to deal with his own fears and tendencies. If a friend told us he had just had an argument with his wife and was going to leave her, we might sit down and counsel them by listening and helping them to sort out the hurt feelings from their long-term wishes. We might point out they had felt this way before but it passed – in other words give feedback they had missed. In a similar way, our various emotions and drives often need this sort of skill employed by ourselves. This unifies us, leading to coping skills as in Paul's dream.

> *Example: 'Walking alone through a small town, I was heading for a place that a group of people, in a street parallel to mine, were also heading for. A person from the group tried to persuade me that the right way to get to the place was along the street the group was walking. I knew the street did not matter, only the general direction. The person was quite disturbed by my independence. It made him or her feel uncertain to have their leader apparently questioned. I felt uncertain too for a moment.' Ivor S.*

A group of people, as in Ivor's dream, can also depict how one meets the pressure of social norms. As social relationship is one of the most important factors outside of personal survival – and survival depends upon it – such dreams help us to clarify our individual contact with society. Human beings have an unconscious but highly developed sense of the psychological social environment. Ivor's dream shows something we are all involved in – how we are relating to humans collectively. Are we in conflict with group behaviour and direction?

Do we conform, but perhaps have conflict with our individual drives? Do we find a way between the opposites? Much of our response is laid down in childhood and remains unconscious unless we review it.

In some dreams, a group of people represent what is meant by the word God. This may sound unlikely, but the unconscious, because it is highly capable at synthesis, often looks at humanity as a whole. Collectively humanity has vast creative and destructive powers which intimately affect us as individuals. Collectively it has performed miracles which looked at as an individual appear impossible. How could a little human being build the great pyramid or a space shuttle? The Bible echoes this concept in such phrases as 'Whatever you do to the least of one of these, you do to me.'

pepper   Warming up one's emotions; livening up the situation; irritation.

perfume, **scent**, **smell**   A smell can remind us of a particular situation or person. Odour attracts, repulses, relaxes or offends. So it depicts feeling responses and intuition, and may summarise what we feel about a person or situation. Frequently in dreams a smell expresses an intuition of something rotten in ones life if the smell is bad. Rotten might mean 'bad' emotions felt in a relationship; a hunch or feelings about something, as in the example; memories. Good smell: good feelings; non-verbalised intimations or love.

> *Example: 'I went back in time in circles, almost as if going unconscious. I went back and back and then there came this awful smell such as I've never experienced. I always felt it was the smell of death. I would wake terrified. One night my husband, a practical and down-to-earth man, said he would read me to sleep to see if it helped me not have the dream. It made no difference, I still had the nightmare. Imagine my surprise though. He said "I knew you'd had the dream again for there was an awful smell in the room for a minute."' Mrs E.C.*

Also explainable by the large number of idioms regarding smell. Idioms: on the right scent; throw someone off the scent; in bad/good odour with; odour of sanctity; smell a rat; smell of grease paint; smells fishy; something stinks to high heaven; like stink; raise a stink; what you did stinks. See: *nose* under **body**.

perspire, sweat   Mostly fear. As we get near to experiencing areas of our memory or inner feelings which disturb us, rapid heartbeat and perspiration are some of the first signs. Occasionally pleasurable exertion. Idioms: in a cold sweat; no sweat; sweat blood; sweat of one's brow; old sweat; sweat it out.

pet   Our natural drives and feelings – such as procreation, desire to be 'petted' – which have been 'house trained' or caged depending on dream – the dream will indicate what one is doing with this side of one's nature; feelings of being like a pet – only being able to do what the person you are dependent upon wishes. Baby pets: if in a woman's dream may signify her maternal drive, her desire for children; one's own dependent Self and feelings. See: **animals**.

petrol   Energy; explosive or dangerous emotions.

petticoat   See: **clothes**.

philosophy of dreams   In attempting to put together the inform-ation gathered from viewing thousands of dreams – not simply at face value, but explored in depth through the emotions and direct associations of the dreamer – a philosophy or view of life arises.

The synthesis of the information gathered suggests that our birth as a physical and psychological being is a paradox. We are unique and at the same time a common undifferentiated process. Psycho-logically we have our identity out of the lives of thousands of humans who preceded us and left the gift of language, of music, art, of concepts and information. Our mental life, our consciousness, is in some very real way formed out of what they left from their life. Our consciousness has been whittled out of the rock of possibilities by the love, the struggle and pain, the endeavour and wit of their lives. Particularly our psyche has been shaped by or modelled on our parents, and the traces in their lives, unknown though they may be, of their parents, backwards for many generations.

Our identity is given to us by the humans who raise us. This sense of Self arises because we are treated as if we were a Self. This, with language, is the creative matrix of our self-awareness. The giving of a name is therefore a miracle which acts as a nucleus around which the many mental connections can be made which form our self-image. Perhaps this is why giving the name in baptism is seen as a holy rite in Christianity.

Our conscious personality can live without ever becoming aware of its connections with other lives except as it meets them in everyday affairs. That its existence has depended upon what was given by countless other lives – that humans constantly create each other through the dynamic flux of communication, consciously and unconsciously – might never be realised. That one's own life is also a part of this creative process, this sea of living consciousness, might never be known. Nevertheless, each individual life constantly takes part in the collective, negatively or positively. This is not a mystical thing, but is plainly observable. Language for instance is not something we created alone. The clothes we wear, the food we eat, the house we live in and the materials it is made of, are all a part of collective skill, effort and knowledge. We exist in this collective creativity all the time. We depend upon it but perhaps seldom acknowledge it. Our unconscious, however, is vitally aware of it and communicates to us as fully as it can considering our frequency of ignoring it, what it sees of our relationship with this collective life process and social activity.

From the point of view of dreams, if our life has given nothing in deed, in love, in rearing of children, in ideas or art, or in common humanity, we are dead – during life and afterwards. Giving and receiving, kinship and symbiosis, growth and decay are the fundamentals of the living process according to dreams. Life is action within the whole.

At death, we face a very real end, a real death. There is no magical escape from this. All that we have been, all we have become, all we gathered and won is lost – finished. But the paradox occurs again. Dreams suggest that out of all we gave of ourselves, out of all we received from the being of others, arises a new existence recreated in a realm of consciousness. This may mean that we continue as living influences in the lives of those who still live. But the suggestion is that something more than this occurs.

phoenix   See: **birds**.

photographs   General: memories; wanting to be remembered or noticed; looking at some aspect of oneself. Looking at family photos: realisation of past influences in one's life; family environment, mentally and emotionally. Taking photos: capturing a realisation; taking notice of something; remembering. Photo of oneself: one's self-image; need to look at oneself or get an objective view. Photos which come to life: the living influence of past experience; our continuing involvement in what the picture depicts; something which we held as a thought, which is taking shape and becoming real. Developing photos: bringing to consciousness what was latent or unrealised before.

physician   See: **roles**.

piano   See: **musical instrument**.

pictures   See: **painting**; **photographs**.

pig   See: **animals**.

pill   An experience you need or are making yourself meet because you think it is good for you; something we 'swallow' because we think it is right – we may 'swallow' lies or excuses; an attempt to deal with internal feelings by external means. A pill we are actually taking: may link with feelings or physical reactions to the drug being taken. Idioms: sugar the pill; bitter pill.

pillow   Comfort; support; may represent someone we rely on or want to be close to. Hugging pillow: feeling alone and needing contact.

pimple   Character blemishes if on face; worry about how one appears to others; sense of not being inwardly clean; feelings about one's spots.

pin   Small ideas, actions or information which help create something or hold things together; one's connection or emotional bond with things. If stuck in: irritation or hurts; irritating or painful sexual intercourse. Idioms: for two pins; don't care two pins; on pins; pins and needles; pin back one's ears; pin one's hopes on; pin someone down; pin something on someone; pin money.

pipe Unconscious connections with others; emotions, or things which you feel are 'on tap'; a difficult way out of a situation; sometimes refers to the experience of being born, especially if accompanied by panic or fear; the 'pipes' in one's body – see number 3 in *the dream as extended perception* under **ESP**. Crawling into pipe: sexual intercourse – sex creates unconscious links with partner; experiencing unconscious connection with others.

pirate See: **roles**.

piston Sexual drive or activity.

pit Feelings or situations one finds it difficult to get out of; feelings about death; feeling trapped or forgotten.

place, **environment** See: **setting**.

placenta Dependence; being depended upon; how one gains nourishment from another.

plait Plaited hair: girlhood. See: *hair* under **body**. Plaiting rope etc.: weaving different influences in one's life together; uniting conflicting feelings or people; a triangle situation.

plane See: **aeroplane**.

planets General: the influence of the abstract or subtle in one's life; desire for the strange or alien. If dreamer has any inkling of astrology, the planet can depict the traditional 'planetary' qualities. Sun: vital energy; the Self; consciousness or awareness. Moon: see: **moon**. Mercury: intuition and the mind. Venus: love; motherhood and femininity; receptivity. Mars: energetic activity. Aggressive action or fire in one's life and feelings; masculinity ruled by passions. Jupiter: growth; expansion in Self and activities; preservation;

freedom from limitations. Saturn: fate; the past catching up with us; retarding influence; emotional coldness; lessons of life which shape our growth; time. Uranus: sudden changes; fluctuation. Neptune: the unconscious influence in daily life; psychic impressions; awareness of death. Pluto: the deep unconscious and death; beyond the ego.

plank   Depends what it is used for in the dream. Can be security in life if flooring – or sense of losing basic support if rotten floor. See: *floor* under **house**, **buildings**. If for making something: one's potential; the materials you have for undertaking a project or 'making something of oneself'. If nailed above one: feeling of being trapped, fear of death; setting up one's own death in the sense of killing one's chances in work or relationship. See: **coffin**; **fence**; **wood**.

plants   Areas of progressive change in one's life; emerging personal qualities; occasionally one's children being helped in their 'growth'. Dead or dying plants: loss of vital enthusiasm; dying pleasure; lost love. See: **flowers**; **weeds**.

plate   If food on plate: what one has a sense of ownership about; what one has received or hopes to receive from others or from one's own efforts; what one has created and now faces. Communal plate: what is available but one may have to compete for or share – in work, relationship, life. Empty plate: one's needs; appetites; receptivity; perhaps status, as in the past only the rich had plates. Idioms: handed to one on a plate; on one's plate. See: **food**.

> *Example: 'I am at a wedding at which we are being served a celebratory chicken lunch. Whilst my back is turned for a moment one of the other guests on the table who is female but who I do not know removes my plate and substitutes it with a plate of food which doesn't contain chicken. When I challenge this, I am told that there is no more. At this I rather petulantly decide to leave the wedding.' Brian Y.*

Brian uses a plate of food to represent the good things he feels are rightfully his in life; but his negative emotions in a relationship with a female rob him of this.

plateau   Reaching a plateau in one's life – a place where things remain the same, where there is little change; a wider and calmer viewpoint of life where one is neither climbing ambitiously or descending and losing what one has gained.

play   See: **film**; **theatre**.

play on words   See: **language and dreams**.

playing   Depends what the 'game' is. Whatever we 'play' at in a dream might just be fun or suggest great seriousness. As humans we use an enormous number of strategies to gain our ends, as explained in Eric Berne's book *Games People Play*. So play in a dream can depict a sense of relaxation; a way of practising something without responsibility; not taking something seriously. Also a game can be a way of playing creatively, exploring feelings, ideas and approaches in a safe way before trying them out in life. This sort of self-allowing, of letting oneself 'want' something without too many serious overtones, can be very creative and the beginning of new developments in life.

The enormous number of idioms on play define some of these 'games'. Idioms: come into play; fair play; foul play; make a play for; make play of; play a part in; play along with; play at; play cat and mouse; play dead/possum; play down; played out; play fair; play false; play for time; play hard to get; play it cool; play no part in it; play on words; play safe; play people off against each other; play the field; play up; play upon a weakness/fear; play up to someone; the state of play; play somebody at their own game; child's play; play ball with; play it by ear; play fast and loose; play gooseberry; play havoc with; play merry hell; play into their hands; play one's ace; play one's cards right; play second fiddle; play the fool; play the game; play the white man; play to the gallery; play with fire; two can play at that game. See: **games**.

plot of the dream   In attempting to understand our dreams, it is important to honour their drama or plot. Dreams appear to be very specific in the way they use the characters, objects and environs occurring in them.

*Example: 'I was walking up a steep hill on a sunny day when
my husband came running down the hill with blood pouring
from his right arm. He couldn't stop running. As he passed me
he called to me for help. I was happy and peaceful and ignored
him. I calmly watched him running fast down the hill, then
continued on my way.' Joyce C.*

Out of the infinite number of situations Joyce could have dreamt
about, this was the one produced. Why? There are many factors
which appear to determine what we dream. How events of the day
influenced us; what stage of personal growth we are meeting – we
may be in the stage of struggling for independence; problems being
met; relationship situations; past business such as childhood traumas
still to be integrated are some of them.

If Joyce had dreamt she and her husband were walking up the hill
the whole message of the dream would have been different. If we
can accept that dream images are, as Freud stated, a form of
thinking, then the change in imagery would be a changed feeling
state and concept. If the language of dreams is expressed in its
images, then the meaning stated is specific to the imagery used.

In processing our dreams, it is therefore profitable to look at the
plot to see what it suggests. It can be helpful to change the situation
as we have done with Joyce's. Imagining Joyce walking up the hill
on a sunny day arm in arm with her husband suggests a happy
relationship. This emphasises the situation of independence and
lack of support for her husband which appears in the real dream.
Seeing our dreams as if they were snatches from a film or play and
asking ourself what feelings or human situations they depict can aid
us to clarify them. As a piece of drama, Joyce's dream says she sees
but does not respond to her husband's plight.

Our internal 'dream producer' has an amazing sense of the subtle
meanings of movement, positioning, and relationship between the
elements used. Some of these are subtle. A way of becoming more
aware of what information our dream contains is to use visualisation.
Sit comfortably and imagine yourself back in the dream. Replay it
just as it was. Remember the whole thing slowly, going through it
again while awake. As you do so, be aware of what it feels like in
each scene or event. What do the interactions suggest? What does it
feel like in the other roles? We can even practise this with other

people's dreams. If we imagine ourself in Joyce's dream and replay it just as she describes it, we may arrive at a feeling of detachment from the husband. If we take the husband's role we may feel a great need which is not responded to as we go 'down hill fast'. In this way we gather a great deal of 'unspoken' information from dreams.

Looking at our own dreams in this way can be more difficult simply because we do not always want to see what is being said about ourselves. See: **amplification**; **dream processing**; **postures, movement, body language**; **settings**; **word analysis of dreams**.

ploughing   Working at preparing or changing oneself or a situation; making way for new growth; using past experience for future growth. Plough: Means of 'ploughing'; male sexuality in its move toward parenthood – sowing the seeds.

plumbing   The way we direct emotions or the flow of feelings; our internal 'plumbing' – intestines, colon, bladder, kidneys, etc. See: **pipe**; **water**.

plunge   Taking a risk; facing uncertainty; going into something unknown or untried.

pocket   General: One's personal secrets or thoughts; Self; sense of ownership or possession; vagina. Trouser pocket: can refer to sexuality; your intimate space that you only allow certain people to enter. Idioms: be in somebody's pocket; in/out of pocket; pocket one's pride; burn a hole in one's pocket; dip into one's pocket; line one's pocket.

point   Anything pointed can refer to male sexuality; reaching a point – arriving at a culmination or change; a meaning; a decision to be made.

pointing   Drawing one's attention to something; feeling at the receiving end of someone's emotions or suggestions. Pointing hand: drawing your attention to something. Pointing stick or gun: aggressive or defensive sexuality or emotions.

poison　Warning to avoid something; something that will not be good for us; attitudes, emotions or thoughts which can harm us; warning against business deal or relationship; possibly related to foods we are eating which are not suitable. Idioms: what's your poison; poison one's mind; poison pen letter; avoid it like poison.

pole　The penis; male sexuality; life force in its positive, expressive aspect.

policeman/woman　See: **roles**.

pool　Our inner world of thoughts, fantasies and feelings; sometimes a sense of unity with living beings – collective consciousness.

pop star　See: **famous people**.

Pope　Father; code of behaviour arising from religious beliefs; God. See: **dream as spiritual guide**.

positions　General: one's stance or position in life; the way one is relating to what is depicted – or the way we feel we are relating to it.

above　General: what is superior or has a wider view or possibility than our present standpoint; sense of inferiority in relationship to what is above us; what we strive for. If we are standing above or high up: having a wider viewpoint; being intellectual; feeling superior or in a position of advantage. Idioms: above all; above and beyond; above asking; above oneself; above board; above one's station; risen above oneself. See: **flying**; **high**; **hill**; **mountain**.

behind　The past; what one has chosen to or wants to forget – left behind; what one is unaware of – as talk behind one's back; what has been learnt or dealt with. People behind dreamer: taking the lead in relationships; being decisive. Idioms: behind the scenes; behind the time; fall behind; put something behind me.

below　Something one feels is 'beneath one'; what is 'below' in the body – so the non-intellectual aspects of Self; something one can now look back on from a detached viewpoint. If below something else, see *above*. Idioms: beneath my contempt; it's below my standards.

close   Intimacy; being made aware of; what one feels connected with or has ties with; near to, in the sense of making a decision – near to leaving home; close to, as 'close to finding the solution'; a situation which is near at hand or being confronted or realised now. Idioms: at close quarters; close-fisted; close on; close to home; that was close.

distant   Barely conscious of; a long time off; something one does not identify with strongly.

in front   The future; what is seen and understood; what is being confronted.

opposite   Meeting or 'facing' a situation; opposition or resistance to decided direction.

side   Supportive feelings as 'by one's side'; as well as; indication of choice as 'what side are you on' or 'who's on my side?' Idioms: from all sides; let the side down; on every side; on the wrong side of thirty; on the right/wrong side; on the side; pass by on the other side; pick sides; put to one side; side by side; side with somebody; take sides; take to one side; the other side – death; safe side; bit on the side; seamy side.

poster   Something the unconscious is trying to show you.

postures, **movement**, **body language**   Even in everyday life, the way we hold and position our body, the inclination of chest and head, the movement of hands, are a means of communication. The apparently intuitive information in some dreams, when investigated, can be traced to an unconscious insight into the languages of the living body. We all have this ability to understand body language, but it seems to be something which is inherited from our ancient forebears, perhaps developed to an intense degree as a survival need prior to the growth of verbal language. It therefore remains a largely unconscious ability. In our dreams, however, it is a major factor in how the dream is structured.

If you cannot find a satisfying description below, imagine yourself making the movement or posture in the dream to see if you can define what the feeling quality is, or what you are saying non-verbally. It can often be of value to make the movement or take up the posture physically instead of in the imagination. By comparing the movement/posture with another one, it can help to clarify its quality.

Example: 'Marilyn was experiencing emotional pain connected with her impending divorce. Marilyn had dreamt of seeing a dinosaur standing in her path, devouring all who approached it. We explored it by having Marilyn find a body posture and movements which for her expressed the feeling of the dinosaur. In doing so Marilyn did not sense anger or aggression, but she did feel like a predator which always had to take to gain her own needs. This feeling immediately reminded her of her family life as a child. She remembered when she was sent shopping as a very young child of three or four, as well as buying what she had been asked for, she purchased some sweets for herself. When she arrived home she was treated as if she had done a terrible thing and that was where she began to feel like a predator. It seemed to her as if her own needs were always gained at the expense of someone else.

With this awareness, she could now see that the dinosaur standing in her path clearly related to her present situation. Bargaining to gain a realistic share of the house and property jointly owned by her husband and herself felt to her as if she were gaining her needs at his expense, like a predator. That made her feel so awful she was almost ready to allow her husband to take all, leaving her without house or money to start again. Her awareness of where the feelings arose from, and the unrealistic part they played in her life, allowed her to relate to the situation with less pain and more wisdom.' From Mind and Movement, *Tony Crisp (C.W. Daniel).*

jump Jumping to: daring; taking a risk; sometimes connected with flying. Jumping to avoid: feeling of threat; anxiety; evasion tactics. Jumping off: getting out of a situation. Jumping at dreamer: unexpected; irritations. Idioms: one jump ahead; the high jump;

jump at; running jump at yourself; jumping down one's throat; jumping off place; jump out of one's skin; jump the gun; jump the queue; jump to it; jump on the bandwagon; jump to conclusion.

kneel Humility; acknowledgement of dependence or co-operation; sense of awe; defeat.

prone Relaxation; letting go of activity; introversion; sex. Also retreat from the world; feeling injured; afraid to stand up for oneself; non-involvement; negative introversion; weakness; death. Idioms: lie low; lie at one's door; lie in wait; taking it lying down. See: *squatting down* and *standing* below.

run General: exuberance; flowing life energy; strong and easy motivation. Running away: avoiding one's own emotions or sexuality; not meeting problems in a way that will resolve them; anxiety about what you are running from; feelings of guilt. Running to: anxiety; responsibility and self-giving; sometimes running toward danger. As if made of lead: held back by one's own hesitations. See: **paralysis**.

> *Example: 'There followed a nightmare of running along streets, round corners, knowing I was being followed and trying to get away. Then I met a friend who also was running away. She took me down a narrow street full of down and outs and prostitutes.' Pauline B.*

Idioms: run for one's money; run of the house; out of the running; on the run; run along; run down; run for it; run out of steam; run out on someone; run up against; run wild. See: **chased**; question 7 in **dream processing**; second example in **emotion, mood**; **lucidity, awake in dreams**; **nightmares**.

sit One's situation at time of dream; status, depending where one is sitting; being relaxed; inactive waiting. Sitting up: becoming more involved. Idioms: sit back; sit for; sit in on something; sit on; sit out; sit something out; sit tight; sit at someone's feet; sit in judgement; sitting target; sit on the fence.

squatting down Sleep; rest; withdrawal; non-involvement. Idioms: feel down; down and out; do someone down; down at heel; down hearted; down with. See: *prone* above.

standing   Our involvement in the exterior world of change, opposites and needs which require expenditure of effort; our 'standing' in
society; what one 'stands' for; being active; confrontation; co-operation with others. Idioms: know where one stands; left standing;
make a stand against; stand alone; stand aside; stand by; stand
corrected; stand down; stand firm; stand in someone's way; stand up
for; stand up to; stand one's ground; stand on ceremony or dignity.

turn   A change; making a new decision.

walk   Motivation and confidence; where you are walking is what
you are meeting in life or where you are going; personal effort in
trying to get somewhere; changing one's relationship with things; a
period of experience you are passing through. Walking up a lane: as
above, but may be memory lane. Idioms: walk over somebody; walk
away with; walk off with; walk on air; walk tall; walk the streets;
walk out on; walk out with.

potter   The drives, creativity, you are shaping your life with, or
being shaped by; the Self.

poverty   Feelings of being inadequate; negative emotions depriv-
ing one of well-being; sense of deprivation; being tight emotionally
and sexually.

prayer   Depending upon feelings in dream could depict looking
for certainty in face of anxieties; seeking approval or authority for
one's desires; expression of pleasure and thanks; seeking co-operation of unconscious faculties to aid one's everyday activities; attempt
to channel the forces of the unconscious. See: **dream as spiritual
guide**.

precipice   If at the top: fear of failure; on the edge of losing
confidence; near to a leap into the unknown or great change. If
precipice drops into a void: death; the unconscious or unknown. If
at bottom: sense of insurmountable obstacle in life.

precognition   As a part of the human survival ability, the capacity to predict the future is a well-developed, everyday part of life. So much so we often fail to notice ourselves doing it. When crossing a road we quickly take in factors relating to sounds, car speeds and our own physical condition and predict the likelihood of being able to cross the road without injury. Based on information gathered, often unconsciously, we also attempt to assess or predict the outcome of relationships, job interviews, business ventures and any course of action important to us.

If a detailed observation were made of the habits of ten people, one could predict fairly accurately what they would be doing for the next week, perhaps even pinpointing the time and place. For instance some would never visit a pub, while others would be frequently there.

Because the unconscious is the storehouse of millions of bits of observed information, and because it has a well-developed function enabling us to scan information and predict from it, some dreams forecast the future. Such predictions may occur more frequently in a dream rather than as waking insight because few people can put aside their likes and dislikes, prejudices and hopes sufficiently to allow such information into consciousness. While asleep some of these barriers drop and allow information to be presented.

Ed Butler's dream below is about his work scene. Each detail was real and horrifying. Shortly afterwards, Rita was burnt just as in the dream.

Example: 'I was startled by the muffled but unmistakable sound of a nearby explosion. While unexpected, it wasn't entirely unusual – the high-energy propellants and oxidisers being synthesised and tested in the chemistry wing were hazardously unstable. When I heard the screams I froze for an instant, recognising that they could only be coming from Rita, the one woman chemist in the all-male department. I rushed to the doorway of her laboratory. Peering through the smoke and fumes I saw a foot sticking out of the surrounding flames. I was only in my shirt sleeves, unprotected, not even wearing my lab coat, but I had to go into the flames. I grabbed Rita by the foot and noticed with horror that her stockings were melting from the heat. I pulled her back into the doorway and tugged at a chain which released gallons of water on her

*flaming body. When satisfied the fire was quenched, even
though my own clothes still smouldered, I ran for the emergency phone.' From* Dream Network Bulletin, *June 1985.*

Some precognitive dreams appear to go beyond this ability to
predict from information already held. So far there is no theory
which is commonly accepted which explains this. A not too bizarre
one, however, is that our unconscious has access to a collective
mind. With so much more information available, it can transcend the
usual limitations when predicting from personal information. The
speculative side of modern physics suggests an extension to this in
saying the origins of our being lie beyond space and time. If we
touch this aspect of ourselves we may transcend our usual time-
bound Self and see things in new ways – one of which might be
precognition.

The next examples are all from Shirley G. Because of lack of
space, only three of the dreams are quoted. Nevertheless, they are
typical of dreams which do not seem to fall into the category of
precognitive dreams arising from unconscious scanning or information already known. See: **ESP in dreams**.

*Example: 'I set out to dream the winner of a horse race each
day for a week.
1. Was driving down a country road and suddenly saw a
glimpse of Emmerdale Farm down a side road. Following day,
chosen horse 'Emmerdale Farm' came in first.
2. Was working in a room when a man popped his head
around the door and shouted excitedly, "John, John, your
uncle's here" and disappeared. I carried on working. Chosen
horse: "Uncle John" came in first.
3. Was walking down a road, called into a house by a friend
to have a chat. On the way out she opened the door and I saw
a completely empty room except for a huge black fireplace.
Door closed and I left the house. Chosen horse: "Black Fire"
which I insisted would only be placed due to "fireplace". Came
in second.'*

pregnancy General: a new area of one's potential or personality
developing; a deepening relationship with one's unconscious is

producing a new area of experience – still unexpressed but developing; a new scheme or creative idea 'hatching'. In a woman's dream: may refer to desire for a child.

If pregnant at time of dream: anxieties regarding pregnancy and birth. Carolyn Winget and Frederic Kapp researched on the dreams of seventy pregnant women. Those women whose dreams included a high percentage of anxiety themes were the ones who delivered their babies in the shortest time – less than ten hours. The conclusion was that by allowing feelings of anxiety in our dreams we are less influenced by anxiety in waking and we can deal with situations more confidently. Someone else pregnant in dream: an aspect of oneself about to bring forth new characteristics; an intuition about that person. See: second example under **baby**; **birth**; third example under *penis* in **body**; **cave**; example under **girl**.

prehistoric   Our own primeval urges and drives such as fear, territorial aggression, mating rituals, survival; urges that have not been integrated fully into our present social situation, perhaps because they were repressed during childhood. Many of our social rituals – such as the father giving the daughter away in marriage which possibly arose out of the need to allay aggression between males and break the father's sexual bond with the daughter – arose from these basic drives. Also our babyhood or prenatal life.

premenstrual tension   Dr Ernest Hartmann carried out studies in connection with people who have stable sleep patterns. His aim was to define whether waking events influenced people's need for sleep. For instance, a loss of boyfriend or a stress situation caused many young women to have an increased need for sleep. Some people who had undergone successful psychotherapy for their emotional difficulties and some meditators found their sleep need was decreased.

Wanting to know more about why these situations changed sleep needs, Hartmann went on to study dream sleep in a group of women who suffered premenstrual tension. This group were prone to depression and irritability during PMT – records show there is an unusually high rate of murder, suicide and admission to psychiatric hospitals during this time. Although Hartmann found this group needed a little more sleep time than a control group, the main feature of change was their increased need for dreaming. Their length of time spent in dreaming increased in relationship to their depression. The conclusion reached was that one of the functions of dreaming is to help deal with difficult states of emotion or anxiety.

presents   Receiving: being affirmed; feeling recognised or loved; gaining something from a relationship. Giving: giving of Self – negative or positive; making love; if it is a present actually received in life, probably relates to giver and circumstances of giving. See: **parcel**, **package**.

priest, **priestess**   One's religious beliefs; one's relationship with religious beliefs; a sense of sin; sympathy; a sense of community; a non-sexual relationship.

prince   The best aspect of the dreamer if male; one's brother or lover/boyfriend if female.

princess   The best aspect of the dreamer if female; one's lover/ girlfriend if male.

prison   Traps we create for ourselves out of our own anxiety, patterns of behaviour and concepts such as right and wrong.

Example: 'I was in a prison cell with two other men. We ate, slept and defecated in the cell. I was standing at the bars of the cell and had the impression of having been in the prison for years. I was shouting and cursing the people who had put me in the prison, full of hate and self-pity. Suddenly I realised that my years of shouting had availed nothing. The only person who was upset by it was myself. I was the victim of my own anger and turmoil. I dropped the attitudes and was free of them. Years went by and one by one I dropped other habits of emotion and thought with which I had trapped and tortured myself. I realised I could be totally free within myself. One morning I woke and sat up on the mattress on the floor that was my bed. The last ghost of inner entrapment fell away. A fountain of joy opened in my body, pouring upwards through me. So intense was it I cried out. The cell mates called a warden. They stood looking at me as I experienced a radiance so strong I felt as if I must be shining. I was aware my joy poured into them, although they thought I was mad. Nothing would ever be the same again.' Andie.

See: *wolf* under **animals**; **cage**, **cell**; **escape**; **holding**; **imprisoned**; **trapped**.

prize   May reflect people having praised dreamer; feeling rewarded; occasionally intuition; feeling good about oneself.

propeller   One's driving force or interest.

prostitute   Dire sexual need unconnected to feelings of care or respect; sexuality breaking out of deadening moral restrictions. Woman's dream: unacknowledged sexual longings; feelings of 'cheapness' or guilt in sex; desire to be more free sexually. Woman dreaming another woman is prostitute: one's own hidden desires; feeling the other woman is promiscuous or might be in competition with her; uncertainty about her own sexual value. Man's dream: wishing a woman was more available; wish that sexual relationships were as simple as an exchange of cash; being ill at ease about his sexual practices; feeling unable to break free of sexual dependence on partner/mother.

psychodrama and dreams   In psychodrama there is no 'interpretation' of a dream. The dreamer unravels the meaning of the dream by acting it out with the help of others. The dreamer acts the main role of him or herself and directs the helpers in the other roles. In dramatising and exploring the dream in this way the obvious as well as the hidden meaning, associations and emotions are made clear. To finish, the dreamer is encouraged to take the dream forward, altering it to what feels more adequate and satisfying. This gives the person opportunity to express and enact what was absent in the dream and provides release from recurring dreams and catharsis where necessary.

psychologist, **psychiatrist**   See: **analyst**.

pub   See: **bar room**.

pulling Doing something about a situation; positive action or expression of will. Being pulled: being influenced by someone or something else; being pulled by one's emotions – perhaps attracted to someone; going along with something – as when 'going with the flow'. Pulled against one's will: being influenced by aspects of one's nature which one feels at odds with; influenced by someone else against one's own inclinations. Idioms: have pull; pull one's socks up; pull out; pull through; pull something off; pull strings; pull the women/men; pull together; pull up one's roots; pull rank.

pulse Feelings about health; anxiety about death.

punishment, torture Depicts the internal pain or fear of retribution that occurs inside us caused by conflict between our social training and internal drives. The more rigidly moral we are, the more hell and punishment we dream about; a means of allaying guilt out of childhood feelings of responsibility for such things as being unloved by a parent (we must have done something awful or be awful), abused by an adult, or the death of a parent.

puns See: **wordplay**, **puns**.

puppet Manipulation or feeling manipulated; feeling powerless against what feels like an external influence – the power of alcohol or drugs.

puppy See: **animals**; **pet**.

purse Something in our nature we value and try not to lose; a woman's sexual feelings; the vagina.

pus Emotions infected by fears, self-doubts, jealousy, etc.; occasionally sign of physical illness.

pushed, pushing Pushing: being positive in what one wants; exerting one's will or effort of will. Being pushed: feeling coerced or taken for granted. Idioms: give someone the push; when it comes to the push; push off; push/press on; push-over; push one's luck; push and shove.

pyjamas   Being casual or intimate; sexuality; difficulty in facing life. In street or public in night clothes: revealing one's sleep, perhaps honest, Self to others; inappropriate attitudes.

pyramid   The Self; wider awareness; integration of Self; death.

quarrel Conflict within the dreamer. See: **people** – it describes some of the main areas of human conflict.

quartz Deep internal processes, such as those shaping the body – consciousness can influence these so the dream may show what relationship exists; the Self. See: **jewels**.

quay Departures; meetings and partings; leaving a phase of life behind or meeting a new one, and how we encounter such changes. See: **beach**.

queen One's mother; a figure we use in dreams to illustrate our need for acknowledgement and personal and public acclaim; also represents one's culture, language and traditions. In some dreams, the king or queen is dreamt about as the dreamer is becoming acclaimed externally, and the dreams may precede this. See: **king**.

Example: 'I was with the Queen and Prince Philip in a public place. We were sitting in easy chairs watching something. I was very aware of being seen by millions of people in company with the Queen. As we sat and talked easily, and I felt very much at ease, I thought how ridiculous it was that we were having to crane our heads, so I gently levitated into the air carrying my seat with me. Then I slowly lowered down to the ground again. I knew this would be interpreted in many different ways by people seeing it. For myself, I wanted to show people it was possible to do and natural to do.

Then I and the Queen were walking together in public,

through streets and countryside. We gradually developed a loving and sensual relationship. Several times I held her full breasts, hands under her clothes. She made no effort to stop this. At a later time I put my hands down onto her belly. She tensed slightly but not in a way to say no. But also there was a lot of laughter and playfulness between us and I was very impressed and moved by how many risks she was taking socially by her obvious enjoyment of our touching and playing in public.' Tony.

Tony is not only seen by millions of people but is also loved publicly, so the dream is obviously dealing with his feelings about acclaim and acknowledgement.

quicksand Feelings of insecurity; emotions that take away our confidence or sense of value or adequacy.

rabbit   See: *rabbit* under **animals**

race   Taking part in life and the human race – perhaps acknowl-edging one's position in the 'race'; competitiveness or feelings of competition. <u>Racing car or bike</u>: competitive drive; sexual energy; daring. See: example in **failure**.

> *Example: 'My husband has a gammy – crippled, damaged – leg in real life. In his dream though he is running in the London Marathon. He is running along with everyone doing okay. He sees the finishing line and all his family are there cheering him on. Then he crosses the finishing line and we all rush forward to hug him. We are all happy except for his son-in-law who is crying. He keeps wondering why his son-in-law is crying.' Edna (LBC).*

I see the dreamer as a man who is near the end of his life looking back and assessing the quality of it. The marathon is his participation in life. He is a part of a 'race' – the human race. The imagery of the marathon is wonderful in depicting this. In it is all manner of human expression. Some participate out of competition. They want to struggle to achieve, to break barriers. Others are there almost crawling on hands and knees. They stay the course despite their condition. Determination, anger, fury, show on their faces. Some are participating for the sheer fun of it, in funny costumes, seeing the comedy of life. Others are putting in this enormous human effort for others to collect funds for charity. Still others just love being with the crowd – meeting, mating, communicating. There are also various ways we take part in this 'human race'. Apart from the various ways of participating by running, the crowd of onlookers are also a vital part of it, as are the recorders, the police, the helpers by the wayside, the officials who organise behind the scenes. The race is all of these in its totality. This is life.

So the dreamer sees himself as a part of all this. He has two good legs because he feels his life has been full and adequate despite the condition of his body. He doesn't feel crippled. At the end, the finishing line, death, he realises he has developed bonds of love with his family which will go with him over the boundary line when his life is finished. But there is pain too as his son-in-law cries. This is most likely caused by the real sense of death and the ending of all the experience of the 'race', all the togetherness and loss of what he has been and done as a young man.

radar   Intuition; one's subliminal sense of other people or of what feelings or 'signals' other people are giving out.

radio   Our sense of what is 'in the air' – messages we are picking up from other people or our environment. Being on the radio: feeling valued; having a sense of something worth communicating; actually communicating.

railway, train   General: opportunity or choices in life; your life direction if on a train, or the direction the events in life are taking you. Carriages: the compartments of our lives. Leaving someone behind or being left behind: feelings about loss of spouse; or break-up of a relationship; being left. Lines or tracks: a communal or generally accepted direction; habitual pathways of thought or action; rigidly fixed to certain attitudes or way of life; inflexibility. Missing the train: feeling left out of opportunity; sense of inade-quacy; held back by one's own hesitations; hidden desire to avoid change or to make one's individual journey. Railway station: moving toward something new; changing senses – i.e. from family to work environment; leaving something behind – a relationship, one's youth; one's ability to change; effort to get somewhere in life or experience something new; parting. The train journey: the aspect of our journey through life which has connections with other people and has a predetermined end, limiting our individual will and passing through certain stages; journey into self-awareness; can refer to ageing and death – especially where there is a feeling of 'departing' or 'time of departure'; the train of thoughts or experiences which carry us through life. Train engine: the energy which takes us through life; libido. Idioms: go off the rails; lose track of something; make tracks for; on somebody's track. See: **airport**; **ticket**.

rain   Depressed feelings or difficulties; emotions which take away enthusiasm and act as a barrier to action; tears and emotional release – an outpouring; other people's emotions 'raining' on one. Also return of feelings after a dry intellectual or unfeeling period; something which gives life or heals. Idioms: come rain or shine; it never rains but it pours; saving for a rainy day.

rainbow   A sense of better things to come; illusion; an awareness of the beauty and value of life in the midst of difficulties. Idioms: chasing a rainbow.

raincoat   See: **clothes**.

rape   Rape in dreams is very different from rape in real life as we create our own dream, so why introduce rape? Perhaps in the example below Mrs B. discovers her own power in the situation as she realises the weakness of the male.

> *Example: 'I tried to turn but my legs were like lead. The man caught me and I fought. He tried to rape me but couldn't do it. As I talked to him I began to feel sorry for him and not frightened. I realised that inside he was a nice person. In the end I found I liked him so much I began to kiss him myself.' Mrs J.B.*

> *Example: 'A man is trying to make love and at the last moment I repel him as I know it will cause a pregnancy. When I was about ten I was raped and for many years had a fear of men.' Anon.*

This is the other side of rape. Rape in this dream may be memories, the effects of which are still apparent in the life of this dreamer causing her difficulties in experiencing warm sexuality.

> *Example: 'The devil attacked a woman. He was invisible. The woman turned black as he raped her. She didn't die. At this point I woke and went to the toilet. On returning to bed I continued the dream, particularly wondering what I was in conflict with in the image of the devil. I found it disturbing and frightening to be confronted by such a powerful opponent. Partly because of the rape, I realised it was repressed sexuality. I then approached the 'black' woman with tenderness and this transformed the devil into available sexual or emotional energy. I tried this again and again. Each time it worked, and I could observe the devil was my sexual warmth and love which had become negative through restraint.' Neil V.*

In this male dream, it is the conflict with his sexuality which causes the 'devilish' rape. When he can find tenderness the negative aspect disappears. Rape also depicts the real evil of another person disregarding our personal needs and feelings, abusing not only the body but particularly the 'person'. Being raped by someone known: feeling anxious about sex with them; fighting off desire for them.

rat   See: *rat* under **animals**.

raven   See: **birds**.

reaching out   The desire for something; attempt to grasp, control or manipulate something or someone depending on dream; extending or giving oneself. Being reached toward: feeling of being asked for something, or demands of other people.

reading   Realisation; recall from memory; scanning internal memory for information.

receptacle – jar, **cup**, **bottle**, **kettle**   Receptive state of mind; our body and what we put into it; what feelings or thoughts we 'contain' or pour out; the womb. See: first example under **fish**, **sea creatures**.

record, cassette, cd, computer disk Can simply be the sort of pleasure we feel on listening to music; the impressions left on us by events, people and therefore memory, but often memory is integrated by the unconscious into insights; information we have gathered; the impression we might leave behind at death – what remains of us; the impression we would like to give others. <u>Idioms</u>: for the record; track record.

recurring dreams If we keep a record of our dreams it will soon become obvious that some of our dream themes, characters or places recur again and again. These recurrences are of various types. A certain theme may have begun in childhood and continued throughout our life, either without change or as a gradually changing series of dreams. It might be that the feature which recurs is a setting, perhaps a house we visit again and again, but the details differ. Sometimes a series of such dreams begin after or during a particular event or phase of our life, such as puberty or marriage.

The theme of the dream can incorporate anxious emotions such as the example below, or any aspect of experience. One woman, an epileptic, reports a dream which is the same in every detail and occurs every night.

In general dreams recur because there are ways the dreamer habitually responds to their internal or external world. Because their attitude or response is unchanging, the dream which reflects it remains the same. It is noticeable in those who explore their dreams using such techniques as described under **dream processing** that recurring themes disappear or change because the attitudes or habitual anxieties which gave rise to them have been met or transformed.

> *Example: 'This dream has recurred over thirty years. There is a railway station, remote in a rural area, a central waiting room with platform going round all sides. On the platform mill hundreds of people, all men I think. They are all ragged, thin, dirty and unshaven. I know I am among them. I looked up at the mountainside and there is a guard watching us. He is cruel-looking, Oriental in green fatigues. On his peaked cap is a red star. He carries a machine gun. Then I looked at the men*

*around me and I realise they are all me. Each one has my face.
I am looking at myself. Then I feel fear and terror.' Anon.*

A recurring environment in a dream where the other factors change
is not the same. We use the same words over and over in speech, yet
each sentence may be different. The environment or character
represents a particular aspect of oneself, but the different events
which surround it show it in the changing process of our psychological growth. Where there is no such change, as in the examples
above, it suggests an area of our mental emotional Self is stuck in a
habitual feeling state or response.

Some recurring dreams can be 'stopped' by simply receiving
information about them. One woman dreamt the same dream from
childhood. She was walking past railings in the town she lived in as
a child. She always woke in dread and perspiration from this dream.
At forty she told her sister about it. The response was, 'Oh, that's
simple. Don't you remember that when you were about four we
were walking past those railings and we were set on by a bunch of
boys. Then I said to them, "Don't hurt us our mother's dead!" They
left us alone, but you should have seen the look on your face.' After
realising the dread was connected with the loss of her mother, the
dream never recurred. Another woman who repeatedly dreamt of
being in a tight and frightening place found the dream never
returned after she had connected it to being in the womb.

Recurring dreams such as that of the railings suggest that part of
the process underlying dreams is a self-regulatory homeostatic one.
The dream process tries to present troublesome emotions or
situations to the conscious mind of the dreamer to resolve the trauma
or difficulty underlying the dream. An obvious example of this is
seen in the recurring nightmare of a young woman who felt a piece
of cloth touch her face and repeatedly woke her family with her
screams. Her brother, tiring of this, one night woke her from her
screams and made her talk about her feelings. His persistence
gradually revealed that she associated the cloth with the burial
shroud of her grandmother. This brought to the surface grief and
feelings about death she had never allowed herself to feel before.
The nightmare never returned. See **dream processing**; **nightmares**.

reflections   Present view or opinion of ourself. Because few of us define how we really see ourselves, the self-image may be largely unconscious, therefore shown as a face which might be different to what we are used to seeing. Also how we feel others see us; may also be aspects of ourselves the unconscious is showing us which we may not have been aware of.

refrigerate   To cool down our emotions or sexuality; to be cold emotionally or sexually; a romance which is cooling off; something we have put on 'cold storage'.

relationship and dreams   Most dreams depict relationships in one form or another. Some dreams, however, specifically show us in a particular relationship. Such dreams are usually highly significant in that they reveal aspects of what we are doing in the relationship that we may not admit or realise consciously. It can therefore be transformative to gain insight into such dreams.

> *Example: 'I was with Lorna and she told me she was pregnant. I said to her this was impossible and it couldn't be my child. She looked at me and shrugged saying "Okay, I'm not pregnant".' Neal C.*

On exploring the dream, Neal realised the enormous feelings involved. He had not realised consciously that Lorna had completely offered herself to him in their relationship. The dream shows him rejecting this complete offering of her sexuality and womanhood and her turning away. This had actually happened, but Neal had not been conscious of what was occurring between them. The dream enabled him to realise how he pulled away from a woman's full flow of self-expression and began to change this.

relatives   See: **family**.

religion and dreams   In most ancient cultures, consideration and even veneration of dreams played a great part. Some groups felt that dream life was more real and important than waking life. Not only were dreams looked to for information about hunting (Eskimo groups), but also for ways of healing physical and psychological ills

(Greek Dream Temples) and insights into the medicinal properties of herbs, barks and clays (African tribal witchdoctors). Common to most of these groups, and evident in the Old Testament, was also the sense that through dreams one had awareness of the transcendental or supersensible. St Peter's dream of the sheet and unclean animals was a turning point in the history of Western society – as was Constantine's dream of his victory if he used the symbol of Christianity.

At its most fundamental, the human religious sense emerges out of several factors. One is the awareness of existing amidst external and internal forces of nature which cause us to feel vulnerable and perhaps powerless. Such natural processes as illness, death, growth and decay, earthquakes, the seasons, confront us with things which are often beyond our ability to control. Considering the information and resources of the times, one of religion's main functions in the past was the attempted control of the 'uncertain' factors in human life, and help toward psychological adjustment to vulnerability. Religions were the first social programmes aiding the human need for help and support toward emotional, mental, physical and social health and maturity. Even if primitive, such programmes helped groups of people gain a common identity and live in reasonable harmony together. Like a computer program which is specific to a particular business, such programmes were specific to a particular group and so are outdated in today's need for greater integration with other races. See: second example in **creativity and problem solving in dreams**.

Dreams also portray and define the aspect of human experience in which we sense a kinship with all life forms. This is the side of spiritual experience through which we find a connection with the roots of our being. While awake we might see the birth of a colt and feel the wonder of emergence and newness; the struggle to stand up and survive; the miracle of physical and sexual power which can be accepted or feared. In looking in the faces of fellow men and women we see something of what they have done in this strange and painful wonder we call life. We see whether they have been crushed by the forces confronting them; whether they have become rigid; or whether, through some common miracle, they have been able to carry into their mature years the laughter, the crying, the joy, the ability to feel pain which are the very signs of life within the human soul. These things are sensed by us all, but seldom organised into a comprehensive view of life and an extraction of meaning. Often it is only in our dreams, through the ability the unconscious has to draw out the significance of such widely divergent experiences, that we glimpse the unity behind phenomena which is an essential of spiritual life – i.e. we all have a liver, we breathe, we have come from a mother, so we share a universal experience.

Example: To quote J.B. Priestley from his book Rain Upon Godshill*: 'Just before I went to America, during the exhausting weeks when I was busy with my Time Plays, I had such a dream, and I think it left a greater impression on my mind than any experience I had ever known before, awake or in dreams, and said more to me about this life than any book I have ever read. The setting of the dream was quite simple, and owed something to the fact that not long before my wife had visited the lighthouse here at St Catherine's to do some bird ringing. I dreamt I was standing at the top of a very high tower, alone, looking down upon myriads of birds all flying in one direction; every kind of bird was there, all the birds in the world. It was a noble sight, this vast aerial river of birds. But now in some mysterious fashion the gear was changed, and time speeded up, so that I saw generations of birds, watched them break their shells, flutter into life, mate, weaken, falter and die. Wings grew only to crumble; bodies were sleek, and then, in a flash bled and shrivelled; and death struck every-where at every second. What was the use of all this blind struggle towards life, this eager trying of wings, this hurried mating, this flight and surge, all this gigantic meaningless effort?*

As I stared down, seeming to see every creature's ignoble little history almost at a glance, I felt sick at heart. It would be better if not one of them, if not one of us, had been born, if the struggle ceased for ever. I stood on my tower, still alone, desperately unhappy. But now the gear was changed again, and the time went faster still, and it was rushing by at such a rate, that the birds could not show any movement, but were like an enormous plain sown with feathers. But along this plain, flickering through the bodies themselves, there now

*passed a sort of white flame, trembling, dancing, then hurry-
ing on; and as soon as I saw it I knew that this white flame was
life itself, the very quintessence of being; and then it came to
me, in a rocket burst of ecstasy, that nothing mattered, nothing
could ever matter, because nothing else was real but this
quivering and hurrying lambency of being. Birds, men and
creatures not yet shaped and coloured, all were of no account
except so far as this flame of life travelled through them. It left
nothing to mourn over behind it; what I had thought was
tragedy was mere emptiness or a shadow show; for now all real
feeling was caught and purified and danced on ecstatically
with the white flame of life. I had never before felt such deep
happiness as I knew at the end of my dream of the tower and
the birds.*

Some North American Indians developed the totem out of similar
processes. In one generation a person might learn to plant a seed
and eat the results. Later someone might see that through fertilisation
more food was produced. Still later someone found that by
irrigating, still more improvement was made. No one individual was
responsible for such vital cultural information, and the collective
information is bigger than any one person, yet individuals can
partake of it and add to it. The totem represented such subtle
realities, as it might in a modern dream; as Christ might in today's
unconscious. That older cultures venerated their collective information and modern humans seem largely apathetic to it shows how our
'religion' has degenerated. Yet utilising the power of the unconscious to portray the subtle influences which impinge upon us and
building the information gained into our response to life is deeply
important.

With the growth of authoritarian structures in Western religion,
and the dominance of the rational mind over feeling values, dreams
have been pushed into the background. With this change has
developed the sense that visionary dreams were something that
'superstitious' cultural groups had in the past. Yet thoroughly
modern men and women still meet Christ powerfully in dreams and
visions. Christ still appears to them as a living being. The transcendental, the collective or universal enters their life just as frequently
as ever before. Sometimes it enters with insistence and power,

because a too-rational mind has led to an imbalance in the psyche – an imbalance in which the waking and rational individuality is one pole and the feeling, connective awareness of the unconscious is the other.

Although it is tempting to think of the transcendent as ethereal or unreal, the religious aspects of dreams are nearly always symbols for the major processes of maturing in human life. We are the hero/ine who meets the dangers of life outside the womb, who faces growth, ageing and death. The awe and deep emotions we unconsciously feel about such heroic deeds are depicted by religious emotion. See: *sheep* under **animals**; *angel, Christ, devil* and *rebirth* under **archetypes**; **church**; **colours**; **dream as spiritual guide**; **evil**; **fish, sea creatures**; example in *whale* under **fish, sea creatures**; *sweets* under **food**; **heaven**; **hell**; **hero/ine**; **mass**; **masturbation**; **old**; **paralysis**.

religious themes See: *angel, blood, Christ* and *devil* under **archetypes**; **church**, **dreams as spiritual guide**; **evil**; **heaven**; **hell**; **religion and dreams**.

remembering dreams Considering that each of us have four or five periods of dreaming each night, most of our dreams are forgotten. But for people who observe family or friends regularly remembering a dream and yet themselves seldom if ever able to recall one, the question arises as to why such a wide divergence occurs.

There are many different reasons why dreams may be forgotten. The most obvious is that we do not give enough attention to our dreaming process. When people become intrigued by what they might be dreaming and develop a motivation to remember, they frequently start recalling several dreams a week. From this standpoint, the reason why some people have always remembered might be that they have always been either intrigued or anxious about their nightly dramas.

The way we rise in the morning has an effect upon this type of memory. If our attention is immediately turned outward on waking, there is little hope of recalling a dream unless it has great power, as might a nightmare. Spending a few moments leaving our mind open to memory aids recall. Any visual or even muscular activity will fill consciousness with new and powerful impressions which might obliterate the subtler impressions of dreaming. Rorschach suggested not opening the eyes and remaining physically still. Tests also showed that passage of time, even a few minutes, between dreaming and attempting to remember, causes many dreams to fragment and be lost. So to remember one must quickly record the dream by speaking it to one's bed mate, using a tape recorder by one's bed or writing it down.

Some dreams have rather misty or fragmentary imagery and themes, while others are clear, concise and dynamic. These latter are more easily remembered. There may be times when we sleep with longer periods of wakefulness, perhaps because we feel cold or uncomfortable in a strange bed, which causes us to remember as we are nearer consciousness. Because dreams occur in cycles during the night, if something wakes us during a dream cycle the memory is easier, if only because less time has elapsed since occurrence. So another method of capturing a dream is to have one's alarm gently sound prior to the time one usually wakes. The last hour or so of sleep includes a long period of dreaming, so waking in this period with intent to remember can often capture the quarry.

There are also psychological reasons for forgetfulness. Dreams often deal with past areas of experience which we do not wish to remember or would rather not be aware of. If we find it difficult to feel emotions or feel uncomfortable with them, it is highly likely we repress dream memory as dreams have a base of high feeling. Experiments have shown that during dreaming, our heartbeat, body movements and breathing frequently reflect intensified emotions. Also, research into what areas of the brain produce dreaming suggest that dreams may be from the 'visceral brain' which is largely non-verbal. If temperamentally we find feeling qualities a foreign language, connecting with a dream would need to be a learnt skill.

rent   Interpersonal responsibility; what we 'pay' for what we have or want. Collecting rent: what we want from others, or what we are getting from them in the way of feelings, influences.

reptiles – lizards, snakes   General: our basic spinal and lower brain reactions, such as fight or flight, reproduction, attraction or repulsion, sex drive, need for food and reaction to pain. This includes the fundamental evolutionary ability to change and the urge to survive − very powerful and ancient processes. Our relationship with the reptile in our dreams depicts our relatedness to such forces in us and how we deal with the impulses from the ancient part of our brain.

Modern humans face the difficulty of developing an independent identity while keeping a working relationship with the primitive, thus maturing and bringing the primitive into an efficiently functioning connection with the present social world. The survival urge at base might be kill or run, but it can be transformed into the ambition which helps an opera singer meet difficulties in his or her career. Also the very primitive has in itself the promise of the future, of new aspects of human consciousness. This is because many extraordinary human functions take place unconsciously in the realm of the reptile/spine/lower brain/right brain/autonomic nervous system. Being unconscious they are less amenable to our waking will. They function fully only in some fight or flight, survive or die situations. If we begin to touch these with consciousness as we do in dreams, new functions are added to consciousness. See: *the dream as extended perception* under **ESP**.

snakes   The Hebrew word for the serpent in the Garden of Eden is *Nahash*, which can be translated as blind impulsive urges such as our instinctive drives. General: many different things, but usually the life process. If we think of a person's life from conception to death we see a flowing moving event, similar in many ways to the speeded-up films of a seed growing into a plant, flowering and dying. The snake depicts the force or energy behind that movement and purposiveness − the force of life which leads us both to growth and death. That energy − like electricity in a house which can be heat, power, sound and vision − lies behind all our functions. So in some dreams the snake expresses our sexuality; in others the rising of that energy up our body to express as digestion − the intestinal snake; as the healing or poisonous energy of our emotions and thoughts.

Snake in connection with any hole: sexual relatedness. A snake biting us: unconscious worries about our health, frustrated sexual impulse, our emotions turned against ourselves as internalised aggression can poison us and cause very real illness, so may be shown as the biting snake. Snake biting others: biting remarks; a poisonous tongue; emotional energy turned against oneself or someone else. A crowned or light-encircled snake: when our 'blind impulses', our instinctive or unconscious urges and functions are in some measure integrated with our conscious will and insight, this is seen as the crowned snake or even winged snake. It shows real self-awareness and maturity. In coils of snake: feeling bound in the 'blind impulses' or habitual drives and feeling responses. Instincts and habits can be redirected, as illustrated by Hercules' labours. Snake with tail in its mouth: sense of the circle of life – birth, growth, reproduction, ageing, death, rebirth; the eternal. Snake coiling up tree, pole, cross: the blind, instinctive forces of life emerging into conscious experience – in other words the essence of human experience with its involvement in pain, pleasure, time and eternity; the process of personal growth or evolution; healing because personal growth often moves us beyond old attitudes or situations which led to inner tension or even sickness. Snake in the grass: sense or intuition of talk behind your back; danger; sneakiness. Colours – green: our internal life process directed – perhaps through satisfied feelings, love and creativity – into a healing process or one which leads to our personal growth and positive change. White: eternal aspect of our life process or becoming conscious of it. Blue: religious feelings or coldness in relations.

The Africans saw the dream of a snake round the leg signified slavery, while the dream of a dragon round the body is a symbol of bondage in Artemidorus.

> *Example: 'A small snake about a foot long had dropped down my shirt neck. I could feel it on the left side of my neck. Fearing it was poisonous and might bite me I moved very slowly. At one point I put my head on the ground, hoping the snake would wish to crawl away. It did not. Then I was near an elephant I loved and hoped it would remove the snake. It did not. Even as I slept I felt the snake was an expression of the attitude of not sharing myself with anybody except family.' David T.*

For months prior to the dream above David had experienced a great deal of neck pain. After discussing the dream with his wife, and realising much of his thinking and feeling was in-turned, the pain disappeared. So the snake was both 'poisoner' and 'healer'. This may be why snakes are used as a symbol of the medical profession.

Example: 'I was in a huge cathedral, the mother church. I wanted to go to the toilet/gents. As I held my penis to urinate it became a snake and reached down to the urinal to drink. It was thirsty. I struggled with it, pulling it away from the unclean liquid. Still holding it I walked to a basin and gave it pure water to drink.' Bill A.

Here the connection between the snake and sexuality is obvious. But the snake is not just Bill's penis. It is the direction his sexual urges take him he is struggling with. Out of his sense of love and connection with life – the cathedral – he wants to lift his drive toward something which will not leave him with a sense of uncleanness. In this sense a snake might be something one wrestled with, depicting the wrestle one has with inner drives and hungers, especially sexuality or anger.

See: **anxiety dreams**; *death and rebirth, the Self* under **archetypes**; **colours**; **dreams and ancient Greece**; snake in cellar under **house, buildings**; **hypnosis and dreams**; **jungle**; **paralysis**.

lizards   General: very much the same as snake, except it lacks the poisonous aspect; awareness of unconscious or instinctive drives, functions and processes. In the example below, the banana is both David's pleasure and sexuality, while the lizard is the creativity emerging from his unconscious through the attention he is giving it – he is looking at the lizard. Chameleon: either one's desire to fade into the background, or adaptability.

Example: 'My wife and I saw a large lizard on the wall near a banana. It was there to catch the flies. The lizard turned so it was facing away from us – head up the wall. We then were able to see it had large wing-like flaps which spread from its head in an inverted V. With amazement we saw on these flaps wonderful pictures, in full colour, of birds. In fleeting thoughts I wondered if the bird 'paintings' were to attract birds, or were some form of camouflage. But I felt certain the lizard had

'painted' these wonderful pictures with its unconscious art.'
David T.

frog Unconscious life or growth processes which can lead to transformation – the frog/prince story; the growth from childhood vulnerability – tadpole to frog – therefore the process of life in general and its wisdom. Frog spawn: sperm, ovum and reproduction.

toad Deeply unconscious drives and processes, such as the biological activities to do with intestines and cells that we might feel squeamish about – might therefore connect with abortion; the power of life in us; a cold-blooded or ugly part of ourselves.

rescue Intervention in our life by someone else's action or emotions; something which changes the situation one is in, or changes mood. Rescuing someone else, or animal: the effort we make, or what we have put into dealing with a relationship difficulty or an internal feeling state. Rescued by animal: the supportive and loving action from the unconscious 'animal' level of ourself.

> *Example: 'I am looking at a scene from the top of a cliff. There are large rocks sticking out of the sea at the bottom of the cliff. As I watch this scene a large black – wild? – horse charges towards the edge of the cliff. It carries on running, straight off the edge of the cliff. I am looking down the cliff to see where it will land. I lose sight of it but I am sure it will hit the rocks and be killed. Then I see it swimming straight out to sea. Sometimes it goes under a wave but its direction is strong. Suddenly I realise what the horse is doing. It has been trained to save lives. It had gone into the sea to rescue some people who would otherwise drown.' Leon C.*

The horse here represents the natural drives in ourselves we have harnessed for generations and made sociable, and lifted to a spiritual purpose.

Also can relate to one's desire to do something admirable or noble, such as saving souls, helping someone in distress and thus having power in life. Rescuing someone of the opposite sex:

breaking the bonds of emotion, sexuality or dependence which tie us to parents or others.

restaurant, café   Sociability; search for emotional or sexual satisfaction; hunger for company or sexuality; because one's sociability might at times be a fear of being alone, might represent this. See: **food**.

riding   Idioms: along for the ride; a rough ride; ride something out; let it ride; ride roughshod; take somebody for a ride; riding high. See: *horse* under **animals**; **car**.

right   See: **left, right**.

ring   General: one's wholeness; one's essential Self. Wedding or engagement ring: the state of the relationship, as in example below, where Mary is 'choking' on or 'can't swallow' her relationship. Heirloom or parent's ring: psychological influence of the family or parent, even if dead. Idioms: have a hollow ring; have a true ring; run rings round someone. See: **shapes, symbols**.

> *Example: 'If I swallow I am going to swallow and choke on my engagement ring. I seem to be trying to stop a ring going down my throat.' Mary S.*

RISC method   The premise of the RISC dream therapy is straightforward: if bad dream scripts make you awaken discouraged and downhearted, rewriting the scripts to improve the endings should lead to better moods.

Dream therapy has just four steps that you can learn on your own:

1. Recognise when you are having a bad dream, the kind that leaves you feeling helpless, guilty or upset the next morning. You need to become aware while you are dreaming that the dream is not going well.
2. Identify what it is about the dream that makes you feel bad. Locate the dimensions that portray you in a negative light – as, for example, weak rather than strong, inept rather than capable, or out-of-control rather than in control.

3. Stop any bad dream. You do not have to let it continue. You are in charge. Most people are surprised to find that telling themselves to recognise when a bad dream is in progress is often all it takes to empower them to stop such dreams.

4. Change negative dream dimensions into their opposite, positive sides. At first, you may need to wake up and devise a new conclusion before returning to sleep. With practice, you will be able to instruct yourself to change the action while remaining asleep.

Quoted from *Psychology Today*, Nov–Dec 1992, excerpt from 'Crisis Dreaming: Using Your Dreams to Solve Your Problems', authors: Rosalind Cartwright; Lynne Lamberg. Accessed via Compuserve.

ritual   See: **ceremony**.

river   The images of rivers used in drama helps us understand their symbolism. The river can be calm, in flood, or even dried up, representing our state of feeling about our energy, sexuality and emotions – the energy which as anxiety can cause illness, or as pleasure can sustain health. Similarly we can drown in the river – drown in despair – float on it – be carried along by prevailing feelings – or cross over, suggesting change or even death.

General: the feelings which flow through us or we are immersed in; the process of life in our body, connecting with emotions, sexuality and changes of mood; the flow and events of our life or destiny. Being in a river: being influenced by or immersed in one's internal flow of feelings and energies. Crossing a river: making great changes. If one is in the water to cross, it means meeting a lot of emotions in the process of change. Seeing someone cross a river: feelings about death – same as falling in the river. Going against the current: resisting one's own feelings; going against prevailing influences or attitudes; going back to the womb. Directing a river: channelling one's emotional or sexual energy. Stagnant river: restrained feelings or sexuality; holding oneself back.

road   General: one's prevailing direction in or approach to life – this direction/approach can be either self-created out of one's own actions or decisions, or arise out of other people's or social influence; the norm in social behaviour, therefore the direction in life taken by many people; one's predispositions; any direction you are taking, such as a love affair, a business, a new attitude; one's public activities. Crossroads or deciding which road to take: Arthur's dream in the second example shows crossroads as depicting our many choices. Arthur's choice involves his attempt to include his wife's needs. The size, richness, cleanliness, number of people, situation of the road shows how you inwardly see either the direction chosen, or the choices confronting you. See: **crossroad**.

Road behind: the past; what you have already achieved or done. Road ahead: the future; aspects of Self not yet expressed; new areas of endeavour. Fork in the road: something to decide; parting from accustomed way or relationship. Hole in road: danger; fears about death; difficulties about direction in life. Unpaved road or track off to one side: going off the beaten track or being side-tracked. Lane: individual direction. Known road: one's associated feelings with that road. Running into road: danger. Going the wrong way up a one-way street: going against prevailing attitudes; defying public opinion. Going out from house into road: how others see you; being in public view. Idioms: on the road to recovery; road hog; end of the road; take to the road; middle of the road; the high road to. See: **track**.

> Example: 'My dream is of an eternal journey, which takes a road that turns into a circle or maze that is endless. Behind me is a large, fat young man with blond hair. I can't get along and he catches up with me. I say, "We can't go back we must struggle on." He takes my wrist. I am trying to hide my fear of him and the pathway, when I wake up.' J.P.

J.P. feels her life is something she must 'struggle on' with, but it is an endless circle of confusion in which she gets nowhere. This illustrates the road as a symbol of one's approach to life. Perhaps it is her fear which creates this sense of life for her.

> Example: 'Janet, my wife, was cycling beside me. We came to the end of a short road. I said we should turn left, but Janet thought we ought to turn right. We got out into the middle of the road without turning either way.' Arthur P.

Example: 'Walking alone along a road through a small town. I was heading for a place that a group of people, in a street parallel to mine, were also heading for. A person from the group tried to persuade me that the right way to get to the place was along the street the group was walking. I knew the street did not matter, only the general direction. The person was quite disturbed by my independence. It made him or her feel uncertain to have their leader apparently questioned. I felt uncertain too for a moment. Then I walked on and came to an open stretch of ground.' Ivor S.

Ivor's dream shows how roads can represent different sorts of social behaviour. To choose one's individual 'road' may be difficult, because others are so sure they know best. Patterns of behaviour such as needing an authority figure to follow, are also here depicted as a road.

rock   Reality, but not just physical reality; the physical world; the eternal as it is met by our waking Self; stability; a remembrance of something or someone important to us. If the rock is sculpted: what our life has expressed to enrich our own spiritual or eternal nature. A small rock or stone: the unconscious sees our personal existence as a part of the material the cosmos is made of – another pebble on the beach. The rock portrays how we shape the material of our nature through our life – similar to the parable of the talents. See: **stone**.

rocket   Male sexuality; feeling threatened from relationship with male; energy to gain greater awareness of oneself.

roles   The different people in our dreams, such as doctor, lawyer, business person or tramp in general represent the different abilities, weaknesses or interests we have ourselves. Even if we know the 'role model' it still depicts that person's quality or skill in ourselves. The only difference might be that our personal reactions to that particular doctor or schoolteacher will also play a part. Roles often play an important part in our self-image. Without an appreciated social role we may feel uncertain and ineffective. Maturity might require the acceptance that we are nothing, but can be many things.

actor/actress   Depending on context, can represent yourself wanting public acclaim, or not expressing real Self – acting a role. Just as someone's life may be 'acted out' on stage or in a film, so actors may represent a showing of facets of your own life, especially inner life; the false image we may be expressing; our attempt to impress others or act a part. <u>Idioms</u>: act a part; act on impulse or information; acting up; caught in the act; as the actress said to the bishop. See: **theatre**.

astrologer   Intuitions, thoughts or concerns about your future; intuition concerning your innate abilities or qualities and where they might lead.

authority figure   Might depict what has arisen in your life out of relationship with father; one's relationship with authority; a view of how one uses power of authority.

bus conductor   How we give someone authority in a group situation, although we may be more capable than they; the part of Self concerned with paying our way; feelings helping or standing in the way of reaching our goal.

captain   The daring, doing, positive side of Self; how we relate to father figures or dominant authoritative male; the side of our nature which is capable or is in touch with the wider issues in our life and makes decisions out of comprehensive awareness.

captive, prisoner   Many emotions, anxieties, moods or ideas 'captivate' us, or act as means of denying free expression to our own talents, sexuality or well-being. Fear of illness might stop us going on holiday, thoughts that only the privileged can make it in business might stop us developing ideas we have. In this sense we, or areas of our potential, can be imprisoned or made captive. Using **dream processing** and the allied methods can help to define what is restraining us and find freedom from such restraints. See: *wolf* under **animals**; **cage**, **cell**; **escape**; **holding**; **imprisoned**; **trapped**.

carpenter   The creative but practical part of us; the side of us which tends to create with old ideas and attitudes – the wood – but perhaps is not very radical; sometimes the Self. See: *Christ* under **archetypes**.

conjurer   Depending on dream, might be the ability to change our moods or attitudes easily, which is commonplace yet at the same time magical ability humans have – in this way we might pull out of a deep depression and suddenly become creative; or perhaps the youthful side of Self which forever wants magical or idealistic answers to life situations and relationships; trickery.

convict   See: *captive, prisoner* above.

cook   The active and practical side of our nature which can transform inedible aspects of a relationship or situation into something which satisfies us; the sense of responsibility which 'feeds the family'; female reproductive ability – puts one thing in the oven (sperm and ovum) and out comes something else (baby); need for or ability to nourish oneself and provide for physical, emotional, mental and spiritual needs. <u>Idioms</u>: cook the books; cook someone's goose; cook up; what's cooking.

cripple   Emotional hurts; parts of us injured by trauma or twisted by such withheld feelings as anger or jealousy.

dentist   Depends on your relationship with dentists – fear of being hurt; the courage and ability to deal with painful areas of experience; father's distressing sexual attentions, or rape feelings; need for care of what comes out of our mouth such as things we say, opinions, criticism.

doctor   Our dependence upon authority figure for a sense of wholeness or to deal with anxiety; the healing process within us – the unconscious wisdom we have concerning our body's needs and well-being. The doctor might give us advice for instance; anxiety about health; desire for intimacy or to be looked at. <u>Idioms</u>: doctor something; have an animal doctored; doctor the accounts.

farmer   Feeling easy with sexuality and material world; practical, down-to-earth feelings; care of 'animal' side of Self; earthy wisdom. See: **farm, farmyard**.

fireman   How we deal with our passions or outbursts of emotion or anger; dealing with misplaced energy.

judge   Feelings of guilt; self-criticism or judgement; how we are relating to someone whose judgement means a lot to us; social condemnation.

king   See: **king**; **queen**.

leader   Our relationship with authority figures or the generally accepted ideas which people take to guide their life; the relationship with the leader might show how much responsibility we are taking for our own lives; feelings of being responsible, as in parenthood or professional capacity. See example in **road**.

lover   If one's lover: your present feelings or fears about the relationship. If dream lover or someone else: your sexual desires or needs; sexuality which is either not accepted, or not expressed in present relationship. See: **affair**.

magician   Sometimes the Self – the magical abilities the unconscious has which are seldom tapped; one's potential. Black magician: the negative or selfish ways we might use our power or internal insights and wisdom; the shadow or unacknowledged side of Self. See: *conjurer* above.

monk   Influence of religious teachings; difficulty in meeting sexuality and emotional and financial independence; awareness of spiritual.

nun   Sexual purity; fear of sex; religious feelings; one's sister.

pirate   Our own piratical or plundering urges or what we feel plundered by; sense of having someone else take what is important to us.

policeman/woman   General: sense of what is socially right or wrong – our feelings of what others would dislike or punish us for; our social rules of conduct rather than our innermost sense of rightness, therefore inhibitions; feelings of guilt or shame. Policewoman: as general, but more emphasis on moral issues connected with feeling values.

sailor   One's ability to meet the storms and calms of life.

salesman   Someone seeking to influence you; opportunity; one's business sense. In a woman's dream: perhaps a hint of things you want – a lover or a new romance – that you are not admitting to yourself; the man in your life trying to get what he wants at your expense.

scientist   Creative rational mind; intellectual curiosity; in some dreamers the fear of rational critical people or looking at oneself analytically; insight into the unconscious through rational investigation.

secretary   The other woman; practical business side of Self supporting creative action.

seductress or seducer   Sexual desires; sexual drives which have not been matured into satisfactory expression in relationship with real person; sexual longings unattached to present partner; fantasy of being loved.

servant   Social roles – top dog/under dog feelings; feeling you are treated like a servant, or treating someone else like one; class distinctions.

shepherd   Being in contact with instinctive or feeling reactions in Self; the Self. See: *Christ* under **archetypes**; **farmer**.

shopkeeper   May relate to work if dreamer works in a shop or store; relates to how one supplies one's needs – or who supplies one's needs – therefore might show feelings about parents. It might throw light on how you gain your needs from other people or decisions about what you want from life or others.

soldier   If in opposition with: things we feel in conflict with; our internal conflicts and involvement with the 'wars' or trauma we have experienced. If soldier or united with soldiers: our willingness or ability to face internal conflicts and hurts; daring to confront the difficulties of life. In woman's dream: inner conflicts; feeling threatened regarding relationship with a male. Military service: feeling bound by social or personal disciplines or restrictions; learning strengths and self-discipline to meet internal conflicts.

stranger   Unknown aspect of oneself; part we avoid 'meeting' in everyday life.

teacher   Relationship with authority figure; learning situations; something to learn or teach.

thief Fear we might lose something or that what we have gained will be taken; unacknowledged desires; desire to take from others; conflict of will; feelings of having been induced into a sexual encounter or fear of sex. See: **stealing**.

victim Being the victim: feeling victimised; often depicts the chip on our shoulder. We may have been hurt sometime and go on bemoaning our fate. The 'chip' may be useful in avoiding real responsibility or in hiding from trying out one's positive creativity or sexuality. Thus we avoid possible failure or further hurt. Other person as victim: may still be as above; the hurts and damage received from relationship with others; passive anger – by being the victim we get someone else to be a bastard and can·thus sneer at them because we have manipulated them; hidden desires to avoid success, perhaps as a way of hurting parent. See: **victim**.

waiter, waitress Wanting to be waiting on; feeling you are being made to wait on others; word play for waiting around for someone else.

See: **baker**; **barber**; **beggar**; **chemist**; **gardener**; **inventor**; **nurse**; **potter**; **victim**; **waiting**.

room　See: **house, buildings**.

root　See: **tree**.

rope　If tied by: what is holding us back from expressing; strength turned against oneself. Tying someone else: restraints we use to hold back particular parts of our feelings or drives; sometimes sexuality.

rose　See: **flowers**.

round　See: **shapes, symbols**.

ruins　See: **house, buildings**.

running   See: **postures**, **movement**, **body language**.

rust   Negligence; sense of ageing; seeing how transitory worldly things are.

sack The womb; death; getting the sack.

sacrifice May refer directly to feeling someone is or will make you a scapegoat; sometimes connected with decision making – we cannot have all things at once, so we are willing to sacrifice one thing for another; occurs in some dreams where a change is occurring in one's personality – parts of our nature we once identified with can now be allowed to die to the process of growth. Also sacrifice depicts a strange fact of human psychology. Some aspects of oneself grow in strength and maturity by letting them 'die'. While we maintain a behaviour pattern or belief, it stays in its habitual form. When we let go of it a new approach can emerge.

saddle Influencing something or somebody by our will; feeling constrained to support someone else; in control. If thrown from a saddle: out of control.

sadism Anger from childhood hurts – sometimes the inability to face the real emotional pain of one's own hurts as a child; lack of real sexual satisfaction, perhaps because of lack of emotional development.

sailing How we are feeling about or handling our life. The images in sailing lend themselves to depict human endeavours to work with the tides and influences of life. Dealing well with wind and waves: suggests being able to meet internal and external pressures, emotions and drives, and using them to advantage. Being overwhelmed or sinking: finding emotional, sexual drives and anxieties too much

346

to cope with. <u>Idioms</u>: plain sailing; sail against the wind; sail close to the wind; sail into something; sail under false colours; set sail; trim one's sails; take the wind out of someone's sails. See: **boat**, **ship**.

sailor   See: **roles**.

salad   Sometimes a direct reference to the body's need for such foods; lack of meaty – sexual – experience.

salt   The subtle qualities we bring to our activities which transform them from empty trivialities into meaning or savour; zest; may sometimes refer to the body's reaction to salt. <u>Idioms</u>: above/below the salt – in or out of honour; salt a mine; salt something away; with a pinch of salt; worth one's salt; salt into a wound; salt of the earth.

sand   Lack of security; passage of time; lack of emotion or nourishment; abrasiveness or irritations. <u>Idioms</u>: built on sand; sands of time are running out; bury one's head in the sand. See: **desert**.

satan   The things in Self, or in the world, which we feel frightened of, or feel we cannot control; the influence of dry intellectualism or materialism. See: *devil* under **archetypes**.

satellite   Communication between the more global or cosmic awareness of the unconscious and our everyday waking Self. <u>If in satellite</u>: might suggest loss of a down-to-earth attitude; global view. <u>Being attacked from satellite or UFO</u>: thinking and feeling has been split from realistic evaluation, perhaps because internal pain is scrambling communications.

sausage   Penis or male sexuality; down-to-earth experience. <u>Idioms</u>: not a sausage.

savings   Sense of security; what we have not expressed; one's potential.

saw   See: **tools**.

scales   Justice; conscience; trying to make a decision – weighing the information; fair play; trying to find a balance.

scar   Influences still remaining from past hurt.

school   The learning process; what we learnt at school – not lessons but interrelationships, class structure, competitiveness, authority, mortification, group preferences, etc.; habits of behaviour or feeling reactions developed during those years – puberty occurs at this time and confronts us with many new feelings, choices and drives. School friend: your own attitudes developed in school as you are 'meeting' them in the present. School clothes: social attitudes or moral rules learnt at school. Places in school: particular abilities we have – library: our knowledge and learning ability; stored information. Gymnasium: taking risks in learning something new; daring; physical health. Classroom: study; relationship with authority.

Can sometimes refer to feelings of rejection or aloneness due to the stress faced by many children on leaving their mother for the first time to attend school. See the third example.

> *Example: 'I am back at school on the first day of the new school year. At this point it can vary slightly, but I always feel out of place, usually because I am older than the other girls now or – most common – because my uniform is incorrect and it is time for assembly – I went to a very strict convent school. There is always some feeling of panic and quite often loneliness.' P.H.*

P.H. is still uncomfortable about who she is as a person. The influence of the school years still nags at her that she ought to be other than she is. Not having a nature that easily conformed, she was led to feel isolated and an alien.

> *Example: 'In the bathroom area, a school class was being held, so I had to wait for my bath, steam would be bad for the books. I didn't have any soap with me but I was going to wash my hair and could use the shampoo.' Leonie K.*

Leonie is getting rid of attitudes or a self-image developed at school, shown as shampooing her hair. The new attitudes of letting off steam would not have been acceptable at school. <u>Idioms</u>: of the old school; tell tales out of school; old school tie; well schooled. See: *teacher* under **roles**.

Example: 'Working on a dream with P. The dream included reference to a school. Children were on their way to school and waving goodbye to their mothers. I was surprised at the intensity of emotion P. displayed when she looked at the saying goodbye, and then suddenly realised that this was the child's first taste of leaving home, saying goodbye to mother.'

science, **sleep and dreams**   In 1937, through the use of the electroencephalograph (EEG) measuring tiny electrical brain impulses, Loomis and his associates discovered that the form of brain waves change with the onset of sleep. The next leap forward in understanding came when Aserinsky and Kleitman found rapid eye movements (REM) in 1953. In 1957 the REM were linked with dreaming. This defined sleep into two different observable states, REM sleep and NREM (non-rapid eye movement) pronounced non-REM sleep. Within NREM three different stages have been identified. These are defined by the different EEG patterns of electrical activity in the brain. They are measured by the height (amplitude) of the waves and frequency of the up and down movement. There are also electrical changes occurring in the muscles (EMG) and in movement of the eyeballs (EOG).

While awake the height is low and frequency fast. As we relax prior to sleep, the EEG shifts to what are called alpha waves, with an eight to twelve cps (cycles per second).

Stage one of sleep is the transition between this drowsy state of alpha waves to sleeping, in which theta waves occur with three to seven cps. In this first stage we experience random images and thoughts. This lasts about ten minutes followed by stage two, in which 'sleep spindles' occur which have twelve to fourteen cps on the EEG. These last from a half to two seconds with 'K' complexes following, which are slow, large EEG waves. About half our sleep period is spent in this second stage of sleep. Deep sleep is reached when our brain exhibits delta waves, with half to two cps.

After approximately an hour and a half from falling into deep sleep, an exciting change occurs. We return to level two and REMs occur. Suddenly the brain is alert and active, though the person is asleep and difficult to wake. This level has been called paradoxical sleep because of this fact. Voluntary muscular activity is suppressed and the body is essentially paralysed. Morrison has pointed out that although the brain is transmitting full muscular activity messages, these are usually suppressed by an area of the brain in the pons. But bursts of short actions occur, such as rapid eyeball jerks, twitches of the muscles, changes in the size of the pupil, contractions in the middle ear, and erection of the penis. It may be that similar excitation occurs in the vagina. Also, 'autonomic storms' occur during which large erratic changes occur in heart rate, blood pressure, breathing rate and in other autonomic nervous system functions. These are the changes accompanying our dreams.

If we slept for eight hours, a typical pattern would be to pass into delta sleep, stay there for about seventy to ninety minutes, then return to stage two and dream for about five minutes. We then move back into delta sleep, stay for a short period and shift back to level two, but without dreaming, then back into level three. The next return to stage two is longer, almost an hour, with a period of dreaming lasting about nineteen minutes and also a short period of return to waking. There is only one short period of return to stage three sleep which occurs nearly four hours after falling asleep. From there on we remain in level two sleep, with three or four lengthening periods of dreaming and returns to brief wakefulness. The average amount of body shifting is once every fifteen minutes.

Contrary to popular belief, our dreams are not caused by eating certain foods before bedtime, nor by environmental stimuli during sleeping. Dreaming is caused by internal biological process. The large brain cells in the primitive brain stem fire spontaneously about every ninety minutes, sending random stimuli to cortical areas of the BRAIN. As a consequence, muscle-control, memory, sensory and cognitive areas of the brain are randomly stimulated, resulting in the higher cortical brain attempting to make some sense of it. According to the research this gives rise to the experience of a dream.

The question of whether dreams have intentional, or actual personal, meaning is not answered by this research. Many psycho-therapists maintain that while the neurological impulses from the brain stem may activate the dreaming process, the content or meaningful drama of dreams is caused by unconscious needs, wishes, desires, and everyday concerns of the dreamer. Thus, such psychotherapists subscribe to the phenomenological-clinical, or 'top-down' explanation, which holds that dreams are intentionally meaningful messages from the unconscious. The neurological, or 'bottom-up' explanation maintains that dreams have no intentional meaning.

facts and figures

- In undergoing 205 hours of sleep deprivation, four healthy males showed various physiological and psychological changes. Some of these were headache, lack of concentration, hallucination, memory loss, tremor and in some, paranoia. In all cases one night's sleep restored normal functioning.
- One in ten people who complain of excessive daytime drowsiness suffer from sleep apnea, which is a stoppage of breathing while asleep.
- A condition called narcolepsy causes sufferers to fall asleep at inappropriate times – while making love, walking, playing tennis, working.
- As we age we usually sleep less. Our REM sleep in particular decreases sharply.

scissors Cutting remarks; cynicism; sharp tongue; anger; fear of or feelings about castration – female castration expressed in cutting off breasts – the cutting off of developing sexual characteristics in body and mind; sometimes refers to separation or independence – as in cutting umbilical cord – or death; cutting something or someone out of one's life; cutting off or cutting out feelings.

screw Male sexuality; intercourse; security. Idioms: got a screw loose or missing; put the screws on someone; have a screw, or screw you.

scurf Thoughts; ideas; opinions.

sea Most of the activities which underlie our physical and mental life are beyond our awareness. Occasionally something – an ache in the chest, a strange emotion which unsettles us – may emerge into consciousness, then disappear. The sea, with its surface and hidden depths, lends itself to depicting this human experience of known and unknown regarding Self. The enormity of the sea is also a visible image of the enormity of our own inner world – most of it unknown – and also the relationship we have with the universe which we exist in yet know so little about. The sea holds vast treasures, curiosities and our history. Not simply because life emerged from the sea, or our blood is as salt as the ancient sea, but because so many ships and shorelines are now beneath the waves. Sometimes these can be recovered and this depicts our remembering or making conscious.

General: the boundary between unconscious and conscious; our processes of life and the origins of our life; the wisdom, still non-verbalised because locked in process rather than insight, of our existence; source of the huge life drives, such as that which urges us toward independence, mating and parenthood; a symbol of infinite energy or consciousness in which human existence is only a tiny part; the waves of experience we face in life, some acceptable, some threatening.

Going under the sea: bringing internal contents to consciousness; remembering the womb experience; letting our ego surrender a little; looking at death. If there is a sense of hugeness or depth: going beyond the boundaries of experience usually set up by our conscious Self or ego. Waves: impulses, feelings and emotions, such as sexuality, anxiety, anger. Tide: rising and falling of feelings such as love, pleasure or sexuality; may refer to ageing when going out; tide in our affairs. Idioms: all at sea; plenty more fish in the sea; lost at sea. See: **beach**; **fish**, **sea creatures**.

> *Example: 'My husband and I were standing looking at the sea's surface. It was just falling night. I saw a mass of dark shapes, thought it would be a school of fish. Then we were looking at water birds, maybe ducks, again dark shapes as the light had almost gone. Then there was a hole in the sea, like a belly button. I was wondering what it was, how was it being made, was there something under the water? Something very big was coming up to the surface very close to me. It shot me to wake.'*
> *Ginny Q.*

Ginny and her husband had been exploring the content of their dreams. The image of the sea shows Ginny sensing there are enormous depths to her own being and something big – a previously unconscious complex of insights and feelings – is becoming conscious.

Example: 'A small speed boat was at sea. But the sea dissolved anybody who fell in. One man fell in but held himself together as a blob of water and jumped back to the speed boat. I remember the words "The sea is a great solvent".' Tim P.

Tim is aware of his unconscious sense of being a part of the huge sea of life or energy. In it one might lose sense of identity. In the end, identity is 'held together' by one's own belief in oneself.

Example: 'I am either standing at the edge of the sea or near, when suddenly enormous tidal waves appear in the distance and are coming closer. I know they will engulf me, I turn and run away. Sometimes they do overtake me, other times I wake up.' Mrs A.V.

We can run from pleasure and wider insight, just as much as from pain or fear.

Example: 'On the first night I slept with my present wife I noticed she struggled with her breathing. While she was asleep I spoke to her suggesting she would relax and allow her breathing to be easy. Within moments she responded. This encouraged me and I suggested her whole body would relax, and the barriers within her dissolve, allowing healing and well-being to be experienced. Within ten minutes she suddenly awoke and told me a dream.

She was at the rear of a house sunbathing with her family, feeling very relaxed and happy. As she sank into the enjoyment, waves like a tidal wave began to roll up her body. The pleasure was so intense she woke up.' Tony C.

seance Meeting the unconscious as if it were spirits; concern about death or the dead; intuition.

searching Usually indicates an attempt to find such as a past way of life – like wanting to have childhood lack of responsibilities; a lover from the past; trying to find an answer to a pressing problem; searching for one's identity or sense of value in a particular setting. Also may indicate a feeling of having lost something – youth; sexual appeal; creativity; motivation. <u>Idioms</u>: searched high and low; a searching look; search me. See: **looking**.

searchlight Focused attention; concentration; insight.

seasons Times or periods of one's life. See: **autumn**; **spring**; **summer**; **winter**.

secret of the universe dreams Writers commonly quote the experience of William James who, while under anaesthetic dreamt he found the secret of the universe. What he was left with was the doggerel 'Higamus Hogumus women are monogamous – Hogumus Higamus, men are polygamous'. Their conclusion is that dreams cannot be truly revelatory. While it may be true to say that some such dreams contain little which adds to the dreamer's understanding, many dreams give insights which profoundly alter the dreamer's future attitudes or actions.

Revelatory dreams are more common to men than women. It may be that more men concern themselves with questions of what the universe is. If the dreamer creates a mental or emotional tension in themselves through the intensity with which they pursue such questions – and we need to accept that often such intensity arises out of anxiety regarding death and one's identity – then the self-regulatory process of dreaming might well produce an apparent revelation to ease the tension. On the opposite tack, research into mental functioning during dreaming, or in a dream-like state as in research using LSD, show that there is an enormously increased ability to access associated ideas, allow feeling responses and achieve novel viewpoints. Freud pointed out that dreams have access to greater memory resources and associated ideas. P.H. Stafford and B.H. Golightly, in their book dealing with LSD as an aid to problem-solving, say that this dream-like state enables subjects to 'form and keep in mind a much broader picture . . . imagine what is needed – for the problem – or not possible . . . diminish fear of making mistakes.' One subject says, 'I had almost total recall of a course I did in thermo dynamics; something I had not given any thought to in years.'

Although humans have such power to scan enormous blocks of information or experience, look at it from new angles, sift it with particular questions in mind and so discover new connections in old information, there are problems – otherwise we would all be doing it. The nature of dream consciousness, and the faculties described, is fundamentally different to waking awareness which limits, edits, looks for specifics, avoids views conflicting with its accepted norm and uses verbalisation. A non-verbal, symbolic scan of massive information is largely lost when translated to waking consciousness. My experience is that the content of revelatory dreams is almost wholly lost on waking. If the individual explores the dream while awake, however, and dares to take consciousness into the realm of the dream, then the enormous waves of emotional impact, the massive collection of details, the personality-changing influence of major new insights can be met. The reason most of us do not touch this creative process is for the same reason most of us do not attempt other daring activities – it takes guts. See: **creative dreaming**.

secrets learnt from dreams   One of the great secrets observed from over thirty years of dream watching concerns health. It is that each of us carry within us fears about our health, or about our own personal adequacy. This is natural enough, but in dreams these feelings are shown as being like a hypnotic suggestion for the body to be ill. These negative emotions are like bad infections or viruses we have contracted. To counteract their influence we must take time to feel the basic force for life and survival in us. Become aware of the force that is constantly renewing body and mind. Imagine it pervading every part of you and work with it toward healing and renewal. Whatever feelings of pleasure you can find, let them spread to areas of pain or discomfort. Let them fill your body and restore it.

The second great secret is that behind the façade we may erect to tell people who we are, each of us wants to be capable of loving and supporting at least one other human being. We want at least one other person to be glad we exist. This secret of love permeates our sexual drive. Even the sex cells – the sperm and ovum – when they meet, burst asunder and give themselves completely to each other. Dreams suggest we have an urge toward this at a personal level. We deeply desire our lover to so open to us, and we to them, that we take them into ourselves and are enriched by the merging of the other personality without compromising our independence. If you are frightened of this giving of yourself, you remain frustrated in a large degree. And one of the great themes in dreams is the constant reminder of the fears and hurts that stand in the way of such love. See: second example in *wife* under **family**.

The third great secret is about death. A huge number of dreams reviewed for this book are about death. Most of them reflect the fears and images we have of death and show us running from these painted masks. Many such images are what we have inherited from our culture, through its lack of positive statements about death. The secret witnessed in dreams is that if you dare stop running from these emotions and cut-out cartoons of death, with their maggots and rotting bodies, you will break through the screen the images are projected upon. The wondrous reality of life will be waiting for you there, ready to share the love and transformation that lies in death. Dare to challenge the mirage. See: second example in **creativity and problem solving in dreams**.

> *Example: 'I was Jesus walking among the people in today's world. I was in a crowded shop-like building and could see lots of people out on the street gathering for a communal procession. I walked the other way through a corridor, passing people going out to the front way. It was then I knew that people were getting closer with the intention of shooting me. I kept walking to the area that I was intent on reaching which was a group of my people. I came out of a door and saw them sitting in small groups talking amongst themselves. I walked up to a table where a couple were sitting, very engrossed in each other. I sat down with them, reaching out with my hand to touch the women saying, "Do not be afraid, I am going to be shot." As soon as I said it I felt the shot go through me. Then several more. I stood up and saw a man take aim and shoot me, I wasn't afraid, just stood there feeling the bullet go through. I then began to walk amongst the crowds knowing that I was shot several times. The top of my head was blown off, all my*

brains had gone and still I walked with the crowds. I saw the
blood and brains on the ground and wondered at the marvel
of still being there. I felt it was the Crucifixion of myself/Jesus.'
Hyone

A fourth secret is that we can communicate with the deeply
unconscious aspects of our nature such as body processes. Dreams
portray the life process as intelligent and purposive, as something
existing in all things and synthesising all individual experience. Life
as presented by the unconscious is responsive to our own actions
and attitudes. If we care for and love the innate process of our being,
such as daring to face the cultural and childhood sources of internal
pain and heal them, then life loves us, responds more fully to us, and
opens its treasures to us.

sedative   Attitudes we use to stop ourselves feeling anxiety or
emotions. This may be dangerous to our health if feelings such as
guilt or grief remain unfelt.

seed   Sperm or ovum; new idea arising out of past experience; a
suggestion; a new possibility or potential.

seeing, saw, sight   This is one of the major aspects of dreaming.
Unless we are born blind, virtually every dream shows us looking at,
seeing or viewing the events, objects, environment and people of
the dream. In a word count from a sample of 1,000 dreams, the
words *see, saw, look, looking* occurred 1,077 times. This is the
highest occurrence of any words in the sample. Next were *feel,
feelings, felt* with a score of 855, and *house, houses* with 412.

This suggests that dreams are almost entirely about giving attention
to, being aware of, being confronted by, considering or realising some
aspect of the enormously wide range of experience which human
consciousness meets. Therefore, whatever appears in the dream
shows we are giving some thought to, feeling or confronting what is
depicted. During each day we meet, in sensory impressions, in
memory, in emotion, in thought, a huge variety of things. It is therefore
of great interest what comparatively few subjects our spontaneous
dream response chooses to give attention to out of all the range. It
seems likely these chosen areas are important to us.

Looking at something implies our attitudes or response to what is seen. Being looked at by someone else in the dream suggests seeing oneself from a viewpoint which is not our norm. By actually attempting to stand in the role of the other person, as described in **dream processing**, we can become conscious of this different viewpoint. By standing in our own role in the dream, and actually taking time to consider what it is we are 'seeing' and the impressions involved, we can 'see' or become aware of what the dream is getting us to look at regarding ourselves.

The view a person has in their dream, the environment they see, reflects how they see life and themselves. It shows the narrowness or wideness of their 'vision'. The example below shows Debbie viewing a huge landscape and sea. The size and space of it shows the depth and breadth of her mind. See example in *whale* under **fish**, **sea creatures**.

Idioms: from the look of things; look after; look askance at; look at; look before you leap; look blue; look down on; look for; look forward to; look into; look out; look over something; look small; look the other way; look up to; look for a fight; not like the look of; as far as I can see; as I see it; do you see what I mean; I'll see about that; I see; see over something – overseer; see eye to eye; see life; see red; see which way the wind blows; catch sight of; get out of my sight; in sight of; lose sight of; out of sight out of mind; second sight; at first sight. See: **searching**.

semen Essence of masculinity; the sense of one's personal identity, but also the potential one has as an individual. Thus the withholding of sperm in the dream might be the non-giving of Self, warmth, emotion, bonding.

serial dreams Many people report recurring dreams, but these are of two types. One is the dream that recurs much the same in every feature. The other – serial dreams – are those that slowly change and evolve. Serial dreams might be about something like learning to fly in a long series of dreams, or exploring territory or a house that you only slowly penetrate. Sometimes they are about a relationship that is at first difficult, but gradually becomes more accessible and enjoyable.

Such dreams usually reflect changing attitudes and skills in oneself. For instance, a man who was confronting his own fears concerning sex experienced a series of dreams in which at first he had difficulty getting close to and loving a woman. The dreams evolved into ones in which he satisfyingly made love.

The theme of these serial dreams usually gives a clue to the area of our personality the changes refer to. Common themes are gaining of confidence; learning skill in relationships; developing courage to go beyond usual boundaries of anxiety and thus take risks such as starting one's own business; discovering latent potential in oneself.

settings   The environment in which the action of the dream takes place signifies the background of experience which supports the situation dealt with in the foreground.

> *Example: 'I was near a lake in the countryside. Everything was frozen. I saw some horse droppings still steaming and this seemed to be the only living thing around.' Kevin K.*

Kevin's comments on this are that the frozen lake and countryside express his feelings about the world around him. He sees it as cold and uninviting. It is frozen and there is no life in it for him. That is, he cannot find anything in life to excite him or have meaning. The horse dung, he realised, is the resource he can use to change his life. The dung can be manure or food for growth, or fuel to burn for energy and heat. This made him feel that there is a way to transform his old unsatisfying patterns of 'frozen' emotions into something growing and satisfying.

So Kevin's dream setting illustrates his view of the world – that it is a cold uninviting place. So it is the feeling state he lives within most of the time.

> *Example: 'I was in a crowd around a church.' Efrosyni G.*

If we looked at the rest of Efrosyni's dream we might lose the impact of this very first 'scene-setting' statement. If we look up **crowd**, we find under, Talking to, leading or part of crowd at a central event: 'An impulse or idea which unifies many parts of one's own nature.' So here is something which Efrosyni is deeply interested in. Many of her feelings are involved in it. Looking up **church** we find, 'Religious feeling or beliefs, including moral code, or our feelings about organised religion.' So it is against the setting of Efrosyni's religious beliefs the rest of the dream drama unfolds.

Example: 'I was in a house with old clothes and was washing up.' Mrs P.R.

The entry on house says it is P.'s everyday feeling state, her general image of herself. The old clothes are a sense of being old or unattractive. Washing up suggests she feels there are things to clear up concerning what is happening in her life. But it also suggests she sees herself as unexciting. Having clarified that – she feels old and uninteresting and this needs to be cleaned up or dealt with – the very next part of the dream explodes into view with meaning. 'My daughter's husband-to-be came in. I admired the way he dressed and he turned his back on me.' At the end of her dream P. feels 'lost and rejected'. By clarifying the opening scene, it seems likely P. looks at her daughter in her new romance – P. being fifty, a divorcee and at the tail end of a 'whirlwind romance' – and feels jealous. Maybe she even hopes to attract her daughter's man away from her, but he indicates there is no hope. Basically, after her romance, P. feels unwanted and rejected. The helpfulness of the dream, however, is that the first scene shows P. the sort of feelings about herself she is living in daily – feelings of being old and uninteresting. Shifting those feelings can change the way others react to her.

sewing   Creating a new attitude; changing old habits; healing a hurt or tear in a relationship if mending.

sex and identity   Many dreams show how we gain much of our identity out of our sexual relationship or lack of it. Men and women often feel they are inadequate or lacking in personal worth if they are not in a relationship where their partner is fascinated by them sexually. As suggested in the entry on **individuation**, our sense of personal value and positive existence may be built on many things, but can ultimately become less dependent upon particulars such as physical attractiveness or sexual partnership.

While the identity is still dependent upon sexual partnership, lack of sexual intercourse can produce powerful feelings of loneliness, loss of self-esteem and a strange feeling of isolation and distance from other people – especially one's sexual partner. This brings about an urge to establish sexual contact again and illustrates the dependence one has upon sex for a sense of well-being.

sex in dreams   Although sex is symbolised in many dreams, where it appears directly it shows that the dreamer is able to accept their sexual urges and hurts more easily. What is then important is to attempt an understanding of what setting or drama the sexual element occurs in. Our psychological and sexual natures, like our physical nature, never stand still in development unless a pain or problem freeze them at a particular level of maturity. Therefore, our sexual dreams, even if our sex life is satisfactory, show us what growth, what new challenge is being met.

> *Example: 'My lover was standing behind me and John, my husband, was standing in front of me. I was asking John to have sex with me and at the same time thinking, "Oh hell, if he does he will think we have something going between us." I felt no flow towards John but felt somehow I was trying to tell my lover that I was desirable.' Sally A.*

Sally's dream needs no interpretation. Such clear dreams show that Sally is ready to be directly aware of what she is doing in her relationships. If the sex in the dream is deeply symbolised, it suggests the dreamer is less willing to be aware of their motivations or connected painful feelings. Even though Sally's dream was clear, it was still dealing with an area of her sexuality she was not clearly conscious of. If she had been aware, it is doubtful that she would have dreamt it.

> *Example: 'I was in a farmyard. A small boy climbed all over the bull. It became terribly angry. It had been chained without attention too long. Now it tore away and sought the cows. The gates were closed, but the bull smashed through the enclosing fence. I rushed to the fence and sat astride it, but on seeing that the bull smashed it like match wood I looked around for some safe place. The bull charged the first cow to mount it, but so*

terrible was its energy and emotion that it could not express as sex. It smashed the cow aside as it had done the fence. Then it rushed to the next and tossed it over its head, charging and smashing the next. I climbed into somebody's garden, trying to get out of the district.' Arthur J.

Although this dream depicts Arthur's 'chained' sexual drive using the bull, it is still fairly obvious. If we consider the setting and plot of the dream, as suggested above, we see that Arthur is desperately trying to avoid responsibility for or trying to escape his own sexual drive – figuratively 'sitting on the fence'.

Example: 'My husband and I were walking down a road. We were going in the same direction together. I started to sing with a very happy feeling but then felt I should stop because he would say the happiness was because I had had sex. I sensed he knew what I was thinking as I walked along. He then quietly began to sing and the dream ended with me smiling to myself. We had had sexual cut-off for four weeks but had made love that afternoon.' Joan W.

In talking about this dream, Joan said she felt it slightly embarrassing to admit that sex gave her feelings of happiness. She liked to believe she was perfectly happy without it. It is probably out of the slight conflict between her conscious attitude and her feeling of well-being after sex that the dream was produced.

General information about sex in your dreams Whenever a healthy man dreams he experiences an erection, no matter what the subject of the dream. It is likely that women also experience such stimulus during their dreams.

While dreaming you can safely allow any form of sexual pleasure you desire. Don't let the useful morals of waking life intrude into your dreams. If your sexual dreams are frustrating or do not lead to deep pleasure, drop the fears and limiting attitudes that are blocking the full flow of your excitement.

Your longing for sexual partners that isn't openly expressed will attempt to become real in your dreams. It doesn't mean that you are dissatisfied with your present partner if you have sex with other people in your dreams. All of us have such secret longings and it is healthy for them to be allowed as we sleep.

Sometimes sexual pleasure is depicted in dreams as a tidal wave, or a snake, or something you may be resisting. This is because full sexual bliss floods the whole body, releasing tensions, bringing peace and a healing action physically and psychologically. To achieve this, learn to let go of rigid self-control and be ready to be emotional.

Enjoying sexual pleasure with an animal, such as being kissed or licked by a cat, is the way dreams describe your own sexual urges at their most uncomplicated and basic level. It doesn't mean you are weird. In such dreams you are dropping the complicated social rules that usually direct how you express yourself.

The energy behind the sexual drive is enormously important. It can flow in many different ways. It not only expresses as genital sex but also in caring for others. If it is blocked illness can result. Your dreams show in detail just how you are dealing with this most important area of your life and what is standing in the way of satisfaction and health. Do not accept the ready-made formulas of popular sexual norms. Your dreams will show your own intimate and unique needs. Remember your dreams and be enriched by them.

See: **adolescent**; **affair**; **animals**; *devil, Christ, shadow* under **archetypes**; **bag**; **banana**; **bed**; example in **bite**; **black person**; *breasts* and *penis* under **body**; **bud**; **candle**; **cane**; **castration**; **ceremony, ritual**; **clothes**; **compensatory theory**; **cuckoo**; **cup**; **dam**; **dance**; third example in **danger**; **defence mechanisms**; **dragon**; **drum**; **ejaculation**; **emotions, mood**; second example under **evil**; fourth example under *husband* in **family**; **feelings**; **homosexuality**; **horns**; **hostility**; example in *door* under **house, buildings**; **hypnosis and dreams**; **insects**; **jungle**; **kiss**; **left, right**; **lift**; second example under **light**; **man**; **masturbation**; **mirror**; **murder**; **nest**; **oval**; **pole**; **prostitute**; **purse**; **rape**; **refrigerate**; **religion and dreams**; first example under **reptiles – lizards, snakes**; **sadism**; **sex while asleep**; **wordplay, puns**.

sex while asleep This fairly common dreaming experience demonstrates powerfully how dreams are an expression of a self-regulatory or compensatory action in the psyche and body. Charles in the example below says he had been restraining his sexual activity. This shows the enormous gulf which can exist between what we will to do as a conscious personality and what our being needs to do or wishes to do outside of conscious decision making. The 'glamour and fantasy' Charles describes are regular features of how these deeper needs make themselves known or attempt to coerce the conscious mind into fulfilling the need. If we reject the fantasy, the unconscious processes will attempt a more radical approach, as in actual physical movement while we sleep. This may have given rise to ideas about possession or devils in past ages when it was not understood that we can split our mind by such conflicts. Fear of the 'possessing' influence actually heightens its power through suggestion. Much better to understand what one's needs are and seek an acceptable fulfilment. See: **abreaction**.

> *Example: 'Many times in my adult life I have woken to find I have made love to my wife while asleep. Or I wake to discover myself in the middle of the sexual act. At such times I have usually been avoiding my sexual drive and it has burst through to fulfil itself while I was asleep or under the sway of dreams. For instance most times this has happened I have been in the middle of a dream in which there is a sense of absolute imperative that I must make love/have sex. It is like being lost in a storm of glamour and fantasy or a vision in which I am totally involved. The whirl of the "dream" is towards the wonder, totality of the need to have sex. As this imperative is expressed in my still spontaneous, dreaming physical action, the experience of sex is also visionary and enormous.' Charles W.*

shade, shadow Feeling 'put in the shade'; feelings still overshadowing one from past experiences or relationships; feeling inferior; protection; occasionally a sense of the dead or fear of the unknown; negative emotions. Idioms: afraid of one's shadow; shades of; shadow of one's former self; worn to a shadow. See: *the shadow* under **archetypes**; **shadowy figure**.

shadowy figure In the example, Gloria is meeting her own feeling of fear. This is obvious because the shadowy thing felt the fear also.

In fact it is the feeling of fear. Such shadowy figures are our own rejected emotions or potentials. It is the aspect of ourselves we reject, the secondary side of our personality, its non-dominant traits. See: *the shadow* under **archetypes**.

> *Example: 'A shadow thing came very quickly up the stairs along our corridor and into the bedroom, over to the bed to bend over me. I felt fear as I never felt it before and I started to make a noise. It was also the shadow making the noise and it was frightened and moved towards the window. I felt sorry it was frightened too, but then it was too late as it had gone. I woke up making a howling noise. My husband said he felt the fear in the room strongly too.' Gloria F.*

shampoo   Attempt to clear away thoughts or attitudes which are not useful or interfere in a clear thinking. See: *hair* under **body**; second example under **school**.

shapes, **symbols**   These are a visual presentation of our own internal or psychological structure. Because the mind and emotions in some ways appear so abstract, it is difficult to have a clear image of our differences compared with other people, or to see changes which occur through maturing. Shapes, symbols and patterns give us a clear image of our inner world. See example in *spiral* below.

centre, middle   Emphasises the importance of the thing, person or animal in that position; conflict, where the middle is between opposites; obstruction when something might be in the middle of the road, corridor, etc.; feelings of being involved, when in the middle of a crowd for instance. When something is in the middle of a circle or square can represent the Self or spirit. Idioms: middle of the road; piggy in the middle; centre of attention.

circle   Oneself; personal identity; wholeness; it suggests a good harmony between all the aspects of our being – thus a feeling of pleasure, centredness and openness, physical, mental and spiritual; may be used to depict the Self; eternity; female sexuality. If the circle is irregular, suggests imbalance or lack of harmony. Idioms: go round in circles; come full circle; vicious circle; circle of influence/ friends.

crescent   Femininity; the vagina; the process of feminine creativity. Crescent moon: the beginning or ending of something to do with one's feelings or inner life.

cross   Difficulties or tribulations we carry, perhaps unnecessarily; human life and its whole spectrum of experience, physical, sexual, mental, emotional, cosmic – painful and delightful; wrongness as with tick being correct, cross being wrong or forbidden; completion as when crossed off list; the body, upon which consciousness is nailed or fixed during life. If cross upright as +: being upright; correct; self-assertion; balanced. If cross as x: the four extremities; reaching out; crossing out.

diamond   Choices or direction, like the compass needle.

line   Distance; movement; movement in space or time. Tangled line: changes and decisions in life; indecision or confusion. Zigzag line: movement; change; the basic pleasure or achievement of leaving one's mark.

mandala   This is any circle or square within which shapes, objects or other symbols appear. The mandala can be a square garden with round pond in it – square with circle in – etc. It depicts what we have done with our life, what qualities or balance we have achieved through our own effort or self-responsibility. It shows whether we have dared meet the darkness and light in our nature and bring balance, whether we have found the courage to have our boundaries of thought and viewpoint split asunder by a greater vision or despair, and what we have done with the pieces of wonder and pain we have found. See: **mandala**; *spiral* below.

oblong   An area of our experience – may be sex, mind, etc.; boundaries of our awareness or what we dare let ourselves experience; physical reality; oneself contained within the boundaries of our experience and social and personal constraints.

patterns   Concepts or realisations, made up of interblending pieces of information and experience; the order or chaos of our inner world of thoughts and feelings; the patterns we live by, such as habits and beliefs; insight into the cycles or patterns underlying human and animal life; the actual patterns of one's pulse and breathing – these may be represented by patterns of dots for the pulse and wavy or short lines may represent breathing.

sphere, ball   General: wholeness; an 'all-round' view or a rounded character. Ball: interaction between two people, sexual and other-wise – the 'ball' is in your court – in that throwing the ball may show someone trying to get one's attention and response. Ball games or being thrown a ball: challenges, prowess, competition in the game of life; having and letting go; sex play; masturbation; a man's 'balls'; wholeness. Idioms: have a ball; ball at one's feet; one's eye on the ball; start the ball rolling; new ball game; play ball with someone; he has/hasn't the balls. See: *the Self* under **archetypes**; **games**.

spiral   Things we repeat over and over like habits; movement toward greater awareness or insight.

> *Example: 'We walk around, go upstairs, and I notice a staircase leading to a room or rooms. The stairs are painted in the green too, and they go up square, about eight steps in a flight, but round and round – spiral. I am scared by them, don't want to go up, but am curious. We move in and nobody but myself has really taken any notice of the stairs. Nobody has been up. Halfway up I can see there is a glass roof, the wooden frames painted green. I am terrified but have to go on. Then I wake. Next dream I got up there. It smelt very musty. Lots of draw sheets covering things. I bent to lift a sheet. It was raining. I could hear it thrashing on the glass. Then I woke.' Ann H.*

In this example we have the spiral and the square combined in the stairs. In this way the dream manages to combine many different ideas such as climbing to the unknown, spiralling or circling something, and the squareness or down-to-earth nature of what is being discovered. There are things we have learnt, yet not realised consciously. Like a jigsaw puzzle, we have all the pieces and we sense the connection, but we have never formed it into a conscious thought or verbal idea. It therefore remains as a feeling sense or hunch, but not a rational idea. Ann is spiralling toward or circling around such a realisation. She is frightened because it may be difficult – she may realise that all the years of marriage point to having been used as a doormat.

square   Down to earth; reality; the physical experience; stability; the materialising of an idea, feeling or plan. Leonardo Da Vinci's diagram of the man in the circle within the square represents a complete balance of the various aspects of human nature – as he may have achieved himself. See: *mandala* above; **mandala**.

star   Aspiration; the spiritual aspect of Self. Six pointed: personal harmony between physical, mental and spiritual. Five pointed star: one's body, oneself and one's sensed kinship with all life.

triangle   Oneself being capable of 'standing'; the three major aspects of human nature – body, personal experience and impersonal consciousness; similar to the number three – see: **numbers**. The triangle with point upwards: depicts the physical aspects of human nature moving toward the personal or conscious. Triangle with point downwards: the areas of consciousness moving toward physical expression. Triangles linked in Star of David: complete balance in human nature. Sometimes the points of the triangle are used to represent three stages of human development of awareness. The first is undifferentiated or preconscious stage. The second is the sense of individuality, feeling 'otherness' in regard to the world. The third is the relationship of the Self to the 'other' in people and the world.

shark   See: **fish, sea creatures**.

sheep   See: **animals**.

shell   The defence we use to avoid being hurt emotionally or to defend the integrity of our identity. See: **fish, sea creatures**.

shine   Containing a lot of our personal energy. See: **aura; light**.

ship   See: **boat, ship**.

shit   See: **excrement; toilet**.

shiver   Fear or conflict; excitement; getting near to release of unconscious material. Idioms: give one the shivers; send shivers up one's spine.

shoes See: **clothes**.

shop Desires; something we are looking for or want – love, fame, sex; place of work or business. Idioms: shop around; set up shop; shut up shop; talk shop; closed shop. See: *shopkeeper* under **roles**.

shot, shooting To be shot: a traumatic injury to feelings, often in parental or other close relationship. It need not be something dramatic like being assaulted, but can be a quiet injury like not bonding emotionally with parents; feeling as if you have been a target for other people's ridicule or attack. Someone or something else shot: still usually refers to dreamer. Dreamer shooting someone or something: anger; fear or defence against meeting feelings or insights; aggressive sexuality. Idioms: get shot of; shot across the bows; shot in the arm; all shot to pieces; shot in the dark. See: example in **abreaction**.

shovel, spade Introspection; the work of digging into our memories; uncovering our past experience.

shrink If dreamer or people shrink: return to a childhood feeling state or point of view; losing face or feeling 'small'. If other things shrink: they are becoming less threatening or interesting or play less of an important part in one's life; are seen as connected with the unconscious, aspects of which are often seen as of 'little' significance, yet are full of the sort of power which motivates or undermines our resolves.

sick Bad feeling you are discharging; feeling sick of a relationship or situation; being pregnant. Idioms: fall sick; make one sick; sick and tired of; sick as a dog; sick to death of.

sight See: **seeing, saw, sight**.

signature Agreement; what one wills; one's mark in the world; oneself.

silence Uneasiness; unspoken feelings; expectancy; being unable to voice one's feelings; condoning; absence of life – death; the silence – non-existence or void – out of which personal life emerges.

sing   Expressing one's inner feelings, one's real Self; touching the flowing feelings of our lives; other people's self-expression and daring.

sinking   Despairing; losing ground; loss of confidence. Idioms: be sunk; sinking feeling; sink or swim; sink to someone's level. See: second example in **falling**.

sister   See: **family**.

size   How important we see something, or what feeling impact it has on us, or how we feel in relationship to the person or object.

big, large   Importance; relationship – as when we feel small beside somebody with a 'big' reputation. Idioms: big of somebody; big brother; big fish/noise/wheel/shot; big guns; big head; go down big; big time; too big for one's shoes/boots.

little, small   Of little importance; feeling 'small'; relating to childhood. See: **shrink**.

skating   See: **ice**.

skeleton   Feelings about death; part of your own ability or basic strength, feelings or talent you have 'killed off' or allowed to die at some time.

sky   The mind; our potential. Dream scenes such as the sky opening and people or objects appearing, or threatening things falling from the sky are graphic descriptions of how suddenly a new thought or viewpoint or event appears from nowhere; or for no apparent reason anxious or depressing thoughts occur 'out of the blue'. Floating or flying in sky: avoiding anxiety; escape into day dreaming or the mind; having a wider awareness of a situation; exploring potential. Colour or mood of sky: our view of life at the moment. Idioms: sky's the limit; sky high; pie in the sky; out of the blue. See: **flying**; **space**.

sleep   Sleep is one of the most mysterious of human experiences. It is the polar opposite to waking awareness, with its focused sense of personal existence and external sensory impressions. From this point of view, there are several levels of conscious life. The first is waking awareness; the second is dreaming sleep – immersion in symbolic representation and the acceptance of these as real; the third is lucidity within a dream – the awareness of dream imagery as symbols and recognition of the symbols being personal creations and not external reality; the fourth is dreamless sleep, or awareness beyond ego, symbols, thoughts or emotions.

American sleep research laboratories in recent years have pointed out that the invention of the electric light bulb has disoriented normal sleep patterns. Millions of people suffer sleep disorders or sleep starvation. According to the National Commission on Sleep Disorders Research, the 1989 Exxon Valdex oil spill in Alaska was the result of the third mate falling asleep while piloting the ship. Similarly, the melt-down at the Three Mile Island atomic power plant in Pennsylvania in 1979 which almost led to a massive nuclear explosion was also caused by a technician being asleep and failing to hear an alarm.

Forty million Americans are estimated to be chronically ill with sleep disorders. Few people recognise their condition and its cause, however. Signs of it are chronic tiredness and needing constant stimulants to keep going during the day; constant falling asleep during work, talks, driving; inability to wake easily in the morning. As sleep plays an equally important part in healthy long life as nutrition and exercise, it is important to assure its quality. If our pattern and quality of sleep is disturbed, we may fail to notice the influence of such drinks as coffee, chocolate and alcohol, all of which disturb sleep.

One of the major sleep disorders is called sleep apnea. This condition causes the sufferer to stop breathing for periods of ten seconds to a minute or more. The person is therefore aroused to waking state, or near it, over and over during the night. This may underlie the recurrent nightmare some people have of feeling suffocated. This condition, if suspected, needs a doctor's help.

Insomnia is the largest sleep disorder and of course it covers all causes. Psychologist Peter Hauri, director of the Mayo Clinic's insomnia programme and co-author (with Shirley Linde) of *No More*

Sleepless Nights (John Wiley & Sons) says about 60 per cent of all cases of chronic insomnia stem from mental or physical ailments. These include depression, sleep apnea and periodic limb movements (which usually involves leg jerks, repeated every few seconds for hours on end). Sleepers may awaken numerous times, but so briefly that awakenings go unremembered in the morning.

To help oneself get a better quality of sleep if you suffer insomnia, use the following suggestions:

- Keep a twenty-four-hour record showing good and bad nights of sleep. Closely observe connections between events and sleep. Hauri says one woman suspected her insomnia was triggered by phone calls in the evening, her supervisor's foul moods and 'times I felt like speaking up but didn't'. Her log showed, however, that she slept badly only after phone calls from her fault-finding mother. No other daytime events, no matter how irritating, wrecked her nights.

- Develop your own insights or theories about what is causing you to sleep badly from the observations you make.

- Hauri says chronic insomniacs sabotage their own sleep by constant fretting. The more they worry, the more they toss and turn. The worse they sleep, the more they tend to worry. Some people say their minds start to race as soon as they turn off the lights. 'It's not that you worry too much,' Hauri tells them, 'but that you do it at the wrong time.' He suggests scheduling thirty minutes earlier in the day as worry time. Sit in a quiet place. Write each worry on a separate 3 × 5 inch card. Sort the cards into categories. Take each in turn and think about it until you decide what to do. Write that plan of action down.

- A period of vigorous exercise or soaking in a hot bath also helps. Both raise core body temperature. Recent research shows that cooling down afterwards helps induce and deepen sleep. The timing is important. Exercise three to six hours before bedtime. Take your bath two to three hours before; keep adding hot water as necessary to keep your temperature up.

- Reserve bed just for sleep. Do not watch TV, eat or drink in bed. These hinder the habit of associating bed with sleep.

- Sex is okay in bed if it leaves you feeling relaxed.

- Don't drink any caffeine or alcohol after 2pm.

- Avoid napping during the day. Save sleep for bed unless you find it improves your night-time sleep.
- Go to bed and get up at the same time each day. The body is like an animal that loves regular activities.
- If you are involved in highly demanding creative work, sailing a boat single-handed across the Atlantic or fighting a forest fire, break your sleep into short chunks. Even fifteen minutes at a time can keep you going. Do not attempt complete sleep avoidance, tests have shown the drive for sleep becomes compulsive and dangerous.

sleep apnea   See: **sleep**.

sleep disorders   See: **science and sleep**; **sleep**; **sleep movements**; **sleep rocking**.

sleep movements   Adrian Morrison at the University of Pennsylvania, investigating narcolepsy – a condition producing sleep in the middle of activity – found that a small area of the brain, the pons, suppresses full muscular movement while we dream. If this area is damaged or suppressed humans or animals make full muscular movements in connection with what is dreamt. He observed that cats would stalk, crouch and spring at imaginary prey. These very important findings suggest a number of things:

1. The unconscious process behind dreaming, apart from creating a non-volitional fantasy can also reproduce movements we have not consciously decided upon. This shows we have at least two centres of will which can direct body and mental processes.
2. Christopher Evans, linking with the work of Nicholas Humphrey at Cambridge University, sees the movements of the dreaming cats as expressions of survival 'programs' in the biological computer. These programs or strategies for survival need to be replayed not only to keep in practice, but also to modify them in connection with the influx of extra experience and information. In the human realm, our survival strategies and the way we relate to our social, sexual, marriage and work roles may also be replayed and modified in our dreaming.

    Such movements are not linked simply to survival or social

'programs'. An important agenda in dreaming is releasing painful emotions or trauma and moving toward psychological growth. Also, the process producing these movements does not keep strictly to the realm of sleep. It is observable that many muscular spasms, ticks or unwilled waking movements arise from this source – the 'will' of the unconscious – attempting to release trauma or initiate a necessary programme of psychological growth. That such 'dream' activities as spontaneous movement or verbalisation should occur during waking would appear to suggest that a dream must occur with them. Research shows this is unlikely. It does, however, show that a dream may be imagery produced to express this mental, muscular, emotional 'self-regulation'. The imagery may not be necessary if the process is consciously experienced.

Because the self-regulatory process produces spontaneous movements, emotions and verbalisation, it is likely there is a connection between it and many ancient religious practices such as Pentecostalism, Shaktipat in India, Subud in Indonesia, Qi Gong in China and Seitai in Japan. These are forms of psychotherapy practised by other cultures. They create an environment in which practitioners can allow spontaneous movement and fantasy while awake. Because consciousness is then involved and can co-operate with the self-regulating or healing activities of the unconscious, such practice can lead to better health and utilisation of unconscious functions. The older religious forms of this practice relied on belief systems of spirits or gods. Once the connection between these practices and the dream process is realised, much in them which was obscure becomes understandable. In my books *Mind and Movement* and *Liberating the Body*, I explain the connection between the dream process, self-regulatory healing, extended perception and waking consciousness. See: **abreaction**; **dream as therapist and healer**; **sleep walking**.

sleep rocking   Ian Oswald (as related in his book *Sleep*, Penguin) observed active rocking in some children and adults during sleep. These rocking movements were very powerful, occurring at a rate of one per second during REM sleep. They occur more frequently in the blind or to people institutionalised during childhood. As rocking is a movement used by primates and humans to comfort themselves during stress or unhappiness, it is possible that the rocking accompanies disturbing dreams. The dream probably evokes unhappy feelings or conditions from the past. As the person used rocking to cope with their past distress, it occurs as an habitual accompaniment of the distressing dream.

sleep walking   Very common with some people, especially during adolescence or times of stress. Sometimes accompanied by hallucinations. Sleep walking is normal as an occasional event in children. If the child is agitated, excited or acting in a manner to injure themselves during the sleep walking, then it may be a sign of emotional distress.

The same applies to adults. Many sleep walkers perform complex acts without coming to harm. A young Portsmouth boy drove his father's car twenty-seven miles before waking in Southampton. The police checked his story and did not charge him. But sometimes severe injury is inflicted either upon themselves or others. During a dream phone-in on London Broadcasting Company, a man told me of his experience of smashing through a glass window, cutting an artery and nearly bleeding to death. In America and Britain, homicidal acts have been committed while the person claimed to be sleep walking and the people involved were acquitted of murder.

Because of such powerful activity during sleep, many people who experience this type of sleep walking are worried about what they might do to a partner sleeping next to them. In most cases one wakes as the contact is made, or the involved person wakes one, but the element of risk cannot be denied.

Where such worry exists, hope can be gained by understanding what was observed with many men who began to sleep walk after war combat. In their cases the movements, speech and emotions were observably connected with trauma that occurred during their war experience. The self-regulatory process in dreams was thereby attempting to release the tension, horror or emotional pain of the events. Where these emotions could be met consciously, perhaps with the help of a psychotherapist, the sleep movements stopped. This suggests that dramatic activity while sleep walking has similar roots and can be dealt with.

sleeping Not being aware; avoidance of feeling or looking at something; surrender of waking Self; withdrawal from involvement with others. Idioms: lose sleep over; sleep around; put it to sleep; sleep in; sleeping partner; sleep like a log; let sleeping dogs lie; sleep off; sleep on something; sleep together; sleep with; sleep rough.

smell See: **perfume, scent, smell**.

smoke Intuition of danger or anxiety about danger; smouldering passions or emotions. Idioms: go up in smoke; put up a smoke screen; no smoke without fire. See: **fire**.

smoking Anxiety; something controlling our decisions – habits; sometimes connects with hidden sexual desires; comfort or a change in mood, such as might occur when we meet a friend.

snail Vulnerability – its shell depicting our defence against being hurt; feelings of repulsion for some people. Probably repulsion regarding 'squirmy' feelings regarding their body or sexuality.

snake See: **reptiles – lizards, snakes**.

snow Depending on feeling reaction to the snow: emotional coldness or frigidity; pureness; beauty. Skiing or winter sports: freedom, relaxation.

soap Cleansing or melting of emotions resulting in a feeling of release or well-being; feeling one needs to 'clean up one's act' in some way, or 'come clean'; sense of grubbiness; guilt or conscience.

soldier See: **roles**.

son See: **family**.

soup A hunger being satisfied. See: **food**.

south The genital area of Self; warmth, lightness, feelings.

space Space in a building: one's potential or what has not been used up in activity yet; opportunity; sense of independence and freedom. Cosmic space: beyond thinking or limited concepts and ego boundaries; beyond what is established already; being out of touch with reality. Awareness of space: awareness of experience going beyond the present view of the world one has created. The realisation one's personal experience is not all there is.

spectacles   See: **glasses**.

speed   Intensity of feelings; growing anxiety; feelings of not being able to cope with events.

spice   Sex; pleasure.

spider   See: **insects**; **web**.

spirits   Feelings or intuitions about the dead or death; fears concerning one's own unconscious memories or feelings – i.e. being haunted by the past; intuitions arising from one's own mind and awareness as it exists beyond the preconceptions and boundaries of prejudice or fear. Idioms: be with someone in spirit; high/low spirits; public spirit; spirit away; spirit is willing. See: *devil* under **archetypes**; **ghosts**; **masturbation**; **sex while asleep**.

splinter   Minor irritation; hurtful words or ideas; harboured ideas which bring negative feelings or pain.

spring   New growth; what was latent emerging; a new start in business or relationship; childhood or youth. Spring of water: free-flowing feelings; rejuvenating energy. See: **water**.

stab   Feeling 'wounded' by someone else's remarks, actions or attitude; aggressive sexuality. See: **weapons**.

stage   See: **theatre**.

stairs   See: *stairs* under **house**, **buildings**.

stars   Intuitions about the cosmos; the perhaps almost unnoticeable promptings or motivations which occur through life leading us in a particular direction – destiny; hopes or wishes. See: *star* under **shapes**, **symbols**.

starvation   Something in oneself not given due attention; the impoverished and ignored aspect of Self; attempts to deny the body because there is anxiety about its needs and urges.

station   See: **railway**.

statistics   Below are figures based on a word count of 1,000 dreams. If we look at the entry on 'man' below, the number 304 appears beside it. This means the word 'man' appeared 304 times within the 1,000 dreams. The word beside it, 'men', appeared ninety-one times. These are totalled to make the next figure 395, which is the number of times reference to man/men appeared in the dreams. The figure 1 in the next column shows that within the group headed 'people and family', the words man/men had the highest score. The word 'people' came second scoring 345. The figure in the third column shows the overall position under all the headings, making man/men the sixth highest score, with 'see, seeing, looking' the highest.

People and family

Baby 85 Babies 4	103	9
Boy	70	14
Child 71 Children 111	182	6
Daughter	64	15
Father 69 Dad 10	79	12
Friend 136 Friends 60	196	5
Girl	85	10
Husband	197	4
Man 304 Men 91	395	1	6
Mother 122 Mummy 3 Mum 12 Mother's 22	159	7
People	345	2
Person	76	13
Son	80	11
Wife	106	8

Woman 175 Women 41	216	3

Objects

Bus	51	6
Car	124	4
Clothes 54 Wearing 48 Dressed 53	155	2
Fire	44	8
Table	50	7
Tree 32 Trees 36	68	5
Water	164	1
Window 103 Windows 32	135	3

Doing

Driving	80	11	
Fall 41 Falling 30	71	12	
Finding, Found, Finds	297	2	12
Flying, Fly, Flew	98	10	
Hold, Holding, Held	142	8	
Give 44 Gave 23	67	13	
Ran 83 Run 61 Running 64	208	4	
Sleep, Sleeping, Slept	106	9	
Sat 47 Sit 112 Sitting 20	179	7	
Standing 141 Stood 52	193	6	
Swim, Swimming, Swam	59	14	
Take, Took, Taking	248	3	
Wait, Waiting, Waited	56	15	
Walking 165 Walk 68 Walked 134	367	1	9
Work, Worked, Working	194	5	

Body

Arm 43 Arms 67	110	2
Body	79	5
Breast, Breasts	36	8
Ear, Ears	5	12
Eye 20 Eyes 46	66	6
Face	97	3
Hand 107 Hands 62	169	1
Hair	41	6
Head	96	4

Leg, Legs	56	7	
Mouth	30	10	
Nose	9	11	
Teeth, Tooth	34	9	

House and home

Bed	153	4	
Bedroom	66	8	
Door, Doors, Doorway	311	3	
Floor	103	6	
Home	134	5	
House, Houses	412	1	4
Room, Rooms	390	2	8
Stair, Stairs, Steps	98	7	

Psyche

Decide 9 Decided 41 Decision 6	56	18	
Fear 58 Terrified 45 Scared, etc. 86	189	9	
Feels 187 Feelings 244 Felt 424	855	2	2
Happy	63	17	
Heard, Hear	97	13	
Keep, Kept	102	12	
Knew 177 Know 106	283	6	
Realise	38	19	
Remember 104 Remembering 13	117	11	
Say 69 Saying 99 Talking 113 Talk 113	394	3	7
See 293 Seeing 411 Looking 373	1077	1	1
Sex, Sexual, Sexuality	94	14	
Take, Taking	174	10	
Tell, Told	193	8	
Think 72 Thinking 41 Thought 226	339	4	10
Tried, Trying	298	5	11
Want, Wanting, Wanted	200	7	
Watch, Watching	71	16	
Wonder 47 Wondering 26	73	15	

Orientation and size

Above	46	10	

Behind	100	9	
Bottom	44	11	
Down	404	2	5
High	100	9	
Large and big	296	3	13
Left	166	5	
Low	21	13	
Right	130	7	
Side	149	6	
Small	171	4	
Top	115	8	
Under	40	12	
Up	424	1	3

Life events

Birth, Born	23	3
Death, Dying, Dead, Died	276	1
Married, Marriage, Wedding	65	2

Animals

Bear 15 Bears 4	19	4
Bull	14	5
Cat	24	3
Cow	9	6
Dog 51 Dogs 14	65	1
Elephant	19	4
Horse 30 Horses 16	46	2
Lion	5	8
Monkey	4	9
Mouse	2	10
Pig	1	11
Wolf	7	7

Colours

Red	52	5
Orange	2	9
Yellow	13	8
Green	59	4
Blue	61	3

Violet	1	10
Gold	26	6
Silver	14	7
Black	86	2
White	101	1

statue, **idol** An unfeeling or 'dead' part of Self; feeling that someone is unresponsive or cold. Idol: values you have erected, false or otherwise.

stealing Taking love, money or opportunity under false pretences; not giving as good as you get; feeling you are undeserving or unloved and what you get is stealing because it is given unwillingly. Being stolen from: feeling cheated or not respected; may refer to sexuality or love – do you give it, or does it feel as if it is taken from you?; can also refer to death – that life is being 'stolen' from one. Idioms: steal one's heart; steal someone's thunder; steal the show.

steam Emotions under pressure; expressed emotions; something transitory. Idioms: getting steamed up; full steam ahead; get up steam.

steeple A landmark in one's life; may also refer to the body, as 'bats in the belfry' does, suggesting the head. The top of the steeple is the mind and wider awareness; male sexuality.

steps Effort made, or to make, to get somewhere. See: *stairs* under **house**, **buildings**.

sterilise Fear of illness; reference to infection in the body; cleaning out sources of negative feelings or hurts.

stiffness Sensing that you are either holding yourself back in relationships or endeavours or you are too formal; anxiety or tension.

stone Hardness, loss of feeling or unfeeling. Idioms: cast the first stone; leave no stone unturned; stone dead; stone deaf; blood out of a stone; stony broke; heart of stone; stoned. See: **rock**.

storm Anger; emotional outburst; feeling battered by events or emotions; difficulties. If storm is approaching: a sense of difficult times ahead; anger or passion building up. Idioms: bend before the storm; storm in a teacup; take by storm; weather the storm.

strangle Holding back feelings; trying to kill emotions or sexuality. Most of our feelings create sounds such as laughter or crying, a sigh, words of anger or love, cries of pain. The attack on the neck is therefore usually an attempt to stifle these. See: **danger**; third example in *door* under **house**, **buildings**.

string Attempts to make something secure; mending a situation or relationship; trying to hold something together – a business, a marriage; connection with others. Idioms: have someone on a piece of string; hold the purse strings; string along; string someone along; strung up; no strings attached; pull strings; apron strings.

submarine Ability to meet the depths of feelings in the unconscious, as well as functioning all right in the everyday world. See: **boat**, **ship**.

sucking Emotional hunger; experiencing childhood longings, dependence or feelings. Being sucked at: If other than child/parent relationship, feeling one's energy drained; having a sense of another person, or an aspect of oneself, being parasitic – not giving as well as receiving – or having baby needs. Idioms: Suck up to someone; bloodsucker.

suffocating Usually to do with a sense that the external environment or one's inner attitudes or fears are threatening to kill one's pleasure in living; feeling imprisoned by another person's will or emotional pressure and demands; there may be a connection with some sleep problems, so see section on sleep apnea in **sleep**.

sugar Pleasure; substitute for relationship or love; may refer to body health. Idioms: all sweetness and light; be sweet on someone; a sweet tooth; the sweets – rewards – of.

suicide Remembering that most people in dreams depict an aspect of oneself, this may be illustrating that we lack pleasure in life or have little to live for in the way of satisfaction; suicide may also be a sign of interiorised anger, where instead of admitting our anger, we destroy parts of our own feelings; may depict business or relationship suicide. If it is someone we know: often shows us hoping person will get out of our life; intuition.

suitcase General: the womb; what one carries inside oneself such as longings, attitudes, fears; how we see ourselves socially – the luggage might be a sign of status, how we rate oneself; also a symbol of independence or going somewhere. See: **bag**.

Example: 'In last night's dream the baby I dream about incessantly had been locked in a suitcase but was quite unscathed when taken out, except that it was very dirty, but still not crying. I do not have any memories in connection with these babies and the only feelings I have are those of remorse that I have neglected the baby. I have had four children of my own, none of whom were ever neglected in this way.' Mrs C.

Mrs C. uses the suitcase in at least two ways. One is her womb or reproductive ability. Although she has had four children, this does not stop her unconsciously desiring more. The second is what 'luggage' – emotional feelings, urges, thoughts – she carries.

summer Mid-life; success; fruitfulness; pleasure; warmth.

sun Warmth; vitality; conscious awareness; the Self or source of one's life energy; the radiant life energy of the father as an inner power. Sunlight: being aware; warmth; positive feelings in body and mind; relaxation; health. Sunbathing: allowing the flow of inner energies to give pleasure. Sunrise: realisation; a new start; childhood; hope and energy to grow. Midday: maturity; middle life; time to be working at one's life. Sunset: old age; death; return to latent period prior to a new birth. See: *death and rebirth* under **archetypes**; **time**.

surgery A surgery: one's health, emotional or physical. Having surgery: feeling 'got at' by someone; having someone 'get under one's skin'; difficult but healing changes in Self; feelings about surgery if imminent.

swallowing   Holding back emotions; swallowing words or anger; taking in something. Idioms: swallow one's pride; he/she swallowed it.

swamp   Feelings which undermine confidence and well-being; might depict feelings about a relationship, perhaps with mother. See: example in **insects; sink**.

sweeping   Clearing away outmoded attitudes, anxieties or emotions; getting feelings about someone out of one's life. Idioms: make a clean sweep; sweep someone off their feet; sweep something under the carpet; sweep the board; sweep the floor with.

sweets   Pleasure; rewards. See: **sugar**.

swimming   General: confidence in dealing with the sort of impacts, anxieties or emotions which cause some people to 'go under', either in relationships, running a family or business; being able to meet the many influences, urges and thoughts in which we exist; expressive motivation; trusting oneself, life and one's sexuality; there is an element of personal survival in swimming. A parent dreaming about its child swimming might very well be considering whether they will 'sink or swim' in their dealings with life. Swimming against the current or tide: meeting opposition, either from within or others; moving against general opinions; feeling difficulties. Swimming underwater: taking awareness into what was unconscious; looking within; seeing what goes on under the surface in relationships, etc. Swimming with other people: sharing common feelings, goals, etc.; connections with others. Diving in: taking the plunge in a new activity, relationship or way of life. Hanging about not getting in: hesitation about a change or something new in life. Idioms: in the swim; swim against the tide; sink or swim. See: **diving; drowning; pool**.

Example: 'I looked at a large pool where a river surfaced. A

*woman swam in it and was going to enter tunnels leading
away from it. As I watched I saw some huge crocodiles swim
toward her. With great speed and confidence she swam away,
obviously being able to match the threat.' Laurie V.*

Laurie explored the dream and found the swimming expressed his
growing confidence in meeting feelings which in past years had led
to depression.

swing　Like rocking, may refer to way we relax ourselves when
facing stress – see: **sleep rocking**; self-gratification, sex or masturbation; feelings of pleasure; daily ups and downs. <u>Idioms</u>: get into
the swing of things; go with a swing; in full swing.

symbols and dreaming　Words are themselves symbols of
objects, ideas or feelings. Whether we look at mathematical equa-
tions, a film, a novel or a business logo, each involves the use of
symbols. When we look at a thermometer we lose sight of it as a real
object and see it as temperature. Throughout our everyday life we
use things symbolically without noticing. A name on the label of
goods may depict quality to us. A face can represent love or brutality.
In the struggle toward human awareness, and its increasingly subtle
use of symbols such as language to think and express with, there
must have been stages of development. That is a side of 'history'
seldom given attention, yet it is very important. Perhaps our dream
'thinking' is using an earlier form of symbols, one which might have
been more an everyday event prior to language.

Even though we exist as an individual integrated with today's
world, our earlier levels of thinking still exist. Unconsciously we still
see the thermometer as temperature; the car as status, independence
or ease in getting to work; inside our house as an expression of
ourselves – if we didn't we would not take pains to make it nice for
guests. Through these unconscious feeling connections or symbolic
views we have of things, dreams create their store of images and
scenes. Processing a dream is an attempt to discover what values we
ourselves unconsciously place upon the people, animals, objects
and situations around us.

The way we unconsciously use symbols relates to more than
simply our dream life and feeling connections with such things as a

car. Because symbol 'thinking' is now partly unconscious and links with more basic emotional responses, we often unconsciously use symbols in our body and life. A physical disability or illness can sometimes symbolise a powerful emotion or hurt the person cannot meet consciously. Often people take on a profession that symbolises important fears or attitudes they have. A Jewish doctor who worked with me as a client was the only child of two people who were the sole survivors in their families of the Holocaust. He discovered during analysis that his motivation to become a doctor arose because he knew within himself that one could be killed for simply being a Jew. Doctors were the last ones you killed. See: **unconscious**.

syringe   Intercourse; a sense of what influence other people's opinions or criticism is having on us; for some – drug dependence. See: **injection**.

table   See: **furniture**.

tablet   See: **pill**.

tadpole   Sperm; a baby, so perhaps pregnancy; our feelings about prenatal life. See: *frog* under **reptiles – lizards, snakes**.

tail   As the tail can be raised and lowered can refer to sexual excitement; the penis; what we are carrying with us from the past.

talisman   Feelings or beliefs we use to ward off anxiety, loss of confidence, or sense of inadequacy.

talking   General: sense of being in contact with whatever is depicted; expressing what one feels and thinks; standing up for what one believes or feels strongly about. Difficulty in speaking or not speaking: restrained anger or difficult feelings; anxiety or lack of confidence; absence of real contact or communication. Speaking and not being understood: feeling of not being listened to; frustration. Idioms: on speaking terms; know someone to speak to; nothing to speak of; speak as one finds; speak for someone; speak out; speaks for itself; speak volumes; speak with forked tongue; speak one's mind. See also: *mouth* under **body**; **silence**.

talking in sleep   Most people who have kept a dog have witnessed it bark while it is obviously dreaming. Calling out during a disturbing or active dream is common in humans also. Some people sleep talk so frequently, they worry in case they disturb the

388

sleep of others or say things they regret. In some cases they will even respond to questions. One such person told me that she went to her mother's room and asked her about whether or not to get married. The dreamer was single, so the subject of the talk may have been bothering her. Perhaps the most prolific and creative of sleep talkers was **Edgar Cayce** – see his entry. See: **sleep movements**.

tame   Developing a relationship with the animal aspect of Self; taking away sexual drive.

tangled   Confusion; tangle or difficult ties in a relationship. <u>Bodies tangled together pleasurably</u>: intimacy; acceptance.

tank   Defensive aggression. <u>Water tank</u>: the womb – especially if fairly small and containing fishes or tadpoles; one's inner feelings and processes.

tap   Emotions – turning them on and off; tapping one's resources; depicts how well we can get our needs satisfied.

tapestry   Reflection of one's inner condition or history; the tapestry of life experience, its richness and symmetry. See: *patterns* under **shapes**, **symbols**.

target   One's aims or motivations; the Self; vagina. <u>Idioms</u>: sitting target.

taste   Likes, dislikes, desires and standards. The words used to describe taste often refer equally as well to feelings – bitter, sweet, sour. <u>Idioms</u>: bad taste; taste blood; have a taste for; leaves a nasty taste; acquired taste.

tattoo   Indelible memory of an experience or relationship – might relate to pain also; tribal or group identity.

tax   Feeling 'taxed'; what we owe to life and society for our existence; how much of Self we want to give.

taxi   Desire for help; other people's influence in your life; help you have to pay for. See: **car**.

tea   Sociability; uplift or energising influence; allowing oneself to 'drink in' one's surroundings or experiences. See: **drink**.

teacher   See: **roles**.

teddy bear   Desire for comfort; wanting sympathy and love which cannot hurt us or respond negatively; childhood state of relationship.

teenage girl's love dreams   If you are a teenage girl, your dreams help you flower into the unique woman you potentially already are. No matter what you look like, no matter what your skin colour, you have an innate beauty. It is the secret processes of life that are transforming you into a woman. Being female is something you share with women of every race throughout history – yet *you* are unique.

There are three major themes you may notice in your dreams. One of the most important is the emergence of your sexual abilities as a woman. In all warm-blooded animals sex is not just the urge to join two bodies genitally. It also involves desires to attract and bond to a mate; the urge to have a child and the strength to care for and protect your children. Your dreams are a safe place where you practise or unfold these emerging facets of yourself. Dreams allow you to work out any difficulties in letting these qualities flower. So you will probably dream of a man you fancy and enjoy the pleasure of touching and loving. You will also encounter the fears or pains standing in the way of such a meeting.

In some dreams you may also experience being pregnant and even having a baby. These are very positive signs that you are meeting your physical and emotional changes well.

Example: 'I'm fourteen and had a dream of having a baby boy. I don't know who my husband was. I am sitting in a house with no roof and all my family come to see my baby and said it was special. It was night time. When I looked into the sky there were three moons. Two of them were shaped like a lady with a baby in her arms.' Sam (Teletext).

Sam's dream shows a great sense of beauty and ease about her ability to have a baby.

You are moving toward becoming physically, emotionally and financially independent of whoever parents you. This will show in dreams such as feeling trapped by Mum or Dad, perhaps fighting them, or even seeing them die. Such death is a way of saying you can survive alone. Sometimes these dreams of independence centre around what clothes you wear. You might be wearing other people's clothes or arguing with your mother about what you can dress in. Other people's clothes represent how you might be modelling yourself on someone else or feeling pressured to do so.

Your dreams link you with the deepest mysteries and gifts of life. Unfolding your womanhood means receiving many new powers and abilities. The power of full physical sex and pleasure; the power of emotional strength and gentleness; the power of creativity; the feeling of being a part of life and the world. Be daring enough to meet any difficulties and fears necessary to claim these powers. Use them – don't be used by them. They are yours to claim. Meanwhile, may the force – of dreams and womanhood – be with you.

teeth   See: *teeth* under **body**.

telepathy   See: **ESP and dreams**.

telephone   Desire or attempt to communicate; attempt to make contact with an aspect of oneself or someone else. Dreamer not answering phone: avoiding contact or communication; someone is trying to 'get through' to you. No reply to dreamer's call: feeling someone is out of contact with you, not aware of your feelings. 999 call: probably a crisis in your relationship or life; reaching out for help; moral dilemma. Telephone number: if it is of someone known, most likely an attempt to communicate with that person – see **numbers**. See: **fax machine**, **fax**.

Example: 'I want to telephone somebody but find the dial on the telephone will not work or I cannot find the numbers on the dial. Even though I know where the nine hole is I cannot seem to dial 999.'

telescope   Taking a 'closer look' at whatever is being viewed; making something bigger than it is.

television   TV set: the function of seeing what is going on, or what is the news from within oneself. Watching TV: watching one's internal activity, values, politics; relaxation. Television personality: see: **famous people**.

temple   See: **church**.

temptation   Conflict between different aspects of Self – perhaps sexual urges and social fears, or personal boundaries.

tennis   See: **games**, **gambling**.

tent   One's relationship with natural forces in Self; feeling of being on the move, not putting down roots; getting away from everyday responsibilities.

tests   Measuring oneself against others; self-assessment; feelings of being compared or criticised or self-criticism; stress caused by competitive work situation or need for qualifications. Medical tests: concern about health.

thaw   Change in emotional responses; forgiveness; melting of frigidity or emotional distancing through withdrawal of feelings.

theatre   General: observing the 'play' of one's own thoughts and feelings, hopes, fears and fantasies; acting something out and not being real. On stage: feeling in the public eye or wanting to be noticed; going through a 'stage' of one's life. The stage: a situation you are meeting or in the midst of, perhaps demanding you play a particular role. Looking at stage: what is claiming one's attention at present; looking within oneself; experimenting with or exploring an idea; role or situation. Idioms: set the stage for; stage fright; stage-manage; act a part; act of God; act on; catch somebody in the act; get in on the act; get one's act together; act one's age; play the fool.

thermometer Concern about health if medical thermometer; one's emotional warmth or lack of it.

thirst To have an inner need for something; to long for satisfaction, probably in regard to one's emotional or spiritual needs, but can be sexual too. See: **drink**.

throat Self-expression; vulnerability. Idioms: at each other's throats; cut-throat competition; cut one's own throat; lump in the throat; jump down someone's throat; ram something down someone's throat; stick in one's throat. See: *neck* under **body**.

thunder Repressed emotions being released; warning of emotional outburst; external difficulties. See: **storm**.

ticket The price we pay to achieve something or get somewhere; sense of right to something, therefore confidence; sometimes ability or correct view of something. Idioms: that's the ticket; just the ticket; meal ticket; work one's ticket.

tickle Attempt to release tension, to break down barriers of reserve; prelude to sexual intimacy; sexual pleasure.

tide See: **sea**.

time of day The passage of time in our life; our age; our sense of ease or pressure.

the daylight hours Our conscious waking life; our area of choice and ability to make decisions. Most dreams deal only with one day. Where several days pass in the same dream, or even longer periods: the dream is expressing periods of change; different stages of growth in one's life; or very different conditions through which one has lived or might live. Being late: feeling we have left something too late or we have missed out on something; realising we have not acted quickly enough to avert a situation; avoidance of responsibility.

afternoon and evening The end of life; middle or old age; the more subtle feeling areas of experience or relationship.

hours of the day   May refer to age; period of life, twelve noon being mid-life; something that happens at that time of the day; 11 o'clock may be the eleventh hour. See: **numbers**.

midday   Mid-life; fully awake as opposed to the unconscious.

morning   Our youth or the first part of our life; energy; enthusiasm.

night   Night can be so many things these have to be illustrated by examples. In the first example below the night depicts feelings of relaxation, pleasure and sexual encounter. This aspect of night also suggests feeling the absence of the workaday world; time for reflection and being by oneself; intimacy with others; introspection.
Night in the second example shows a period of difficult change in the dreamer's life. It represents a period of darkness or depression; loneliness; difficulties; sometimes negative feelings about old age and death.
In the third example, Sam is experiencing areas of his unconscious or unknown Self, thus the secrecy, as he probably has hidden something from himself. This aspect of night suggests turning our attention inwards to an extent where we discover insights, memories or mysteries which were previously unknown to us. These can be painful areas of our experience, or very positive and life enhancing realisations. It depicts the times in life when feelings arise from within when we are alone, or in a receptive mood – or go in search of who we are.

Example: *'Three of us were on our way to a lively night out and I suggested a short cut through Richmond Park.' Jasmine C.*

Example: *'It was a very dark night with thunder and lightning, heavy rain and high winds. I am in a waiting room at Heathrow airport.' Mrs W.*

Example: *'I was creeping through a field at night. In darkness I and others were trying to accomplish some secret act, rather as spies or underground agents might. I also remember another where I was near a house at night. There was some special reason for getting to the house. Again an "agent" sort of feeling.' Sam K.*

Idioms: it's about time; all in good time; at one time; do time; for the time being; half the time; gain time; have no time for someone; lean times; time after time; time flies; behind the times; big time. See: **dark**; **light**; **sun**.

toad   See: **reptiles – lizards**, **snakes**.

toilet   The actual room: privacy; our need for time where we are not always considering what others need or want of us, but can do what we want. If it is a bathroom and toilet: possibly includes the need for cleaning up one's sexual attitudes or general attitude to others and Self. Toilet bowl: the part of us which can deal with the body wastes and the emotions we need to discharge; female sexual organ; 'sexpot'. Going to the toilet: expressing oneself; releasing feelings, often creative; letting go of tightly held attitudes, the past, or sexuality; acceptance of one's own natural drives and needs. What we put down the toilet: what we consider to be the least important or most unpleasant aspects of ourselves or our experience; what we want to get out of our lives – my small son, who had depended for long years on a dummy, one day decided he no longer wanted to have that dependency or be seen as needing it. He took the dummy out of his mouth, put it down the toilet and flushed it away.

> *Example: 'I am in a toilet and people can see me. Sometimes the walls fall down. Once I looked around and everyone was watching me.'*

This relationship with the toilet usually shows that one needs more privacy and time to oneself.

> *Example: 'I go to the toilet and it is full up to the brim. It is disgusting and I can't go.' Alan (LBC).*

Alan went on to say he is often awake in his dreams and if anything unpleasant happens he wakes himself to avoid it.

Alan shows great difficulty in meeting the very biological, blood and guts, and sexual side of himself. This may lead to living a very intellectual or sweetness and light sort of life; occasionally suggests the body needs cleansing. Not being able to go to the toilet: as with Alan above – a difficulty in expressing the more natural and down-to-earth aspects of Self; holding back sexuality or emotions; being selfish and not sharing or 'giving' of oneself.

Example: 'I was watching my teddy bear go to the toilet. It fell down and disappeared.' Jackson S.

Jackson was very young and just learning to sit on the toilet by himself. His dream shows him meeting the fear of falling down it. He has seen things disappear for ever and this disturbs him. He uses his bear as himself. This aspect of toilet can depict the magical, hidden or unseen world into which we disappear in sleep – the unconscious.

tomato   Passion; sexuality; if dream shows body reactions, may show personal reaction to tomato as food. See: **eating**; **fruits**.

tomb   Feelings or insights about death; fears we face when beginning the meeting with contents of our own unconscious; unconscious family influences. If bodies in tomb: our own potential; aspects of Self which 'died' in the past or were buried, perhaps by the immediate needs of bringing up children or some other aspect of outer life. If trapped in tomb: illustrates a withdrawn or autistic aspect of Self – a part trapped by fears or pain; how we bury our living potential by withdrawing from difficulty, pain or *life*. See: **cemetery**; **grave**.

tools   General: practical abilities we have; suggestion of things we might need to do in our life – hammer out a situation with someone, cut away old attitudes, drill through resistances to discover our real feelings, etc.; male sexuality in different aspects.

drill   Working through the emotions and fears which resist our insight; sex when there is little feeling contact or there are fears preventing intimacy.

hammer   Aggression; desire to hammer home one's point; energy to break through resistances or break old patterns of behaviour.

saw   Energy to reshape old attitudes; wordplay on *see*; sex as the relationship meets hesitations; masturbation.

torch   Confidence in meeting the dark or unknown aspects of Self; insight. See: **searchlight**.

tornado   Emotions and urges against which we feel powerless and which may become obsessive. See: **storm**; **wind**.

torpedo   Unconscious or unadmitted sexual drive which could be destructive; unconscious aggression.

tortoise   Our vulnerable feelings or hurts which hide behind a defensive shell – perhaps of shyness, introversion or withdrawal, or could be anger. See: example in the unofficial Christ under **archetypes**; *crab* and *shell fish* under **fish**, **sea creatures**; **shell**; **snail**.

touching   General: being aware of; becoming conscious; meeting and becoming intimate; contacting. Touching also sometimes shows a linking up with something, as when a person touches a power line and gets shocked. This suggests we have 'touched' feelings or drives which are a shock to us.

Often directly or indirectly sexual, as in the example below. The absence of touching in otherwise intimate scene: can suggest lack of ability to reach out or express one's needs for contact; a passive attitude in which you want the other person, or a more automatic aspect of oneself, to take responsibility and risks. Active avoidance of touching: as illustrated in second example, shows feelings of anger. The anger may be passive, but such avoidance of contact is as vicious as hitting. The dreamer moves toward a healthier state by expressing her anger.

Touching is also a means of communicating our emotions or intentions. This can be love, anger, sympathy or, as with the third example, a statement which attempts to break down insularity. Albie's dream also shows another aspect of touching, which is its use to produce a change. Albie wanted to leave a mark, make a change in the man who is an aspect of himself.

> *Example:* '*My husband came over to me with his arm out to touch me but I was so angry I put my arm up to shield myself from his touch and then began to throw things at him to express how angry I was feeling.*' *Susie R.*

> *Example:* '*The man was so superior in his attitude, and patronisingly arrogant about the last children, that I cursed him with a touch, saying, "May you lose children of your own."*' *Albie G.*

<u>Idioms</u>: get in touch; keep in touch; lose touch; lose one's touch; out of touch; touch and go; touch someone; touched up; touch something off; touch upon; common touch; Midas touch; touch bottom; soft touch; touch wood.

tower   Something we have built or created in our life. As such it can be an outer achievement or erection of inner attitudes such as defensiveness, isolation, insularity or an attempt to reach the heights of awareness or recognition. Also male sexuality and drive which may not be expressed satisfactorily and thus be the source of aggression toward females and society. This also has the elements of insularity and defence. Occasionally heightened awareness, as in the lighthouse dream of Priestley in the entry **religion and dreams**.

> *Example:* '*The devil was trying to force me to make love to a girl. I wanted to leap off the tower and fly away, but it was high and I was frightened I would fall.*' *Quentin C.*

Quentin is fifteen and facing his emerging drive of love and sex. The woman in the tower is his idealised relationship with the opposite sex. Actual intimacy is threatening and he wants to 'fly' from it but feels this would be failure. The devil is his own life pushing to grow, but felt as threatening.

town   See: **capital**; **city**, **town**.

toy   Childhood attitude to life or people; not taking something or someone seriously, but just 'playing' at life or love; can also show an attitude of play that is positive and creative – not killing one's creativity by being too serious; the toy dream may be a way of 'playing' with emotions and sexuality which allows the dreamer to explore and mature in these areas in a safe way. Toy animal or cuddly toy: a childhood attitude to one's natural drives; one's desire for a non-threatening emotional or sexual relationship. See: **doll**; **games**, **gambling**.

track   A little-used, unconventional, or more natural way of going about something. Idioms: off the beaten track; in one's tracks; lose track of something; make tracks for; hard on someone's track; on the right/wrong track; track record; on the track of; blaze a trail. See: **railway** for railway track; **road**.

train   See: **railway**.

tramp, **drop-out**   General: the ignored or little expressed side of oneself; a threatening aspect of oneself; the 'yes but' syndrome – I would make an effort in life *but* I'm broke, people put me down, others are against me, I come from a broken home; the 'I've had a hard time in life', 'life owes me a living', feeling. In a woman's dream: may refer to the negative feelings and thoughts connected with your urge toward personal identity and success – 'a woman can't make it in the world', 'it's a man's world', 'my husband puts me down', feelings and attitudes.

transformation   Any dream in which an obvious change occurs in one of the dream figures shows transformation. Each of us go through major transformations during growth – not just physically as when we change from a toothless baby to a walking, toothy child, but also psychologically.

Example: 'On a hot summer day I was walking with a beautiful black woman through countryside. She stopped and told me she had a problem. To show me she pulled down the strap of her dress. On her shoulder the black skin was peeling to reveal golden white skin underneath. She said that if she kept seeing me she would become completely white. She was

going to ask advice from her mother about what to do. As we
walked on two black men fought with me. They wanted to take
her back to the village. I woke feeling I was winning.'
Paraphrased from The Way of The Dream, *Fraser Boa*
(Windrose).

Here the dreamer is relating well to his own feelings of sexuality and
sensuality. However, he is beginning to see a female partner as a real
person, not just as his sexuality paints her. Also, the reference to
seeking advice from the mother suggests his ability to love is still not
freed from emotional and erotic connections with his mother, and
needs transforming. One often hears people, even in their forties,
saying 'It is difficult developing a relationship with that person
because my mother doesn't like them.' The dreamer 'fights' the
opposing drives which want to take the man's love back to the
village – his childhood level of love – thus he moves toward
becoming independent in love and life. The transformation is
toward mature love and relatedness.

For a further description of the major areas and themes of
transformation, see **individuation**.

transparent   Available to insight and awareness; something we
can 'see through' – therefore suggesting gaining discernment; may
also show us feeling vulnerable because others can see parts of our
nature usually hidden – or that we are revealing more of Self.

trapped   Not being able to break free of old fears, attitudes or
relationships; being held by beliefs or religious views not conducive
to personal growth.

Example: 'After our first baby was born I had such nightmares
my doctor gave me a tranquilliser to take before going to sleep.
I have taken one at bedtime for thirty-six years! I am too afraid
not to take it, but I still have dreams.' Margaret S-W.

Although this is not a *dream* about being trapped, Margaret is
trapped by fears which she never faces. Such fears can stay with us
for a lifetime, so it is much more economical and satisfying to meet
the difficulties they represent. Margaret's fears might be represented

by a dream such as the next example.

> *Example: 'I am trapped in a small brick room with no way out.*
> *I shout for someone to help me. Then either a huge bird or*
> *creature with arms tries to catch me and I scream myself*
> *awake.' Karen S.*

Karen had lived through a divorce, an unhappy love affair, the loss of a baby. In the dream the figure who comes after she has called for help might save her, but her fears make her reject it. Perhap's Karen's feelings about men paint them as monsters. Whatever her past males may have been like, with such feelings, it is Karen herself who is the prisoner and suffers loneliness. Trapped dreams can also depict feelings we have about work, about lack of opportunity, and so on. It must be remembered that the dream puts into images one's own feelings about the situation, not the external thing itself. See: *wolf* under **animal**; **cage**, **cell**; **escape**; **holding**; **imprisoned**.

travelling   What you are doing with your life – thus your destiny or direction in life; the direction or function of your personal growth at time of dream; the movement of life through the ageing process. Travelling without a goal: having no aim in life; confused about direction; taking life as it comes. Going on holiday: moving toward giving yourself more free time; growth toward allowing yourself to fulfil your needs instead of always considering other people. Travelling to an island: becoming more independent; isolating oneself. Travelling alone: independence; loneliness. Travelling with others: involvement with others; relationship; social relationships; how you compare yourself with others; what feelings and attitudes influence you. See: **aeroplane**; **boat**, **ship**; **railway**; **road**.

treasure   The riches of the Self – the wonder, wisdom or value of one's own life in its wholeness; something one has had to face difficulties to gain, such as personal achievement, mature love, self-realisation, wholeness; something which is enormously valuable in bringing wholeness and health to oneself – such as a balancing of dry intellectual achievement with deeply felt love, or an introverted personality with outward activity.

trees   General: the tree depicts the living structure of our inner Self.
Its roots show our connection with our physical body and the earth,
our family background and influences and cultural roots; its trunk,
the way we direct the energies of our being, shows growth, sex,
thought, emotion. The branches are the abilities, directions and
many facets we develop in life – varied and yet all connected in the
common life process of our being. The tree can also symbolise new
growth, stages of life and ageing, with its spring leaves and blossom,
then the falling leaves. The top of the tree or the end of the branches
are our aspirations, the growing vulnerable tip of our personal
growth and spiritual realisation. The leaves may represent our
personal life which may fall off the tree of life – die – but what gave
it life continues to exist.

The tree is our whole life, the urge which pushes us into being and
growth. It depicts the force or process which is behind all other life
forms – but seen as it expresses in our personal existence.

The phrase 'family tree' describes a way the unconscious uses the
image of a tree to represent something that is a reality internally.
Within the unconscious there is an awareness that our present
personality is built upon the lives and character of our forebears. So
our face may be presented as upon the top or surface of the tree, but
behind our faces lie the lives of our ancestors stretching back
throughout the ages.

In some old manuscripts, pictures show a man lying on the
ground and his penis growing into a tree, with fruits, birds and
perhaps people in its protective shade. This illustrates how one's
personal life energy can branch out from its source in the basic
drives and become creativity, fruitfulness, something given to
others. The tree can also represent the spine and the different levels
of human experience – physical, sensual, sexual, hungers, emotions,
relatedness, communication, thought, self-awareness.

A wood or collection of trees: the natural forces in one's own
being, therefore one's connection with or awareness of the unconscious; other people's personal growth and connection with Self.
Dead tree: past way of life; something which was full of life for you
in the past, but is now dead; dead relative. Falling tree: sense of
threat to one's identity; loss of relative. Christmas tree or other
evergreen: the eternal aspect of our transitory experience. Human or
animal hanged on tree: personal sacrifice; the death of some part of

Self so further growth can occur – death of dependence so independence can arise; surrender; the pains and struggles, the sense of crucifixion occurring in the maturing process. Oak: strength; masculinity. Flowering tree: fertility; femininity. Idioms: top of the tree; family tree; bark up the wrong tree. See: *death and rebirth* and *the Self* under **archetypes**; second example in *wife* under **family**; fifth example in **flying**; **individuation**.

The first example in **climb** shows the tree depicting the child's sense of her life as it might develop or grow in the future. Climbing it shows her exploring what it might be like to grow up. At about eight most children unconsciously develop a philosophy which enables them to meet the difficulties of meeting the growth of self-awareness, which includes the knowledge of death at the end of life. The dreamer looks at this by having the baby fall out of the tree. Death is seen as the bluebird which flies away.

> *Example: 'I flew low over small trees which were just coming into leaf. They had beautiful, soft, green leaves. I knew it was autumn and the leaves were only just coming out because it had been a cloudy, overcast summer. I felt the leaves would have time to mature because the sun would be out in the autumn and the trees would not die.' Colin C.*

Colin dreamt this in his early fifties at a time when he felt frustrated by not being able to achieve a regular source of income or, more important, feel satisfied with what he had achieved in life. The flying shows him taking an overview of his situation. The poor summer represents his feelings that the years of his life which should have been most productive had been poor – literally, the sun had not shone on his endeavours. But he feels encouraged because he senses that his personal 'summer' is still to come, and his many endeavours – the trees – would not prove unproductive.

trespassing   Feeling that you are not respecting someone else's boundaries or wishes – or vice versa.

tunnel   Pathways you have created into your unconscious; ways you have evolved to deal with innermost feelings and memories; exploring inner ideas or tendencies; vagina or being in the womb;

strategies developed to reach our inner resources and bring them to the surface. See: last example in *death and rebirth* under **archetypes**; second example in *penis* under **body**; **corridor**; examples in **dark**; **enclosed**; **end**; **swimming**.

UFO Our mind has the ability to view our experience as a whole rather than in parts. What we sense unconsciously in this way is presented to the conscious mind as images such as UFOs or circles of light.

The ball of light or fire: this is a common waking experience as well as a dream image which occurs when the person touches their sense of wholeness as described above. We see this mentioned in the description of Pentecost – the flame on top of the head – and may account for cases of people seeing flying saucers.

> *Example: 'A flying saucer dropped a man on our lawn. He was seven feet tall and stood in a ring of light. The sky was vivid pink and a peculiar aeroplane flew over. It was the shape of a cross.' Mrs A.*

The circle, the light, the shape of the cross and the big man are all symbols of the Self. See: **dream as spiritual guide**; **hallucinations**, **hallucinogens**; **satellite**; **unconscious**.

umbilical Dependence upon others for one's needs; emotional tie to mother; prenatal life.

umbrella The coping skills we use to ward off difficult feelings and changes in circumstance.

unconscious As dreams apparently emerge from what has been named the unconscious, it is helpful to understand ideas regarding it and something of its nature.

In ancient cultures we occasionally find hints regarding the unconscious, but no definite statements as were presented by Freud. In the dream theories worked out by the Iroquois American Indians, they believed that through dreams the hidden or unconscious area of psyche makes its desires known. See: **Iroquoian dream cult**. The Greek stories of the Underworld also clearly depict common unconscious activities.

In general, however, many ancient peoples developed concepts of exterior agents such as devils, angels, spirits and God to account for phenomena which today we connect with the unconscious. The first philosopher to talk clearly of an aspect of the mind being unconscious was Leibniz (1646–1716). He observed that one often recalled at a later date some detail of experience which at the time one was unaware of. One must therefore have observed it unconsciously. So in general the word means anything we are not generally aware of in our being.

Freud's concept of an unconscious element of human nature which influenced conscious behaviour was strongly resisted. It was disturbing to many people and questioned the idea of humans being the 'captain of their soul'. The Freudian slip has become one of the popular examples of the influence of the unconscious. Saying to guests arriving at our house, 'I'm so sorry – I mean glad – you could come' suggests one's real feeling was sorrow at their arrival, not gladness. There is a story of a faculty member of Oxford University who asked the guests at a function to toast the Queen, his actual words were 'Let us toast our queer dean.' But such slips might be seen as attempts to conceal our real feelings rather than evidence of unconscious motivations.

Taking into account not only Freudian and Jungian approaches to the unconscious, but something of more recent research, the term unconscious must be taken to represent many functions and aspects of Self, rather than something we can neatly define. Therefore, we might think of the term as being like the word *body*, which means a whole spectrum of organs, functions, chemical processes, neurological events, systems, cell activities, as well as one's experience of these.

In general a helpful way of thinking about the unconscious is to realise its function in memory and skills. For instance a mass of your experience is presently not in your conscious awareness. It is therefore unconscious. But if I pose the question – What is your present home address? – what was unconscious a moment ago becomes known and communicable. Millions of other bits of information lie unconscious in you at any one moment, along with skills not being accessed and other functions not used. So in this sense your conscious Self is a tiny part of your total potential.

There is also an action of the unconscious level of mind that scans our life experience, that attempts a healing process in the psyche and, through these, urges us toward actions or experience that is more expressive of our total Self rather than the one-sidedness of conscious viewpoints. Dreams not only reflect this drive arising from wholeness, but also present potentials we have which we ignore because they lie outside our daily experience.

memory   Penfield's experiments with memory, along with the experiential side of Humanistic psychology, suggest that most if not all of our experiences are retained in a level of memory we seldom have access to. Our everyday experience of accessing parts of our memory, and only occasionally touching other parts, is an example of this. Even prenatal life has been shown to leave memory, although it is not verbal. The word unconscious can refer to the memories which we have little access to, or have not been able to recall since their inception, but which can be recalled under special circumstances.

communication   Careful research into speech shows that we constantly use a miracle of mental functioning in communicating with each other. Each sentence we hear spoken undergoes enormous forms of analysis. Each word is taken and a meaning sought. This is compared with other meanings depending on context in sentence, conversational direction, speaker and speaker's tone. At unbelievable speed, we formulate our response, with similar search and comparisons, as well as filters controlling social situation, mood, status of person being addressed, and so on. All this takes place with almost no awareness, so we can think of it as a process of the unconscious. Factors which govern subjects spoken of and choice of words are also largely unconscious.

information processing   According to modern theory, the amount of information the human brain can hold is more than is held in all the books in the Library of the British Museum. Gradually, it is becoming recognised that information gathered is not simply what we 'learn' from vocal communication, or read, or set out to learn. In fact an unimaginable amount of information gathering has gone on prior to speech and goes on at an unimaginable speed prior to school years.

Consider a small preschool child walking into the garden. It has learnt gradually to relate to muscular movement, balance and its own motivations and feeling reactions in a way enabling it to walk. It has already grasped thousands of bits of 'information' about such things as plants in the garden, the neighbour's cat, the road outside, possible dangers, safe areas. Stupendous amounts have already been absorbed about interrelationships. An idea of 'reality' in the sense of what is probable and what would be dangerously out of norm has been formed.

We gather information in ways little recognised. How our parents relate to their environment and other people is all recorded and learnt from, bringing about enormous 'programming' regarding how we later act in similar circumstances. As explained in the entry on the **dream as spiritual guide**, we have great ability to 'read' symbols, ritual, art, music, body language, architecture, drama and extract 'meaning' from them. So we have immense stores of information from these sources.

Work done with people exploring their dreams over a long period suggests that some of these information resources are never focused on enough to make conscious what we have actually learnt. Sometimes, it is enough simply to ask oneself a question to begin to focus some of these resources. Such questions as: What social attitude and response to authority did I learn at school? What feeling reaction do I get when I am in the presence of – someone you know well? These questions may help to bring to awareness aspects of information gathered but remaining unconscious. These unfocused or unconscious areas of information can explain why we have apparently irrational feeling responses to some people or situations.

the body   A lot of what we call the unconscious are basic physiological and psychological functions. For instance, in a modern house when we flush the toilet we do not have to bring a bucket of water to fill the cistern again. A self-regulating mechanism allows water to flow in and switches it off when full. This is a clever built-in function that had to be done manually at one time. Nowadays we have built into some dwellings fire sprinklers or burglar alarms. Through repeated actions over thousands or millions of years, many basic functions, or functions only switched on in emergencies, have been built into our being. We do not need to think about them, just as we do not have to give awareness to the fire sprinkling system or toilet each time we walk through a room or flush the toilet. They are therefore unconscious.

Research with animals done in connection with rewards and conditioned reflex have shown that an animal can do the ·most amazing things by gradually leading it toward a certain performance by rewarding it each time it gets nearer to the goal. It can increase the circulation of blood to its ear, slow its heart, and in fact influence body functions which were thought to be completely involuntary. Where human beings have learnt to use some of these techniques – such as raising the temperature of an arm at will, helping to increase the efficiency of the immune system – the actual processes still remain unconscious. In general, however, the functions of the body are thought to be outside of our awareness and so are one of the areas of the unconscious.

species behaviour and habits   As a species, humans have certain norms of behaviour, many of which we share with other animals. We tend to find a partner of the opposite sex and produce children. We care for our children. We have strong feelings about territory. In groups this becomes nationalism and, like ants or some group animals, we fight to defend our territory. We elect leaders and have complicated rituals regarding group status or personal 'face'. We seek outward signs of our status and wherever possible we show them.

Many individuals barely recognise these drives. Yet they are powerful enough when manipulated to gather huge armies of people who then march to their death. They are behind enormous hostility between neighbours and nations. Although irrational, and not in our best interest to be influenced by, millions of us are moved by them as if we had little will of our own. The feelings behind them, although seldom acknowledged directly by our conscious Self, are often raised to religious status. The procreative drive, the election of leaders, the parental and child-raising urges, are all to be seen in the Christian religion as the bones behind the robes and rituals. If it is not based on these mighty urges and biological drives, why does Catholicism ban the contraceptive and divorce? Or make a giant figure out of the Pope? Or worship a woman with a baby in her arms?

Dreams reveal that much of human life arises out of these patterns. The patterns are in us unconsciously. We often venerate the 'norm' of these patterns and raise them, religiously or politically, to a level of tremendous importance. The problem is that many of these patterns are no longer serving us well. They are habits developed through thousands or millions of years of repetition. While they remain unconscious we find it difficult to redirect them or even admit to their influence in our life.

There are, of course, many other aspects of the unconscious, such as memories of childhood trauma, the dream process, the image formation process and sensory apparatus. It is enough to begin with if we recognise that a lot of ourselves and our potential remains unknown to us because it remains unconscious or a part of our unconscious processes.

under, underneath   The person we are beneath our social mask; the feelings and urges we have but may not admit to others or even ourselves; the less expressed or capable side of our nature; something we hide. If dreamer is under something or someone: feeling suppressed; feeling weighed down or worried about something; feeling the underdog. If dreamer sees something under them: feeling the top dog; seeing one's inferior, not-as-capable functions or Self; looking down on others; having a wider view. Idioms: come under; down under; under one's wing; under the weather; under the thumb; under one's hat; under a cloud; under one's nose; under the counter; under the influence. See: **above**.

underground   Under the ground: the usually hidden side of ourselves; our unconscious depths of experience – ancient strata of psychological and physiological processes in us; parts of Self we have ignored or buried. Underground, subway: our journeys into what is usually unconscious in us – such as realisation of childhood traits still active in us as an adult, meeting repressed sexuality, discovery of unexpressed potential or insight; something alternative we are considering or involved in – as in 'underground' newspaper. See: **tunnel**.

undress   Revealing one's real feelings; revealing one's sexual feelings; being intimate. See: **clothes**.

unearth   Bring to consciousness; reveal to oneself or realise; become aware that one has buried feelings about a past love, old hurts, etc.

uniform   Identification with a role, such as soldier or nurse; identification or conformity with collective likes and dislikes – being 'in' with the group; social pressure to conform; feeling a sense of being accepted by a group or work situation; social correctness. See: first example in **school**.

university   Individual potential and learning ability; something important you are learning; something important you have to offer. See: **school**.

up, upper   Looking through dreams in which the words 'up', 'upwards', 'upper' or 'upstairs' are used, again and again one sees the same feeling as that expressed in the example below – getting away from being 'pulled down' by difficult feelings, by depression, by everyday duties, by difficulties in relationships, and so on. It expresses the technique we use when worried, such as reading a book, being entertained, having a drink – anything to take our attention away from the difficult feelings. This does not remove the anxieties. It would be longer lasting if we faced them and transformed them. Also moving upwards of course depicts positive change; shifting toward mental activity; gaining a wider view of things; promotion. Idioms: One up on; on the up and up; up a gum tree; up and down; ups and downs; up the pole; up the wall; up the spout; up to the hilt.

Example: 'When I was very small probably even preschool I often dreamt of flying. I was mostly dressed only in my short vest and usually floating upwards to escape adults who were clawing at my legs to pull me down.' Miss G.C.

urine, **urinate**   Release of tension; letting go of restrained feelings; release of sexual feelings; other people's sexual attitudes – or their negative sexual attitudes; the flow of life through us.

Dreams in which we try to go to the toilet but it is mysteriously locked or closed may be due to the need to pee during the night.

using symbols to change habitual life problems   One of the major aspects of dreams is their representation in symbols and drama of inner conflicts and problems. Because some dreams resolve lifelong problems, we can assume the dreams that do not solve personal difficulties, may at least be attempts to do so.

The problem solving dreams present a life situation in the form of an external event in which we participate, usually with deep emotional and mental involvement. The transformation in ourselves occurs because we are led through the experience and events of the dream to the point where a shift occurs. The dreams that do not solve problems are those that simply replay the difficulty without moving on to a change in the events to bring a shift of feelings and realisation. Once we realise that this is a fundamental process our mind uses in problem solving, we can take it up consciously and make use of it, extending its efficiency far beyond the level occurring without conscious help.

To put this into plain language, supposing painful childhood events had left someone with the habit of building a powerful shield between themselves and others. Suppose this barrier was like a great metal shield they erected every time they felt slightly hurt, thus stopping them from prolonged intimacy with others. To attempt a change in this habit, one need not wait for a dream. If the situation has been seen, the first step is to create a pictorial representation of it just as a dream does. So in this case the person could be depicted as having powerful great doors which could be shut whenever anyone came close.

The next step is to act this out alone or with one or two other people who are sympathetic to the technique. It can even be done by imagining – fantasising – the action. The person could act out closing their powerful doors and excluding people. So far this simply represents the negative habit the person has built into their life, but this is important because it makes it real for the person. The next step should be taken slowly, and with as much openness to emotions and delicate feeling responses as possible. This is to enact a shift from the problematical position. So the person might try opening their doors – but not automatically – with sensitivity to what fears, emotions they experience in doing so.

This should be repeated until it can be done with ease and without negative fears and hesitations.

utopia   Escape from our difficulties or internal pains; sense of one's own wholeness.

vacation See: **holiday**.

vaccination Ideas or feelings received from someone else – depending upon how you feel in the dream, what has been received can aid in meeting negative influences in life; influence of other people in your life; may be similar to injection and suggest sexual intercourse. See: **injection**.

vagina See: *vagina* under **body**.

valley Being down to earth; outward activity; fertility; depression or gloominess; female sex organs – Cwm in Welsh means the valley between the hills; occasionally associated with death – valley of the shadow of death.

vampire The fear associated with emotional or sexual relationships; feeling that someone is too demanding; the sense of not being able to be independent of one's parent/lover and feeling any personal independence or will is sucked away by them. We create this creature out of our own doubts or fears. If a man is afraid of sex – afraid his mother/lover will disapprove if he has any sexual feelings of his own – the fear and perhaps anger will sap any good feelings about a sexual relationship. Every time they have sex, such a man or woman will feel bad afterwards, perhaps sucked dry, even 'dead', because they still do not really wish to give of themselves. The fear or anger about not having a will of their own and still being emotionally dependent on mother/father turns back upon them, depicted as the vampire.

Example: 'I had a breach birth and arrived blue with near suffocation. When I relived this experience in therapy I felt my body trapped, and I was struggling for my life. I was imprisoned in a woman's body and it was killing me. As I witnessed this I realised like an explosion of insight how my difficulties with women and sexuality had arisen. There was no way I could happily put my dick back in a woman when one had nearly killed me.' John B.

vanish   Thoughts and feelings constantly appear and then disappear, sometimes never to be seen or captured again. This is the magical world of mind and emotion, where things emerge out of the vast world of the unconscious and vanish again. Therefore vanishing suggests one is losing awareness of something. Person or animal who vanishes: love for someone who has gone; something we realised or learnt which we have lost sight of; an autonomous part of Self which we cannot yet direct. See: **autonomous complex**.

vase   Womb; receptivity; our ability to contain something. With flowers: sense of beauty and growth emerging out of receptivity; could be brothers and sisters.

vault   The womb; our store of resources; sexual potency; memories; unrealised wisdom.

VD   Sense of uncleanness in sexual life or an unhealthy sexual attitude; feeling infected by another person's sexual attitudes; awareness of the fears and hurts that infect one's sexual life.

vermin   See: *mouse* and *rat* under **animals**; **insects**.

victim   Feeling victimised; having a passive relationship with others or one's own internal aggression; the aspect of Self which one has injured or murdered by repression or moral condemnation. See: **aggression**; **murder**; *victim* under **roles**.

village   One's childhood; quiet homely feelings; rural or unsophisticated in a business or commercial sense; past values. Village of one's birth, childhood or home: the values and attitudes which prevailed at that period. See: **town**.

vine   One's connections with family and ancestors; growth or fruitfulness of parts of Self; the spiritual in one's life. Idioms: clinging vine. See: **tree**.

violin   Innermost feelings; heartfelt feelings or urges. See: *music*; **musical instrument**.

virgin   General: state of being which is free of preconceptions; receptivity; girlhood, boyhood or innocence. In a woman's dream: oneself if still a virgin; a daughter; that one has had sex doesn't mean that one's girlhood feelings actually were met and mated with. These might very well reappear in a new relationship or in a phase of one's marriage. In a man's dream: one's feeling Self which is receptive; one's soul or psyche; the aspect of oneself which can connect with expanded awareness because it can rid itself of preconceptions.

visions   See: **ESP in dreams**; **hallucinations**, **hallucinogens**; **religion and dreams**; **unconscious**.

vitamin   Intuition about health needs; anxiety about health – hypochondria; thoughts or feelings which are healthy – for instance, the confidence which one might gain by taking vitamins, might be healthier for one than the vitamins.

voice   General: expression of oneself, not simply ideas but also subtle feelings or realisations. Spontaneous speech or a voice that speaks through or to one: our personality or mind is not a totally unified whole. We do not identify with some aspects of Self. Because we disown them, they become split from our main expression. Contacting them may be like meeting a stranger – thus in dreams they are shown as exterior to Self, or a separate voice, perhaps disembodied. Also some aspects of Self express spontaneously – see **autonomous complex**. The voice may therefore be one's intuition; expression of unconscious but not integrated parts of Self; fears; the Self being met in the dream.

Example: '*I was going mad. I was crawling around on my hands and knees and wailing and behaving in a most peculiar manner. I actually felt mad. But inside my head a tiny voice kept saying, "You aren't completely insane yet – there's still a chance." People around me kept saying to each other. "We think she's possessed by devils." My sane voice then said "Make the sign of the cross, cast out the evil spirit." I kept trying to do that but my hands wouldn't or couldn't complete the sign. I woke still feeling disturbed.' Margaret F.*

Margaret has fears about her sanity. The voice here is that of her unconscious speaking from a more whole view of her being. Such a voice may very well be the voice of one's fears and confusion, however.

Example: '*My present lover, Tony, and a man I had loved years before were standing side by side. A voice was telling me to go to Tony.' Miranda L.*

Here, Miranda's unconscious is summarising her feelings and helping her transfer her feelings of love connected with the past to her new lover.

void   See: **abyss**.

volcano   Long-held emotions or hurts. If erupting: emotional release – possibly hurts from many years past will surface, and if allowed, express in a healing way.

vomit   Discharge of feelings and ideas that one's system finds irritating or poisonous to well-being.

vortex   See: **whirlwind**, **vortex**.

voyage   A new undertaking, relationship or way of life. Sometimes the voyage of discovery into one's inner life. See: **boat**, **ship**; **travelling**.

vulture   See: **birds**.

waiter, **waitress**   See: **roles**.

waiting   Looking to others or circumstances for your cue. Idioms: waiting in the wings; lady in waiting; wait on someone hand and foot; a waiting game; lie in wait. See: *waiter, waitress* under **roles**.

wake up   To realise something; to 'wake up' to one's situation; to come out of a period of withdrawal. Idioms: rude awakening; wake up to something; wide awake.

walking   See: **postures**, **movement**, **body language**.

wall   General: our defensive attitudes; feelings of security; social barriers; boundaries created by anxiety or view of life – a nationalistic attitude might act as a barrier to seeing other viewpoints on history. Our dependence upon our physical senses gives a boundary to our awareness, and a wall may also express such a frontier of our awareness. Walls of a favourite house: might be our feelings of security in our marriage or family which give us defence against the 'storms' of life. Wall of prison or trap: fear; pain; ignorance; prejudice; anger; sense of being an outsider; family attitudes or responsibilities one feels restrained or trapped by. Idioms: drive somebody up the wall; go to the wall; writing on the wall; back to the wall; head against a brick wall; fly on the wall. See: **fence**; *wall* under **house**, **buildings**.

> *Example: 'I went to the top of the turret and saw all the men getting ready to defend the castle if attacked. They had arrows*

*and a lot of men were standing on little ledges on the outside
of the wall with no protection, and I knew they were very brave
to face an attack as sooner or later they would have been hit.'
Anna R.*

Here the wall is obviously to do with defending the dreamer against
attack. Such a wall might be made out of our aggressive feelings,
with religious dogma which might defend us against fears and
uncertainty, or from tightly controlled behaviour and emotions.

wallpaper   Surface appearance of things; the surface layers of
your own feelings and awareness; cover-up.

wand   Personal influence over others; power of suggestion; spell
we cast over another's feelings or decisions; male sexuality. Idioms:
wave one's magic wand.

wanting   Wanting is a primal drive which through socialisation we
may crush and thereby lose contact with what we want from our
own feelings and needs. In doing so we may also lose much of our
decisiveness and creativity.

*Example: 'I still want him all to myself. We never touch or kiss
or anything in the dreams, and I want him to, but would never
let on I wanted this. I am a bit coy in my dreams.' Pauline B.*

Pauline is dreaming about a past lover who she has tried to forget,
but when we underline the 'wants' we see how strong her feelings
are. Looking at dreams in this way helps us define what our desires
are.

*Example: 'The older man still wanted something from me. I
didn't want to be involved with him at all and yet had to be
polite, etc. so he wouldn't hit out at me/us. We needed some
kind of contact with this man. I lent forward and kissed him
on his face and drew back quickly as I didn't want to give
anymore than that. I had a fear that he would want more.'
Sandra O.*

Sandra had divorced an older husband and was living with a younger man. The complication of her 'wants' is shown in the dream. When it is a 'don't want' in the dream, it is helpful to change it to a positive. 'I didn't want to go with my mother' could become, 'I wanted to do my own thing.' Because what we want is complex and often in conflict, our dream characters may want something which we oppose, as in the following example.

> *Example: 'To escape from a man chasing me, I decided I must get a taxi home. Got in one driven by a woman who wanted to take me to the man who was chasing me. Woke up sweating.'* Ann G.

The female taxi driver represents Ann's urge to integrate the male part of herself, seen as the man chasing her, but Ann is in conflict with and fearful of this part of herself.

war   Internal conflicts – there might be a bloody battle between one's moral code and sexual needs for instance; or between what we allow ourselves to feel and the self-healing process which attempts to release childhood pain; or between intellect and body needs or emotions. Idioms: in the wars; on the warpath; war of nerves; declare war. See: **air raid**; *unofficial Christ* under **archetypes**; **attack**; **bomb**; **fight**; *soldier* under **roles**.

warehouse   See: *warehouse* under **house**, **buildings**.

warmth   Often appears alongside sunlight and comfort in dreams; physical comfort and well-being; supportive family feelings; love, cheerfulness or hopefulness; feeling of emotional situation 'warming up'.

warning   Warning bell, voice or signal: intuition that something needs attention in our life, internally or externally. Being warned by someone else or voice: sense of not living up to our own standards; something we have noticed unconsciously but need to become consciously aware of.

washing   General: getting rid of negative feelings such as despair or self-doubt; fears about health – neurotic phobias about one's own wholeness. Washing hair: changing one's attitude; altering the way one thinks about something or one's viewpoint. Washing vagina or penis: clearing negative sexual feelings; dealing with the results of pent-up sexuality or reproductive drive. Hanging up washing: allowing change to come into one's life; letting other people see one's new attitudes. In a mother's dream: may refer to caring for the family emotionally. Washing hands: getting rid of feelings about something you have done or been involved in. Idioms: all come out in the wash; lost in the wash; it won't wash; wash dirty linen in public; wash one's hands of. See: **bath**; **soap**.

wasp   See: **insects**.

watch, **wrist**   If a present probably relates to giver or circumstances of giving. See: **clock**; **presents**; **time**.

watching   Being aware of; observing something – perhaps something you have noticed from everyday events but not made conscious, or something about Self; watching out for what other people are doing to you – suspicion; learning something or trying to understand. Idioms: be on the watch for; watch out; watch one's step; watch over; watch someone like a hawk. See: **seeing**, **saw**, **sight**.

water   General: emotions, moods and flow of feeling energy – because of the nature of water it lends itself to depicting aspects of how we relate to emotions. For instance one can 'drown' in or feel swept away by some emotions. At other times we can feel cleansed and refreshed. It also represents our potential to experience many emotions because water can take any shape or move in so many ways. How we relate to the water shows how we are meeting our emotions and moods.

Entering water: entering into strong feelings such as might arise in a relationship or new job; sexual relationship; emotions which might stand in one's way – as a deep lake might, or turgid water. Deep water: the depths of one's inner life. Hot water: strong emotions; facing difficult situations such as social criticism. See example in Introduction. Electricity and water: emotions which can generate very powerful reaction to a situation such as jealousy or anger.

Idioms: make water; muddy the waters; tread water; water something down; turn on the waterworks; water under the bridge; hold water; in hot water; head above water; pour cold water onto something. See: **fluid**; **rain**; **river**.

Example: 'I am in deep water, no evidence that it is the sea. I am wearing my heavy brown coat. I have no fear, no feeling of cold and I pleasantly just sink.' Mrs B.

Mrs B. is in her eighties and is preparing for death in her dreams. The water in her dream has the feeling of being womb-like, suggesting that she senses death as a return to a womb-like feeling state with possible rebirth.

Example: 'I was then standing in front of a series of glass water tanks. I had apparently written an article about the balance between intellect and emotion, which had presented emotion in a way to show its equal value with intellect. The tanks had water flowing through them with a series of valves. This demonstrated the different relationships between intellect and emotion. Some tanks were beautifully clear and colourful, showing the right balance. The unbalanced ones had weed growing in them. I was then in a lift with a young woman. We moved close together and kissed. This moved my feelings so much I felt a great melting feeling in my abdomen, and a lot of body sensation against her body.' Anthony F.

Anthony's dream perfectly illustrates how water refers to the emotions and flowing body feelings.

Example: 'I was in a hospital ward – maybe for children. I was there to help them. In the ward was a large oblong tank full of water. I got into the water. I realised all the sick people in the ward bathed in the water – not soap just immersion. This produced feelings of revulsion. I felt I would take into myself their sickness. I also thought that if I drank the water it would show the patients a positive attitude towards their sickness. They would no longer be afraid and this would be a factor in their healing.' Anthony F.

Another of Anthony's dreams in which he is looking at how to meet anxious feelings about his health. He sees that a more positive conscious attitude heals the childhood fears.

water creatures   See: **fish**, **sea creatures**.

weapons   Guns, rockets, knives, axes, spears, etc., depict our desire to hurt someone, or if we are being shot or hurt in the dream, how we have internalised our own aggression or past hurts or fear of being hurt; also defence against fears or being hurt. If we shoot or stab someone or something, we need to consider what part of ourselves we are turning our aggression upon. If we kill or injure a recognisable person, we may be harbouring the desire to hurt or kill that person, even if only in reputation. All weapons can represent male sexual drive or aggressive sexuality. The situation in which the action takes place defines what the weapon expresses. Ineffective weapons depict feelings of inadequacy. A work tool used as a weapon depicts our skill or authority turned against ourselves or someone else – as might happen if a doctor got sexual favours through his position. See: **rocket**; **shot**.

arrow   Something that has really got into us, like hurtful words or actions; or being pierced by a powerful emotion such as love; turning our attention inwards in a wounding way; sometimes a message, perhaps of love or endeavour.

gun   Penis; male sexuality; anger; confidence in defending oneself against criticism, etc.; fears or anxieties; attitudes we use as a defence against our own emotions or realisations – a man might feel depressed about growing old and defend himself against these with positive thoughts; also the bulldozer emotions we sometimes use against others, like a pistol held to their head. When shot by gun: feeling hurt, wounded; being the target of criticism or hurtful remarks; fear of sex. Idioms: shot in the arm; shot across the bows; shot to pieces; shot in the dark; long shot.

knife   Penis, cutting intellectual insight, aggression – depending on how used in the dream; an attempt to wound someone. Idioms: get one's knife into someone; on a knife edge; under the knife – surgery; cut it out; cut the air with a knife.

sword   Because it often has a cross as a handle the sword has mixed meanings. Erection; social power; justice; spiritual strength. Sword hanging by a thread: threats hanging over one. When sheathed: the soul or self in the body. Heirloom: a heritage of attitudes from one's family; willpower or discrimination. Consider background of dream for meaning. Idioms: cross swords with someone; double-edged sword; sword of Damocles. See: **cross**.

See: **attack**; **fight**; **shot**; **war**.

weather   Changing external situations, or internal response to situations; our moods and emotions. The following idioms give indications of the meaning. Idioms: sunny disposition; things don't look so bright; things will brighten up; it never rains but it pours; like living under a cloud; things are a bit rough/stormy/overcast. See: **cloud**; **flood**; **lightning**; **rain**; **snow**; **thunder**.

web   A sticky situation you feel yourself in; feeling caught up in something that might trap you; a web of lies; the symmetry of the Self.
  Quoting from *Women's Ways of Knowing* (Basic Books), 'webs and nets imply opposing capacities for snaring or entrapment and for rescuing or safety. They also suggest a complexity of relationships and the delicate interrelatedness of all so that tensions and movement in one part of the system will grow to be felt in all parts of the whole. In the complexity of a web, no one position dominates over the rest. Each person – no matter how small – has some potential for power; each is always subject to the actions of others. It is hard to imagine other ways of envisioning the world that offer as much potential for protection to the immature and the infirm.' See: *spider* under **insects**.

wedding   See: **marriage**, **wedding**.

weeds   Things you have developed in your life which are not contributing much or might even be stopping more positive personal growth; misplaced endeavour or energy. See: **plants**.

weight   General: seriousness; sense of a burden or responsibility; importance. Weight of someone on dreamer: feeling they are being too dependent or a burden in one's life. Idioms: carry weight; pull one's weight; throw one's weight around; worth one's weight in gold. See: **fat**.

well   Access to one's deepest resources of life – therefore personal spiritual wisdom or information from the unconscious; the source of one's 'well-being'; the vagina; a view into one's depths. See: **water**.

werewolf   See: **animals**; **vampire**.

west   Where the sun sets – death or the end of something; physical life; down-to-earth Self.

whale   See: **fish**, **sea creatures**.

wheat   Wisdom of experience; the harvest of life experience; fruitfulness.

wheel   The ability to meet changes, to be mobile. Large water or fun-fair wheel: the ups and downs of life; the wheel of life – birth and death; karma. Idioms: behind the wheel; set the wheels in motion; take the wheel; wheeling and dealing; wheels within wheels; oil the wheels; spoke in one's wheel. See: **shapes**, **symbols**.

whip   Hurtful remarks; angry feelings; sexuality which has as its base a desire to hurt; desire to control through threats or pain. Idioms: whip hand; whipping boy.

whirlwind, **vortex**   Conflict – energies storming in one.

white person   Depends on skin colour of dreamer. If black: feelings about whites; or if known, what you feel about them. If white: same as any person dream.

widow   Married woman dreaming of being a widow: fears of losing husband; desire to be free of husband.

wife   See: **family**.

wig   False ideas; unnatural attitude. <u>If dreamer wears wig</u>: feelings about being bald. See: *hair* under **body**.

wind   The movement of consciousness or mind; the hidden influences in our life; ideas and conceptions which move us. <u>Flying with the wind</u>: uplift of sexual energies into the mind to become a wider view or an integration of experience; upliftment. See: **tornado**.

window   See: **house**, **buildings**.

wine   See: **alcohol**.

winter   Emotional coldness; an unfruitful period of one's life; old age; death.

wireless   <u>General</u>: what we listen to or hear going on around us or inside us; company; other people's 'noise'. <u>Inside wireless</u>: our mind; inside oneself.

wise man   Father; the Self; what we have learnt from our active experience. See: *the Self* under **archetypes**; example in **cliff**.

witch   The fears or difficult feelings and relationship habits we have developed in our relationship with our mother. Because these feelings are now part of ourselves, if female, we can of course become the witch in relationship to someone else. Also vindictiveness, jealousy, etc.

> *Example: 'I talked about my mother, she was standing before me in full anger and blaming me for bringing out the witch in her. She said look at my eyes, they were horrid to see, all red and angry and she was dark.' Lesley M.*

wizard   See: *magician* and *conjurer* under **roles**.

woman   A woman in a woman's dream: an aspect of herself, but often a facet of herself she is not immediately identifying with. The example below helps make this plain. Mo explored her feelings about the dream characters. It all fell into place when she asked herself what she had 'lost' recently. She had left a lover of some years standing. This gave her a lot more freedom and new opportunity, depicted by the baby, but also muddled feelings of loss. Her Australian friend represents her feelings of grieving for the 'death' of her relationship. Her muddled feelings arise because she both loves the new life which opens up, but grieves the death of her romance.

A woman's sister and female children: particularly used to represent herself. The character of the dream woman – loving, angry, businesslike, lazy, sexual – give a clue to what part of the dreamer it is referring to. If the dream woman is a person known well, the above can still be the case, but the woman may represent what the dreamer feels about that person. A woman younger than the dreamer: oneself at that age. An older woman: could be the dreamer's mother; her feelings about ageing; her sense of inherited wisdom. Two women and the dreamer: conflicting feelings or drives. One woman one man: behaviour patterns arising from parental relationship. A goddess or holy or Oriental woman: the dreamer's highest potential; what she is capable of but may not yet have lived; her intuition and wisdom transcending her own personality.

In a man's dream: his present relationship with his own feeling and intuitive Self; his sensitivity and contact with his unconscious through receptivity; or how he is relating to his female partner. The latter is especially so if the woman in the dream is his partner. An old woman: usually the dreamer's mother. The woman, because she is his feelings, is obviously also his sexual desires and how he meets them. A younger woman: can depict his desires for a woman of that age, or his more vulnerable emotions. Two women and the dreamer: an 'eternal triangle' situation; conflicting feelings. If one woman and one man: depicting relationship; pattern of behaviour developed in relationship with parents. Oriental woman: the aspect of mind and emotions that links the conscious personality with its unconscious transcendental wisdom and intuition, and perhaps the capacity to love.

*Example: 'I gave birth to a baby girl I named Charlotte. I had
mixed emotions about this, uncertainty, excitement. I wanted
to share the news with my friends. I phoned one, a woman in
Australia. I told her with enthusiasm, but she listened quietly
and remained silent. I felt uneasy, then she said "We lost Luke"
– her son – "the week before." I then woke with muddled
feelings.' Mo.*

*Example: 'On a raised mobile platform a goddess stood. I loved
her and flew to her, skimming above the heads of the people.
I talked to her. She told me the only love I could receive from
her was that which I gave to a human woman. Inasmuch as
I gave love to a human female, she would love me. She was all
women.' Andrew P.*

The example shows Andrew meeting his archetypal conception of a
woman, his ideal. But he understands that you cannot love an ideal.
His love must find a real woman. Through a real love he would call
love from out of himself, out of his unconscious reserve.

For the conditions or situations of the woman, see under
appropriate entries, such as **illness**, **murder**, **swimming**, etc. See:
the great mother under **archetypes**.

womb   General: the state of existence or consciousness in which
we have grown; the state or condition prior to our development of
personality – this can be personal, but it also relates to all human
creatures, so is historical or evolutionary. It is a condition without
ego, with a sense of being life itself; fears connected with birth and/
or sex. Going back to the womb or to the condition of withdrawal
or autism: regression to the 'womb' state of awareness – therefore
perhaps a time of not being able to meet the stress of having a
personality with self-awareness – a time of gaining respite and
perhaps touching one's roots of being in order to gain new strength.

So much of our foundations of experience are connected with our
experience of prenatal life and birth that we may need to touch these
experiences to heal or free parts of our nature for further growth.
See: **balloon**; *nest* under **birds**; *vagina* under **body**; **breath**;
catacomb; *blue* under **colour**; **dark**; **deep**; **descending**; **hole**;
hollow; example in *room* under **house**, **buildings**; **igloo**; **individ-**

uation; **receptacle**; **recurring dreams**; **river**; **sack**; *under the sea* under **sea**; **suitcase**; **tank**; **tunnel**; **water**.

wood Wooden things: the past, or structures of thought or behaviour we have built, which originally had life but are now habitual; being 'wooden' lacking life or feeling. Wooden room or house: a part of our nature which has been carefully cultivated or created out of past experience. For woods see **tree**.

wood with trees Allowing oneself to be natural, and for the mind and emotions to move in their own way.

wool Warmth; gentleness; motherhood; protective fuzziness of thought and feeling; ideas. Knitting wool: creativity; ideas or thoughts we knit together. Idioms: Wool-gathering; woolly thinking; pull the wool over someone's eyes.

word analysis of dreams Having written a dream down, by using highlighting pens to make all matching words the same colour, one can immediately see the main issues in some dreams.

> *Example:* 'We walk around, go upstairs, and I notice a staircase leading to a room or rooms. It goes up square, about eight steps in a flight, but round and round – spiral. I am scared by them, don't want to go up, but am curious. We move in and nobody but myself has really taken any notice of the stairs. Nobody has been up. In one dream I try to go up but the children are scared for me. They plead, "Don't go up Mum, just forget them." Then I wake. In the next dream I wait till they are asleep. Halfway up I am terrified but have to go on. Then I wake. Next dream I got up there. Then I woke.' Ann H.

Ann's dream theme recurs, so is important to her. In marking just some of the words we see that the 'up' or 'go up' is important. Childhood fears hold Ann back for a while, but she dares to climb. If we look at the entries for **climb** and **stairs**, we see they depict taking steps toward exploring the unknown, daring to explore one's potential or opportunities.

By marking the words in this way we might also highlight certain statements otherwise hidden in the dream. Particularly watch out for the connections with the word 'I', such as I want; I do; I will; I have; I know; I cannot; etc.

> *Example: 'I want to withdraw' – 'I was full of sadness but was trying not to show it' – 'I felt keyed up and ready to fight.'*

Taking such statements out of context and looking for connections with everyday feelings or situations often throws considerable light on the dream. If what you realise is then considered in connection with the plot of the dream, the viewpoint your unconscious has on the situation might become evident. For instance, the statement 'I felt keyed up' occurred within a classroom situation and helped the dreamer understand the anger generated at school. See: **amplification**; the comments on **dream processing** in the Introduction; **dream processing**; **plot of the dream**; **postures**, **movement**, **body language**; **settings**; **symbols and dreams**.

wordplay, puns   According to Freud, one of the major processes of the unconscious is condensation. This means that within one element in a dream, such as the strange room we dream we are in, or the unusual name a person has in the dream, are condensed many associated emotions, memories or ideas. Talking about a pea pod which appeared as part of her imagery, Constance Newland shows how it represented her father's penis. The pea associated with pee or urine, and the pod with a seed carrier, the testicles.

Freud gives the example of a patient who dreamt he was kissed by his uncle in an 'auto'. The patient immediately gave his own association as auto-eroticism. A psychologist whose patient dreamt she was going on a trip on a boat called 'Newland' correctly inferred that the patient was getting better because the name suggested new territory traversed.

One woman dreamt about a busy intersection and realised it was referring to inter-sex-on. So we need to consider how we might be unconsciously playing with words, then check if this helps us gain insight. Phrases are also used in the same way. We might see such words as 'I felt a prick', 'keeping it up was difficult', 'dead end' and so on, in writing down our dream. See: introduction to **colours**; **names of person or place**.

work   At work: concerns or issues connected with one's work or lack of it. Working: actively trying to change a situation in one's life – one might be working at one's marriage or learning something, depending on dream surroundings.

> *Example: 'I am working in a hospital in outpatients. Nobody is there. My two children appear. I know I have to find them somewhere to sleep. I lay them on seats, tell the only nurse I can find that I am going to find them a bed. I know where the children's ward is but I can't find it. When I eventually find it all the side rooms are filled. I know I have been a long time so I start to panic, worried my children are missing me and worried night sister will have found them. I pass a military meeting. As I continue the men come out and I get caught in the cross-fire and am shot in the leg. I am now terrified. I have to get back to the children. Night sister must have found them by now and if not what will they be doing? When I got back they are there with night sister.' Laramie F.*

Laramie works as a nurse, was divorced just prior to the dream and was obviously concerned how her work affected her children. This internal conflict – the cross-fire – injures her confidence, hence the shot leg. Idioms: have one's work cut out; set to work; worked up; work like a horse; work off; work out; dirty work; donkey work; spanner in the works.

world   The sphere of one's experience; one's own world of awareness and activity; the way one experiences the world/life; the personal interaction one has with the 'world'. End of the world: end of the way you have been experiencing or relating to life; fears or feelings about death; anxieties about external events; big change in one's personal growth. Other worlds or dimensions: new ways of experiencing oneself and life; new paradigm; breakthrough to new realisations. Idioms: a world of; on top of the world; out of this world; think the world of; best of both worlds; small world.

worm   Feeling insignificant or ineffective; something you treat as insignificant, the penis. Worms: ill health; health worries. Idioms:

even a worm will turn. See: **maggots**.

worship   Worshipping: opening oneself to the influence of what is being worshipped – an idea, a person, an object. Worshipped: inflated sense of Self.

wound   Hurt feeling; trauma from the past. If wounding someone: desire to hurt someone or to destroy some aspect of oneself. If pierced: apart from hurt feelings, may also show one being opened by new experiences, even love.

writing   Thinking about something; sorting out one's ideas and decisions; leaving one's mark in life; expressing one's inner feelings and ideas; one's personal history. What someone you know has written: what you feel about them; their influence in your life and mind.

x Sometimes represents an error; X marks the spot; ten; the cross; an unknown quantity.

x-rays Something influencing your life unconsciously; seeing into a situation or oneself; fear of illness.

yacht See: **boat**.

yawn Boredom; tiredness; unconscious trying to say something – yawning is a movement arising from the self-regulatory process. See: **sleep movements**.

yeast Ideas or intangible influences which can yet change one's life or situation.

yes Wherever we say 'yes' to a person or situation in a dream, we are opening to the influence of that aspect of ourselves. It is important to define what leads us to agreement in the dream. Is it that we say yes because of feelings that we ought, should, or it was expected? Was the yes out of anxiety? Was it said because that was what we agreed with, or was the most useful response? See: **no**.

yogi The Self; withdrawal from outward activity.

youth Oneself at that age; the attitudes and responses developed at that age. If dreamer younger than youth: one's potential of growth and change; the part of Self growing toward that age. See: **boy**; **girl**.

433

zero   See: **numbers**.

zip   Connections with others; one's ability to be 'open' or 'closed' with others.

zodiac   Where an animal or figure of one's birth sign appears – such as a lion in a Leo's, bull in Taurean's, twins in Geminian's dream – this frequently represents the dreamer's basic personality traits. Often it depicts the natural urges the personality meets in itself, but which may not be expressed. How one deals with the animal or figure shows one's relationship with what is felt to be one's basic Self and potential. See: **planet**.

zoo   One's natural urges and instincts, such as sexuality, parental caring, social grouping. What is happening to the animals shows how one is relating to the natural side of oneself, and how it is responding to one's conscious attitudes and activities. Life processes in us are not inert. They constantly respond to what we do and what we are. See: **animals**.

Bibliography

Aaronson and Osmond, *Psychedelics*, Doubleday, 1970.

Adler, Gerhard, *Studies in Analytical Psychology*, International Universities Press, 1967.
Adler's view of dreams.

Ackroyd, Eric. *A Dictionary of Dream Symbols*, Blandford, 1993.

Alex, William, *Dreams, the Unconscious and Analytical Therapy*, C. G. Jung Inst. of SF, 1992.

Becker, Raymond De, *The Understanding of Dreams*, Hawthorn, 1968.

Bro, Harmon, *Edgar Cayce On Dreams*, Warner Books, 1970.

Bro, Harmon, *Edgar Cayce – Seer Out Of Season*, Aquarian, 1990.
Biography of Edgar Cayce.

Brook, Stephen, *The Oxford Book of Dreams*, Oxford University Press, 1983.
A dream anthology, from pre-Christian to present times.

Bunker, Dusty, *Dream Cycles*, Para Research, 1981.

Caldwell, W.V., *LSD Psychotherapy*, Grove Press, 1969.
Caldwell travelled widely in the USA and Europe visiting and studying results in the practices or clinics of psychiatrists using LSD

as a psychotherapeutic tool. In the book he gives an excellent synthesis of the mass of information and experience gathered. In doing so he maps the heights, depths and fantasies of the human psyche in a way that is beyond any particular school of thought. Such a map is of great use to anyone seriously investigating dreams.

Campbell, Joseph, *Myths To Live By*, Paladin, 1988.
Wonderful reading, although not directly about dreams. Campbell shows how human beings create myths, no matter what their culture or historic period. This myth-creating faculty is obviously linked with dreaming and portrays life and death as the unconscious sees them.

Campbell, Joseph, *The Portable Jung*, The Viking Press, 1974.

Cannegeiter, Dr C.A., *Around The Dreamworld*, Vantage Press, USA, 1985.

Capacchione, Lucia, *The Creative Journal*, Newcastle Pub. Co., 1993.

Caprio and Hedberg, *At a Dream Workshop*, Paulist Press, 1988.

Chetwynd, Tom, *Dictionary for Dreamers*, Paladin, 1974.
Good dictionary.

Circlot, J.E., *A Dictionary of Symbols*, Routledge & Kegan Paul, 1962.

Clift, J.D. and W., *Symbols Of Transformation*.

Cooper, J.C., *An Illustrated Encyclopaedia of Traditional Symbols*, Thames & Hudson, 1993.

Corriere, Karle, *Dreaming and Waking*, Peace Press 1980.
Exploring the idea of whether, if we meet the feeling content of dreams, they gradually cease to be symbolic. A landmark in dream theory.

Cotterell, Arthur, *A Dictionary of World Mythology*, OUP, 1986.

Coxhead and Hiller, *Dreams – Visions of the Night*, Art & Imagination, 1993.

Crisp, Tony, *Do You Dream?* Spearman, 1971.

Crisp, Tony, *Dream Dictionary*, Optima, 1990.

Crisp, Tony, *Mind and Movement*, C.W. Daniel Co Ltd, 1987.
Considers the problem solving or self-regulating psychological and physiological process underlying dreaming. It also considers how the process which produces dreams underlies many other puzzling phenomena such as ESP, abreaction, flashbacks to past events, etc.

Crisp, Tony, *The Instant Dream Book*, C.W. Daniel Co Ltd, 1984.
Explain techniques which can be used to transform the fears and emotions of dreams without analysing them. It also considers the different areas of dream activity such as body dreams, problem-solving, extra sensory, sexual dreams, etc.

Crisp, Tony, *Liberating The Body*, Aquarian, 1992.
Using the dream process to use resources of the unconscious for health and intuition. An update of *Mind and Movement*.

Dee, Nerys, *Your Dreams and What They Mean*, Aquarian, 1984.

Delaney, Gayle, *Living Your Dreams*, Harper & Row, 1988.

Diamond, Edwin, *The Science of Dreams*, Eyre & Spottiswoode, 1962.
A fascinating collection of researched information on dreams.

Edinger, Edward, *Ego and Archetype*, Shambhala, 1991.

Evans, Christopher, *Landscapes of the Night*, Victor Gollancz, 1983.
The computer theory of dreaming, with excellent survey of other theories.

Fagan and Shepherd, *Gestalt Therapy Now*, Harper Colophon, 1970.
Contains an explanation of Fritz Perls' approach to achieving insight into one's dreams.

Faraday, Ann, *Dream Power*, Hodder & Stoughton, 1972.
Good basic textbook, written for lay people, but intelligently.

Faraday, Ann, *The Dream Game*, Harper & Row, 1974.

Fay, Maria, *The Dream Guide*, Centre For The Healing Arts, 1978.

Fordham, Freida, *Introduction To Jung's Psychology*, Penguin Books, 1972.

von Franz, Marie-Louise, *On Death and Dreams*.

von Franz, Marie-Louise, *The Way Of The Dream*, Windrose, 1988.
Recorded conversations with von Franz taken by Frazer Boa – a transcript of the film *The Way Of The Dream*.

Freud, Sigmund, *The Interpretation of Dreams*, Allen & Unwin, 1955.
The first of all modern dream books.

Fromm, Erich, *The Forgotten Language*, George Allen & Unwin, 1952.
This is subtitled *An introduction to dreams, fairy tales and myths*.

Garfield, Patricia, *Creative Dreaming*, Ballantine, 1974–81 edition.
Clear description of taking dreams to satisfaction.

Gaskell, G.A., *Dictionary of All Scriptures and Myths*, Crown, 1960.

Gendlin, Eugene, *Let Your Body Interpret Your Dreams*, Chiron, 1986.

Green, Celia, *Lucid Dreams*, IPR, 1968.
The foundation research on lucidity in dreams.

Hadfield, J.A., *Dreams and Nightmares*, Penguin, 1954.
Hadfield proposes a biological theory of dreams which stands between Freud, Jung and more modern theories. It is also an interesting book.

Hall, Calvin S., *The Meaning of Dreams*, Harper & Row, 1953.
Hall worked a lot with series of dreams and with content analysis.
This is the result of his research, written in easily readable form.

Hall, Calvin S., *Jungian Dream Interpretation: A Handbook of Theory and Practice*,

Hamilton, Edith, *Mythology*, New American Library, 1991.

Hannah, Barbara, *Encounters With The Soul: Active Imagination*, Sigo, 1981.

Harding, M. Ester, *The I and the Not I*, Princeton UP, 1965.

Harris, Thomas, *I'm OK – You're OK*, Pan Books, 1975.

Heyer, G.R., *Organism of The Mind*, Kegan Paul, 1933.
Although Heyer is not writing directly about dreams, the book is an interesting commentary on what was being discovered by Analytical Psychology in the early part of the twentieth century.

Hillman, James, *Re-Visioning Psychology*, Harper, 1975.

Hobson, J. Allan, *The Dreaming Brain*, Penguin, 1990.
Latest information on research into dreams and the brain. A good section on understanding dreams – not as things with hidden meanings, but as straightforward expressions of our own unique Self.

Hodgson and Miller, *Self Watching*, Century, 1982.

Hubbard, Ron, *Dianetics*, Bridge, 1985.

Jacobi, Jolande, *The Way Of Individuation*, Hodder & Stoughton, 1967.
Explanation of Jung's concept of the stages in becoming a person.

Jobes, Gertrude, *Dictionary of Mythology Folklore and Symbols, Parts 1 and 2*, Scarecrow, 1962.

Johnson, Robert A., *Inner Work: Using Dreams and Active Imagination for Personal Growth*, Harper & Row, 1986.

Jung, Carl, *Dreams*, Ark Paperbacks, 1986.
Very technical consideration of the subject.

Jung, Carl, *Man and His Symbols*, Aldus, 1964.
The breadth and depth of dreams. It is in paperback, excellent reading.

Jung, Carl, *Modern Man in Search of a Soul*, Kegan Paul, 1933.

Jung, Carl and Wilhelm, Richard, *Secret of the Golden Flower*, Kegan Paul, 1942.
Jung's commentary on this ancient Chinese book on meditation is wonderful reading for those seriously interested in their own inner life.

Kelsey, Morton, *Dreams – A Way to Listen To God*, Paulist Press US, 1978.

Kent, Caron, *The Enigma Of The Body*, an unpublished manuscript.

Kent, Caron, *The Puzzled Body*, Vision Press, 1969.

Kluger, Yechezkel, *Dreams and Other Manifestations of the Unconscious*.

Langs, Robert, *Decoding Your Dreams*, Unwin Hyman, 1989.
A good basic handbook on learning to discover the wealth of information and wisdom in one's own dreams.

Layard, John, *The Lady Of The Hare*, Faber & Faber, 1944.

Leach, Maria, *Standard Dictionary of Folklore Mythology and Legend*, as author, 1949.

Lee, S.G.M. and Mayes, A.R. (eds), *Dreams and Dreaming*, Penguin, 1973.

Lincoln, J.S., *The Dream in Primitive Cultures*, The Cresset Press, 1935.

Ling and Buckman, *Lysergic Acid and Ritalin in The Cure of Neurosis*, Lambarde Press, 1964.

MacKenzie, Norman, *Dreams And Dreaming*, Bloomsbury, 1989.

Mahoney, Maria, *The Meaning in Dreams and Dreaming*, Citadel Press US, 1987.

Martin, P.W., *Experiment in Depth*, Routledge & Kegan Paul, 1964. Martin was one of the early pioneers, along with Rev. Leslie Weatherhead, who started helping people to explore their own dreams adequately – i.e. without the psychiatrist.

Mathews, Boris, *The Herder Symbol Dictionary*, Chiron Publications US, 1993.

Mattoon, Mary Ann, *Understanding Dreams*.

Mindell, Arnold, *Dreambody: The Body's Role in Revealing The Self*, Sigo Press, 1982.

Mindell, Arnold, *Working With The Dreaming Body*, 1984.

Moon, Sheila, *Dreams of A Woman*, Sigo, 1991.

Murray, Alexander, *Who's Who in Mythology*, Studio, 1992.

Newland, Constance, *Myself and I*, Frederick Muller Ltd, 1963. Suffering frigidity, Constance Newland successfully underwent a number of psycho-analytical sessions using the drug LSD. The connection with dreaming is the enormously rich and potent fantasies she met and dealt with during her analysis. The book is therefore a powerful description of the world one meets in dreams, and the personal fears and forces which underlie the strange imagery of the unconscious.

O'Conner, Peter, *Dreams And The Search For Meaning.*

Oswald, Ian *Sleep*, Penguin, 1966.
The great landmark in researched basis of sleep and dreams.

Partridge, Eric, *Origins*, Routledge & Kegan Paul, 1966.

Rainer, Tristine, *The New Diary*, Angus & Robertson, 1980.

Rawson, Wyatt, *The Way Within*, Vincent Stuart, 1965.
Interesting results of a dream group working together over some years. Arising from the work of P.W. Martin.

Reed, Henry, *Getting Help From Your Dreams*, Inner Vision.

Reich, Wilhelm, *The Function of the Orgasm*, The Noonday Press, 1961.

Rennick, Teresa, *Inner Journeys*, Turnstone Press, 1984.
Handbook on the use of visualisation and fantasy in problem-solving and personal growth. It is useful to work with dream images in this way, especially in taking the dream forward toward satisfaction.

Rossi, Ernest, *Dreams And The Growth Of The Personality*, Pergamon, 1972.

Russon, Richard, *Dreams Are Wiser Than Men.*

Sanford, John A., *Dreams and Healing*, Paulist Press US, 1978.

Sechrist, Elsie, *Dreams– Your Magic Mirror*, Cowles, 1968.
Expressive of the Edgar Cayce view of dreams.

Shohet, Robin, *Dream Sharing*, Thorson, 1985.
Working as a dream group.

Stafford and Golightly, *LSD – The Problem Solving Drug*, Award and Tandem Books.

Stevens, William Oliver, *The Mystery of Dreams*, George Allen & Unwin, 1950.
Examples of different types of dreams.

Talbot, Michael, *The Holographic Universe*, Grafton Press, 1991.
Not directly about dreams, but fascinating reading for those trying to understand the dimension out of which dreams occur, and occasionally reach beyond the normal.

Tart, Charles, *Altered States of Consciousness*, Doubleday Anchor, 1969.
Has a whole section on dreaming and self-induced dreams.

Taylor, Jeremy, *Dreamwork*, Paulist Press, 1983.

Ullman and Krippner, *Dream Telepathy*, Turnstone, 1973.
Researched results of telepathy during dreaming.

Ullman and Limmer, *The Variety of Dream Experiences*, Delacorte, 1979.

Ullman and Zimmerman, *Working With Dreams*, Crucible, 1989.

deVries, Ad, *Dictionary of Symbols and Imagery*, North Holland Pub. Co., 1974.

Walker, Barbara G., *The Woman's Encyclopaedia of Myths and Secrets*, Harper & Row, 1983.

Weatherhead, Leslie, *Psychology In Service Of The Soul*, Epworth Press (Sharp), 1929.

West, Katherine L., *Crystallising Children's Dreams*.

Whitmont and Perera, *Dreams: A Portal to the Source*, Routledge, 1991.

Williams, Strephon K., *Jungian-Senoi Dreamwork Manual*, Aquarian Press, 1991.

Wiseman, Ann Sayre, *Nightmare Help*.

Zeller, Max, *The Dream, The Vision Of The Night*, Sigo, 1990.

Zimbardo, Philip, *Psychology and Life*, Scott, Foresman and Company, USA, HarperCollins, 1992.

Zweig, Stefan, *Mental Healers*, Cassell, 1933.
Contains a chapter on Anton Mesmer.

Useful Addresses

In the UK a nightmare clinic has been formed. Chronic sufferers who need help can write with a SAE to Mary Burgess, Nightmare Research Group, Tyson West Two, Bethlem Hospital, Beckenham, Kent, BR2 3BX.

BOOK SHOPS SPECIALISING IN DREAMS AND PSYCHOLOGY

Changes Bookshop,
242 Belsize Road,
London, NW6 4BT
Tel: 071 328 5161.

Compendium Bookshop,
234 Camden High Street,
London, NW1
Tel: 071 485 8944.

Mysteries,
9 Monmouth Street,
Covent Garden,
London, WC2
Tel: 071 240 3688.

COURSES

Atsitsa/Skyros Holidays,
92 Prince of Wales Road,
London, NW5 2NE
Tel: 071 267 7085.

CAER,
Rosemerryn,
Lamorna,
Penzance,
Cornwall, TR19 6BN
Tel: 0736 810530.

Association of Humanistic Psychology,
12 Southcote Road,
Tufnell Park,
London, N19 5BJ
Tel: 081 607 7852.

Institute of Dream Analysis
Tel: 071 794 8717.

MAGAZINES

Human Potential,
5 Layton Road,
London, N1 OPX
Tel: 071 354 5792.

I to I Magazine,
92 Prince of Wales Road,
London, NW5 2NE
Tel: 071 267 7085.

Charles Berlitz's World of Strange Phenomena Omnibus

Charles Berlitz

Bringing together three volumes of Charles Berlitz's collections of bizarre and intriguing phenomena, this bumper omnibus edition contains enough evidence of paranormal occurrences to puzzle even the most hardened of sceptics. Inside you'll find the amazing stories of:

* Roy Cleveland Sullivan, the man struck by lightning on seven separate occasions

* The vultures of Gettysburg, who every year return to roost on the hills where some of the bloodiest fighting took place over a century ago

* Bart Hughes, the Dutch doctor who drilled a hole in his head and lived

... plus hundreds of other nuggets of eerie ephemera and creepy coincidences. Thought-provoking, sometimes downright spooky, the stories in *Charles Berlitz's World of Strange Phenomena* are proof that, even in this technological world, some things just defy explanation.

The Final Prophecies of Nostradamus

Erika Cheetham

Erika Cheetham's final, long-awaited volume of
Nostradamus's prophecies, presented for the first time
since 1568 in the original text.

Since Nostradamus's predictions first appeared in
print, his reputation has grown through the centuries
and throughout the world. This French physician, seer
and astrologer foresaw the historic events of his
own and future times with remarkable clarity.

In this volume, Erika Cheetham presents fresh translations
and interpretations of Nostradamus's last prophecies - and
focuses on new and startling predictions through to
the end of this millennium, which are specifically
indicated to aid the reader.

Other bestselling Little, Brown titles available by mail: